# Rick Steves'

# SWITZERLAND

# 2007

# Rick Steves'

# SWITZERLAND
# 2007

AVALON
TRAVEL

# CONTENTS

# RESORT TOWNS

# Top Destinations in Switzerland

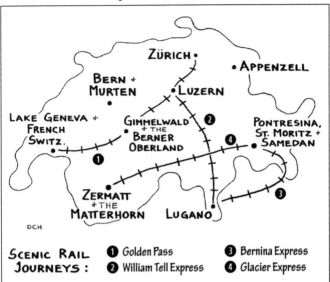

ZÜRICH •

• APPENZELL

BERN +
MURTEN

• LUZERN

LAKE GENEVA +
FRENCH
SWITZ.

GIMMELWALD
+ THE
BERNER
OBERLAND

PONTRESINA,
ST. MORITZ +
SAMEDAN

ZERMATT
+ THE
MATTERHORN

LUGANO

DCH

SCENIC RAIL
JOURNEYS :

**1** Golden Pass

**3** Bernina Express

**2** William Tell Express

**4** Glacier Express

# INTRODUCTION

Little, mountainous, efficient Switzerland is one of Europe's most appealing destinations. Wedged neatly between Germany, Austria, France, and Italy, Switzerland melds the best of all worlds—and adds a healthy dose of chocolate, cowbells, and cable cars. Fiercely independent and decidedly high-tech, the Swiss stubbornly hold on to their quaint traditions, too. Join the cheesemakers high atop an alp, try to call the shepherds on an alphorn, and hike through some of the world's most stunning mountain scenery.

This book breaks Switzerland into its top big-city, small-town, and rural attractions. It gives you all the information and opinions necessary to wring the maximum value out of your limited time and money in each of these destinations. If you plan three weeks or less in Switzerland, this lean and mean little book is all you need... unless you're a skier. Note that this is a fair-weather book—with a focus on the highlights of summertime fun.

Experiencing Switzerland's culture, people, and natural wonders economically and hassle-free has been my goal for three decades of traveling, tour-guiding, and guidebook writing. With this book, I pass on to you the lessons I've learned, updated for 2007.

*Rick Steves' Switzerland* is a tour guide in your pocket. The book includes a balance of cities and villages, mountaintop hikes and lake cruises, thought-provoking museums and sky-high gondola rides. It covers the predictable biggies while mixing in a healthy dose of Back Door intimacy. Along with Luzern, the Matterhorn, and the Glacier Express, you'll experience windswept Roman ruins and ramble through traffic-free alpine towns.

The best is, of course, only my opinion. But after spending half my adult life researching Europe, I've developed a sixth sense for what travelers enjoy. Just thinking about the places featured in this book makes me want to yodel.

## This Information Is Accurate and Up-to-Date

This book is updated every year. Most publishers of guidebooks that cover a country from top to bottom can afford an update only once every two or three years (and, even then, it's often by e-mail or fax). Since this book is selective, covering just the best destinations in Switzerland, it's easy to update it in person each summer.

The prices, hours, and telephone numbers in this book are accurate as of mid-2006. Even with annual updates, things change. Still, if you're traveling with the current edition of this book, you're using the most up-to-date information available in print (for the latest, see www.ricksteves.com/update). Also at our Web site, you'll find a valuable list of reports and experiences—good and bad—from fellow travelers who have used this book (www.ricksteves.com/feedback).

Use this year's edition. People who try to save a few bucks by traveling with an old book are not smart. They learn the seriousness of their mistake...in Switzerland. Your trip costs about $10 per waking hour. Your time is valuable. This guidebook will save you lots of time.

## About This Book

This book is organized by destination, each one a mini-vacation on its own, filled with exciting sights and homey, affordable places to stay. In the following chapters, you'll find these sections:

**Planning Your Time** offers ideas on how best to use your limited time at each destination.

**Orientation** includes tourist information, public transportation tips, and easy-to-read maps.

**Self-Guided Walks** takes you through interesting neighborhoods, with a personal tour guide in hand.

**Sights** provides a succinct overview of Switzerland's most important sights, with ratings:

▲▲▲—Don't miss.

▲▲—Try hard to see.

▲—Worthwhile if you can make it.

No rating—Worth knowing about.

**Sleeping** describes my favorite hotels, from budget deals to splurges.

**Eating** serves up good-value restaurants, ranging from inexpensive *Stübli* to fancier options.

**Transportation Connections** lays the groundwork for your smooth arrival and departure, explaining connections by bus, train, and plane.

The **appendix** is a traveler's tool kit, with telephone tips, a list of festivals and holidays, a climate chart, tips on metric conversion, and survival phrases in German, French, and Italian.

Browse through this book, choose your favorite destinations, and link them together. Then have a great trip! Traveling like a temporary local, you'll get the absolute most out of every mile, minute, and dollar. As you travel the route I know and love, I'm happy you'll be meeting some of my favorite Swiss people.

# PLANNING

## Trip Costs

Five components make up your trip cost: airfare, surface transportation, room and board, sightseeing and entertainment, and shopping and miscellany.

**Airfare:** Don't try to sort through the mess. Find and use a good travel agent. A basic round-trip flight from the US to Zürich costs $600–1,300 (even cheaper in winter), depending on where you fly from and when you go. If your trip extends beyond Switzerland, consider saving time and money by flying "open jaw" (flying into one city and out of another; for instance, into Zürich and out of Paris).

**Surface Transportation:** For a two-week whirlwind trip of all my recommended destinations, allow $430 per person for public transportation (second-class, 15-consecutive-day Swiss Pass, plus reservation fees for scenic trains) or $500 per person for a car rental (based on two people sharing a two-week rental, including parking fees, gas, and insurance). Car rental is cheapest if arranged from the US. Train passes are normally available only outside of Europe, but most Swiss passes are also sold at Swiss train stations. These passes come in such a wide selection that most travelers save money with a railpass, even for short visits (see "Transportation," page 17).

**Room and Board:** You can easily manage in Switzerland on an average of $100 a day per person for room and board. A $100-a-day budget per person allows $15 for lunch, $20 for dinner, $5 for snacks, and $60 for lodging (based on 2 people splitting the cost of a $120 double room that includes breakfast). That's doable. Students and tightwads do it on $45 a day ($20 per hostel bed, $25 for groceries).

# Budget Tips

Switzerland is pricey, but there are ways to stretch your dollars. For example, many expensive alpine lifts offer discounted "early bird" tickets for the first trip of the day. Train trips get cheaper when you choose the right railpass (see all the deals on page 20); the Swiss Pass not only covers trains, but also many museums (see below). Cut down on restaurant costs by having scenic picnics and seeking out self-service cafeterias (often attached to department or grocery stores), which offer delicious food at a fraction of the cost of dining out.

## Save on Sightseeing with the Swiss Pass

The Swiss Pass railpass—offering consecutive-day or flexi-day coverage of Switzerland's trains, boats, and buses, and a 50 percent discount on lifts—also covers admission to more than 400 Swiss museums. This is a swinging deal for most travelers.

You can use your Swiss Pass to cover museum admission only during its validity period. For a consecutive-day pass, that means from the day you activate your pass (that is,  use it for the first time) until the last day it's valid for travel. If you have a flexipass, visiting a museum uses up a day of your pass—to get the most out of your pass, use it for a museum either on the same day you arrive at that destination or on the day you depart.

The following sights, which are covered in this book, are free with the pass (for a full list of covered museums, see www .museumspass.ch):

**Zürich**—Swiss National Museum and Rietberg Museum.

**Luzern**—Rosengart Collection, Picasso Museum, Depot History Museum, Bourbaki Panorama, Glacier Garden, Alpineum, Swiss Transport Museum, Richard Wagner Museum, Museum of Art Luzern, and the Museum of Natural History, plus Fortress Fürigen Museum nearby.

**Bern**—Museum of Fine Arts and Paul Klee Center.

**Near Murten**—Roman Museum in Avenches.

**Near Interlaken**—Swiss Open-Air Folk Museum at Ballenberg.

**Zermatt**—Alpine Museum.

**Appenzell Region**—Folk Museums in Appenzell Town, Stein, and Urnäsch.

**Lausanne**—Collection de l'Art Brut, Olympic Museum, and City History Museum.

**Lake Geneva Region**—Château de Chillon.

**French Swiss Countryside**—Castle and H. R. Giger Museum in Gruyères.

**Sightseeing and Entertainment:** In big cities, figure $5–10 per major sight, $3 for minor ones, and about $50 for each major alpine lift. Though hiking is free, lifts to some of the best high-altitude trails aren't. An overall average of $25 a day works for most. Don't skimp here. After all, this category is the driving force behind your trip—you came to sightsee, enjoy, and experience Switzerland.

**Shopping and Miscellany:** Figure $2–3 per coffee, beer, and ice-cream cone. Shopping can vary in cost from nearly nothing to a small fortune. Good budget travelers find that this category has little to do with assembling a trip full of lifelong and wonderful memories.

## When to Go

The "tourist season" runs roughly from May through September. Summer (July–Aug) has its advantages: the best weather, snow-free alpine trails, very long days (light until after 21:00), and the busiest schedule of tourist fun. In late May, June, September, and early October, travelers enjoy fewer crowds, milder weather, and the ability to grab a room almost whenever and wherever they like.

During the *Zwischenzeit* ("between time," that is, between summer and ski seasons, roughly April, early May, late Oct, and Nov), the cities are pleasantly uncrowded—but the weather can be iffy, and resort towns such as Zermatt and Mürren are completely dead (with most hotels and restaurants closed).

During ski season (Dec–March), mountain resorts are crowded and expensive, while cities are quieter (some accommodations and sights are either closed or run on a limited schedule). The weather can be cold and dreary, and nighttime will draw the shades on your sightseeing before dinnertime. You may find the climate chart in the appendix helpful. Pack warm clothing for the Alps, no matter when you go.

## Sightseeing Priorities

Depending on the length of your trip, here are my recommended priorities. Assuming you'll be traveling by train, I've taken geographic proximity and transportation connections into account.

| | |
|---|---|
| 3 days: | Berner Oberland |
| 5 days, add: | Luzern |
| 7 days, add: | Bern and Lausanne, connecting with Golden Pass scenic rail journey |
| 10 days, add: | Zermatt and Appenzell, linking with Glacier Express train |
| 14 days, add: | Lugano and Pontresina area, connecting with Bernina Express and William Tell Express train rides |

16 days, add:  Zürich and Murten
21 days, add:  More day trips (central Switzerland, French Swiss
               countryside), more hikes, and time to slow down

The map on page 9 and the two-week itinerary on page 8 include everything in the top 14 days, plus modifications for a longer or shorter trip.

## Travel Smart

Your trip is like a complex play—easier to follow and really appreciate on a second viewing. While no one does the same trip twice to gain that advantage, reading this book in its entirety before your trip accomplishes much the same thing.

Reread this book as you travel, and visit local tourist information offices. Upon arrival in a new town, lay the groundwork for a smooth departure; write down the schedule for the train or bus you'll take when you depart. Buy a phone card or carry a mobile phone, and use it for reservations and confirmations—most Swiss people who work with tourists speak some English.

Design an itinerary that enables you to visit the sights at the best possible times. As you read this book, make note of festivals, colorful market days, and days when sights are closed. Saturday morning feels like any bustling weekday morning, but at lunchtime, many shops close down through Sunday. Sundays have pros and cons, as they do for travelers in the US (special events, limited hours, closed shops and banks, limited public transportation, no rush hours). Popular places are even more popular on weekends—especially sunny weekends. Many sights are closed on Monday (head for the hills).

Plan ahead for banking, laundry, Internet stops, and picnics. To maximize rootedness, minimize one-night stands. Mix intense and relaxed periods, villages and cities, mountains and museums. Every trip (and every traveler) needs at least a few slack days. Pace yourself. Assume you will return.

Enjoy the hospitality of the Swiss people. Ask questions. Most locals are eager to point you in their idea of the right direction. Wear your money belt, bring along a pocket-size notebook to organize your thoughts, and practice the virtue of simplicity. Those who expect to travel smart, do.

Perhaps more than anywhere else in Europe, weather plays a huge factor in your sightseeing in Switzerland. The mountains are stunning—if it's not raining. But bad weather needn't ruin a trip. Switzerland has plenty of rainy-weather options. And it's so small and has such a slick train network that you can easily double-back later in your trip to visit the mountaintop hideaway that was clouded over your first time through.

Be flexible. For maximum spontaneity, consider traveling

without room reservations (realizing that this comes with some risk). For example, you might plan on three days split between the city of Bern and the mountainous Berner Oberland region. If it's raining as you approach the area, head for Bern. If it's sunny, make a beeline for the mountains, then hit Bern on your way out of the area. To help you decide, tune into TV stations and Web sites that show the weather in various parts of the country. Many high-altitude observation decks come with 24-hour cameras that pan slowly back and forth, showing you exactly what you'll see when you get up top (for example, www.swisspanorama.com for the Berner Oberland, www.zermatt.ch for Zermatt).

# RESOURCES

## Tourist Information Offices

### In the US

The Swiss national tourist office in the US is a wealth of information. Before your trip, get the comprehensive "Welcome to the Best of Switzerland" brochure and request any specifics you want (such as regional and city maps, festival schedules, and hiking information). Call 877-794-8037 or visit www.myswitzerland.com (info .usa@myswitzerland.com).

### In Switzerland

Your best first stop in any new city is the tourist information office (abbreviated in this book as **TI**). Throughout Switzerland, you'll find TIs are usually well-organized and have English-speaking staff. Take full advantage of their help. Try to arrive, or at least telephone, before it closes. Have a list of questions ready, and pick up maps, brochures, and walking-tour information.

As national budgets tighten, many TIs have been privatized. This means they become sales agents for big tours and hotels, and their "information" becomes unavoidably colored. While TIs are eager to book you a room, you should use their room-finding service only as a last resort. TIs can as easily book you a bad room as a good one—they are not allowed to promote one place over another. Book direct, using the listings in this book.

## Rick Steves' Guidebooks, Public Television Show, and Radio Shows

With the help of my staff, I produce materials to help you plan your trip and travel smoothly.

**Guidebooks:** This book is one of a series of 30+ books on European travel that includes country guidebooks, city and regional guidebooks, and my budget-travel skills handbook, *Rick Steves' Europe Through the Back Door*. All are annually updated.

## Switzerland's Best Two-Week Trip by Train

| Day | Plan | Sleep in |
|-----|------|----------|
| 1 | Arrive Zürich, head to Appenzell | Appenzell or Ebenalp |
| 2 | All day for Appenzell and Ebenalp | Appenzell or Ebenalp |
| 3 | Leave early for Luzern | Luzern |
| 4 | Luzern | Luzern |
| 5 | William Tell Express to Lugano | Lugano |
| 6 | Bernina Express to Pontresina area | Pontresina |
| 7 | Pontresina area (St. Moritz, Samedan, lifts and hikes) | Pontresina |
| 8 | Take Glacier Express; if good weather, head for Zermatt; if bad weather, consider going straight to Lausanne (see below) | Zermatt |
| 9 | Zermatt, Matterhorn-view lifts and hikes | Zermatt |
| 10 | If good weather, spend more time in Zermatt, go late to Lausanne; if bad weather, leave early for Lausanne | Lausanne |
| 11 | Take the Golden Pass to the Berner Oberland. If good weather, go early; if bad weather, linger in Lausanne/Lake Geneva area and leave late | Berner Oberland (Gimmelwald or Mürren) |
| 12 | All day for lifts and hikes in the Berner Oberland | Gimmelwald or Mürren |
| 13 | More time in the Berner Oberland | Gimmelwald or Mürren |
| 14 | Early to Bern, then on to Zürich | Zürich |
| 15 | More time in Zürich, or fly home | |

Zermatt isn't worth the trip in bad weather. If your reservations are flexible, consider skipping that leg and going straight to Lausanne (take the Glacier Express only to Visp, then change for Lausanne). If you have extra time in Switzerland, I'd suggest spending it in (listed in order of priority): Murten and Bern, Zürich, Lausanne and the Lake Geneva area, Lugano (relaxing) or the Luzern area (day trips). For a short trip of a week or so, I'd just focus on the Berner Oberland, Luzern, and Bern. (If you're wondering whether to focus on the Berner Oberland or the more famous Zermatt/Matterhorn region, see the sidebar on page 177.)

**Railpass:** The best railpass for this itinerary is a 15-consecutive-day Swiss Pass ($322 second class, $483 first class, 15

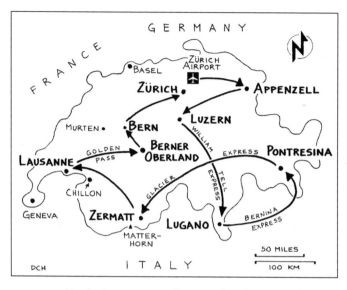

percent less for 2 or more traveling together; figure an additional $100 total in reservation fees for all the scenic rail journeys). While this pass doesn't cover mountain lifts, it does earn you a 50 percent discount on most of them.

**By Car:** While this itinerary is designed to be done by public transportation, it can be done by car with a few modifications. Obviously, you won't take the scenic rail trips. Instead, drive from Appenzell straight to the Pontresina area, then continue through Tirano and on to Lugano (via Lake Como in Italy). From Lugano, drive to Zermatt (crossing again through Italy) and resume the above itinerary, visiting Luzern at the very end before returning to Zürich. Note that the French Swiss countryside and the area around Murten merit more time if you have a car.

**Beyond Switzerland:** Note that Switzerland, right in the middle of Western Europe, splices neatly into a multi-country trip by car or train. For instance, the Appenzell region is a likely gateway to Germany's Bavaria or Austria's Tirol (Innsbruck). Italy's Lake Como is a stone's throw from Lugano or Ticino (in fact, the Bernina Express bus drives right alongside it)—and Milan is not much farther. If you're in Lausanne, you're literally looking at France (across Lake Geneva)—a handy train ride whisks you to Lyon or Chamonix. And big Swiss cities are efficiently connected via night trains and fast day trains to destinations in all of these countries and beyond.

My phrase books—for German, French, Italian, Spanish, and Portuguese—are practical and budget-oriented. My other books include *Europe 101* (a crash course on art and history), *European Christmas* (on traditional and modern-day celebrations, including Switzerland's), and *Postcards from Europe* (a fun memoir of my travels over 25 years). For a complete list of my books, see the inside of the last page of this book.

**Public Television and Radio Shows:** My television series, *Rick Steves' Europe,* covers European destinations. My weekly public radio show, *Travel with Rick Steves,* features interviews with travel experts from around the world. All the TV scripts and radio shows are at www.ricksteves.com. Listen to the shows at any time—or download them onto your MP3 player to take along on your trip.

## Other Guidebooks

Especially if you're traveling beyond my recommended destinations, you may want some supplemental travel information. When you consider the improvements they'll make in your $3,000 vacation, $30 for extra maps and books is money well spent. Especially for several people traveling by car, the extra weight and expense are negligible. One good tip can save the price of an extra guidebook.

The *Lonely Planet* guide to Switzerland is thorough, well-researched, and packed with good maps and hotel recommendations for low- to moderate-budget travelers. The similar *Rough Guide to Switzerland* is written by insightful British researchers.

Students and vagabonds like the highly opinionated *Let's Go: Austria and Switzerland* (updated by Harvard students, has thorough hostel listings). *Let's Go* is best for backpackers who have railpasses and are interested in the youth and nightlife scene.

The popular, skinny *Michelin Green Guide: Switzerland* is excellent, especially if you're driving. Michelin Guides are known for their city and sightseeing maps, dry but concise and helpful information on all major sights, and good cultural and historical background. English editions are sold in Europe at gas stations and tourist shops.

Note that none of the above-mentioned books are updated annually; check the publication date before you buy.

## Recommended Books and Movies

To get in the mood for your trip, consider these books and films, which take place partly or entirely in Switzerland.

**Non-Fiction:** *La Place de la Concorde Suisse* (by John McPhee, in English); *Living Among the Swiss* (memoir by Michael Wells Glueck); *Why Switzerland?* (socioeconomic commentary by Jonathan Steinberg); *The White Spider* (by Heinrich Harrer, on the

---

## Begin Your Trip at www.ricksteves.com

At our travel Web site, you'll find a wealth of free information on European destinations, including fresh monthly news and helpful tips from thousands of fellow travelers.

Our online Travel Store offers travel bags and accessories specially designed by Rick Steves to help you travel smarter and lighter. These include Rick's popular carry-on bags (wheeled and rucksack versions), money belts, totes, toiletries kits, adapters, other accessories, and a wide selection of guidebooks, planning maps, and DVDs.

Choosing the right railpass for your trip—amidst hundreds of options—can drive you nutty. We'll help you choose the best pass for your needs, plus give you a bunch of free extras.

Travel agents will tell you about mainstream tours of Europe, but they won't tell you about Rick Steves' tours. Rick Steves' Europe Through the Back Door travel company offers more than two dozen itineraries and 400+ departures reaching the best destinations in this book...and beyond. You'll enjoy great guides, a fun bunch of travel partners (with small groups of generally around 25), and plenty of room to spread out in a big, comfy bus. You'll find European adventures to fit every vacation length. To get our Tour Catalog and a free *Rick Steves Tour Experience* DVD (filmed on location during an actual tour), visit www.ricksteves.com.

---

first Eiger ascent in the 1930s); *The Climb Up to Hell* (by Jack Olsen, on a 1957 Eiger climb); and *A Tramp Abroad* (by Mark Twain).

**Fiction:** *The Magic Mountain* (by Thomas Mann); *Hotel du Lac* (by Anita Brookner); *A Farewell to Arms* (by Ernest Hemingway); *Daisy Miller* (by Henry James); *The Prisoner of Chillon* (epic poem by Lord Byron); *The Night Manager* (by John le Carré); *I'm Not Stiller* (by Swiss author Max Frisch, available in English); and *Heidi* (children's book by Johanna Spyri).

**Flicks:** *Three Colors: Red* (1994); *Five Days One Summer* (1982); *The Eiger Sanction* (1975); *Third Man on the Mountain* (1959); and *Heidi* (1937). In addition, the following 007 films feature scenes of James Bond skiing in Switzerland: *Goldeneye* (1995); *A View to a Kill* (1985); *The Spy Who Loved Me* (1977); *On Her Majesty's Secret Service* (1969, with scenes of the Schilthorn, in the Berner Oberland); and *Goldfinger* (1964).

## Maps

The black-and-white maps in this book, drawn by Dave Hoerlein, are concise and simple. Dave, who is well-traveled in Switzerland, has designed the maps to help you locate recommended places and get to local TIs, where you'll find more in-depth maps (usually free) of the city or region. Better maps are sold at newsstands and bookstores, which have a good selection, especially in touristy areas. Before you buy a map, look at it to make sure it has the level of detail you want. For drivers, I recommend a 1:400,000-scale map of the whole country, or even larger-scale maps of particular regions. Train travelers usually manage fine with the freebies they get with their railpass or from the local tourist offices.

## PRACTICALITIES

**Red Tape:** Americans need a passport, but no visa or shots to travel in Switzerland. It's a good idea to pack a photocopy of your passport in your luggage in case the original is lost or stolen.

Switzerland isn't a member of the European Union, so you'll generally need to show your passport when you cross borders. And remember, when you change countries, you must also change telephone cards, postage stamps, and *Unterhosen*.

**Time:** In Switzerland—and throughout this book—you'll be using the 24-hour clock. It's the same through 12:00 noon, then keep going—13:00, 14:00, and so on. For anything over 12, subtract 12 and add p.m. (14:00 is 2:00 p.m.).

Switzerland is six/nine hours ahead of the East/West Coasts of the US.

**Shopping:** Swiss shops are generally open Monday through Friday 9:00–18:30, Saturday 8:00–16:00, and closed Sunday. They are often open later on Thursdays. Shoppers interested in customs regulations and VAT refunds (the tax refunded on large purchases made by non-residents) can refer to page 15.

**Discounts:** While discounts for sightseeing and transportation are not listed in this book, youths (under 18) and students (only with International Student Identity Card—www.isic.org) often get discounts—but only by asking.

**Metric:** Get used to metric. A liter is about a quart, four to a gallon. A kilometer is six-tenths of a mile. I convert kilometers to miles by cutting them in half and adding back 10 percent of the original (120 km: 60 + 12 = 72 miles, 300 km: 150 + 30 = 180 miles).

**Watt's Up?** If you're bringing electrical gear, you'll need a two-prong adapter plug (sold cheap at travel stores in the US). You may also need a converter to deal with the increased voltage. Travel appliances often have convenient, built-in converters; look for a voltage switch marked 120V (US) and 240V (Europe).

**News:** Americans keep in touch in Europe with the *International Herald Tribune* (published almost daily via satellite).

Every Tuesday, the European editions of *Time* and *Newsweek* hit the stands with articles of particular interest to travelers in Europe. Sports addicts can get their fix from *USA Today*. Good Web sites include www.europeantimes.com and http://news.bbc .co.uk. Many hotels have CNN or BBC television channels.

# MONEY

## Banking

Bring plastic—ATM, debit, or credit cards—along with several hundred dollars in hard cash as an emergency backup. Traveler's checks are a waste of time (waiting at banks) and a waste of money (paying to purchase and then cash checks).

Before you go, verify with your bank that your card will work. Also inquire about "international transaction" fees (which can be up to $5 per transaction). Alert your bank that you'll be making withdrawals in Europe; otherwise, they may not approve transactions if they perceive unusual spending patterns. Bring an extra card in case one gets demagnetized or eaten up by a temperamental machine.

The best and easiest way to get cash is to use Switzerland's readily available, easy-to-use ATMs (with English instructions). To withdraw cash, you'll need a card that can withdraw money from your bank account, plus a PIN code (numbers only, no letters on European keypads). The German word for cash machine is *Bankomat* or *Geldautomat*. Many ATMs don't issue receipts with your transaction, so you may want to write down the amount you've withdrawn.

---

### Exchange Rates

I've priced things throughout this book in the local currency. Switzerland, which isn't a member of the European Union, has retained its traditional currency, the Swiss franc.

**1 Swiss franc (SF) = about 80 cents, and 1.25 SF = about $1.**

One Swiss franc is broken down into 100 rappen (or centimes, in French Switzerland). To roughly convert prices from Swiss francs into dollars, subtract one-fifth (for example, 50 SF = about $40). There are coins for one, two, and five francs, plus several coins for very small denominations of rappen. The small coin with real value is the 50-rappen (marked with 1/2 rather than 50—worth about 40 cents). In a handful of change, it's easy to identify as the only one with ridges.

## Damage Control for Lost or Stolen Cards

If you lose your credit, debit, or ATM card, you can stop people from using your card by reporting the loss immediately to the respective global customer-assistance centers. If you promptly report your card lost or stolen, you typically won't be held responsible for any unauthorized transactions on your account, although many banks charge a liability fee. Call these 24-hour US numbers collect: Visa (tel. 410/581-9994), MasterCard (tel. 636/722-7111), and American Express (tel. 336/393-1111).

At a minimum, have the following information ready: the name of the financial institution that issued you the card, along with the type of card (classic, platinum). Ideally, plan ahead: Pack photocopies of the backs of your cards (with the collect-call numbers), and write down your card numbers on a separate piece of paper that doesn't have your name on it. Providing the following information allows a quicker cancellation of your missing card: full card number, whether you are the primary or secondary cardholder, the cardholder's name exactly as printed on the card, billing address, home phone number, circumstances of the loss or theft, and identification verification (such as your birth date, your mother's maiden name, or your Social Security number—memorize this, don't carry a copy). If you are the secondary cardholder, you'll also need to provide the primary cardholder's identification verification details. You can generally receive a temporary card within two or three business days in Europe.

In case you need a bank in Switzerland, they're generally open Monday through Friday from 8:00 to 17:00. Post offices (business hours) and train stations (long hours) usually change money if you can't get to a bank.

Just like at home, credit or debit cards work easily at larger hotels, restaurants, and shops. Visa and MasterCard are more commonly accepted than American Express. Smaller businesses prefer payment in local currency. If you have lots of large bills, break them at a bank, especially if you like shopping at mom-and-pop places; they may not have huge amounts of change.

Even in safe Switzerland, you should use a money belt (a pouch with a strap that you buckle around your waist like a belt and wear under your clothes). Thieves target tourists. A money belt provides peace of mind. You can carry lots of cash safely in a money belt, and given bank and ATM fees, you should.

Don't be petty about getting money; it's inefficient and expensive to visit ATMs frequently to withdraw a minimum amount of cash each time. Withdraw a week's worth of money, stuff it in your money belt, and travel!

## Tips on Tipping

Tipping in Europe isn't as automatic and generous as it is in the US—but for special service, tips are appreciated, if not expected. As in the US, the proper amount depends on your resources, tipping philosophy, and the circumstance, but some general guidelines apply.

**Restaurants:** Tipping is an issue only at restaurants that have table service. If you order your food at a counter, don't tip.

At restaurants with a wait staff, service is included, although it's common to round up the bill after a good meal (usually 5–10 percent; so for an 18.50 SF meal, pay 20 SF). Give the tip to your server when you pay your bill rather than leaving coins on the table. Or do as locals do: When the waiter announces or writes down your total, you say how much you'd like the bill to be (for example, for an 8.10 SF meal, give a 20 SF bill and say *"Neun Franken"*—"Nine francs"—to get 11 SF change).

**Taxis:** To tip the cabbie, round up. For a typical ride, round up to the next franc or two on the fare (to pay a 13-SF fare, give 15 SF); for a long ride, to the nearest 10 (for a 75-SF fare, give 80 SF). If the cabbie hauls your bags and zips you to the airport to help you catch your flight, you might want to toss in a little more—but not more than 10 SF. However, if you feel like you're being driven in circles or otherwise ripped off, skip the tip.

**Special Services:** Tour guides at public sites sometimes hold out their hands for tips after they give their spiel; if I've already paid for the tour, I don't tip extra, though some tourists do give a franc or two per person, particularly for a good tour. For minivan tours and for private guides, it's customary to tip a little more. There's no need to tip for excursions that simply provide transportation and offer no commentary. I don't tip at hotels, but if you do, give the porter a franc or two for carrying bags and leave a few francs in your room at the end of your stay for the maid if the room was kept clean. In general, if someone in the service industry does a super job for you, a tip of a couple of francs is appropriate...but not required.

**When in doubt, ask:** If you're not sure whether (or how much) to tip for a service, ask your hotelier or the TI; they'll fill you in on how it's done on their turf.

## VAT Refunds and Customs Regulations

**VAT Refunds:** Wrapped into the purchase price of your Swiss souvenir is a Value Added Tax (VAT) of 7.6 percent (one of the lowest in Europe). If you make a purchase of more than 530 SF at

## Why No Swiss Euros?

You can't help but wonder why the efficient Swiss are stubbornly hanging on to their old franc while surrounded by countries basking in the ease and convenience of the euro. The answer is simple: It's too expensive for the Swiss to change. The Swiss enjoy lower mortgage interest rates and a more stable currency than the rest of Europe. But even more importantly, a huge part of the Swiss economy is based on providing a safe and secret place for wealthy people from around the world to stash their money. When bank fees are figured in, people who "save" in Swiss banks actually earn negative interest—they *pay* the Swiss to keep their money. Compliance with European Union regulations in order to join the euro zone would mean the end of Switzerland's secret banking industry. The Swiss are not inclined to deal such a devastating blow to their economy.

But even though Switzerland hasn't officially adopted the euro, the majority of Swiss hotels, restaurants, and shops (especially in touristy areas) accept smaller euro bills. Most businesses will not take euro coins or larger bills, and you'll usually get bad rates (and your change in Swiss francs). Many coin-operated phone booths even accept euros (marked with a big yellow €). If you're just passing through the country, never fear: Your euros will work. But if you're staying a while, get some Swiss francs...you'll save money and they're prettier.

a store that participates in the VAT refund scheme, you're entitled to get most of that tax back. Personally, I've never felt that VAT refunds are worth the hassle, but if you do, here's the scoop.

If you're lucky, the merchant will subtract the tax when you make your purchase (this is more likely to occur if the store ships the goods to your home). Otherwise, you'll need to do all this:

- **Get the paperwork:** Have the merchant completely fill out the necessary refund document, called a "cheque." You'll have to present your passport at the store.
- **Get your stamp at the border or airport:** Have your cheque(s) stamped at the border at your last stop in Switzerland by the customs agent who deals with VAT refunds. It's best to keep your purchases in your carry-on for viewing, but if they're too large or dangerous (such as knives) to carry on, then track down the proper customs agent to inspect them before you check your bag. You're not supposed to use your purchased goods before you leave. If you show up at customs wearing your new lederhosen, officials might look the other way—or deny you a refund.

- **Collect your refund:** You'll need to return your stamped documents to the retailer or its representative. Many merchants work with a service, such as Global Refund (www .globalrefund.com) or Premier Tax Free (www.premiertaxfree .com), which have offices at major airports, ports, or border crossings. These services, which extract a 4 percent fee, can refund your money immediately in your currency of choice or credit your card (within two billing cycles). If you have to deal directly with the retailer, mail the store your stamped documents and then wait. It could take months.

**Customs Regulations:** You can take home $800 in souvenirs per person duty-free. The next $1,000 is taxed at a flat 3 percent. After that, you pay the individual item's duty rate. You can also bring in duty-free a liter of alcohol (slightly more than a standard-size bottle of wine), a carton of cigarettes, and up to 100 cigars. As for food, anything in cans or sealed jars is acceptable. Don't bring home meat (even if it's dried and cured), cheeses, or fresh fruits and veggies. To check customs rules and duty rates, visit www .customs.gov.

## TRANSPORTATION

### By Car or Train?

Because Switzerland's train network is excellent, I recommend using public transportation here. Only a few areas—like the Appenzell region and the French Swiss countryside—are better by car. Cars are an expensive headache in the bigger cities.

### Trains

Trains are generally slick, speedy, and punctual, with synchronized connections. They're also clean, roomy, and, as of 2006, entirely non-smoking. Few places in Switzerland are out of reach of the train system, though some frustrating schedules make the more out-of-the-way recommendations (such as Taveyanne in the

French Swiss countryside) not worth the time and trouble for the less determined.

**Information:** Switzerland has a train info number you can dial from anywhere in the country: toll tel. 0900-300-3004. For Swiss timetables, visit Germany's excellent all-Europe timetable, http://bahn.hafas.de/bin/query .exe/en, or the Swiss site, www.sbb.ch/en. At most train stations, attendants will print out a step-by-step itinerary for you, free of

## Public Transportation

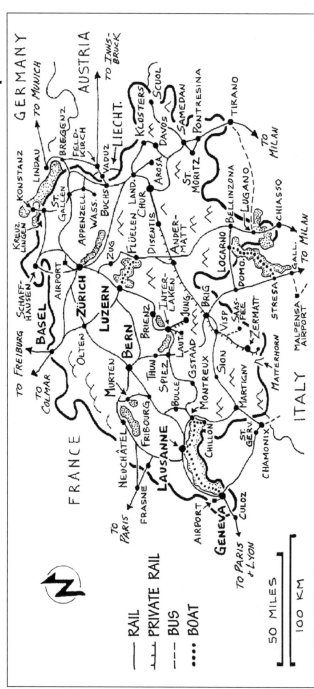

charge. Major stations also have handy travel offices offering general help. Swiss trains and stations are marked "SBB CFF FFS." All those letters mean the same thing ("Swiss Federal Railways"), in three different languages: German, French, and Italian.

**Tickets:** If you're traveling without a railpass, get train tickets at the station—either at the ticket windows, or at the easy-to-use machines. Though you may see some people buying their tickets from conductors on the train (for an additional 5 SF), don't assume you can do so on all trains. If the side of the train displays a yellow-eye logo, you need to get a ticket before boarding, or risk being fined 80 SF.

## Swiss Railpasses

Because of high ticket prices, railpasses are a good deal in Switzerland, even for a three-day trip. But for such a little country, Switzerland has a dizzying array of train passes and deals. Here are the most popular ones:

The **Swiss Pass** is the basic version, covering all trains, boats, and buses, plus admission to most Swiss museums (see page 4), and offering a 50 percent discount on lifts. It comes in both consecutive-day and flexipass versions. Both versions completely cover the cost of any transportation for a specified number of days (but do not cover seat or overnight-train reservations).

If you're traveling with at least one other person, get the "Saver" version of the pass, which is 15 percent cheaper than individual passes. Second class (available to any age) is 33 percent cheaper than first class. For specific passes and prices, see page 21.

The **Half-Fare Travel Card** gives you a 50 percent discount on all national and private trains, postal buses, lifts, and steamers (99 SF for 1 month, sold only in Switzerland). This can save you money if your Swiss travel adds up to more than $160 in point-to-point tickets. The **Swiss Card** is a variation on this, sold only in the US and at a few border stations. It includes the same 50 percent discount and adds two train rides: one ride from any point of entry (such as the German border or Zürich's airport) to any other point in Switzerland and one back from that point to any border ($179 first class, $133 second class).

**Regional passes** cover all travel—including trains, buses, boats, and lifts—in a particular area, such as the Berner Oberland (Berner Oberland Pass, see page 125), Zermatt area (see page 189), or Central Switzerland, around Luzern (Tell-Pass, see page 82). Buy these (in Switzerland, not the US) only if you're very focused on a single region, but note that there's usually no need to have both a regional pass and an all-Switzerland pass (or Eurailpass).

Other deals include the **Swiss Family Card,** allowing children under 16 to travel free with their parents (20 SF per child at Swiss stations, or free with Swiss train passes when requested with purchase in the US).

For more details on all of these passes, see www.ricksteves.com/rail.

## Eurailpasses

If you're also traveling to other counties, consider a Eurail Selectpass, which gives you up to 15 travel days (within a 2-month period, allow about $600) in three, four, or five adjacent countries—choose among Switzerland, Germany, Austria, France, Italy, and other Western European countries. An 18-country Eurailpass is cost-effective only if you're doing a whirlwind trip of Europe (allow roughly $800 for 3 weeks). Like the Swiss Pass, these come in Saverpass versions (15 percent cheaper for two or more traveling together); unlike the Swiss Pass, if you're over 26, you have to buy a first-class pass.

## Railpass Bonuses and Discounts

If you buy a railpass, know what extras are included—for example, boat cruises on the big Swiss lakes are covered by most railpasses. In addition, Swiss railpasses can get you free entry to many museums and discounts on many mountain lifts. Always ask. Note that while Eurailpasses include some deals in Switzerland beyond simple trains (such as on some mountain lifts), the discounts and coverage of these passes generally aren't as extensive as the Switzerland-only passes (for example, lifts in Zermatt are discounted and postal buses nationwide are free with a Swiss Pass, but both are full price with a Eurailpass).

If your railpass is a flexipass (that is, it covers a certain number of days in a given span, rather than consecutive days), it's worth knowing when, and when not, to use up your flexi-days. Trips that are merely discounted, rather than free with the pass—most notably many mountain lifts—don't use up a day of your pass. Any time you use the pass for a free trip, however, you have to use up a day. Keep in mind that it makes sense to pay out of pocket for, say, a short boat or train ride rather than use up a valuable day of your pass for it.

If you have a Swiss flexipass (rather than a Eurailpass), note that when you're *not* using a travel day, your pass gets you a 50 percent discount on all rides taken before the use of your last travel day. Unlike flexipasses for most other countries, a Swiss flexipass expires once you've used up all your travel days—even if that's well before the end of the one-month time frame noted on your pass. It can be smart to use your first travel day near the beginning of your trip, and your last travel day near (or at) the end of your trip;

# Railpasses

Prices listed are for 2006 and are subject to change. For the latest prices, details, and train schedules (and easy online ordering), see my comprehensive *Guide to Eurail Passes* at www.ricksteves.com/rail.

"Saver" prices are per person for two or more people traveling together. "Youth" means under age 26.

## SWISS PASS AND SWISS FLEXIPASS

| | Individual 1st Class | Individual 2nd Class | Saver 1st Class | Saver 2nd Class | Youth 1st Class | Youth 2nd Class |
|---|---|---|---|---|---|---|
| 4 consecutive days | $278 | $185 | $236 | $158 | $209 | $139 |
| 8 consecutive days | 395 | 264 | 336 | 225 | 297 | 198 |
| 15 consecutive days | 483 | 322 | 411 | 274 | 363 | 242 |
| 22 consecutive days | 561 | 374 | 477 | 318 | 421 | 281 |
| 1 month | 622 | 415 | 529 | 353 | 467 | 312 |
| 3 days in 1 month flexi | 264 | 176 | 224 | 150 | N/A | N/A |
| 4 days in 1 month flexi | 318 | 212 | 270 | 180 | N/A | N/A |
| 5 days in 1 month flexi | 372 | 248 | 316 | 211 | N/A | N/A |
| 6 days in 1 month flexi | 426 | 284 | 362 | 241 | N/A | N/A |
| 8 days in 1 month flexi | 495 | 330 | 421 | 281 | N/A | N/A |

Covers all trains, boats, buses, and most museums plus 50 percent off high mountain rides, and—if you have a flexipass—50 percent off any ride taken between your counted "flexi" days. Kids under 16 free with parent, otherwise half of full fare.

## SWITZERLAND–AUSTRIA PASS or
## FRANCE–SWITZERLAND PASS

| | Individual 1st Class | Saver 1st Class | Youth 2nd Class |
|---|---|---|---|
| 4 days in 2 months | $328 | $280 | $228 |
| Extra rail days (max 6) | 38 | 33 | 27 |

The fare for children 4–11 is half the adult individual fare or Saver fare. Kids under age 4 travel free.

## GERMANY–SWITZERLAND PASS

| | Individual 1st Class | Saver 1st Class | Youth 2nd Class |
|---|---|---|---|
| 5 days in 2 months | $349 | $298 | $244 |
| 6 days in 2 months | 385 | 328 | 270 |
| 8 days in 2 months | 458 | 390 | 322 |
| 10 days in 2 months | 530 | 453 | 372 |

The fare for children 4–11 is half the adult individual fare or Saver fare. Kids under age 4 travel free.

## Map key:

Approximate point-to-point one-way second-class rail fares in US dollars. First class costs 50 percent more. Add up fares for your itinerary to see whether a railpass will save you money.

## Lift Lingo

The Swiss have come up with a variety of ways to conquer peaks and reach the best viewpoints and trailheads with minimum sweat. Known generically as "lifts," each of these contraptions has its own name and definition—use the right terms, and impress your new Swiss friends.

**Cogwheel Train:** A train that climbs a steep incline using a gear system, which engages "teeth" in the middle of the tracks to provide traction. Also known as "rack-and-pinion train" or "rack railway."

**Funicular:** A car that is pulled by a cable along tracks up a particularly steep incline, often counterbalanced by a similar car going in the opposite direction (meaning you'll pass the other car exactly halfway through the ride). Funiculars, like cogwheel trains, are in contact with the ground at all times.

**Cable Car:** A large passenger car, suspended in the air by a cable, which travels between stations without touching the ground. A cable car holds a large number of people (sometimes dozens at a time), who generally ride standing up. When a cable car reaches a station, it comes to a full stop to allow passengers to get on and off.

**Gondola:** Also suspended in the air by a cable, but smaller than a cable car— generally holding fewer than 10 people, who are usually seated. Gondolas move continuously, meaning that passengers have to hop into and out of the moving cars at stations. Also, while cable-car lines usually have two big cars—one going in each direction—gondolas generally have many smaller cars strung along the same cable.

Confusingly, the "car" compartment of a cable car is sometimes referred to as a "gondola."

then you can use your flexipass throughout your entire trip for transportation discounts on the days you're not using travel days. It's confusing, but once you figure out the system, you can make it work to your advantage.

### Train Notes

**Scenic Rail Journeys:** In addition to being convenient for transportation, many of Switzerland's trains are also breathtakingly scenic. Several trips are particularly beautiful, and billed as special "theme" routes for tourists. For many visitors, these are a Swiss highlight, and I've devoted an entire chapter to them (see page 253).

**Private Lines:** Switzerland has some privately owned train lines. For instance, a large segment of the Glacier Express scenic journey is private. Private lines are usually covered by Swiss rail-passes, but not covered by Eurailpasses (though Eurailpasses can get you discounts on certain trips). If your railpass doesn't cover an entire journey, pay for the "uncovered" portion at the station before you board the train.

**Check Your Bags:** If you're town- or mountain-hopping through Switzerland by train, you can lighten your load by sending your baggage ahead (drop it off at the station, pay 10 SF with ticket or railpass, 40 SF without, maximum 55 pounds). Your bag will show up within 24 hours of your arrival (usually faster), and will be held for five days (after that, you're charged 3 SF/day).

**Bike 'n' Rail:** Hundreds of local train stations rent bikes for about $5 a day, and sometimes have easy "pick up here and drop off there" plans. For mixing train and bike travel, ask at stations for information booklets.

## Car Rental and Leasing

Car rental is cheapest if arranged in advance from home. Call various companies, look online, or arrange a rental through your hometown travel agent, who can help you out if anything goes wrong during your trip. Rent by the week with unlimited mileage. (For longer trips, consider leasing; see below.) Note that it costs less to pick up your car in Zürich than at the airport. Auto Europe is one of many good companies (www.autoeurope.com).

Expect to pay about $500 per person (based on 2 people sharing the car) for a small economy car for two weeks with unlimited mileage, including gas, parking, and insurance. I normally rent a small, inexpensive model like a Ford Fiesta. For a bigger, roomier, more powerful but still inexpensive car, move up to a Ford Focus or VW Polo. If you drop your car off early or keep it longer, you'll be credited or charged at a fair, prorated price. Always keep your receipts in case any questions arise about your billing.

**Insurance:** For peace of mind, I spring for the Collision Damage Waiver insurance (CDW, about $15–25 per day), which limits my financial responsibility in case of an accident. Unfortunately, CDW now has a high deductible hovering at about $1,200. When you pick up your car, many car-rental companies will try to sell you "super CDW" at an additional cost of $10–20 per day to lower the deductible to zero.

As an alternative, some credit cards offer zero-deductible collision coverage (similar to CDW) for no charge to their customers. Quiz your credit-card company on the worst-case scenario. You have to choose either the coverage offered by your car-rental company or by your credit-card company. This means that if you go with the credit-card coverage, you'll have to decline the CDW offered by the car-rental company. In this situation, some car-rental companies put a hold on your credit card for the amount of the full deductible (which can equal the value of the car). This is bad news if your credit limit is low—particularly if you plan on using that card for other purchases during your trip.

Another option is to buy CDW insurance from Travel Guard ($9/day plus a one-time $3 service fee covers you up to $35,000, $250 deductible, US tel. 800-826-4919, www.travelguard.com). It's valid throughout Europe, but some car-rental companies refuse to honor it, especially in Italy and the Republic of Ireland. Oddly, residents of some states (including Washington) are not allowed to buy this coverage.

In summary, buying CDW from the car-rental company—along with the supplemental insurance to buy down the deductible, if you choose—is the easiest but priciest option. Using the coverage that comes with your credit card is cheaper, but can involve more hassle. If you're taking a short trip, an easy solution is to buy Travel Guard's very affordable CDW. For longer trips, look into leasing (see below).

**Leasing:** For trips of about 17 days or more, leasing is the best way to go. By technically buying and then selling back the car, you save lots of money on tax and insurance. Leasing provides you with a brand-new car with unlimited mileage and a 24-hour emergency assistance program. Car leases must be arranged from the US. One of many reliable companies offering lease packages is Europe by Car (US tel. 800-223-1516, www.europebycar.com).

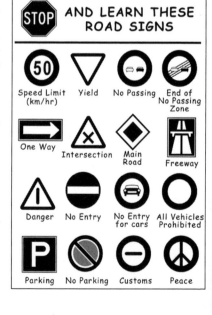

STOP **AND LEARN THESE ROAD SIGNS**

Speed Limit (km/hr) — Yield — No Passing — End of No Passing Zone

One Way — Intersection — Main Road — Freeway

Danger — No Entry — No Entry for cars — All Vehicles Prohibited

Parking — No Parking — Customs — Peace

## Driving

You can get anywhere quickly on Switzerland's fine road system, the world's most expensive per mile to build. Drivers pay a one-time, 40-SF fee for a permit to use Swiss autobahns—check to see if your rental car already has one (if not, buy it at the border, gas station, or car rental agency). Anyone caught driving on a Swiss autobahn without this

## Driving: Distance and Time

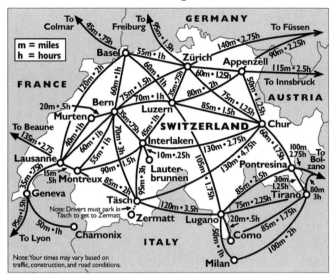

tax sticker is likely to be stopped and fined. Seat belts are required, and two beers under those belts are enough to land you in jail.

For driving in Switzerland, your US driver's license is all that you need. If you're also planning to drive in Austria and Germany, you're strongly advised to get an International Driving Permit (at your local AAA office or online at www.aaa.com—costs $10 plus 2 passport-type photos).

Use good local maps and study them before each drive. Learn which exits you need to look out for, which major cities you'll travel toward, where the ruined castles lurk, and so on.

Know the universal road signs (shown in this chapter and explained in charts in most road atlases and at service stations). *Dreieck* (literally, "three corners") means a Y in the road; *Autobahnkreuz* is an intersection. Exits are spaced about 20 miles apart and often have a gas station (*bleifrei* means unleaded), a restaurant, a mini-market, and sometimes a tourist information desk. Exits and intersections refer to the next major city or the nearest small town. Look at your map and anticipate which town names to watch out for. Know what you're looking for—miss it, and you're long autobahn-gone. When navigating, you'll see *nord, süd, ost, west,* or *mitte*.

To get to the center of a city, follow signs for *Zentrum* or *Stadtmitte*. Ring roads go around a city. For parking, you can pick up the "cardboard clock" (*Parkscheibe*, available free at gas stations, police stations, and *Tabak* shops) and display your arrival time on the clock and put it on the dashboard, so parking attendants can see you've been there less than the posted maximum stay.

# COMMUNICATING

## Language Barrier

Switzerland has four official languages: German, French, Italian, and Romansh (an obscure Romantic tongue). Most of the destinations in this book are in the German-speaking territory. No matter where you are, most young or well-educated people—especially those in larger towns and the tourist trade—speak at least some English. Still, you'll get more smiles by using the local pleasantries. See the German, French, and Italian "Survival Phrases" in the appendix.

In German-speaking Switzerland, locals speak sing-songy *Schwyzertütsch* (Swiss German) around the house, but in schools and at work, they speak and write in the same standard German used in Germany and Austria (called "High" German, or *Hochdeutsch*—though many Swiss prefer to call it *Schriftdeutsch*, or "Written German"). The standard greeting is a hearty *Grüezi* (GREWT-see). "Thank you" is derived from French, but pronounced a little differently: *Merci* (MUR-see). They also sometimes use the more German-like *Dunkcha* (DOONK-chah).

German—like English, Dutch, Swedish, and Norwegian—is a Germanic language, making it easier on most American ears than Romance languages (such as Italian and French). German is pronounced just as it's spelled. There are a few potentially confusing vowel combinations: *ie* is pronounced "ee" (as in *Bier,* the German word for "beer"); *ei* is pronounced "aye" (as in *nein,* German for "no"), and *eu* is pronounced "oy" (as in *Deutsch,* German for "German"). Written German always capitalizes all nouns.

Give it your best shot. The locals will appreciate your efforts.

## Telephones

Smart travelers learn the phone system and use it daily to reserve or reconfirm rooms, get tourist information, reserve restaurants, confirm tour times, or phone home.

### Types of Phones

You'll encounter various kinds of phones in Switzerland.

Swisscom **public pay phones** are everywhere. Some take only insertable phone cards (see below), some only coins, some take both, and some (marked with a yellow €) even accept euro coins.

**Hotel room phones** are fairly cheap for local calls, but pricey for international calls.

**American mobile phones** work in Europe if they're GSM-enabled, tri-band (or quad-band), and on a calling plan that includes international calls. With a T-Mobile phone, you can roam using your home number, and pay $1–2 per minute for making or receiving calls.

Some travelers buy a **European mobile phone** in Europe (but if you're on a strict budget, skip mobile phones and use phone cards instead). For about $125, you can get a phone that will work in most countries once you pick up the necessary chip (about $30) per country. Or you can buy a cheaper, "locked" phone that only works with a SIM card from the country where you purchased it (about $50–100, includes $5–20 worth of calls). If you're interested, stop by any European shop that sells mobile phones; you'll see prominent store window displays. You aren't required to (and shouldn't) buy a monthly contract—buy prepaid calling time instead (as you use it up, buy additional minutes at newsstands or mobile-phone shops).

## Paying for Calls

You can spend a fortune making phone calls in Switzerland...but why would you? Here's the skinny on different ways to pay, including the best deals.

Swiss **phone cards** are just about the only thing that's actually cheaper in Switzerland than in other countries. Dialing direct from a Swisscom public pay phone with an **insertable phone card** *(Telefonkarte)* to the US costs just eight cents a minute, plus a 35-cent connection charge. This is your cheapest bet for both domestic and international calls. These cards are sold at post offices and many newsstand kiosks. Simply slide it into the slot on the phone, wait for a dial tone and digital readout to show how much value remains on your card, and dial your domestic or international call. The cost of the call is automatically deducted from your card.

In case you'll be traveling in neighboring countries, note that their official insertable phone cards are more expensive for international calls. In those countries, it's smart to buy a special **international phone card** with a scratch-to-reveal personal identification number (PIN). With these cards, the cost for international calls plummets to about a nickel per minute. Since you don't have to insert them in the phone, they can also be used from hotel rooms.

Either type of phone card works only in the country where it's purchased. If you use coins to make your calls, have a bunch handy. Or look for a metered phone ("talk now, pay later") in the bigger post offices. Avoid using hotel-room phones for anything other than local calls.

**Dialing direct from your hotel room** without using an international calling card is usually quite expensive for international calls. (I always ask first how much I'll be charged.) Keep in mind that you might have to pay for local and occasionally even toll-free calls.

**Receiving calls in your hotel room** is often the cheapest way to keep in touch with the folks back home—especially if your family has an inexpensive way to call you (either a good deal on their long-distance plan or a prepaid calling card with good rates to Europe). Give them a list of your hotels' phone numbers before you go. As you travel, send your family an e-mail or make a quick payphone call to set up a time for them to call you, and then wait for the ring.

**VoIP (Voice over Internet Protocol),** which is an option only for those traveling with a laptop computer, allows VoIP users to talk with each other for free via their computers over a fast Internet connection. Look into Skype (www.skype.com) and Google Talk (www.google.com/talk).

**US calling cards** (such as the ones offered by AT&T, MCI, and Sprint) are the worst option. You'll nearly always save a lot of money by using a Swiss phone card.

## How to Dial

Calling from the US to Switzerland, or vice versa, is simple—once you break the code. The European calling chart on page 286 will walk you through it. Remember that Swiss time is six/nine hours ahead of the East/West Coasts of the US.

**Dialing Within Switzerland:** All phone numbers in Switzerland are 10 digits (without area codes) that can be dialed direct throughout the country. For instance, to call a recommended Swiss hotel in Gimmelwald, you'd dial the same number (tel. 033-855-1658) whether you're calling from the Gimmelwald cable-car station or from Zürich.

**Dialing International Calls:** For a listing of country codes, see the appendix. When making an international call to Switzerland, first dial the international access code of the country you're in (011 from the US or Canada, 00 if you're calling from Europe), then Switzerland's country code (41), and then the local number *without* its initial 0. So, to call the Gimmelwald hotel from the US, you'd dial 011 (US international access code), 41 (Switzerland's country code), and 33-855-1658 (local number without the initial 0).

To call my office in Edmonds from anywhere in Europe, I dial 00 (Europe's international access code), 1 (US country code), 425 (Edmonds' area code), and 771-8303.

## E-Mail and Mail

**E-mail:** Many travelers set up a free e-mail account with Yahoo, Microsoft (Hotmail), or Google (Gmail). Internet cafés are available at just about every destination in this book, giving you reasonably inexpensive and easy Internet access. Your hotelier can direct you to the nearest place. Many hotels have Internet terminals in their lobbies for guests, and small places are accustomed to letting clients (who've asked politely) sit at their desk for a few minutes just to check their e-mail. Some hotels offer Wi-Fi wireless connections for travelers with laptop computers.

**Mail:** Even when post offices are closed, you're never too far from a yellow mailbox with an automated stamp dispenser (most train stations have one). Type in the value of stamp you want (postcard or letter to the US: 1.40 SF economy, 1.80 SF express), insert coins, and press the pound key. These machines don't give change, so if you have any amount left in the machine, print out a stamp for that amount and use it toward your next postcard.

To arrange for mail delivery, reserve a few hotels along your route in advance and give their addresses to friends. Phoning and e-mailing are so easy that I've dispensed with mail stops altogether.

If you need to mail items home (be warned, it's expensive), you can buy boxes and tape at most post offices.

## SLEEPING

In the interest of smart use of your time, I favor hotels and restaurants handy to your sightseeing activities. Hotels are expensive in Switzerland, so I've scoured the options and presented you with the best values, from $15 bunks to plush $180 doubles.

Accommodations in Switzerland are normally very comfortable and come with breakfast. Plan on spending $80–130 per hotel double, and $60–80 for a double with the bathroom down the hall in a cheap hostel-type place or a private home. A triple is much cheaper than a double and a single. While hotel singles are most expensive, private accommodations *(Zimmer)* have a flat per-person rate. Hostels and dorms always charge per person. Especially in private homes, where the boss changes the sheets, people staying several nights are most desirable. One-night stays are sometimes charged extra.

In recommending hotels, I favor small, family-run places that are central, inexpensive, quiet, clean, safe, friendly, English-speaking, and not listed in other guidebooks. I also like local character and simple facilities that don't cater to American "needs." Obviously, a place meeting every criterion is rare, and all of my recommendations fall short of perfection—sometimes miserably.

# Sleep Code

To give maximum information in a minimum of space, I use these codes to describe accommodations listed in this book. Prices listed are per room, not per person. When a range of prices is listed for a room, the price fluctuates with room size and/or season.

**S** = Single room (or price for 1 person in a double).

**D** = Double or Twin. Double beds are usually big enough for non-romantic couples.

**T** = Triple (often a double bed with a single bed moved in).

**Q** = Quad (an extra child's bed is usually cheaper).

**b** = Private bathroom with toilet and shower or tub.

**s** = Private shower or tub only (the toilet is down the hall).

According to this code, a couple staying at a "Db-150 SF" hotel would pay a total of 150 Swiss francs (about $120) for a double room with a private bathroom. The hotel accepts credit cards or cash in payment.

I've divided the rooms into three categories, based on the price for a standard double room with bath:

$$$ **Higher Priced**
$$ **Moderately Priced**
$ **Lower Priced**

But I've listed the best values for each price category, given the above criteria.

Any room without a bathroom has access to a bathroom in the corridor (free unless otherwise noted). All rooms have a sink. For environmental reasons, towels are often replaced in hotels only when you leave them on the floor. In cheaper places, they aren't replaced at all, so hang them up to dry and reuse.

Unless I note otherwise, the cost of a room includes a breakfast (sometimes continental, but more commonly buffet). The price is usually posted in the room. Before accepting, confirm your understanding of the complete price. I appreciate feedback on your hotel experiences.

## Making Reservations

It's possible to travel at any time of year without reservations, but given the high stakes, erratic accommodations values, and quality of the gems I've found for this book, I'd recommend calling for rooms at least several days in advance as you travel (especially in mountain resorts during summer weekends). Book farther in advance for holidays (see page 288).

If there's any reason to travel without reservations, it's to remain flexible, so you can modify your itinerary as you go to adapt to the weather (spending rainy days in cities and sunny days in the mountains). If tourist crowds are minimal, you might make a habit of calling between 9:00 and 10:00 on the day you plan to arrive, when the hotel knows who'll be checking out and just which rooms will be available. I've taken great pains to list telephone numbers with long-distance instructions (see "How to Dial," above). Use the telephone and the convenient phone cards. Most hotels listed are accustomed to English-only speakers. Some hotel receptionists will trust you and hold a room until 16:00 without a deposit, though many will ask for a credit-card number.

*Honor your reservations or cancel by phone: Trusting people to show up is a hugely stressful issue and a financial risk for B&B owners.* I promised the owners of the places I list that you will be reliable when you make a telephone reservation; please don't let them (or me) down. Being a little late is no problem if you are in telephone contact—and phone calls are cheap. Don't needlessly confirm rooms through the tourist offices; they'll take a commission.

If you know exactly which dates you need and really want a particular place, reserve a room from the US before you leave. To reserve from home, contact the hotel by e-mail, phone, or fax. (Note that mom-and-pop pensions, which can get deluged by e-mail and faxes, are not always able to respond immediately to a message you've sent). E-mail is free, phone and fax costs are reasonable, and simple English is fine. To fax, use the form in the appendix (e-mailers can find it online at www.ricksteves.com/reservation). A two-night stay in August would be "2 nights, 16/8/07 to 18/8/07." (Europeans write the date day/month/year, and European hotel jargon uses your day of departure.)

If you receive a response from the hotel stating its rates and room availability, it's not a confirmation. You must confirm that you indeed want a room at the given rate for the agreed-upon dates. (Don't just assume you can extend upon arrival; take the time to consider in advance how long you'll stay.)

Hotels may require one night's deposit to hold a room. Usually a credit-card number and expiration date will be accepted as the deposit. Faxing your card number (rather than e-mailing it) keeps it private, safer, and out of cyberspace. If you do reserve with a credit card, you can pay with your card or cash when you arrive; if you don't show up, you'll be billed for one night. Reconfirm your reservations a day or two in advance for safety. Ask about the hotel's cancellation policy when you reserve—sometimes you have to cancel as far as two weeks ahead to avoid being charged.

## Camping, Hosteling, and Other Budget Beds

Campers can manage with *Let's Go* listings and help from the local TI (ask for a regional camping list). Your hometown travel bookstore also has guidebooks on camping in Europe. You'll find campgrounds just about everywhere you need them. Look for *Campingplatz* signs. You'll meet lots of Europeans—camping is a popular middle-class-family way to go. Campgrounds are cheap (about $10 per person), friendly, safe, more central and convenient than rustic, and rarely full.

If you're traveling alone, hosteling is the best way to conquer hotel loneliness. Hostels are also a tremendous source of local and budget travel information. They usually cost $15–25 per night (cheaper for those under 27) and serve good, cheap meals and/or provide kitchen facilities. Anyone of any age can hostel in Switzerland. While there are no membership concerns for private hostels, International Youth Hostel Federation (IYHF) hostels  require membership ($28 per year, sold at hostels in most US cities or online at www.hihostels.com, US tel. 202/783-6161). Those without cards simply buy one-night guest memberships for 6 SF.

If you plan to stay mainly in hostels, bring your own sheet (or pay extra at each place to rent one). While many hostels have a few doubles or family rooms available upon request for a little extra money, plan on gender-segregated dorms with 4–20 beds per room. Many hostel receptionists may say over the telephone that their hostel is full, but still hold a few beds for people who drop in. Follow signs marked *Jugendherberge* (with triangles) or with the logo showing a tree next to a house. If you get there and find that the hostel really is full, the staff can direct you to budget accommodations nearby.

Choose your hostel selectively. Hostels can be cozy mountain chalets, serene lakeside villas—or antiseptic spaces overrun by noisy school groups (most common on summer weekends and on school-year weekdays). While IYHF hostels are clean and predictable, they can also have an institutional feel. The independent hostels, sometimes called "backpackers," tend to be smaller than IYHF hostels, with fewer regulations and no school groups. I prefer these informal private hostels, which are usually more fun and more intimate-feeling than the IYHF variety—perfect for getting to know fellow travelers and hostel owners. Some of the hostels are even geared for special-interest guests, such as bicyclists or families traveling together. (For a list of some independent hostels, see www.swissbackpackers.ch.)

A fluffy straw bed awaits at a number of farms that have opened up their hay lofts to sleepy tourists. It's a fun hostel alternative, and more comfortable than you'd think (see www.abenteuer -stroh.ch/en for details).

Many hotels, restaurants, and campsites provide dormitory-style accommodations. Look for the word *lager,* which indicates cheap dorm beds—often a loft lined with mattresses. These slumber mills may be less charming than cozy hostels, but they're cheap and convenient.

For serious hikers and climbers, mountain huts are an essential alpine experience. Don't expect ski-lodge comfort: These practical, adventurous places are simple, offering a warm place to sleep and (usually) breakfast and dinner. Most mountain-hut guests are long-distance hikers, connecting one hut to another along an extended hiking trail. You'll pay about $15 a night for your bunk and grub (see www.sac-cas.ch for more information).

## EATING

The Swiss eat when we do and enjoy a straightforward, no-nonsense cuisine. Specialties include delicious fondue, rich chocolates, a melted cheese dish called raclette, *Rösti* (hash browns), fresh dairy products (try muesli with yogurt), 100 varieties of cheese, and Fendant—a good, crisp, local white wine.

### Restaurants and Budget Options

There are many kinds of restaurants. Hotels often serve fine food. A *Gaststätte* is a simple, less expensive restaurant. A *Weinstübli* (wine bar) or *Bierstübli* (tavern) usually serves food. Mountain huts—called *Hütte*—generally have hot chocolate and hearty meals.

If you're not too hungry, order from the *kleine Hunger* (small hunger) section of the menu. Many restaurants offer half portions, which is a great relief on your budget (although two people save even more by sharing one full portion).

Most restaurants tack a menu onto their door for browsers and have an English menu inside. Only a rude waiter will rush you. Good service is relaxed (slow to an American). To wish others "Happy eating!" offer a cheery *"En Guete!"* When you want the bill, ask for *"Die Rechnung, bitte."* (See the "Survival Phrases" in the appendix for more tips.)

Swiss restaurants are expensive, but there are several excellent budget alternatives. The Co-op and Migros grocery stores are the hungry hiker's best budget bet; groceries—while about 50 percent more than US prices—are a huge savings over any restaurant. These supermarkets also often come with cheap non-smoking self-service cafeterias, with good food at much lower prices than restaurants with table service. In most big cities, you'll find Manor department stores, which usually feature wonderful self-service eateries called "Manora"—with lush salad bars, tasty entrées, and fresh-squeezed juices (I've listed several specific Manora locations in this book). Bakeries are another great place for a snack or affordable light meal.

## Swiss Cuisine

Here at a crossroads of Europe, the food has a wonderful diversity: heavy *Wurst*-and-kraut Germanic fare; delicate, subtle French cuisine; and pasta dishes *all'Italiana.*

Aside from clocks and banks, Switzerland is known for its cheese. Gruyère cheese is hard, with a strong flavor; Emmentaler is also hard, but milder. Appenzeller is the incredibly pungent cheese from the northeast of Switzerland, with a smell that verges on nauseating...until you taste it. Two of Switzerland's best-known specialties are cheese-based.

*Käse fondue* is usually Emmentaler and Gruyère cheese melted with white wine, garlic, nutmeg, and other seasonings. You eat it with a long fork, dipping cubes of bread into it. Raclette is cheese slowly melted by a special appliance; as it softens, scrape a mound off and eat it with potatoes, pickled onions, and gherkins. (In restaurants, raclette often comes as little slices of cheese already melted.)

Another must-try dish, most typical in the mountains of the German-speaking areas, is *Rösti:* traditional hash browns with alpine cheese, often served with an egg cracked over it...yum.

Of course, each region has its own specialties. In French-speaking Switzerland, white wine and heavy cream are used in many dishes, and horsemeat (formerly imported from Eastern Europe, now imported from the US, New Zealand, and Australia) is common. The cuisine in eastern Switzerland (Pontresina, St. Moritz) uses chestnuts in many forms, wild mushrooms, and air-dried beef. Southwestern Switzerland (Zermatt area) specializes in all kinds of cheese, and their favorite white wine is Fendant.

Despite all the cheese and potatoes, the Swiss tend to be health-conscious. Menus often feature a *Fitnessteller* ("fitness plate")—usually a large mixed salad that comes with a steak, chicken, or fish. *Bio* means organically grown, and a *Biolädeli* is a store that sells organic products.

Swiss wine (about two-thirds white) is good, but expensive.

## How Was Your Trip?

Were your travels fun, smooth, and meaningful? If you'd like to share your tips, concerns, and discoveries, please fill out the survey at www.ricksteves.com/feedback or e-mail me at rick @ricksteves.com. I personally read and value your feedback. Thanks in advance—it helps a lot.

Try the dry, white Fendant, great with cheese dishes. If you're in Murten, sample the local Vully wine. Fruity St. Saphorin grows on the slopes above Lake Geneva. Menus list drink size by the tenth of a liter, or deciliter (dl). Order wine by the *Viertel* (quarter liter, or 8 oz.) or *Achtel* (eighth liter, or 4 oz.). Order it *süss* (sweet), *halb trocken* (medium), or *trocken* (dry). You can say, "*Ein Viertel Weisswein* (white wine), *bitte* (please)." *Rotwein* is red wine; a *Pfiff* is two deciliters (about 8 oz.) of red wine. *Bocalino* is a small, decorated eight-ounce ceramic jug with a light Swiss red wine called Dole.

Swiss beer is surprisingly good and inexpensive. Each pub has one brand of a local beer on tap, with others available in bottles. The standard size is a *Stange* (33 cl, or centiliters); the smaller size is called a *Herrgöttli* (20 cl). Beer mixed with lemon-flavored pop is called a *Panaché*. In summer, this light beer is refreshing.

Instead of Coke, try a local favorite: Rivella, a carbonated, vitamin-rich soft drink made with 35 percent milk serum. Its unusual (but not unpleasant) taste doesn't resemble milk at all; it's more like chewable vitamins. It comes in three colors: red is regular, blue is low-calorie, and green is mixed with green tea. Tap water—which many waiters aren't eager to bring you—is *Leitungswasser*. They would rather you buy *Mineralwasser* (*mit/ohne Gas*, with/without carbonation).

As an alternative to hot chocolate, try Ovomaltine. The Swiss have a fondness for this hot drink—a malt-derived vitamin supplement, flavored with chocolate so kids will drink it. (In the US, our Ovaltine is an Asian variation on this drink—considered by the Swiss to be a cheap copy.)

And, of course, there's chocolate. The Swiss changed the world in 1875 with their invention of milk chocolate. Nestlé, Suchard, and Lindt are the major producers. Stroll the chocolate aisle of a grocery store and take your pick.

## TRAVELING AS A TEMPORARY LOCAL

We travel all the way to Europe to enjoy differences—to become temporary locals. You'll experience frustrations. Certain truths that we find "God-given" or "self-evident," such as cold beer, ice in drinks, and bottomless cups of coffee, are suddenly not so true. One of the benefits of travel is the eye-opening realization that there are logical, civil, and even better alternatives. A willingness to go local ensures that you'll enjoy a full dose of Swiss hospitality.

If there is a negative aspect to the image the Swiss have of Americans, it is that we are big, aggressive, impolite, rich, loud, superficially friendly, and a bit naive. Americans tend to be noisy in public places, such as restaurants and trains. Our raised voices can demolish Switzerland's reserved ambience. Talk softly. While the Swiss look bemusedly at some of our Yankee excesses—and worriedly at others—they nearly always grant us individual travelers all the warmth we deserve.

Judging from all the happy postcards I receive from travelers who have used this book, it's safe to assume you'll enjoy a great, affordable vacation—with the finesse of an independent, experienced traveler. Thanks, and happy travels—*gute Reise!*

# BACK DOOR TRAVEL PHILOSOPHY
### From *Rick Steves' Europe Through the Back Door*

Travel is intensified living—maximum thrills per minute and one of the last great sources of legal adventure. Travel is freedom. It's recess, and we need it.

Experiencing the real Europe requires catching it by surprise, going casual..."Through the Back Door."

Affording travel is a matter of priorities. (Make do with the old car.) You can eat and sleep—simply, safely, and enjoyably—anywhere in Europe for $100 a day plus transportation costs. In many ways, spending more money only builds a thicker wall between you and what you traveled so far to see. Europe is a cultural carnival, and, time after time, you'll find that its best acts are free and the best seats are the cheap ones.

A tight budget forces you to travel close to the ground, meeting and communicating with the people, not relying on service with a purchased smile. Never sacrifice sleep, nutrition, safety, or cleanliness in the name of budget. Simply enjoy the local-style alternatives to expensive hotels and restaurants.

Extroverts have more fun. If your trip is low on magic moments, kick yourself and make things happen. If you don't enjoy a place, maybe you don't know enough about it. Seek the truth. Recognize tourist traps. Give a culture the benefit of your open mind. See things as different but not better or worse. Any culture has much to share.

Of course, travel, like the world, is a series of hills and valleys. Be fanatically positive and militantly optimistic. If something's not to your liking, change your liking. Travel is addictive. It can make you a happier American as well as a citizen of the world. Our earth is home to six and a half billion equally precious people. It's humbling to travel and find that people don't envy Americans. Europeans like us, but, with all due respect, they wouldn't trade passports.

Globe-trotting destroys ethnocentricity. It helps you understand and appreciate different cultures. Regrettably, there are forces in our society that want you dumbed down for their convenience. Don't let it happen. Thoughtful travel engages you with the world—more important than ever these days. Travel changes people. It broadens perspectives and teaches new ways to measure quality of life. Rather than fear the diversity on this planet, travelers celebrate it. Many travelers toss aside their hometown blinders. Their prized souvenirs are the strands of different cultures they decide to knit into their own character. The world is a cultural yarn shop, and Back Door travelers are weaving the ultimate tapestry. Join in!

# SWITZERLAND

 Switzerland is one of Europe's richest, best organized, most expensive countries. Like the Boy Scouts, the Swiss count cleanliness, neatness, punctuality, tolerance, independence, thrift, and hard work as virtues...and they love pocketknives. Their high income, a great social security system, and the spectacular Alps give the Swiss plenty to be thankful for.

Nearly half of Switzerland, Europe's most mountainous country, consists of uninhabitable rocks, lakes, and rugged Alps. Despite the country's small size, it is unusually diverse. Its wild geography has kept people apart historically, helping its many regions maintain their distinct cultural differences. Switzerland is at a linguistic crossroads of Europe, with four official languages: German, French, Italian, and Romansh (an obscure Latin dialect spoken by a tiny group in the southeast).

Historically, Switzerland is one of Europe's oldest democracies, yet women didn't get the vote until 1971. Born when three states (cantons) united in 1291, the Confederation Helvetica grew to the 26 cantons of today. (The "CH" decal on cars doesn't stand for chocolate.) The country is named for the Celtic Helvetia tribe that lived here back in Roman times. The Confederation Helvetica government is decentralized, and cantonal loyalty is very strong.

Stubbornly independent (or maybe just smart), Switzerland loves its neutrality, and stayed out of both World Wars. But it's far from lax when it comes to national defense. Every able-bodied man serves in the army and stays in the reserve. Each house has a gun and a fully stocked bomb shelter. (Swiss vacuum-packed emergency army bread, which lasts two years, is also said to function as a weapon.) Switzerland bristles with 600,000 rifles in homes and 12,000 heavy guns in place. Airstrips are hidden inside mountains, accessed by camouflaged doors. With the push of a button, all road, rail, and bridge entries to Swiss territory can be destroyed, sealing off the country from the outside world. Sentiments are changing, though, and Switzerland has come close to voting away its entire military. Today, you can visit once-hidden military installations, now open to the public as museums (for an example, see page 89).

## Switzerland Almanac

**Official Name:** The Confederation Helvetica, or Switzerland, has a different name in each of its four official languages: Schweizerische Eidgenossenschaft (German), Confédération Suisse (French), Confederazione Svizzera (Italian), and Confederaziun Svizra (Romansh). Locals shorten those to "Schweiz," "Suisse," "Svizzera," and "Svizra."

**Population:** Switzerland's seven million people (similar to Virginia) are almost exclusively of European heritage—German, French, or Italian—though the ever-increasing immigration of foreigners concerns many natives. Three out of five Swiss speak German as their main language, one in five speaks French, seven percent speak Italian, and about half of one percent speak Romansh. The populace is 42 percent Catholic, 35 percent Protestant, two percent Orthodox, four percent Muslim, six percent other or unspecified, and 11 percent unchurched.

**Latitude and Longitude:** 47°N and 8°E, similar latitude to Washington State or Quebec, Canada.

**Area:** 16,000 square miles; twice the size of New Jersey, or half the size of South Carolina.

**Geography:** Switzerland sits at the crossroads between northern and southern Europe. The Alps are Europe's high point and continental divide, from which the major rivers flow—Rhine, Rhône, Danube, and Po. Switzerland's highest point is the 15,200-foot Monte Rosa (specifically, the summit called Dufourspitze), along the Italian border. Though Switzerland is mostly mountainous, the center of the country consists of rolling hills and large lakes.

**Biggest Cities:** One in seven Swiss lives in or near Zürich (pop. 366,000 in the city; 1.3 million in the metropolitan area). Geneva has 185,000 people, and Basel has 166,000. The capital is Bern (pop. 127,000).

**Economy:** Like a fine watch, Switzerland's economy just keeps on ticking. The Gross Domestic Product is $264 billion, similar to Washington State. Its per capita GDP of $35,300 is among Europe's highest (but still 15 percent less than

In 2002, Switzerland legalized marijuana use. When polls showed that more than 30 percent of the country had used marijuana, the Parliament decided to decriminalize the drug, rather than criminalize a third of its population. But, while not wanting to clog its prisons with petty pot smokers, the country doesn't want to be known as another Holland, either. So the law remains a bit ambiguous: The Swiss can possess and use pot, but they can't sell

the US). The franc is strong, workers are highly skilled, and unemployment is half the European Union average. Blessed with hydropower and using nuclear technology, Switzerland generates 99 percent of its electricity with virtually no oil. Though not a European Union member, Switzerland conforms to EU standards to stay competitive. Major Swiss money-makers include banking (especially secret, private accounts from around the world), insurance, watches (from top-of-the-line pieces to inexpensive Swatches), chemicals and pharmaceuticals, Nestlé chocolate, tourism, and precision instruments—Swiss-made equipment helps make everything from clothing to ballpoint-pen tips to parts for the Mars exploration rover.

**Currency:** 1 Swiss franc (SF) = 100 Rappen = about $0.80; 1.25 SF = about $1.

**Government:** Founded in 1291 as a confederation of cantons, the country is still a model of federalism, balancing the needs of its different linguistic/ethnic groups. No single political party (or two or even three parties) dominates the political landscape. The president (likely Micheline Calmy-Rey in 2007), chosen by the legislature, serves for just one calendar year. The two-house Federal Assembly consists of the 46-seat Council of States and the 200-seat National Council, elected for four-year terms.

**Flag:** Switzerland's white cross on a red background may have been the inspiration for the red-on-white symbol of the International Red Cross.

**The Average Swiss:** He or she is 40 years old (four years older than the average American), has 1.43 children, and will live to be 80. A typical Swiss man serves at least 260 days of compulsory service in the military. The average woman spends two hours a day on housework. He or she travels about 1,300 miles a year on a train, the equivalent of crossing the country six times. Sixteen percent of the average Swiss income goes to taxes, and 20 percent of the household budget is spent buying insurance. Every month, the average Swiss eats two pounds of chocolate and drinks a quart of alcohol.

it. Each spring, there's a push for stricter control. Word gets out that Switzerland is no haven for pot, and then things ease up.

The costs of a night on the town are high. More and more locals call sitting on the pavement around a bottle of wine "going out." Hotels with double rooms less than $100 are rare. Even dormitory beds are expensive. If your budget is tight, be sure to chase down hostels (many have family rooms) and keep your eyes peeled for *Matratzenlagers* ("mattress dorms"). Hiking is free, though major alpine lifts run around $50.

While Switzerland's booming big cities are cosmopolitan, traditional culture survives in the alpine villages. Spend most of your time getting high in the Alps. On Sunday, you're most likely to enjoy traditional music, clothing, and culture. August 1 is the festive Swiss national holiday.

## A Swiss Timeline

Switzerland has a unique and impressive story—forging unity from diversity, and somehow remaining above the fray when Europe goes ballistic. Despite four languages, diverse geography, ill-defined borders, and many religious sects—and despite being surrounded by continental Europe's four big powers (France, Germany, Austria, and Italy)—the Swiss cantons banded together to form an independent federal system that still works today.

**500,000,000 B.C.:** The ocean floor is rocked by earthquakes that fold the earth upward, creating the Alps.

**53 B.C.:** Julius Caesar defeats the Helvetia, a Celtic tribe. The Romans' language, Latin, would eventually evolve into the French, Italian, and Romansh languages spoken in Switzerland today.

**c. A.D. 300:** Germanic tribes invade and settle.

**c. 600:** An Irish missionary named Columbanus arrives and converts the pagan Swiss to Christianity.

**800:** Swiss lands are part of Charlemagne's empire, later called the Holy Roman Empire, under German kings.

**1256–1273:** During a period in which no emperor rules, the Swiss develop a measure of independence. When Austrian Hapsburgs are brought in to reign, the Swiss resent foreign control.

**1291:** On August 1, Swiss citizens swear the oath, "We will be a single nation of brothers..." and rise up against Hapsburg rule. The three cantons of Uri, Schwyz, and Unterwalden unite, proclaiming independence and democratic institutions. In a legend of the time, the Swiss William Tell refuses to bow to the Hapsburg hat, a symbol of their power. As punishment, he's forced to shoot an apple off his own son's head. He does so, then leads a rebellion. In fact, the Swiss often outbattled the more powerful Hapsburgs, but they had to fight for two full centuries to drive out the Hapsburgs, earning a reputation as Europe's fiercest warriors. Swiss mercenaries (like the Swiss Guards that protect the Vatican today) became a major export.

**1332:** Luzern joins the Swiss Federation, soon followed by more cantons.

**1499:** A treaty makes Switzerland independent in fact, if not in name.

**1500s:** During the Reformation, Switzerland is bitterly divided, but offers a haven for free thinkers. Ulrich Zwingli establishes Protestantism in Zürich, John Calvin (a Frenchman) brings followers to Geneva, and Erasmus (from Holland) teaches at Basel.

**1648:** The Treaty of Westphalia officially makes Switzerland independent.

**1798:** French revolutionary forces occupy Switzerland and try to establish a strong central government. It doesn't stick, so Napoleon restores canton power (1803).

**1815:** The Congress of Vienna proclaims Switzerland with today's borders.

**1848:** Amid a Europe-wide wave of liberal reforms, Switzerland's tradition of democracy is established in a constitution. The new Confederation features a modern, bicameral parliament modeled after America's form of government, but with less power given to the executive branch.

**1864:** The International Red Cross is founded by a Genevan.

**1872–1882:** The Gotthard railway is built over the Alps. A wave of breathtaking mountain engineering follows, taming much of the Alps and bringing vacationers safely and effortlessly to previously unheard-of heights.

**1914–1918:** In World War I, Switzerland declares neutrality, and Geneva serves as the postwar seat of the League of Nations (a forerunner to the United Nations).

**1939–1945:**  When World War II breaks out, 850,000 Swiss men grab their rifles and mobilize to protect the borders while they declare neutrality. Critics charge that, though neutral, Switzerland's open trade policies helped supply Nazi Germany.

**c. 1945:**  After the war, their policy of neutrality leads the Swiss to refuse membership in the UN, NATO, and the EU.

**1989:**  The final canton (Appenzell) grants women the right to vote.

**2002:**  Switzerland joins the United Nations, but decides to hold off on EU membership.

**2003:**  Landlocked Switzerland wins the world's most prestigious sailboat race, the America's Cup.

**2007:**  Today, Switzerland's 26 cantons are autonomous, part of a loose federalist democracy. Four political parties rule in an ever-changing array of coalitions, as they have since World War II.

# ZÜRICH

Zürich is one of those cities that tourists tend to skip right through. Since it's a transportation hub, people fly in or change trains here, but don't give stopping a serious thought. The local graffiti jokes: *Zürich = zu reich, zu ruhig* ("too rich, too quiet"). But even though you won't find a hint of Swiss Miss in Switzerland's leading city—and with limited time, I'd certainly spend it up in the mountains—Zürich is surprisingly comfortable and enjoyable for a quick visit. There's much more to Switzerland than yodeling and alpine–meadow–munching cows.

Zürich was founded by the Romans in 58 B.C. as a customs post. Roman Turicum eventually became Zürich. It gained city status in the 10th century, and by the 19th century it was a leading European financial and economic center. Today, it's home to the world's largest gold marketplace and fourth largest stock exchange (after New York, London, and Tokyo). Assuming you've got the money to enjoy it, Zürich is by many measures the world's most livable city. Its 366,000 people (1.3 million in greater Zürich) are known for their wealth and hard work. Zürich is the only place in Switzerland where you'll see men in ties running in the streets.

## Planning Your Time

While Luzern and Bern provide more charming urban experiences, Zürich is worth a quick visit. With two weeks in Switzerland, I'd spend a day here. Begin by visiting the impressive Swiss National Museum, then wander along the river, using my self-guided walk (see page 47), and take a river/lake cruise. With less time, do only the self-guided walk. With more time, take your pick of the many art museums.

# ORIENTATION

Zürich sprawls around the northern tip of the long, skinny Lake Zürich (Zürichsee). The grand Bahnhofstrasse cuts through Zürich's glitzy shopping center, connecting the train station and the country's top historical museum (Swiss National Museum) with the lakefront in a 15-minute walk. Running parallel to that, across the Limmat River, is the Niederdorf neighborhood—a vibrant, cobbled, Old World zone of colorful little shops, cafés, and restaurants.

## Tourist Information

A helpful TI is located in the great hall of the train station (under the fat blue angel; May–Oct Mon–Sat 8:00–20:30, Sun 8:30–18:30; Nov–April Mon–Sat 8:30–19:00, Sun 9:00–18:30; tel. 044-215-4000, www.zuerich.com). Pick up their city guide and map, browse the racks of brochures, and ask about their daily walking tours. This TI sells a one-day **Swiss Pass** not available elsewhere in the country (95 SF, covers most museums and unlimited second-class travel on trains, buses, and boats throughout Switzerland).

For a whirlwind visit, consider the **ZürichCARD,** which covers transportation by train, tram, bus, and boat; admission to 43 museums; a 50 percent discount on the city walking tour; and "welcome drinks" in many restaurants (15 SF/24 hrs, 30 SF/72 hrs, sold at TI). The one-day card will pay for itself if you do the walking tour and at least one museum or boat cruise in a day.

**Tours:** You can tour Zürich on a **guided walk** (2 hrs, 20 SF, 10 SF with ZürichCARD, leaves from TI mid-April–Oct daily at 15:00, Sat–Sun also at 11:00) or by **bus** (2 hrs, 32 SF, May–Oct daily at 9:45, 12:00, and 14:00). The TI has details on both tours.

## Arrival in Zürich

**By Train:** The slick train station (with a TI and shopping mall—see beginning of self-guided walk, below) is on the north end of town; to reach most of the recommended hotels, cross Walchebrücke bridge in front of the station.

**By Plane:** From Zürich Airport (Flughafen Kloten), catch a train to the train station downtown (5.80 SF, 15 min, departures every 10 min 5:00–24:00) rather than take a 50-SF taxi ride. For more on the airport, see page 62.

## Getting Around Zürich

A ticket good for one ride on the trams and buses costs 2.40 SF (2-hour ticket for 3.80 SF, 24-hour transit pass for 7.60 SF). All transportation is covered by the ZürichCARD, mentioned above.

## Helpful Hints

**Bikes:** A city program called "Züri rollt" allows you to borrow a bike for free (leave passport and 20-SF deposit, May–Oct daily 7:30–21:30, various locations, including Swiss National Museum and the Opera, look for *Züri rollt* or *Velogate* signs). For more info, ask the TI or visit www.zuerirollt.ch.

**Laundry:** Try **Waschsalon Anker** (Tue–Fri 13:00–19:00, Sat 10:00–14:00, closed Sun–Mon; small load-8 SF, big load-10 SF; take tram #2 or #3 to Bezirksgebäude, then walk past the cinema down Ankerstrasse to Ankerstrasse 9; tel. 043-243-3831). **Easy-Waschservice** is larger but farther away (Mon–Fri 8:30–12:00 & 13:30–18:30, Sat 12:00–16:00, closed Sun, take tram #13 to Zwielplatz, Limattalstrasse 236, tel. 044-342-4565).

**Phone System Change:** Until recently, all Zürich phone numbers began with 01; now they begin with 044. However, the 01 numbers will continue to work through March 2007, and you may still see numbers printed this way in older sources.

## SELF-GUIDED WALK

### Welcome to Zürich

This handy walking tour is the perfect orientation for travelers blitzing Zürich from the train station. It crisscrosses the river,

connecting the city center's main sights en route to the boat dock for a lazy lake-cruise finale (or a quick tram back to the station). Allow about an hour for the walk.

**Train Station:** Zürich's central station has great energy. This major European transportation hub handles 2,000 trains a day, including InterCity expresses to many major capitals. Built in 1870, its vast main hall was once lined with tracks. Today, it's a farmers' market (Wed 11:00–20:00) and community hall—busy with concerts, exhibitions, and even beach volleyball. The station sits above a vast underground modern shopping mall (open late—until 20:00—and on Sundays).

Above you, find the fat blue angel, Zürich's "Guardian Angel" protecting all travelers. The angel, who's been here since 1997 to celebrate the 150th anniversary of the Swiss rail system, looks toward the **Swiss National Museum,** just across the street. It's the best museum in town, offering an essential introduction to Swiss history. To maximize your education, tour this museum before starting the walk (see page 56).

# Welcome to Zürich Walk

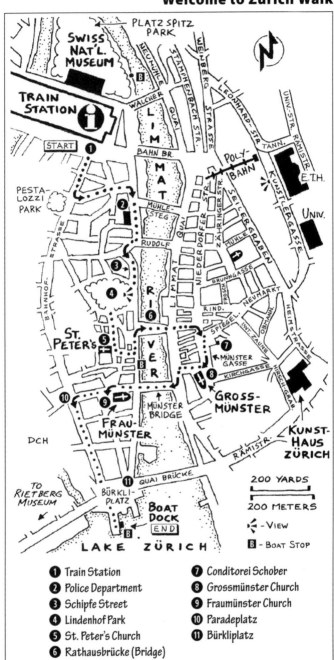

1. Train Station
2. Police Department
3. Schipfe Street
4. Lindenhof Park
5. St. Peter's Church
6. Rathausbrücke (Bridge)
7. Conditorei Schober
8. Grossmünster Church
9. Fraumünster Church
10. Paradeplatz
11. Bürkliplatz

• *The station fronts Zürich's main shopping boulevard...*

**Bahnhofstrasse:** Bahnhofstrasse, stretching from here to the lake, is lined with all the big-name shops. Head on down.

On the right, the only **park** along this pedestrian- and tram-only boulevard is dedicated to Zürich's most important teacher, Johann Heinrich Pestalozzi (1746–1827). He promoted the notion, still prevalent in today's Switzerland, that a good education should be available for everyone (not only for sons of rich families). Parks like this are rare in central Zürich because of sky-high property values—among the most expensive in the world.

Turn left just before the park onto Beatengasse, and walk toward the Limmat River. Then go right onto Werdmühlestrasse, and head toward Werdmühleplatz (following signs to *Stadtpolizei*), and make a short stop at the **Police Department,** facing the river. Don't be shy—show your ID and enter for a free peek at an amazing wall painting by Swiss artist Augusto Giacometti. His famous *Hall of the Flowers* (*Blüemlihalle*, 1926), awash in bright colors, reflects the relief and joy the artist felt when World War I ended.

• *From here, walk along the river upstream toward the church spires (without crossing the river). Back when the city's trade depended on river traffic, this small riverside street, called* **Schipfe***, was Zürich's harbor. Pass a fun riverside eatery (Restaurant Schipfe 16—see "Eating," page 62) and an arcade. Twenty yards before the ugliest bridge in Switzerland, head uphill two blocks, and then right up Pfalzgasse, to enjoy a great view from another park...*

**Lindenhof:** Important forts and strategic buildings stood on this hilltop square from Roman times through Carolingian times. But when Zürich became a free city in the 13th century, the townspeople destroyed the fort and established a law forbidding any new construction. The citizens realized that whoever lived on this hill would rule over the city—and they didn't want any more rulers. Today, this is a people's square, where locals relax under linden trees (for which the square is named) and enjoy the commanding city view.

Survey Zürich beyond its river. The **university** (behind the green spire) is the largest in Switzerland, with 25,000 students. Left of that is Zürich's renowned technical college, the ETH (Eidgenössische Technische Hochschule, or Federal Institute of Technology), with 15,000 students. The ETH has graduated 25 Nobel Prize winners, including Albert Einstein and Wilhelm Röntgen (who discovered X-rays). The university and ETH terrace offers a great city viewpoint (which you could visit later by taking tram #6 or #10 to the ETH stop). The boats moored under the street are traditional farmer delivery vehicles, sculled with one oar like Venetian gondolas. Lining the far side of the river, Niederdorf is the lively restaurant, café, and bar district (see "Eating," page 60).

## Switzerland's Zwingli Reformation

Today's Evangelical Reformed Church of Switzerland was founded by Huldrych Zwingli (1484–1531), who preached in Zürich from 1519 through 1531. A follower of the humanist philosopher Erasmus of Rotterdam, Zwingli believed that the true foundation of the church was based on preaching the Holy Scriptures freely. In 1522, most of German-speaking Switzerland embraced Zwingli's ideas—and that required leaving the Roman Catholic Church.

Zwingli was 33 in 1517, when German church reformer Martin Luther posted his revolutionary *95 Theses* (which questioned the practice of selling forgiveness, salvation, church offices, and so on). Within two years, sellers of indulgences were refused entry to Zürich. As the Reformation swept Switzerland, things heated up. In 1523, rioters were storming churches, and authorities called for an orderly removal of all images in Zürich houses of worship (except stained glass windows).

The new, reformed Swiss church let priests marry. (Zwingli—like Luther—promptly took advantage of this freedom.) Fancy Masses were replaced by simple services. At Zürich's main church, the Grossmünster, preachers studied Latin, Greek, and Hebrew in order to translate the Bible into the people's German. In 1531, the Zwingli Bible (the first complete Bible translated into German) was published. It's still used today (like the King James Bible is in English).

Zwingli gave the Swiss church an unusual austerity: no altar, no pictures, and for a while, not even any music. Church services focused on preaching. Holy Communion was celebrated only on holidays. This puritanical simplicity permeated Swiss society in general. Zwingli (no fan of the "separation of church and state")

On a clear day, you can see the Alps (behind the twin domes).

• *Take the stairs just left of the chess players down to Strehlgasse, and follow Glockengasse, passing to the left of the Golden Bell. Continue down tiny Robert-Walser-Gasse—passing a characteristic eatery, Reblaube Gaststube, made famous by visits from Goethe in 1779—to St. Peterhofstatt, a square with Zürich's oldest church.*

**St. Peter's Church:** Founded in the seventh century, this church has one of Europe's largest clock faces (28 feet in diameter). The town watchman used to live above the clock. If he spotted a fire, he would ring the alarm and hang a flag out of the window

established an ironclad city law: The government's duty was to oversee public worship, and only preaching true to the Bible was to be tolerated.

But Zwingli's reforms were by no means universally supported. Oh, it was a mess: Switzerland's Protestant movement split over baptism. Luther and Zwingli split over the Eucharist (is Christ's body really *in* the bread, or there only in a spiritual sense?). And, as old-school Catholics predicted, putting the Bible into the hands of regular people brought chaos—enabling every Tom, Dick, and Hans to "carve his own path to hell." Switzerland was embroiled in a religious civil war, as Protestant cantons fought Catholic ones. In 1531, while fighting as a "citizen soldier," Zwingli was killed in battle. His friend and partner Heinrich Bullinger succeeded him as the leader of German-speaking Swiss Protestantism.

Bullinger collaborated with John Calvin as Swiss Protestantism matured. The Protestant focus on preaching promoted the translation and interpretation of the Bible. Everyone was reading the Bible directly, which promoted literacy. The Reformation provided a basis of the autonomous community spirit, strong work ethic, and high literacy of a prosperous Switzerland for the future. The Swiss church became a place where equals would meet and worship God. Zwingli's heritage included transferring the notion of social charity from being a church phenomenon to being the social welfare responsibility of any self-respecting modern state. The foundations of Swiss democracy and its present social policies are rooted in Zwingli's teaching. And these Swiss reformers planted the seeds of what became the Presbyterian Church in the United States.

facing the blaze. This system seems to have worked—Zürich never suffered a major fire. In the 18th century, this church had such a well-loved preacher, Johann Kaspar Lavater (1741–1801), that people reserved their seats for Sunday Mass. The minister, a friend of Goethe, had long discussions over glasses of wine with the "German Shakespeare" in the nearby Reblaube Gaststube, mentioned above.

**From St. Peter's Church to the Grossmünster:** Continue past the church on Schlüsselgasse and take the first left, down the narrow Thermengasse (Bath Street).

Under your feet are excavations of a **Roman bath,** discovered by accident in 1984. A sketch on the wall shows the bath. Studs elevated the floor, which was heated from below.

The lane empties out on **Weinplatz,** a wine market of centuries past (notice the grape-picker on the fine little fountain). Zürich's fountain water, which is regularly checked for quality, is as good as bottled mineral water. A wall mural inside the Barchetta bar shows the medieval river action. (Note the dock here for river and lake cruises—see page 54.)

The city's oldest bridge, the **Rathausbrücke,** goes back to Roman times. Cross the bridge, passing the 17th-century, Renaissance-style City Hall, and walk a block uphill to Marktgasse—the gateway to the bustling **Niederdorf** neighborhood. To the left, down Niederdorfstrasse, is the best place for colorful streets, fun shopping, restaurants, and nightlife. You can explore this area now...or, better yet, tonight.

To continue our walk, go the opposite direction (right), heading down **Münstergasse.** At #19, pop into Schwarzenbach, which still advertises "merchandise from the colonies" out front and sells things the old-fashioned way inside (in loose bags, by the weight). Inhale. Pick up 100 grams of dried bananas from Togo or some Thai sticks...coconut, of course. Across the street, Zürich's popular Conditorei Schober, a riot of silk flowers, serves famously good (and expensive) hot chocolate and champagne truffles. Try not to look at the kinky knights on the plaque opposite #17.

• *Ahead is the "big cathedral" (literally)...*

**Grossmünster:** It was here that Huldrych Zwingli sparked the Reformation in German-speaking Switzerland (see "Switzerland's Zwingli Reformation" sidebar, page 50). The domes of its towers (early examples of neo-Gothic) are symbols of Zürich. They were rebuilt following a 1781 fire, and after much civic discussion, were left a plain stone color. Step inside and sit down...let the strength and purity of the 12th-century Romanesque architecture have its way with you. The simple round arches feel strong, and the wide triumphal arch separating the nave from the altar makes you feel like a winner.

The impact of the architecture is made stronger since it's uncluttered—Zwingli's reforms led to a clean sweep of Catholic decor in 1519.

In the front are three choir windows by Augusto Giacometti (c. 1933, perhaps Switzerland's most famous modern artist, known for his gnarled and stretched-super-thin metal statues). Mary and the baby Jesus meet the three kings bearing their gifts, while angels hover above with offerings of flowers. In the crypt (stairs below altar), you'll see an original 15th-century statue of Charlemagne (a copy now fills its niche on the river side of the church exterior). The church is free and open daily (9:00–18:00, pick up English bio of Zwingli). For 2 SF and 200 steps, you can enjoy a fine city view from atop the tower (Mon–Sat 9:15–17:00, Sun 12:30–17:00).

Leaving the church, go right and into the corner, where a door leads to a fine Romanesque cloister ringed with fanciful 12th-century carvings (free, Mon–Fri 9:00–18:00, closed Sat–Sun). Upon entering, take eight steps to the left and meet the sculptor (self-portrait on the highest arch).

• *Cross the river to another tall-steepled church.*

**Fraumünster:** This was founded as an abbey church for a convent out-side the town walls in 853. The current building, which sits on the same footprint as its Carolingian predecessor, dates from 1250. With the Reformation of Zwingli, the church was taken by the Zürich town council in 1524 and—you know the drill—gutted to fit Zwingli's taste. Today, it's famous for its windows by Chagall, described in the "Fraumünster's Chagall Windows" sidebar on the next page.

**From the Fraumünster to Lake Zürich:** From the church, Poststrasse (continuing away from the river) takes you back to Bahnhofstrasse and the busy **Paradeplatz.** Survey the scene: The train station is a 10-minute walk to your right, and the lake is a few minutes to your left. You're facing Sprüngli, Zürich's top café for the past century. Its "Luxemburgerli" macaroons—little cream-filled, one-inch macaroon-meringue hamburgers—are a local favorite (you can buy just a couple; if you buy 100 grams, you'll get a selection of 12). The café upstairs offers elegant finger-sandwich lunches. To the right is Credit Suisse (with a ground floor full of fancy shops). A bit farther (at #31) is the fine little Beyer watch museum (the watchmaker's personal collection, in the basement of his watch shop; 5 SF, Mon–Fri 14:00–18:00, closed Sat–Sun).

Finish this walk at the lake. Turning left, follow Bahnhofstrasse to Bürkliplatz and the boats. **Lake Zürich** is 17 miles long, 2.5 miles wide, and—because it's relatively shallow—warm enough for swimming. From here, you can enjoy the lakeside promenade (a fine strolling path 3 miles in either direction, left is sunnier) or a short cruise (see below). Tram #11 zips you back to the station, and so will the riverboat-bus (described below).

## Fraumünster's Chagall Windows

The church's claim to fame is its 30-foot-tall stained glass windows by Marc Chagall (1887–1985), the Russian-born French artist. Chagall gave an exhibit in Zürich in 1967. It was such a hit that the city offered the world-famous artist a commission. To their surprise, the 80-year-old Chagall accepted. Having stood in the church's spacious chancel (50 feet by 40 feet by 60 feet), he intuitively felt it was a place where his unique mix of religious themes could flourish.

For the next three years, he threw his heart and soul into the project, making the sketches at his home on the French Riviera, then working in close collaboration with a glass-making factory in Rheims. After the colored panes were made, Chagall personally painted the figures on with black outlines, which were then baked into the glass. Chagall spent weeks in Zürich overseeing the installation and completion.

His inimitable painting style—deep colors, simple figures, and shard-like Cubism—is perfectly suited to the stained glass medium. Blending Jewish and Christian traditions, Chagall created a work that can make people of many faiths comfortable.

The five windows (left to right) depict Bible scenes, culminating in the central image of the crucified Christ:

**1. The Prophets (red):** The prophet Elisha (bottom) looks up to watch a horse-drawn chariot carry his mentor Elijah off to heaven. Further up, Jeremiah (blue in color and mood) puts his hand to his head and ponders the destruction of wicked Jerusalem. Up in heaven (top), a multicolored, multifaceted God spins out his creation, sending fiery beams down to inspire his Prophets on earth. This window is artificially lit, as it's built into an interior wall.

**2. Jacob (blue—Chagall's favorite color):** Jacob (bottom, in deep purple amid deep blue) dreams of a ladder that snakes up to heaven, with red-tinged angels ascending and descending, symbolizing the connection between God above and Jacob's descendants (the Children of Israel) below.

## SIGHTS AND ACTIVITIES

**Cruises on Limmat River and Lake Zürich**—There are two basic boat-ride options: 1) small, low-floating buses that take local commuters and joy-riding visitors up and down the river and to points nearby on the lake; and 2) big, romantic lake ships taking tourists on longer rides around Lake Zürich. All boats leave from Bürkliplatz (lake end of Bahnhofstrasse) and are covered by railpasses (but it costs a flexi-day—handy if you're already using that day for a train trip to or from Zürich). None of the

**3. Christ (green):** The central, biggest window depicts the central figure in God's plan of salvation—Jesus Christ, who as the Messiah fulfills the promises of the Old Testament prophets. Mother Mary suckles baby Jesus (bottom) amid the leafy family tree of Jesus' Old Testament roots. The central area is an indistinct jumble of events from Christ's life, leading up to his crucifixion. The life-size Christ is crucified in a traditional medieval pose, but he's surrounded by a circle that seems to be bearing him, resurrected, to heaven. Chagall signed and dated the work (1970).

**4. Zion (yellow):** King David (bottom right) strums his harp and sings a psalm, while behind him stands his mistress Bathsheba, who gave birth to Solomon, the builder of Jerusalem's temple. At the end of history, an angel (top) blows a ram's horn, announcing the establishment of a glorious New Jerusalem, which descends down (center), featuring red, yellow, and green walls, domes, and towers.

**5. The Law (blue):** Moses, with horns of light and the Ten Commandments (top), looks sternly down on lawbreaking warriors on horseback wreaking havoc. At the bottom, an angel (in red) embraces the prophet Isaiah (very bottom) and inspires him to foretell the coming of the Messiah (in red, above the angel). Bible scholars note that Isaiah (who predicted the Messiah) points from this window across to King David (in window four), whose descendant was Jesus (born on the same level in window three), who fulfills the promise.

Everyone comes away with a different interpretation of this complex work, which combines images from throughout the Bible. The tall, skinny windows seem to emphasize the vertical connection between heaven above and earth below, both bathed in the same colored light. Some think Chagall used colors symbolically: blue and green represent the earth, while red and yellow are heavenly radiance. But all recognize that the jumble of images—as complex as God's universe—reaches its Point Omega in the central act of Christ's crucifixion.

boats comes with commentary.

The riverboat-buses (very low, to squeeze under the bridges) make a 60-minute loop around the Zürich end of the lake and down the river to the train station and Swiss National Museum (2/hr, daily 10:00–22:00, schedule posted at pier 6, buy ticket on boat; 3.80 SF for any ride, short or long; free with 24-hr transit pass or ZürichCARD). These buses can be handy for connecting the lake and the Swiss National Museum.

The big, touristy, lake-only boats run daily from spring through fall (7.60 SF for basic 90-min version, 2/hr, 11:00–19:00).

They also offer longer trips, jazz and dinner cruises, and so on. The ticket kiosk is near pier 1; boats depart from piers 1 through 6.

▲**Swiss National Museum (Schweizerisches Landesmuseum)**—This massive museum, in a neo-Gothic castle next to the train station, presents a wide range of artifacts from Swiss history. In the late 19th century, it was clear that the world was changing, and the Swiss wanted to protect their unique heritage. A national competition was held, and Zürich (promising to provide a piece of land, pay for construction, and donate an impressive collection) won the privilege of hosting the country's National Museum. The quirky building is a mish-mash of architectural themes from around the country. The museum, while huge and entertaining, is decidedly old school—but a slick new wing is planned to open in 2008 (5 SF, covered by ZürichCARD and Swiss Pass—see page 4, Tue–Sun 10:00–17:00, closed Mon, Museumstrasse 2, tel. 044-218-6511; good café in courtyard that leads into Platzspitz Park, www.musee-suisse.com).

Here are a few highlights, by floor: The basement features exhibits on medieval bookmaking and winemaking, an intricate diorama of the pivotal Battle of Murten (see page 114), and a room of huge church bells with an inviting rubber mallet (unique in Europe...bang away). The ground floor has pre-Reformation church art—all the fancy stuff the Protestants gutted from the churches so they could "concentrate." There's also a Zwingli room about the Reformation in Switzerland and medieval living rooms. On the first and second floors are living rooms from the Renaissance and the 18th and 19th centuries. The third floor is home to a small toy exhibit, plus traditional folk costumes from around the country.

**Platzspitz Park**—What used to be a riverside hangout for drug addicts has been cleaned up and—apart from a rusty needle here and there—is now a safe, friendly place for a scenic picnic (free, daily 6:00–21:00, behind train station and Swiss National Museum, clean WC). From here, you can take a riverboat-bus down the river and around the lake (included in 24-hour transit pass or ZürichCARD, departures at :05 and :35, see above).

**Kunsthaus Zürich**—Switzerland's top collection of modern art includes Swiss artists (Alberto Giacometti, Johann Heinrich Füssli, and Ferdinand Hodler) as well as international greats such as Munch, Picasso, Kokoschka, Beckmann, Corinth, Monet, and Chagall. The younger generation is also represented, with works by Rothko, Merz, Twombly, Beuys, Bacon, and Baselitz (10 SF, covered by ZürichCARD and Swiss Pass—see page 4; Tue–Thu 10:00–21:00, Fri–Sun 10:00–17:00, closed Mon; tram #3, #5, #8, or #9, or bus #31 to Kunsthaus stop, Heimplatz 1; tel. 044-253-8484, www.kunsthaus.ch).

**Rietberg Museum**—Filling historic villas set in a beautiful park, this museum houses art from Asia, Africa, America, and the South Pacific (12 SF, covered by ZürichCARD and Swiss Pass—see page 4; Tue–Sun 10:00–17:00, Wed–Thu until 20:00, closed Mon; tram #7 to Museum Rietberg stop, Villa Wesendonck, Gablerstrasse 15; tel. 044-206-3131, www.rietberg.ch).

**E. G. Bührle Collection**—This collection is a must for lovers of the French Impressionists, their forerunners, and their followers. Here you'll find exceptional paintings by Manet, Degas, Cézanne, Monet, Renoir, Gauguin, van Gogh, Picasso, and Braque. You'll also see a smattering of Dutch Baroque and 18th-century Venetian works, plus religious sculptures from medieval times to the Renaissance (9 SF; Tue, Fri, and Sun 14:00–17:00, Wed 17:00–20:00, closed Mon, Thu, and Sat; tram #2 or #4 to Wildbachstrasse stop, or bus #77 to Altenhofstrasse stop, Zollikerstrasse 172; tel. 044-422-0086, www.buehrle.ch).

## SLEEPING

High season in Zürich is May, June, September, and October. There are about 10 days a year when festivals and conventions send prices higher. My listings are near the train station, ideal for those passing through or leaving on an early-morning train or plane (train to airport: 5.80 SF, 15 min, leaves every 10 min). Zürich introduced a new city tax in 2006. Your hotel may include the tax in its price, or charge you an extra 2.50 SF per person per night; ask when you reserve.

### Across the River from the Train Station

With this efficient, handy neighborhood as your home base, you're a quick stroll away from the train station, Swiss National Museum, riverboat dock, a huge underground mall of services and shops (under the station), and the Niederdorf restaurant and nightlife zone (down Stampfenbachstrasse). To reach these hotels, exit the train station from the huge hall with the "Guardian Angel" sculpture and the TI. Cross the river on the Walchebrücke bridge and continue straight through the passageway to Stampfenbachstrasse, where you'll see Hotels Bristol and Arlette; the Leoneck is two blocks farther away. The Martahaus is a little farther south (toward the lake).

$$$ **Hotel Bristol,** run by Martin Hämmerli and his friendly staff, offers 54 modern and cozy rooms an eight-minute walk from the station. This is a business-quality place with family-run warmth (Sb-115–155 SF, Db-155–200 SF, Tb-195–225 SF, Qb-205–245 SF, 5 percent discount if booked direct with this book in 2007, Internet access, laundry, Stampfenbachstrasse 34, tel. 044-258-4444,

---

## Sleep Code

**(1.25 SF = about $1, country code: 41)**
**S** = Single, **D** = Double/Twin, **T** = Triple, **Q** = Quad, **b** = bathroom,
**s** = shower only. Unless otherwise noted, credit cards are accepted, English is spoken, and breakfast is included.

To help you sort easily through these listings, I've divided the rooms into three categories, based on the price for a standard double room with bath:

$$$ **Higher Priced**—Most rooms 180 SF or more.
$$ **Moderately Priced**—Most rooms between 140–180 SF.
$ **Lower Priced**—Most rooms 140 SF or less.

---

fax 044-258-4400, www.hotelbristol.ch, info@hotelbristol.ch).
Helpful Maggie at the reception desk answers travel questions.

**$$$ Hotel Arlette** is a bit worn, but comfortable, functional, and centrally located in a quiet neighborhood (Sb-120–185 SF, Db-160–250 SF, Stampfenbachstrasse 26, tel. 044-252-0032, fax 044-252-0923, hotel.arlette@bluewin.ch, family Schlotter).

**$$ Hotel Leoneck** offers 78 modern yet kitschy, bovine-themed rooms at a good price. The hotel—and the fine attached Crazy Cow restaurant (daily 6:30–24:00)—somehow manages to make Swiss cows seem cool; enjoy the moo-velous mural in your room (Sb-120–150 SF, Db-150–180 SF, Tb-185–230 SF, Qb-240–280 SF, half are non-smoking rooms, elevator, Internet access, some street noise—ask for quieter back room, Leonhardstrasse 1, tel. 044-254-2222, fax 044-254-2200, www.leoneck.ch, info@leoneck.ch, Herr Gold). From the station, walk 12 minutes uphill (see above), or use the Bahnhofstrasse exit and find tram #10 (direction Bahnhof Oerlikon, two stops to Haldenegg, look for Crazy Cow restaurant).

**$$ Martahaus Hotel,** run by a YWCA-type organization, is open to all and has a special mission to help women and disabled travelers. Despite its youthful-prison ambience, its 100 bomb-hardened rooms feel cozy and perfectly safe (bunk in 6-bed boys' dorm or girls' dorm-38 SF, D-100–115 SF, Db-150–160 SF, T-135 SF, Qb-200 SF, old town side is quiet, street side is 15 percent cheaper and a little noisy, elevator, Zähringerstrasse 36, tel. 044-251-4550, fax 044-251-4540, www.martahaus.ch, info@martahaus.ch). They also run a cheap, not-so-central, women-only guesthouse.

**$$ Zic Zac Rock Hotel,** funky and creaky, is popular with young backpackers. To save money, get a room with a bathroom down the hall. Each of the 51 basic rooms has a different rock-star theme—from Elvis Presley to Led Zeppelin to U2 (S-82–93 SF,

# Zürich Hotels and Restaurants

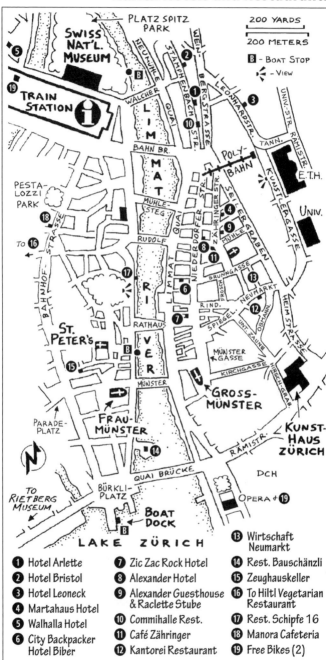

| | | |
|---|---|---|
| ❶ Hotel Arlette | ❼ Zic Zac Rock Hotel | ⓭ Wirtschaft Neumarkt |
| ❷ Hotel Bristol | ❽ Alexander Hotel | ⓮ Rest. Bauschänzli |
| ❸ Hotel Leoneck | ❾ Alexander Guesthouse & Raclette Stube | ⓯ Zeughauskeller |
| ❹ Martahaus Hotel | ❿ Commihalle Rest. | ⓰ To Hiltl Vegetarian Restaurant |
| ❺ Walhalla Hotel | ⓫ Café Zähringer | ⓱ Rest. Schipfe 16 |
| ❻ City Backpacker Hotel Biber | ⓬ Kantorei Restaurant | ⓲ Manora Cafeteria |
| | | ⓳ Free Bikes (2) |

Sb-85–98 SF, D-129 SF, Db-142–164 SF, T-165 SF, Tb-175 SF, Qb-267–307 SF, skimpy breakfast-5 SF, Marktgasse 17, tel. 044-261-2181, fax 044-261-2175, www.ziczac.ch, rockhotel@ziczac.ch).

**$ Alexander Hotel** runs a centrally located guest house (Gästehaus) with 20 affordable rooms, just next door to Raclette Stube restaurant on Zähringerstrasse 16 (see page 61). The guest house rooms are basic and uninspiring, but clean and quiet (Sb-95 SF, Db-140 SF, extra bed-25 SF). Their **$$$ main hotel,** one block away, is expensive (Sb-145 SF, Db-200 SF, air-con, Niederdorfstrasse 40). Both hotels share the same contact information: tel. 044-251-8203, fax 044-252-7425, www.hotel-alexander.ch, info@hotel-alexander.ch.

## Near the Station
**$$$ Walhalla Hotel,** just behind the train station, has 48 modern, spacious rooms (Sb-100–150 SF, Db-140–220 SF, breakfast-16 SF, Limmatstrasse 5, tel. 044-446-5400, fax 044-446-5454, www.walhalla-hotel.ch, info@walhalla-hotel.ch). The lower end of the price ranges apply to their annex rooms, which are modest but clean and comfortable.

## Cheap Beds
**$ City Backpacker Hotel Biber,** buried right in the middle of the Niederdorf action three floors above a restaurant, offers the cheapest backpacker beds in the old center (65 bunks in 6-bed dorms for 31 SF each, no breakfast, lockers, kitchen, Internet access, smoky lobby, street noise at night, no curfew, reception open daily 8:00–11:00 & 15:00–22:00, Niederdorfstrasse 5, tel. 044-251-9015, www.city-backpacker.ch, sleep@city-backpacker.ch).

# EATING

Niederdorf is Zürich's dining district, and the traffic-free Niederdorfstrasse is its restaurant row. While the countless eateries lining this main drag won't offer the best values, the people-watching is hard to beat. Browse the street and survey the eating options (including many colorful ethnic places). All the recommendations below are within a few minutes' walk of this spine of Zürich's people zone. They're listed clockwise, in order from the train station through Niederdorf and back down again along the train-station side of the Limmat River.

**Commihalle Restaurant,** near the recommended hotels, is a popular Italian chain. The 34-SF "Tavolata" special—ideal for big eaters—gets you a dressy antipasto buffet, pasta dish, main meat dish, and dessert-buffet finale (open daily, but "Tavolata" available only Tue–Sat 18:15–21:30, plain but dressy interior, fine outside seating, Stampfenbachstrasse 8, tel. 044-250-5960).

**Raclette Stube** is the place to be if you're looking for cheese—you'll climb into bed smelling like a cheeseball. The menu is classic and simple: just fondue (25 SF) or all-you-can eat raclette (33 SF). The food is heavy: essentially bread, potatoes, and lovingly chosen cheeses. Since these dishes are traditionally eaten in cold weather, this place can feel a little lonely in summer. But in winter, locals love their fondue and raclette—and prefer to eat them out, in places like this, rather than stink up their homes (daily from 18:00, Zähringerstrasse 16, tel. 044-251-4130).

**Café Zähringer** is an artsy, bohemian co-op with a passion for serving reasonably priced healthy food to people who take time to keep life in balance (20-SF daily specials, always good veggie plates, organic produce, salad bar by the weight—just point, also meat dishes, wok dishes, famously good coffee, stay-a-while interior or leafy seating on the square a block from where Lenin lived before heading back to Russia, daily until 24:00, Zähringer Platz 11, tel. 044-252-0500). You may also enjoy the sweet smell of an herb not on the menu.

**Kantorei Restaurant** serves well-presented modern Swiss cuisine with an Italian touch in a classy but unpretentious atmosphere. Sit inside or out on the quiet square next to a fountain (30-SF plates, 17–20 SF daily specials, daily 9:00–24:00, good vegetables, half-portions available, Neumarkt 2, tel. 044-252-2727).

**Wirtschaft Neumarkt,** tucked away in the old town, offers "authentic international" dishes. It prides itself in using only healthy ingredients such as organic vegetables, salads, and additive-free meat—justifying the higher prices. In good weather, the restaurant's long and fun-loving garden is packed with locals eating well under chestnut trees. The upper garden is best, so it's usually filled with diners who made reservations (lunch specials, 30-SF plates, 60-SF three-course meals, Mon–Sat 11:30–14:00 & 18:00–24:00, closed Sun, extensive wine list and good beer on tap, Neumarkt 5, tel. 044-252-7939).

**Restaurant Bauschänzli** is a block inland from the boat docks at Bürkliplatz. Filling a small island in the river, it's a fun-loving and popular self-serve restaurant offering Zürich's best beer-garden experience—like a Munich *Biergarten* without the kraut. Help yourself to beer and wine from big casks (grab the glass or carafe of your choice). *Citro* (lemonade) is mixed with lager to make a shandy (or *Radler*). *Süssmost* is apple juice. The garden is open daily in good weather May through mid-September, followed in fall by a raucous Oktoberfest (daily 11:00–23:00, live Bulgarian folk music daily 15:00–17:00 & 19:15–22:30, Stadthausquai 2, tel. 044-212-4919).

**Zeughauskeller** fills an atmospheric 500-year-old armory

with medieval battle gear (William Tell's crossbow?) and happy eaters enjoying typically Swiss cuisine. Their traditional meals include lots of soft meats (but no cheese—which the Swiss don't like to smell unless they're eating it). *Kalbsgeschnetzeltes*—calf's liver with *Rösti*—is a house specialty and a local fave (15–30-SF plates, daily until 23:00, plenty of beer and wine, near Paradeplatz at Bahnhofstrasse 28, tel. 044-211-2690).

**Restaurant Schipfe 16,** gorgeously and peacefully situated on the river with an old-town view, is part of a city-run organization providing work for hard-to-employ people. Don't expect polished service...but you're contributing to a worthy cause and enjoying healthy and decent food at a very good price (lunch only, 18-SF daily specials, Mon–Fri 10:00–16:00, closed Sat–Sun, Schipfe 16, tel. 044-211-2122).

**Hiltl Vegetarian Restaurant** is a treat for vegetarians. In 1898, Ambrosius Hiltl was fighting rheumatoid arthritis. His doctor said, "No more meat." So Ambrosius established the world's first vegetarian restaurant. Today his great-great-great-grandson, Rolf, carries on the family tradition. While historic photos decorate the walls, the loyal clientele's attention is on the enticing buffet and friendly conversation. At dinner, along with the salad buffet, there's an Indian buffet (endorsed by Indian tourists). Fill your plate, which is sold by the weight—generally 22–28 SF per hearty meal. At lunch, the salad bar is cheaper, but has no Indian options. The à la carte menu comes with delightful salads, curries, and fancy fruit juices. Hiltl's food is legendary for its freshness and lack of preservatives (daily 7:00–23:00, non-smoking, 2 blocks off Bahnhofstrasse where it kinks at Sihlstrasse 28, tel. 044-227-7000).

**Manora,** a non-smoking cafeteria at the Manor department store on Bahnhofstrasse, is reliably good and fast. Choose between a fresh salad bar (big plate-10 SF) and a variety of main dishes (10–15 SF). It's popular with locals—eat early or late (Mon–Fri 9:00–20:00, Sat 9:00–17:00, closed Sun, fifth floor, Bahnhofstrasse 75).

## TRANSPORTATION CONNECTIONS

**From Zürich by Train to: Luzern** (3/hr, 1 hr), **Interlaken** (hourly, 2 hrs, most direct but some with transfer in Bern and/or Spiez), **Bern** (2/hr, 1–1.25 hrs), **Murten** (2/hr, 1.75–2 hrs, transfer in Bern, Fribourg, or Kerzers), **Appenzell** (2/hr, 1.75 hrs with transfer in Gossau or 2.25 hrs with transfer in St. Gallen), **Lausanne** (2/hr, 2.5 hrs), **Chur** (2/hr, 1.5 hrs), **Lugano** (hourly, 3 hrs, some with easy change in Arth-Goldau), **Munich** (nearly hourly, some direct in 4.5 hrs, some 5.25 hrs with transfer in Stuttgart), **Frankfurt** (at least hourly, 4–4.5 hrs, some direct but most with transfer in Basel or Stuttgart).

## Zürich Airport (Flughafen Kloten)

Smooth, compact, and user-friendly, Zürich Airport is a major transportation hub and an eye-opening introduction to Swiss efficiency. There are three levels: 1) train station on the bottom floor, with train info and ticket desk; 2) main level, with a top-end food court, Migros supermarket, fancy souvenir shops, Swiss Post Office (easy to mail things home—pack light), banks, ATMs, and lockers; and 3) departures, upstairs. Eateries and ATMs are plentiful before and after the immigration checkpoint. For flight information, call the automated toll number: 0900-300-313 (press 2 for English).

Upon arrival by plane, pick up a free baggage cart, which you can wheel up and down the escalators. The train station underneath the airport can whisk you about anywhere you'd want to go in Europe, including downtown Zürich (5.80 SF, 15 min, leaves every 10 min 5:00–24:00, much cheaper than the 50-SF taxi ride). Your train ticket into Zürich is good for the following two hours on all city public transportation.

If catching an early-morning flight, don't spend a fortune to stay near the airport (**$$$** Hilton, Db-from 250 SF, tel. 044-828-5050). Sleep near the train station downtown, then zip to the airport in the morning on the frequent and fast train.

**From Zürich Airport by Train to:** Luzern (2/hr, 1.25 hrs), **Interlaken** (hourly, 2.25 hrs), **Bern** (2/hr, 1.5 hrs), **Murten** (hourly, 2–2.25 hrs, change in Fribourg or Bern), **Appenzell** (2/hr, 1.5 hrs with transfer in Gossau, or 2 hrs with transfer in St. Gallen), **Lausanne** (2/hr, 2.25 hrs), **Chur** (2/hr, 1.75 hrs, change at Zürich main station), **Lugano** (hourly, 3–3.25 hrs), **Munich** (4/day direct, 4 hrs, more with multiple transfers, 4.75–5 hrs).

# LUZERN
## and CENTRAL SWITZERLAND

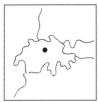

Luzern has long been Switzerland's tourism capital. Situated on the edge of a lake, with a striking alpine panorama as a backdrop, Luzern has drawn visitors such as Goethe and Queen Victoria for centuries. Since the Romantic era, Luzern has been a regular stop on the "Grand Tour" route of Europe. And with a charming old town, a pair of picture-perfect wooden bridges, a gaggle of fine museums, and a famous weeping lion, there's still enough in Luzern to earn it a place on any Swiss itinerary.

Luzern also makes a fine home base for exploring the surrounding region, known as Central Switzerland (Zentralschweiz). A wide variety of boat trips, mountain lifts, and other excursions make fun day trips (described on page 83).

### Planning Your Time

Many visitors home-base in Luzern for a week of side-trips. While I'd rather settle into the high country instead, Luzern is worth at least a full day and two nights. To get the most out of your day, begin with the TI's two-hour walking tour (see "Tours," below), or follow the self-guided walk in this chapter (see "Reuss River Stroll," page 67). Then hit the museums that interest you most: art buffs flock to the Rosengart and Picasso museums; gearheads will have a ball at the Swiss Transport Museum; and geologists dig the Glacier Garden. In the late afternoon, take a peaceful boat trip on Lake Luzern, then wander the town's scenic bridges at sunset.

# Luzern

Luzern (or "Lucerne" in English) is a charming midsize city with about 60,000 residents (and a metropolitan area sprawling to almost 200,000). It sits where the Reuss River meets Lake Luzern (Vierwaldstättersee). South of the river is the train station and bustling new town (Neustadt), and north of the river is the quaint, traffic-free old town (Altstadt). The river is spanned by a series of pedestrian bridges, including two classic wooden ones: the Chapel Bridge, with its famous stone water tower, and the Mill Bridge. Museums, restaurants, and hotels are scattered on both sides of the Reuss.

## ORIENTATION

### Tourist Information

Luzern's helpful, modern TI is right inside the train station (mid-June–mid-Sept daily 8:30–19:30; May–mid-June and mid-Sept–Oct Mon–Fri 8:30–18:30, Sat–Sun 9:00–18:30; Nov–April Mon–Fri 8:30–17:30, Sat–Sun 9:00–13:00; Bahnhofstrasse 3, tel. 041-227-1717, phone not answered on weekends, www.luzern.org).

At the TI, ask about their walking tour (listed under "Tours," below), and pick up the free, handy *City Guide* (loaded with info and museum discounts; see "Helpful Hints," below) and *Cultural Guide* (with music and entertainment listings). Browse through their other literature as well. The TI also provides a free room-booking service (with some great last-minute deals) and sells tickets to various activities around town, such as boat trips. If you have kids (or are one), ask about the pedal boats.

### Arrival in Luzern

Luzern's train station is refreshingly user-friendly. The TI is just off track 3. Most other important services are down the escalators at the front of the tracks, in an underground shopping mall called RailCity. There you'll find the ticket desks, WCs, ATMs, lockers, a convenient self-service cafeteria, a long-hours grocery store, and lots of other shops and restaurants. If all the other stores in town are closed (for example, on Sunday), head for RailCity.

For the quickest route into the old town, ride any escalator down into the underground RailCity and follow signs to *Altstadt* (to avoid having to cross the busy streets above).

In front of the train station is Bahnhofplatz (where buses fan out in every direction) and the pleasant lakefront.

## Helpful Hints

**Sightseeing Discounts with Free "Visitor's Card":** When you check into your Luzern hotel, have them stamp your *City Guide* tourist brochure (free at TI). This stamped brochure becomes a "Visitor's Card" (Gästekarte) that gives you minor discounts at all of Luzern's museums. Remember to carry this brochure with you, and ask for this discount when buying entrance tickets.

**Internet Access:** An Internet point is inside the TI (4 SF/10 min). The cheaper **Inside** is in RailCity (3 SF/15 min, 5 SF/30 min, 8 SF/60 min, Mon–Sat 9:00–21:00, Sun 9:00–20:00). Even cheaper is the city library—Stadtbibliothek—situated in the same building as the Bourbaki Panorama (4 SF/60 min—which is also the minimum charge, 10 SF deposit for plastic card required, Mon 13:30–18:30, Tue–Fri 10:00–18:30, Thu until 20:00, Sat 10:00–16:00, closed Sun, Löwenplatz 10, tel. 041-417-0707, www.bvl.ch). You'll also see other Internet signs scattered around town.

**Post Office:** The main post office (Hauptpost) is kitty-corner from the train station (Mon–Fri 7:30–18:30, Sat 8:00–16:00, closed Sun).

**Bike Rental:** You can rent bikes at the train station to enjoy Luzern's delightful lakeside bike paths (23 SF/half-day, 31 SF/day, 5 SF less with Eurailpass or Swiss Pass).

## Getting Around Luzern

Except for the Swiss Transport Museum, all the sights, hotels, and restaurants recommended in this chapter are within easy walking distance from the station. The Swiss Transport Museum is a 25-minute walk around Lake Luzern. To get there without the hike, catch bus #6 or #8, or take a boat (summer only) to "Verkehrshaus." Buses and all boats depart from Bahnhofplatz, in front of the train station. The TI's *City Guide* includes a map of bus routes. On the bus, the stops for all the major sights are announced in English.

Public transportation prices in Luzern depend on which zones you travel in; a single ticket within the primary zone (Zone 1) costs 2.60 SF. Short rides, up to six stops—which would cover a trip to the Swiss Transportation Museum or the Lion Monument—cost 2 SF. A day pass is 9.50 SF, and a six-day pass costs 47.50 SF.

# TOURS

**Walking Tour**—A two-hour tour in English and German, offered every morning in summer, also includes a short hop on the tourist train to the Lion Monument (18 SF, departs from TI at 9:45, daily May–Oct, 2/week Nov–April).

**Tourist Train**—You can go on the entire 40-minute circuit of the tacky little train, departing from Hotel Schweizerhof (10 SF, 24-SF combo-ticket also includes walking tour and saves 4 SF, headphone commentary, daily April–Oct every hour from 11:00, less frequently off-season, tel. 041-220-1100).

**Local Guide**—Ursula Korner is a good guide (150 SF/2 hrs, tel. 041-248-6048, ursula.korner@ko5ive.com). The TI has a list of other guides.

## SELF-GUIDED WALK

### Reuss River Stroll

This self-guided orientation stroll will give you a brief overview of the town—going up along the Reuss River, then across one of Luzern's famous wooden bridges, then back through the old town. Begin at Bahnhofplatz, the busy zone between the lake and the train station. Stand in front of the big stone arch.

**Bahnhofplatz:** This is the transportation hub of Luzern—and all of Central Switzerland. From the area in front of the station, buses zip you anywhere in town. Along the lakefront, you can catch a boat for a lazy cruise around Lake Luzern. And underneath you is the extensive RailCity shopping mall, honeycombed with pedestrian passageways leading to different parts of town. The big stone **arch** was the entrance of the venerable old train station—built in the late 19th century when Switzerland became a top tourist spot, with Luzern as its main attraction. But it burned down in 1971 and was replaced with the modern station. Today, the arch hides vents for the huge underground parking lot below.

• *The huge, new building with the big overhanging roof (on your right, with your back to the station) is the...*

**Culture and Conference Center (Kultur-und-Kongress-zentrum):** This building, finished in 1998 by Parisian architect Jean Nouvel, features a concert hall that hosts the Luzern Festival, one of Switzerland's biggest music events (mid-Aug–mid-Sept, www.lucernefestival.ch). Lake water is pumped up, into, through, and out of the building; if you wander around its far side, you'll see open channels that go right through the middle of the structure (blocked by benches, so distracted tourists don't fall in), as well as a big pond. The architect claims this design recalls earlier times, when Luzern was swamplands...but it more likely recalls his own original plans for the building. Nouvel wanted to put the center out in the middle of the lake. When he was voted down by the people of Luzern, he decided to surround it with water anyway. The plaza under the roof (which reflects the lake and weather, further incorporating the building into the surrounding environment) is a busy community space popular for open-air concerts.

• *Now walk in the opposite direction from the conference center, across the busy street. Stroll Bahnhofstrasse along the river until you have a good view of Luzern's most famous landmark, the wooden...*

**Chapel Bridge (Kapellbrücke):** Luzern began as a fishing village. By the 13th century, traffic streaming between northern

and southern Europe went through nearby Gotthard Pass—and Luzern became a bustling trading center. In the 14th century, this bridge was built—at an angle, to connect the town's medieval fortifications. As the bridge was part of the city defense system, the "window" openings facing the lake are smaller than the inland side, giving defenders more cover. The octagonal stone **Water Tower** (Wasserturm) predates the bridge by a century.

In 1993, a leisure boat moored under the bridge caught fire, and before long, Luzern's wooden landmark was in flames. (A plaque at the start of the bridge tells the story.) You'll notice the wood is lighter—that is, newer—in the middle of the bridge than at the ends. Chapel Bridge was painstakingly rebuilt, but many of its famous paintings were lost (those still remaining under the wooden roof are the 17th-century originals, but are restored). Boats are no longer allowed under the bridge, it's now strictly non-smoking, and you'll notice tiny security cameras everywhere.

Wander out onto the bridge itself. Notice the colorful paintings overhead, which depict scenes from Luzern and Swiss history. The coats of arms on the paintings tell you which aristocratic families sponsored them. Painting #1 features a legendary giant, an icon of Luzern you'll see all over town. This big boy dates back to the Middle Ages, when mammoth bones discovered locally were mistakenly identified as the bones of a 15-foot-tall human giant. Painting #2 shows an angel shining a divine light on the place where the town would be born (and where, in the eighth century, a monastery was founded). The name "Luzern" is derived from the Latin word for "light." Painting #3 shows Luzern circa 1400—see how the bridge was already part of the city fortifications. Painting #6 shows a bigger city as it looked in 1630. In the middle, a painting features the town's patron saint, Mauritius (a plaque mid-bridge tells why he matters to Luzern).

Any swans out? Locals say they originated as a gift from the French king, Louis XIV, in appreciation for the protection his "Swiss guards" gave him.

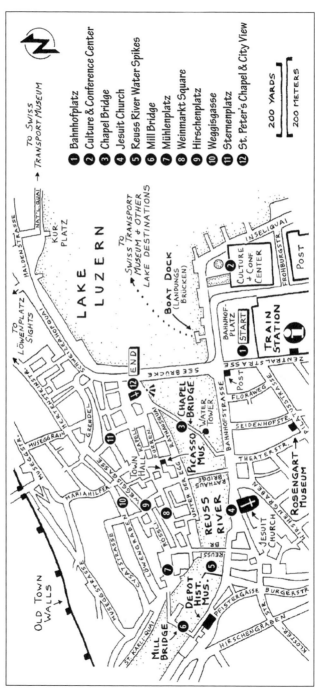

## Reuss River Stroll

1. Bahnhofplatz
2. Culture & Conference Center
3. Chapel Bridge
4. Jesuit Church
5. Reuss River Water Spikes
6. Mill Bridge
7. Mühlenplatz
8. Weinmarkt Square
9. Hirschenplatz
10. Weggisgasse
11. Sternenplatz
12. St. Peter's Chapel & City View

200 YARDS
200 METERS

*Now head back to the train-station end of the bridge, and continue up the river. Enter the big, white...*

**Jesuit Church (Jesuitenkirche):** This was the first major Baroque church in Switzerland (built 1666–1677). Even though

Luzern was a relatively small town back then, the pope wanted to establish a strong presence in Central Switzerland to empower the local Catholics during the tense times of the Protestant Reformation. The interior of the church once dripped with Baroque stucco. It's been retouched in the lighter Rococo style (c. 1750). The decorations on the ceiling celebrate the life (and afterlife) of the great missionary Francis Xavier, a co-founder of the Jesuit order. In front he's shown baptizing native Asians (looking like American Indians). After he dies, you see (in the center) Xavier heaven-bound. In an exuberant setting that includes both this church and Luzern's landmark Chapel Bridge, the bishop and townsfolk gather to wish him Godspeed. Xavier's cart is pulled by an elephant, a leopard, and a camel—commemorating his mission trips to the exotic Far East. Riding his chariot into heaven, he enjoys a hero's welcome (free, daily 6:00–18:30, www.jesuitenkirche-luzern.ch).

• *Back outside, continue strolling downriver past the iron pedestrian bridge (at the narrowest crossing spot, marking the location of Luzern's first bridge in the 12th century) toward Luzern's other wooden bridge. Stop at the spiky fence partially damming up the river.*

**Reuss River Water Spikes:** This big river (pronounced "royce") flows out of the lake. Lake Luzern's main source of water is

snowmelt, which trickles in from streams coming off the surrounding mountains. The water drains out of the lake here on its way to the Rhine. Luzern is responsible for controlling the flow of water, and preventing the flooding of lakeside villages by maintaining the lake level. In the mid-19th century, the city devised and built

a simple yet ingenious extendable dam (*Nadelwehr*, literally, "water spikes"). When the water is highest (in the spring), they remove spikes to open the flow; as the summer wears on and the water level drops, they gradually broaden the dam to keep the water level up. In the winter, they close the dam entirely to keep the lake level high enough for boats.

• *Continuing along the river, you'll pass the Depot History Museum on your left (see "Museums," below) before coming to the wooden...*

**Mill Bridge (Spreuerbrücke):** Unlike the rebuilt Chapel Bridge, this one's original—and the city is determined to keep it that way (try to find the low-profile security cameras). Cross the bridge, appreciating the fine old 17th-century paintings. Painting #1 shows Luzern's favorite giant again with the blue-and-white city and cantonal banners under the double eagle of the Holy Roman Empire. The flip side shows Judgment Day, with some going to heaven and others to hell. As you cross the bridge, notice that each painting includes a skeleton. Townsfolk crossed the bridge daily, and these scenes provided vivid reminders that nobody, in any walk of life, can escape death (an especially poignant message in times of war and plague, when these were painted). Like the other wooden bridge, this bridge was part of the city fortification—its downstream defending wall is higher.

This bridge sits where Luzern's mills were once located (*Spreu* means "chaff"—the sheath surrounding wheat, which was separated from the wheat at the mill). You can see sketches of these mills as you leave the bridge (on the red wall on the left). A turbine that generated power in 1889 sits quiet on the left, but the tradition of harnessing water power continues here. The stream of water spurting into the air (on the right) indicates that the modern hydroelectric plant—underwater below you—is engaged. It creates enough power for 1,000 households.

After crossing the bridge, you find yourself in Mühlenplatz (traffic-free each summer), the square at the entrance to the old town. The riverfront Hug bakery on your right is a good place for lunch or a snack (see "Eating," page 81). The fun facade above Fischer Stube (Mühlenplatz 11) tells the story of the wine god Bacchus (and marks the only down-and-dirty bar you'll see in this elegant town).

• *At the top of the square (under the Swiss Marilyn Monroe), head right on Kramgasse, then take the first left onto Weinmarktgasse, which leads to...*

**Weinmarkt Square:** In medieval Luzern, this square served as a marketplace for wine (as the name implies). The big mural on the decrepit green building at the top of the square looks like the Last Supper, but it's actually the Wedding Feast at Cana, where Jesus turned water into wine. On the right (as you face the mural), the facade of a now-gone pharmacy comes with a wise saying, *Amor medicabilis nvllis herbis* (roughly, "No medicine can cure a broken heart"). Across the square is a modern building with a secret message hiding in its strange zigzags. Start at the top left and read: W-E-I-N-M-A-R-K-T.

• *Leave the square on the left side of the big mural. You'll walk one block to...*

**Hirschenplatz:** This square hasn't always been a square—notice the footprints of two former buildings in the middle. It's named for the Hirschen ("Deer") Restaurant, with the elaborate golden sign. Across from that, try to guess who used to have a shop in the big green building. Yep—the jeweler (see all the rings?). Notice that, along with a happy cupid at the top, death is lurking again. To the right of that building, look for the painting of a famous German writer with the legend, *"Goethe logierte hier 1779."* Goethe—the "German Shakespeare"—visited Luzern, and stayed in a hotel on this corner. The grand facade on the Dornach House, from 1899, celebrates 500 years since the last battle against the Germans (1499). Switzerland has enjoyed a durable understanding that there can be disagreements but no wars with its historically aggressive and militaristic neighbor to the north.

Continue right out of the square onto the busy **Weggisgasse.** As you stroll, realize that every building in the old town—whether new or rebuilt—is required to offer residential apartments to prevent this historic zone from becoming only office space and touristy shops.

• *After a few blocks, you'll come to the Manor department store, with a tasty and convenient top-floor cafeteria (see "Eating," page 82). Turn right after the Manor store and walk one block to...*

**Sternenplatz:** This tiny square is dominated by the colorful facade of the Restaurant Fritschi. The paintings feature symbols from Luzern's annual Mardi Gras cel-  ebration—the city's biggest event, called Karneval here. Karneval is celebrated by Mr. and Mrs. Fritschi, pictured near the top of this building, wearing masks and throwing oranges. Flanking them are their trusty servants, a nanny, and a jester—who, in this case, bear a striking resemblance to the restaurant's owners. Below them is the story of Karneval: The cock calls at 5:00 in the morning the Thursday before Ash Wednesday (on the left), and the people get up to frighten winter away. Mr. and Mrs. Fritschi arrive on their wagon to kick off the festivities (on the right). Flying around the scene are oranges—traditionally tossed from the Fritschis to their adoring fans. This special seasonal fruit, rare in winter, marks the beginning of spring.

Continue down the street at the bottom of the square (Hans-Holbein-Gasse), and you'll stumble on a colorful fountain with masks of Herr and Frau Fritschi and their servants. Continue around to the riverfront, walking around **St. Peter's Chapel,** the namesake of Chapel Bridge—which you've arrived at once again. We finish our walk here, with *the* classic Luzern view: the Chapel Bridge and Water Tower, with Mount Pilatus hovering in the background.

• *From here you may want to take a...*

**Lakefront Stroll:** Consider walking north from here along the lakefront towards the Swiss Transport Museum. The delightful pathway was built during the tourism boom in the 19th century, when this part of the bay was filled in and fancy resort hotels went up—giving this city the nickname "Monte Carlo of Switzerland." Simply follow the tree-lined waterfront promenade (Nationalquai) that begins near the Hofkirche (the big church with the pointy spires). Believe it or not, Luzern's wooden Chapel Bridge used to stretch all the way to that church.

# SIGHTS

## Museums

Luzern is charming enough that simply strolling the streets and bridges and cruising the lake would be enough for a happy day of sightseeing. But the city also offers some fine museums, especially if you're into modern art.

▲**Rosengart Collection (Sammlung Rosengart Luzern)**—In the 1930s and 1940s, wealthy resident Siegfried Rosengart palled around with all-star modern artists, financing and collecting their works. This museum displays the fruits of his labor, with three floors of all the big names from the late 19th and early 20th centuries (15 SF, 13 SF with Visitor's Card, 18-SF combo-ticket also includes Picasso Museum, covered by Swiss Pass—see page 4, good English booklet-2.50 SF, otherwise no English info, daily April–Oct 10:00–18:00, Nov–March 11:00–17:00, a few blocks from the train station in the new town at Pilatusstrasse 10, tel. 041-220-1660, www.rosengart.ch).

The ground floor features an extensive Picasso collection (mostly lesser works from the 1950s and 1960s). Several other Rosengart Picassos were donated to the city, becoming the core of the Picasso Museum across the river (see below). Upstairs are a few early Picassos, as well as works by Braque, Monet, Renoir, Miró, Chagall, Cézanne, Matisse, Modigliani, and Pissarro. In the basement are 125 small works by Paul Klee, displayed chronologically so you can follow the evolution of his career. Watch as Klee discovers colors, and blossoms from a doodler and sometime watercolor artist into a mature painter.

▲▲**Picasso Museum Luzern**—In 1978, the Rosengart family donated eight Picassos to the city of Luzern. Over the years, the collection has grown to fill three floors of a creaky old building next door to the Town Hall. You'll see various Picasso ink sketches, and even a ceramic pigeon. While the "Picassos" here are nothing special, Picasso himself is: More than 200 black-and-white candid photographs of the artist, by American David Douglas Duncan, make this museum a ▲▲▲ experience for Picasso fans. I've seen a pile of Picassos, but never have I gotten personal with him as I did here. Duncan's intimate photos of the artist and his family, scattered around the museum, capture the very human personality of this larger-than-life genius. The photos—taken in Picasso's later years, and many featuring his wife, Jacqueline—provide insight into his artistic process, as well as his lifestyle, showing him at work and at play. As a fly on the wall of his chaotic studio, you'll see Picasso in the bathtub, getting a haircut, playing dress-up, moving to a new house, horsing around with his kids, entertaining his guest Gary Cooper, and getting a ballet lesson from Jacqueline. The excellent English descriptions—which you must borrow when you buy your ticket—are essential for getting the stories behind the photos (8 SF, 7 SF with Visitor's Card, 18-SF combo-ticket includes Rosengart Collection, covered by Swiss Pass—see page 4, 5-SF English brochure, daily April–Oct 10:00–18:00, Nov–March 11:00–17:00, in the Am-Rhyn-Haus at Furrengasse 21, tel. 041-410-1773).

**▲Depot History Museum (Depot Historisches Museum Luzern)**—This cluttered old museum is a "depot" for the accumulated bric-a-brac of Luzern's past (10 SF, 8 SF with Visitor's Card, covered by Swiss Pass—see page 4, Tue–Sun 10:00–17:00, closed Mon, Pfistergasse 24, tel. 041-228-5424, www.hmluzern.ch).

The museum is in one of Luzern's oldest surviving buildings, which used to house military weapons and uniforms. Their collection is just too big to display effectively, so they've come up with an innovative concept: Throw all of their archived stuff together and display it on three crowded floors. You'll wander through shelves of old weapons, stained-glass windows, sculptures, and old-fashioned tourism posters. The items are displayed without much rhyme or reason, and each is labeled with a barcode. You'll use a scanner (included with entry) to scan the items you're interested in and get the history (in English on your handheld screen).

**▲▲Swiss Transport Museum (Verkehrshaus)**—This enormous complex, across the lake from the train station, is the Smithsonian of Switzerland. The vast museum grounds include hundreds of exhibits in several different buildings, covering virtually all modes of transportation. It's a fun excursion, but it's pricey (though covered by Swiss Pass) and a little overwhelming, demanding at least a half-day. If you're in town for only one day, I'd skip this and enjoy the museums and ambience in the old town. But if you have a second day, brought your kids, or are obsessed with trains, planes, and automobiles, this is time well spent.

**Getting There:** From downtown, it's a 25-minute walk to the museum, most of it along a beautiful promenade (see "Riverfront Stroll," page 67). This is a pleasant stroll, even if you're not going to the museum. To make a beeline to the museum, take bus #6 or #8 from the station, and get off at the Verkehrshaus stop (the stop is announced in English, plus you'll see the huge, barrel-shaped, can't-miss-it IMAX theater). For a more scenic approach, catch a boat in front of the train station (to Verkehrshaus; 8.80 SF round-trip, second class, 10 min each way).

**Cost:** 24 SF, covered by Swiss Pass (see page 4). In addition to the exhibits, there are a wide variety of shows and demonstrations (pick up a schedule—and inquire about English-speaking events—as you enter). These include a planetarium show (included in entry price) and an IMAX theater (costs 16 SF extra, www.imax .ch). There are also combo-tickets available (32 SF for museum plus IMAX).

**Hours and Information:** Daily April–Oct 10:00–18:00, Nov–March 10:00–17:00, IMAX shows Fri-Sat until 21:00, Lidostrasse 5, tel. 0848-852-020, www.verkehrshaus.ch).

**Touring the Transport Museum:** Starting in the first building, you'll come across a 30-minute show about the Gotthard Tunnel. Then you'll wander through endless halls of train engines and tram cars. As you exit, you'll be face to face with some Swissair jetliners, and surrounded by pavilions devoted to various vehicles (such as planes, cars, boats, motorcycles, spaceships, and high-mountain lifts). Many of the exhibits are interactive, like the parasailing simulator, where you lie down on a smoothly gliding platform and peer down at the countryside below. Upstairs in the boat and cable-car building, be sure to seek out the **Swissarena**—an enormous (more than 2,000 square feet) aerial photograph of Switzerland (follow signs that look like a Swiss map in a CBS-style eye). This photo map, spread out on the floor like laminated linoleum, is detailed enough to show virtually every single building within Switzerland's borders. Slide on the Swiss slippers, borrow a map and magnifying glass, and glide across Switzerland, looking for the places you've visited so far.

**Other Museums**—Music fans may want to venture out to the **Richard Wagner Museum,** housed in a building where the composer lived (6 SF, 5 SF with Visitor's Card, covered by Swiss Pass—see page 4, mid-March–Nov Tue–Sun 10:00–12:00 & 14:00–17:00, closed Mon and off-season, along the lakefront south of train station at Wagnerweg 27, tel. 041-360-2370). The **Museum of Art Luzern** (Kunstmuseum Luzern), in the lakeside cultural center, features special exhibits of contemporary art (16 SF, covered by Swiss Pass—see page 4, Tue–Sun 10:00–17:00, Wed until 20:00, closed Mon, Europaplatz 1, tel. 041-226-7800, www.kunstmuseumluzern.ch). The **Museum of Natural History** (Natur-Museum), with an emphasis on interactive exhibits, is great for kids (6 SF, 5 SF with Visitor's Card, covered by Swiss Pass—see page 4, Tue–Sun 10:00–17:00, closed Mon, Kasernenplatz 6, tel. 041-228-5411, www.naturmuseum.ch).

## Near Löwenplatz

The following sights are clustered around Löwenplatz, a square that's a 10-minute walk from the old town (or take bus #1 three stops from the train station, direction Maihof, 2 SF). This is the heart of touristy Luzern, with a must-see monument and a trio of tacky but fun attractions. If you're doing the two bigger attractions here (Glacier Garden and Bourbaki Panorama), you might as well buy the **Lionpass,** which saves you money and also includes the Alpineum (17 SF, an 8-SF savings over individual admissions).

I've listed the museums below in descending order of respectability (or ascending order on the international "tacky tourist trap" scale).

▲▲**Lion Monument (Löwendenkmal)**—This famous monument is an essential stop if you're visiting Luzern—if only because when

you get back home, everyone will ask you, "Did you see the lion?" The huge sculpture (33 feet long by 20 feet tall) is carved right into a cliff face, over a reflecting pool in a peaceful park (free, open sunrise to dusk). While it's often overrun with tour groups, a peaceful moment here is genuinely affecting: The mighty lion rests his paws on a shield, with his head cocked to one side, tears streaming down his cheeks. In his side is the broken-off end of a spear, which is slowly killing the noble beast. This heartbreaking figure represents the Swiss mercenaries who were killed or executed defending the French king in the French Revolution. The inscription reads, *Helvetiorum fidei ac virtuti*—"To the loyalty and bravery of the Swiss."

▲**Bourbaki Panorama**—Here's your chance to get right in the middle of a great painting—literally. This exhibit, with a 360-degree painting (on a 33-foot-tall wraparound canvas with a circumference of 360 feet), tells the story of an epic battle. The 1.50-SF booklet explains it all (important, as there's not much English inside) and makes for a good souvenir. Panoramic paintings such as this were in vogue in the 19th century, when realism was king. Standing completely surrounded by a landmark historical event—such as this battle—was a favorite in "reality painting" (8 SF, 7 SF with Visitor's Card, covered by Lionpass and Swiss Pass—see page 4, daily 9:00–18:00, Löwenplatz 11, tel. 041-412-3030, www.bourbakipanorama.ch). Upon arrival, request an English playing of the 10-minute soundtrack of the battle.

The painting depicts the dramatic conclusion of the Franco-Prussian War. For three days in February of 1871, the 87,000-man French Army—led by the panorama's namesake, General Bourbaki—trudged through the snow across the Swiss border. Once in Switzerland, they gave up their weapons and surrendered to the Swiss—who, the story goes, took excellent care of the French, nursing them back to health before sending them home.

The Bourbaki Panorama was painted by Edouard Castres, who was actually there (as a Red Cross volunteer) on that frigid morning. The painting was completed in just five months in 1881; it was thoroughly refurbished in 2000, when several life-size figures were added in the foreground. Sound effects fill the hall as you view the painting. A museum exhibit gives more background on the Franco-Prussian War and Bourbaki's army, as well as details about this and other panorama paintings.

**Glacier Garden (Gletschergarten)**—This complex is a strange sort of mini–theme–park with an eclectic hodgepodge of exhibits, most loosely relating to alpine geology. While it's very touristy, and the various pieces don't quite hang together (such as the fun but out-of-place Hall of Mirrors), it adds up to a pleasant if overpriced activity (12 SF, 10 SF with Visitor's Card, covered by Lionpass and Swiss Pass—see page 4, daily April–Oct 9:00–18:00, Nov–March 10:00–17:00, Denkmalstrasse 4, tel. 041-410-4340, www.gletschergarten.ch).

Pick up the English info booklet as you enter, and follow the numbers on the confusing one-way path. First, you'll walk through the **glacier-grinded grounds** that give the museum its name. While geologists would get a thrill out of this, it was just a bunch of holes to me. Then you'll enter the **museum,** with exhibits about glacial processes, as well as (downstairs) huge 3-D reliefs of late-18th-century Luzern, and the Alps and lakes of Central Switzerland. Back upstairs, you'll cross directly into the **Amrein's House,** an old chalet with some original furnishings and models of traditional Swiss buildings. As you leave, you have the option of hiking up the steep **Tower Walk,** which leads to another old chalet and an observation tower.

At the end, be sure to visit the **Hall of Mirrors.** This undeniably enjoyable attraction, made in 1896 for a national exhibition in Geneva, is a delightfully low-tech fun house. You'll grope your way through twisting corridors—with mirrors on all sides—decorated like a Disneyfied Alhambra. It's confusing, dizzying, and claustrophobic, but goofy fun. As you run into yourself (literally) again and again, you'll lament the poor sap who has to clean the smudge marks off all those mirrors (walk slowly and—if you don't mind looking foolish—with arms outstretched). As you leave, giggling and nauseated, you'll ask yourself: So, what exactly did that have to do with glaciers?

**Alpineum**—This disappointing attraction, overshadowed by its substantial gift shop, displays a handful of paintings and reliefs of famous Swiss mountain peaks and panoramas. These are the same views you'll see if you visit the peaks in person—but in a musty, outmoded, tourist-trap environment. The exhibit also includes English explanations and miniature models of traditional houses, trains, boats, people, and cows. Visit this only if you're also doing the Glacier Garden and Bourbaki Panorama, in which case the Lionpass gets you in free (5 SF, covered by Lionpass and Swiss Pass—see page 4, April–Oct daily 9:00–12:30 & 13:30–18:00, closed Nov–March, Denkmalstrasse 11, tel. 041-410-6266, www.alpineum.ch).

## SLEEPING

Luzern accommodations are expensive. I've listed one big, classic hotel (the Waldstätterhof), a handful of small and basic hotels, and two good backpacker options. The prices here are for high season (April–Oct); you'll pay marginally less off-season. These are all centrally located (except Backpackers Luzern). As the city can be noisy at night, ask for a room on a high floor. In 2006, Luzern added a daily 1.50-SF tax for hotel guests. While most hotels include the tax in their listed prices, some add it to the bill. Confirm with your hotel beforehand.

**$$$ Hotel Waldstätterhof** is a grand old hotel across the street from the train station with reasonable rates for its high level of comfort. Its 80 bright, spacious rooms come with all the amenities (Db-220–260 SF depending on size, pricier suites, Zentralstrasse 4, tel. 041-227-1271, fax 041-227-1272, www.hotel-waldstaetterhof.ch, info@hotel-waldstaetterhof.ch).

**$$$ Hotel des Alpes** is a good bet if you want to sleep right on the river in the old town. Its lobby hides above a busy restaurant, but the 45 rooms are fresh and modern, with new bathrooms. Rooms facing the river cost a bundle and come with beautiful views (riverview rooms: Sb-155 SF, Db-245 SF; back-side rooms: Sb-125 SF, Db-198 SF; some rooms have balconies for the same price, Furrengasse 3, tel. 041-410-5825, fax 041-410-7451, www .desalpes-luzern.ch, info@desalpes-luzern.ch).

**$$$ Hotel Baslertor** and its cheaper annex, **Hotel Pension Rösli** (across the street), offer well-located rooms for various budgets. The Baslertor's 30 rooms, with old, dark furnishings, are more expensive and come in three sizes (small Db-150 SF, medium Db-175 SF, large Db-200 SF, extra bed-25 SF, family deals, elevator, atmospheric breakfast room, small, solar-heated swimming pool). The Rösli pension—an older building with lower ceilings—has six rooms with even older furnishings and no elevator (Db-125 SF). If you need a single, you'll pay the same at either place (125 SF), so you might as well opt for the Baslertor. Both hotels charge 15 SF per person extra for breakfast. Roland runs both from the Baslertor reception desk (Pfistergasse 17, tel. 041-249-2222, fax 041-249-2233, www.baslertor.ch, info@baslertor.ch).

**$$ Hotel Goldener Stern** is a good, solid value offering 16 perfectly acceptable rooms with some street noise over a restaurant (Sb-95 SF, D-100 SF, Db-140 SF, Tb-180 SF, Qb-200 SF, prices fluctuate with demand and length of stay, elevator, church bells ring at night, Burgerstrasse 35, tel. 041-227-5060, fax 041-227-5061, www.goldener-stern.ch, hotel@goldener-stern.ch, Amrein family).

**$$ Hotel Alpha,** once a convent-run boarding house for village girls, is now popular with students and offers 60 stark, institutional rooms, most with toilet down the hall (S-70 SF, twin D-98 SF, twin Db-130 SF, T-135 SF, comfy TV room, Zähringerstrasse 24, at intersection with Pilatusstrasse, tel. 041-240-4280, fax

---

## Sleep Code

**(1.25 SF = about $1, country code: 41)**
**S** = Single, **D** = Double/Twin, **T** = Triple, **Q** = Quad, **b** = bathroom, **s** = shower only. Unless otherwise noted, credit cards are accepted, English is spoken, and breakfast is included.

To help you sort easily through these listings, I've divided the rooms into three categories, based on the price for a standard double room with bath:

**$$$**  **Higher Priced**—Most rooms 150 SF or more.
**$$**  **Moderately Priced**—Most rooms between 100–150 SF.
**$**  **Lower Priced**—Most rooms 100 SF or less.

## Luzern Hotels and Restaurants

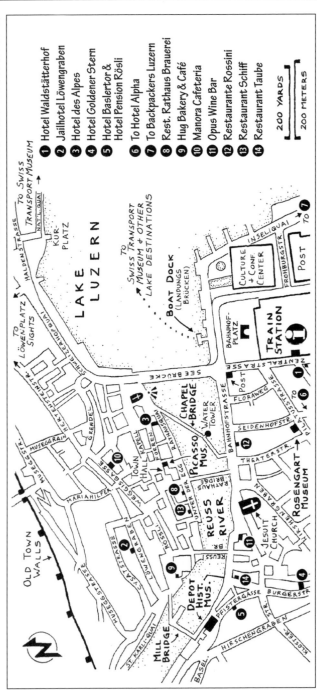

1. Hotel Waldstätterhof
2. Jailhotel Löwengraben
3. Hotel des Alpes
4. Hotel Goldener Stern
5. Hotel Baslertor & Hotel Pension Rösli
6. To Hotel Alpha
7. To Backpackers Luzern
8. Rest. Rathaus Brauerei
9. Hug Bakery & Café
10. Manora Cafeteria
11. Opus Wine Bar
12. Restaurante Rossini
13. Restaurant Schiff
14. Restaurant Taube

200 YARDS
200 METERS

041-240-9131, www.hotelalpha.ch, info@hotelalpha.ch). Located in a pleasant residential area, it's a 10-minute walk or an easy bus ride from the train station (take bus #1, #2, or #10, get off at Pilatusplatz, then walk two blocks on Pilatusstrasse).

**$ Jailhotel Löwengraben** rents clean, functional cells in the renovated former city prison on a nondescript street a few steps from the heart of the old town. As much an experience as a place to sleep, it has 133 beds in 56 cells (3 double beds, but the vast majority—logically—are twins). Cells, which can be a bit stuffy, come with cot-like beds, tiny barred windows, and reinforced doors—so (except for the mod little WCs) it still feels like a prison (Sb-69 SF, Db-98 SF, Tb-144 SF, Qb-180 SF, elaborate wardens' suites-165–200 SF, includes breakfast, non-smoking, Löwengraben 18, tel. 041-410-7830, fax 041-410-7832, www.jailhotel.ch, hotel @jailhotel.ch).

**$ Backpackers Luzern** is calm and well-run, sharing a modern, blocky building with student dorms (Studentenheim) in a peaceful residential area a 15-minute walk south of the train station. There are 30 rooms with balconies, a pair of kitchens for guests (open 16:00–23:00), a welcoming lounge, no curfew, Internet access (10 SF/60 min), and laundry (9 SF per load for full service). The walk to the center is mostly along the lake, through pretty parks and next to a fine beach (29 SF per person in 4-bed rooms, 33–35 SF per person in 2-bed rooms, includes sheets, no breakfast, reception open 7:30–10:00 & 16:00–23:00, elevator, Alpenquai 42, tel. 041-360-0420, fax 041-360-0442, www.backpackerslucerne.ch).

# EATING

While eateries along the river are pricey and a bit touristy, if you have one evening in Luzern, that's where you'll make the best memories. Here's a selection of places with great riverfront ambience (except Manora) and decent prices.

**Hug** is a cuddly named bakery and café right at the old town end of the Mill Bridge, handy for a lunch break in the middle of the sightseeing action. They have pastries and tasty sandwiches for a take-away picnic (3–6 SF, inviting riverside benches are a few steps away), as well as a selection of basic traditional Swiss dishes (like fondue and *Rösti*, 15–20 SF) to enjoy at outdoor tables overlooking the river or in the glassed-in terrace. Many people simply come to sip a coffee or beer, or to savor an ice-cream sundae with a river view (Mon–Sat 7:00–18:30, Sun 10:00–17:00, also open for dinner in summer in good weather, Mühlenplatz 6).

**Opus,** next to the big Jesuit Church, is a trendy wine bar with tasty food. You have several options: meat and fish dishes with international flair (30–40 SF); a lush and varied salad bar (a small plate piled high makes a light and healthy dinner for 16 SF); or your choice of dried meats and cheeses (20–25 SF, choose and cut your own fresh bread to go with it). They always have a couple dozen bottles of wine open and available by the glass. Sit in the upscale, colorful interior; in the candlelit and extremely romantic wine cellar; or out front, right on the river (open long hours daily, Bahnhofstrasse 16, tel. 041-226-4141, www.restaurant-opus.ch).

**Restaurant Rathaus Brauerei** is a lively microbrewery with an ideal riverfront location and a young, helpful staff. It's clearly a local favorite for its Seidel Rathausbier, brewed in such small quantities that you can only get it here. They serve their beer to ladies in a two-deciliter "elegant flute." Special seasonal brews are on the menu board, along with salads, "gourmet" pretzel sandwiches, 30-SF dishes, Swiss-style mac and cheese (20 SF), and the daily three-course 22-SF special—available until it's sold out (open long hours daily, Unter der Egg 2, tel. 041-410-5257).

**Restaurant Taube** is popular both for its traditional Swiss cuisine (great spot for a good *Rösti*, 25 SF), and for its riverside seating (closed Sun, Burgerstrasse 3, tel. 041-210-0747).

**Restaurant Schiff** has scenic riverfront tables in the old town with good food and relatively reasonable prices (plenty of salads, pizzas, most main dishes 25–35 SF, open long hours daily, across the river from Jesuit Church, Unter der Egg 8, tel. 041-418-5252).

**Restaurante Rossini,** a dressy Italian eatery packed with happy eaters, offers good handmade pizzas and pastas (15-SF pizzas, 20–30-SF plates, Mon–Sat 7:30–24:30, Sun 10:00–24:30, across the street from the river at Bahnhofstrasse 7, tel. 041-210-8050).

**Manora,** a cafeteria on the fifth floor of the Manor department store in the old town, is ideal for a fast, tasty, efficient lunch. Choose between a fresh salad bar (big plate-10 SF) or a variety of main dishes (10–15 SF). In good weather, climb the stairs to the outdoor terrace, with views over the rooftops of Luzern. This place is packed with locals and very crowded during peak times—eat early or late, and send your travel partner up top to claim an outdoor table while you buy the food (Mon–Wed 9:00–18:30, Thu–Fri 9:00–21:00, Sat 8:00–16:00, closed Sun, non-smoking, Weggisgasse 5).

## TRANSPORTATION CONNECTIONS

Luzern is marvelously well-situated in Switzerland, with convenient connections to anywhere in the country. Note that Luzern is on both the Golden Pass and the William Tell Express scenic rail lines (see Scenic Rail Journeys chapter).

**From Luzern by Train to: Zürich** (3/hr, 1 hr), **Zürich Airport** (2/hr, 1.25 hrs), **Bern** (hourly, 1 hr; or 2/hr with transfer in Olten,

1.5 hrs), **Interlaken** (hourly, 2 hrs direct to Ost station), **Lausanne** (hourly direct, 2.5 hrs; more with transfer in Olten), **Lugano** (hourly, 3 hrs), **Chur** (hourly, 2.25 hrs, change in Thalwil).

# Central Switzerland:
## Day Trips from Luzern

Luzern is perched on the edge of a super-scenic lake and ringed by family-friendly mountain peaks that are easily conquerable for a price. The city is the perfect springboard for alpine excursions. The following side-trips—including a boat cruise, two different mountain lifts, and a military fortress—are all popular excursions.

If you're serious about day-tripping, consider a **Tell-Pass.** This pass includes two days of free passage on lifts, boats, and several area train lines in a seven-day period (with a 50 percent discount on the other 5 days; 140 SF, or 112 SF with a Swiss Pass, buy at TIs, train stations, and boat docks, April–Oct only, www.tellpass .ch). While this can be a good deal if you're home-basing in the region for a week, it probably won't pay for itself on a quick visit.

Note that the military fortress is open only on weekends from April through October.

**Possible Do-It-All Day Trip:** This plan combines most of these adventures (the fortress, a mini–lake cruise, and the Pilatus mountain lift—up one side and down the other) into one jam-packed day trip. (Note that it must be done on a Saturday or Sunday to include the fortress.) Confirm all the schedules and logistics at the TI before embarking: Take an early train or boat to Stansstad and tour Fortress Fürigen, then have lunch in Stansstad. Catch the 14:00 boat to Alpnachstad (20-min ride), where you ride up the mountain on the Pilatus cogwheel train (departing 14:30, arriving at the summit at 15:00). When you're ready to return to Luzern, catch the gondola for the seven-minute ride down to Fräkmüntegg (4/hr, last departure at 17:15, or 18:00 July–Aug), where you have a chance to do the luge ride before changing to a smaller gondola down to Kriens (they run constantly until 17:30, or 18:15 July–Aug, 30-min ride, don't get off at Krienseregg). In Kriens, walk five minutes following the white signs to *Luzern bus.* (You don't want the bus stop in front of the building.) Bus #1 gets you to Luzern's main station in 10 minutes. Whew!

**Boats of Note:** These boats can help you connect the excursions in this chapter: **Stansstad** (Fortress Fürigen) **to Alpnachstad** (where you catch Pilatus cogwheel train; 6 boats/day, 20–35 min, plus 2 steamboats/day July–Aug, 8.80 SF); **Stansstad to Luzern** (6 boats/day, 60–75 min, plus 2 steamboats/day July–Aug, 14.20 SF); **Alpnachstad to Luzern** (7 boats/day, 90 min, 19.80 SF).

## Lake Cruises

Lake Luzern (or Lucerne) is the English name for the lake, but the Swiss call it the Vierwaldstättersee—"Lake of Four Forest Cantons," since it lies at the intersection of four of Switzerland's states (or cantons, as their political units are called).

On this most-touristed lake in Switzerland, there are a variety of routes and destinations (33 stops in all). Cruises range from a one-hour sampler tour (around Luzern's "harbor") to a full-blown six-hour exploration (to Flüelen, at the far end of the lake, and back again). Some routes are round-trip; on others, you'll get out, explore, and then take the next boat back. Romantics will want to hitch a ride on one of the five old-fashioned paddleboat steamers.

The easiest and most efficient trip is to boat across from the train station to the Swiss Transport Museum (Verkehrshaus, see page 74; 8.80 SF round-trip, second class, 10 min each way). A "castle cruise" makes one-hour (13.20 SF) and two-hour (21 SF) round-trip sightseeing swings around the lake (4/day, from piers 3 or 4). For most, the two-hour circle is about as much of a scenic cruise as the lake deserves. Another easy two-hour excursion is to take the boat from Luzern out to Weggis or Vitznau (under Mount Rigi, across the lake; see "Mountain Lifts," below), then back to Luzern (27 SF round-trip, second class to Weggis, 33 SF to Vitznau). You can buy tickets and get advice on which trip best fits your schedule at the Luzern TI.

Boats leave from in front of the Luzern train station. They're operated by the Lake Lucerne Navigation Company (tel. 041-367-6767, www.lakelucerne.ch). Note that these boats are free with a Eurailpass or Swiss Pass. But remember that if you're using a flexi-pass, the boat trip costs a flexi-day. Doing the lake cruise on the day you arrive or depart—when you're already using a flexi-day for your train transportation—is a smart plan.

## Mountain Lifts

There's no shortage of mountain lifts in Central Switzerland. I've described the two most famous and most accessible from Luzern: Mount Pilatus and Mount Rigi.

### Mount Pilatus

Pilatus looms behind Luzern, offering the city a dramatic back-drop...and an enjoyable destination. While legend dictates that it's

# Lake Luzern Area

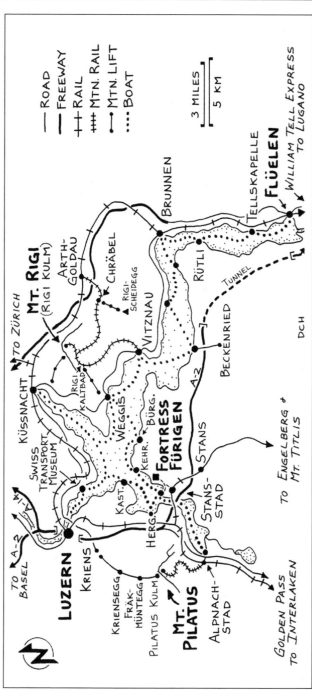

Legend:
— ROAD
— FREEWAY
+—+ RAIL
++++ MTN. RAIL
•— MTN. LIFT
···· BOAT

3 MILES
5 KM

- TO BASEL
- TO A-2
- LUZERN
- KRIENS
- KRIENSEGG
- FRÄKMÜNTEGG
- PILATUS KULM
- MT. PILATUS
- ALPNACHSTAD
- GOLDEN PASS TO INTERLAKEN
- HERG.
- KAST.
- STANSSTAD
- STANS
- TO ENGELBERG & MT. TITLIS
- FORTRESS FÜRIGEN
- KEHR. BÜRG.
- WEGGIS
- RIGI KALTBAD
- KÜSSNACHT
- SWISS TRANSPORT MUSEUM
- TO ZÜRICH
- MT. RIGI (RIGI KULM)
- ARTH-GOLDAU
- CHRÄBEL
- RIGI-SCHEIDEGG
- VITZNAU
- BECKENRIED
- A-2
- RÜTLI
- TUNNEL
- DCH
- BRUNNEN
- TELLSKAPELLE
- FLÜELEN
- WILLIAM TELL EXPRESS TO LUGANO

named for Pontius Pilate—whose body is supposedly in one of its lakes, kicking up a fuss if disturbed—it more likely comes from a Latin word meaning "cloudy." It's also said to be infested with dragons.

You can ascend Pilatus (to the overlook platform, at 7,000 feet, called "Pilatus Kulm") two different ways: by cogwheel train (the world's steepest, at 48 percent grade) or gondola (in three stages).

**By Train:** The cogwheel train leaves from the lakeside town of Alpnachstad—from Luzern, take the S5 train to Alpnachstad (2/hr, 20 min), or take the 90-min boat; cogwheel train runs mid-May–mid-Nov only, goes at least hourly, daily 8:10–17:35, 30 min up, 40 min down; for the best views going up, take a downhill-facing seat on the right side).

**By Gondola:** The gondola leaves from the town of Kriens, virtually a suburb of Luzern (from in front of Luzern train station, take city bus #1 for 15 min to Kriens; gondola goes continuously, daily July–Aug 8:30–17:30, April–June and Sept–Oct until 16:45, Nov–March until 15:45, closes periodically for maintenance Oct–Nov). From Kriens, you'll take a small gondola to Krienseregg (recreation area with trails and playground), then on to Fräkmüntegg (total trip 30 min).

At Fräkmüntegg, you'll have a chance to zip down Switzerland's longest luge ride, called "Dragon Speed" (8 SF, almost a mile long, good weather only, www.rodelbahn.ch). At the fun Suspension Rope Park, you can test your agility high up on seven rope trails with varying degrees of difficulty (25 SF includes material and instruction, July–Aug daily 10:00–17:30; mid-April–June and Sept–mid-Oct Wed–Sun 10:00–17:00, closed Mon–Tue and off-season).

From Fräkmüntegg, it's another seven minutes in a bigger cable car to the observation platform at Pilatus Kulm.

**Costs:** A one-way segment to the top, no matter how you go, costs 29 SF; a round-trip costs 58 SF (with your choice of cogwheel train or gondola for each leg; does not include your transportation between Luzern and the cogwheel train or gondola stations). Eurailpass- and Swiss Pass–holders get a 30 percent discount. When you buy your ticket, tell them which way you want to go up and down (it's most interesting to go up one way, down the other). Don't throw your ticket away, as you'll have to scan it several times until you finally exit the last station. Be warned: Buying a one-way ticket up and hiking all the way down was a fatal decision for two Americans in 2003.

The handiest way to visit Pilatus from Luzern is with the popular **Golden Round Trip** package. This includes the bus to Kriens, the cable car up to Pilatus, the cogwheel train down to Alpnachstad, and a lazy, 90-minute boat trip back to Luzern (or the same route, reversed; 79 SF second class, 43 SF with Eurailpass or Swiss Pass, 14 SF less to return by train instead of boat, May–Oct only). Figure out the best route with the help of Luzern's TI, or check www.pilatus.ch (tel. 041-329-1111, fax 041-329-1112).

**At the Summit:** The summit (Pilatus Kulm) is a family fun zone with plenty of activities, including a "summer toboggan" (Switzerland's longest at more than a mile). Hotel Bellevue acts as the visitors' center, with a good information office, restaurants, a souvenir shop, and free Internet terminals. Hotel Pilatus-Kulm hosts temporary exhibits. Its three restaurants have the original furnishings from 1889; there's also a modern self-service cafeteria. Check out the fancy WC: When you open a door, a red dragon claims the stall for you. The terrace below is full of free and comfortable deck chairs.

**Hikes from Pilatus:** These walks lead to great viewpoints. I've listed them roughly in order of difficulty, from easiest to most strenuous. All leave from the summit, Pilatus Kulm.

Two short **Dragonpaths** lead through tunnels to various viewpoints in the rock. These paths come with signs illustrating dragon tales by the famous Swiss artist Hans Erni.

A 10-minute hike takes you up to **Esel** ("Donkey," commemorating the pre-cable-car days, when Queen Victoria came up to Pilatus on the back of a donkey). Below, Esel hides an impressive part of Switzerland's anti-aircraft defense system. Find the gray, round structures within the imitation rock. Modern missiles behind the camouflage point to the skies. The biggest radar in Switzerland towers above Hotel Pilatus-Kulm in an off-limits military zone.

Hiking to **Tomlishorn** (35 min), you'll spot more camouflaged military installations. Stop at the yellow *Echo* sign and shout your message out to the world. Somebody out there keeps yelling it back.

A 90-minute hike leads to the 6,700-foot cross-capped summit of **Matthorn** (not Matterhorn). This is moderately strenuous—generally uphill, with lots of ups and downs. A visitors' book invites you to sign and leave your impressions on this breathtaking spot.

**Sleeping at the Summit:** You can spend the night on the summit of Pilatus. Linger outside to enjoy the views with the marmots and mountain goats...or head inside for the hotels' free nightly entertainment: movies and a disco on alternating nights. **$$$ Hotel Bellevue** is a modern, round building with 27 rooms—

clean and bright, with Nordic-style furniture (Sb-111 SF, Db-192 SF). **$ Hotel Pilatus-Kulm** is a historic building from 1900 with basic, sink-only rooms (S-77 SF, D-124 SF). Both hotels come with a big breakfast and share the same contact information (tel. 041-329-1212, fax 041-329-1213, www.pilatus.ch, hotels@pilatus.ch).

## Mount Rigi

This long, shelf-like mountain, across the lake from Luzern, provides sweeping views of Central Switzerland (and, on a clear day, Germany and France, too). Even though it's at a lower altitude than Pilatus (5,900 feet), this so-called "Queen of the Mountains" claims to offer the best vistas in the area. The mountain is laced with hiking trails and other attractions to while away an afternoon.

As with Pilatus, there are two ways to approach the topmost viewpoint, Rigi Kulm: via cogwheel train (from Arth-Goldau or Vitznau), or by cable car (from Weggis).

**By Train:** To go by cogwheel train, you have two options: from the town of Arth-Goldau ("behind" Rigi, accessible by train from Luzern), or from Vitznau (right on Lake Luzern, accessible by boat—but not train—from Luzern). The train from Luzern to Arth-Goldau takes 30 minutes; once there, you'll take the cogwheel train up to Rigi Kulm (35 min, departs hourly, coordinated with arrival of certain trains from Luzern, daily 8:00–18:10). Or take the boat from Luzern to Vitznau (about 1 hr), then take a different cogwheel train from there up to Rigi Kulm (30 min, departs hourly, daily 8:40–22:05).

**By Cable Car:** To go by cable car, take the boat from Luzern to Weggis (30–45 min), then board the cable car to Rigi Kaltbad (10 min, departs hourly, Mon–Fri 7:00–18:45, Sat–Sun 8:15–18:45); there you'll switch to the cogwheel train that brings you the rest of the way up to Rigi Kulm.

**Costs:** As with Mount Pilatus, you can go up one way and down the other for maximum experience and the same price. Before ascending, figure out your complete route at the Luzern TI. No matter how you go, the price from the base of the mountain to Rigi Kulm is 35 SF one-way, 58 SF round-trip, plus the cost of getting from Luzern to the cogwheel train or cable-car stations. Figure a total of 90 SF per person for the total round-trip from Luzern (plan on 5–6 hrs). Note that cogwheel train and cable-car prices are discounted 25 percent with a Eurailpass and 50 percent with a Swiss Pass; the train trip from Luzern to Arth-Goldau and the boat trips to Vitznau and Weggis are also included in your pass (but you'll have to use one of your flexi-days). The schedules and prices listed here are for peak summer season (May–Oct); they may vary in shoulder and ski seasons (confirm at Luzern TI, or check www.rigi.ch).

## Fortress Fürigen Museum of War History

Most visitors come to Luzern to confirm all their stereotypical images of Switzerland, and the city happily responds: picture-perfect mountains around a gorgeous lake, surrounded by tidy villages and lush meadows full of happy cows. The Fortress Museum of Fürigen (Festung Fürigen Museum zur Wehrgeschichte) shows you another face of the country—the reason why Switzerland was able to remain peaceful and neutral: its elaborate and secret system of bunkers and fortresses. Unfortunately, this fascinating exhibit is open only Saturday and Sunday, April through October.

Enter through an innocent-looking wooden barrack. The bunker is always chilly, but no worries: Visitors are loaned original Swiss Army coats. Put on your coat, grab the English brochure that explains each room, and you're on your way. The radio station was placed near the entrance to assure clear reception. The living quarters were gas-proof, complete with specially sealed doors and devices to monitor the air for poison. The museum is a petting zoo of 20th-century weaponry. Visitors can fiddle with and even aim guns, knowing all the ammo is now imaginary. Imagine the photo op—you, in a Swiss military uniform, manning a cannon.

Historical photographs take you back to World War II. Fortress Fürigen was built in 1941 as part of a new military strategy: to protect Switzerland with fortresses hidden in the Alps, called *Réduitfestung* (roughly "shelter fortress"—see next page). In case of a Nazi invasion, the Swiss government would retreat to a secret bunker in the Berner Oberland, and Swiss troops would abandon the border regions and gather around this alpine stronghold. Fortress Fürigen was meant to protect roads and rail lines that led from Luzern and Zürich along Lake Luzern into the Berner Oberland. This was one of a network of fortresses in the area. After World War II, they were retooled with a new focus: the threat of the Soviet Union and nuclear war.

Big guns in the fortress could shoot more than six miles, and machine guns protected the immediate access routes to the bunker. This fortress could house and feed 100 people for three weeks. But in 1990, with the end of the Cold War, the practical Swiss decommissioned the fortress, refit it with vintage WWII and early Cold War gear, and opened it to the curious public.

**Cost and Hours:** Entry costs 5 SF, covered by Swiss Pass (see page 4). The museum is open only on weekends from late spring through early fall (April–Oct Sat–Sun 11:00–17:00, closed Mon–Fri and Nov–March, tel. 041-618-7522).

**Getting There:** Fortress Fürigen is near the lakefront town of Stansstad (on Kehrsitenstrasse), below the village of Fürigen, not far from Luzern. It's an easy trip from Luzern by **train** (hourly, :41 past each hour, train S4, direction: Engelberg, 6 SF one-way,

## Swiss Military Readiness

Strolling through a peaceful Swiss village—charming pastoral greenery studded with rustic farmhouses between an Alp and a lake—my friend walked with me to the door of a nondescript barn. He said, "Stand here," and slid open the door to reveal a solitary mighty gun—point-ing right at me. Crossing a field, kicking a stray soccer ball back to a group of happy grade-school-ers, we came to another barn. This time I noticed the "wooden" door was actually metal, with a clever paint job. Inside was a military canteen, now selling snacks to civilians, and a steel ladder leading down into a mili-

tary-gray world that felt like a vast submarine. A network of passages, just big enough for heavily armed soldiers to race down single file, led to a series of gun barns and subterranean command rooms with charts locating other installations in the area.

Switzerland may be famous for its neutrality, but it's been anything but lax defensively. Travelers marvel at how Swiss engineers have conquered their Alps with the world's most-expensive-per-mile road system. But no one designs a Swiss bridge or tunnel without designing its destruction. Each comes with built-in explosives, so, in the event of an invasion, the entire country can be blasted into a mountain fortress.

Even today, you can't get a building permit without an expensive first-class bomb shelter worked into the plan. Old tank barriers (nicknamed "Toblerones" for their shape) stand ready to be dragged across the roads to slow any invasion. Sprawling hospitals are dug into mountains, still ventilated to be kept dry and ready for use. And halfway up alpine cliffs, Batcave-type doors can slide open, allowing fighter jets to zoom into action from hidden airstrips cut out of solid rock. If you're approaching a mountain pass by car, look for the explosive patches ominously checkering the roads near the summit.

But the end of the Cold War in 1989 brought changes even to neutral Switzerland. Western armies began cutting back on their military spending, and Switzerland followed suit, with deep cuts in its defense budget. The Swiss Army met its tighter budget in part by closing many of the 15,000 hidden fortresses that protected the country's strategic roads, train lines, and mountain passes. Some of the forts, such as Fortress Fürigen, have been turned into tourist attractions no more formidable than medieval castles.

15-min ride) or boat (see below).

From the train station in Stansstad, you have two options for getting to the museum: walking direct (15 min) or detouring up to a fun funicular.

To **walk,** follow brown signs to *Festungsmuseum* or *Kehrsiten* (down Bahnhofstrasse to Stanserstrasse, cross and follow signs, right on Achereggstrasse, left passing swimming-pool sign and tennis courts, and finally along the lake).

For the **funicular,** catch the yellow postal bus from the station up to the village of Fürigen (direction: Bürgenstock, tell driver you want to get off at Fürigen). Cross the road and follow *Fürigen* signs left. Pass Hotel Fürigen, and turn left at the parking lot. The gray wooden pavilion is the station of a funky, short, and steep funicular back down to Stansstad. Ring the bell and sit down in the 1923, box-like cabin (3/hr, April–Oct only, 5-min joyride, 4 SF). Exit and follow to the right; the entrance to the fortress museum is just around the corner. Those taking the more dramatic cogwheel train up to Pilatus won't be impressed by this detour.

You can also get to Stansstad from Luzern by **boat** (7/day, 60–75 min, plus 2 steamboats/day July–Aug, 14.20 SF). From Stansstad's boat dock, walk 10 minutes up to the main street (Achereggstrasse) and keep left, following the brown signs for *Festungsmuseum.*

**Drivers** arriving in Stansstad can follow white signs to *Kehrsiten* for lakeside parking (1 SF/hr, free WC, 5-min walk along lake to museum entrance).

# BERN AND MURTEN

Enjoy urban Switzerland in the charming, compact capital of Bern. Ramble the ramparts of Murten, Switzerland's best-preserved medieval town, and resurrect the ruins of an ancient Roman capital in nearby Avenches.

If you like cute, small towns (as I do), make Murten your home base. Otherwise, choose busier Bern.

## Planning Your Time

On a quick trip, big Bern and little Murten—only a half-hour apart by train or car—are each worth a half-day. Either makes a fine day trip or overnight stop. Murten, while easy by train, is even better by car. With a car, I'd sleep in Murten, visit Avenches, and enjoy the view.

Bern is a handy on-the-way stop between other destinations (such as going from the Berner Oberland to Murten or Zürich). If you're day-tripping, put your bag in a locker at the Bern station, spend a few hours taking my self-guided "Welcome to Bern" walk (page 96) and visiting some museums, then catch a late-afternoon train to your next stop. You could combine the destinations in this chapter by ending your busy Bern day in Murten—where you can spend the evening wandering the walls and savoring a lakeside dinner. In the morning, linger in Murten or move on to your next destination.

## Bern and Murten

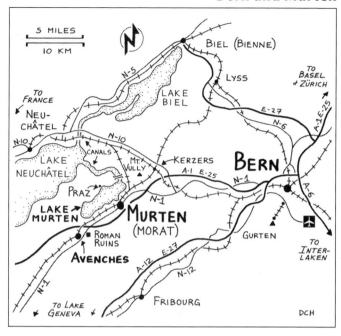

# Bern

Stately but human, classy but fun, the Swiss capital gives you the most delightful look at urban Switzerland. Window-shopping and people-watching along the arcaded streets and lively market squares are Bern's top attractions, but there's more to this city: Enjoy Bern's fine museums, quaint-for-a-capital ambience, and much-adored mascot bears.

The city, founded in 1191, has managed to avoid war damage and hasn't burned down since a great fire in 1405. After the fire, wooden buildings were no longer allowed, and Bern gained its

gray-green sandstone complexion (with stones quarried from nearby). During its 12th- and 13th-century growth spurt, the frisky town grew through two walls. Looking at the map of the city contained within a bend of the Aare River, you can get a sense of how it started with a castle at the tip of the peninsula, and expanded with a series of walls—each defending an ever-bigger city from its one accessible-by-land side. The clock tower marks the first wall (1218). A generation later, another wall was built (in 1256, at today's prison tower). The final wall—where today's train station sits—was built in 1344.

In 1353, Bern became the eighth canton to join the Swiss Federation. Its power ended with the conquest by Napoleon in 1798. But in 1848, Bern rose again to become the Swiss capital.

Today, the German-speaking town has 127,000 people (one-third Protestant and two-thirds Catholic). Its pointy towers, sand-stone buildings, and colorful fountains make Bern one of Europe's finest surviving medieval towns.

# ORIENTATION

User-friendly Bern is packed into a peninsula bounded by the Aare River. The train station is located where the peninsula connects to the mainland. From there, a handy main drag leads gradually downhill, straight through the middle of town past most of the major sights, to the tip of the peninsula (and, across a bridge, the bear pits).

## Tourist Information

Start your visit at the TI inside the train station (June–Sept daily 9:00–20:30; Oct–May Mon–Sat 9:00–18:30, Sun 10:00–17:00; tel. 031-328-1212, www.berninfo.com). Pick up a free map of Bern (and maps for any other Swiss cities you'll be visiting), and browse through their free brochures: general information booklet, museum guide, booklet on bus and walking tours, transit map, monthly *What's On* events guide, and informative leaflets on various sights. There's a second TI at the bear pits (June–Sept daily 9:00–18:00; March–May and Oct daily 10:00–16:00; Nov–Feb Fri–Sun 11:00–16:00, closed Mon–Thu).

Walking **tours** leave daily at 11:00 from the TI at the train station (90 min, 16 SF, June–Sept). Rafting tours are supposedly available by request daily June through September (50 SF, mini-mum 4 people, reserve through TI).

**Sightseeing Pass:** If you plan to visit more than one museum in Bern, get the BernCard—unless you already have a Swiss Pass (see page 4). The BernCard offers admission to many museums and unlimited travel on local public transportation. You can purchase it at the TI and at many Bern museums (19 SF/1 day, 29 SF/2 days, 35 SF/3 days, www.museen-bern.ch).

## Arrival in Bern

**By Train:** Bern's bustling train station is a thriving, multistory mall. The trains almost get lost. On the upper level, you'll find a Migros grocery store (daily 8:00–21:00) and a pharmacy (daily 6:30–22:00). Near the TI are lockers (6 SF) and WCs (2 SF). From the station, it's a 30-minute downhill stroll through the heart of town to the bear pits and Rose Garden. My "Welcome to Bern" self-guided walk (page 96) lays out the most interesting route.

**By Car:** Drivers approaching by freeway should follow *Bern Zentrum* signs, then *Bahnhof,* and *Bahnhof Parking.* There's a huge pay garage behind the train station (Bahnhof). While not the cheapest option, this is your easiest for a quick visit. The old town is essentially car-free (only service vehicles and public transit allowed).

## Helpful Hints

**Blue Monday:** Most of Bern's museums are closed on Monday.

**Internet Access:** The TI has a list of centrally located Internet cafés.

**Jäggi Bookstore,** in the Loeb department store on Spitalgasse, is the closest to the station (2 SF/15 min, pay at cashier, keep receipt and take it to info desk behind stairs, Mon–Fri 9:00–18:30, Thu until 21:00, Sat 8:00–16:00, closed Sun).

**Bookstore: Stauffacher** is a huge bookstore with an entire floor of English books, a fine travel section, and an inviting café with a terrace and good salads (a block below the train station at Neuengasse 34).

**Laundry: Jet Wash** is at Dammweg 43 (Mon–Sat 7:00–21:00, Sun 9:00–18:00, small load-4 SF, large load-8 SF, dryer-4 SF, soap-0.80–1.20 SF). Take bus #20 from the train station (1.90 SF); get off at the third stop (called Lorraine), cross the main street at the pedestrian crossing, turn right, and walk another block along Dammweg, which runs parallel to the main street.

**Bike Rental:** Free loaner city bikes are available during the summer at Bahnhofplatz (to the right as you exit the station). Look for the *Bern rollt* kiosk. Leave your photo ID and a 20-SF deposit (daily 7:30–21:30, www.bernrollt.ch). You can rent bikes year-round at **Velostation,** behind the train-station baggage office (5 SF/day, Mon–Fri 7:00–19:00, closed Sat–Sun).

**Tours: GTK Tours,** run by Robert Home from Tasmania, offers tours of the region by minibus, including half-day cheese tours (28 SF) and chocolate tours (55 SF), departing from the Bern train station. Robert has a passion for showing people the true charms of Switzerland. He offers personalized tours that will avoid touristy places and explore hidden valleys, allowing you to meet authentic Swiss people (tel. 031-762-0028, www.gtktours.ch, tours@gtktours.ch).

## Getting Around Bern

The city is walkable, though the trams can be handy. A standard single ticket costs 3.20 SF, a shorter trip *(Kurzstrecke)* runs 1.90 SF, and a 24-hour ticket is 12 SF. The best plan for exploring the town: Walk from the train station to the far end of town, then catch tram #12 back to the station (buy 1.90-SF *Kurzstrecke* from machine at bus stop, tram goes about every 6 min, www.bernmobil.ch).

# SELF-GUIDED WALK

## Welcome to Bern

This orientation walk begins at the train station and ends at the bear pits, at the far end of town. From the bear pits, you can catch tram #12 or browse your way back to your starting point, which is the...

**Train Station:** The station is a bright and airy shopping center, with a first-class TI (next to train information center), long-hours exchange desk, and all the shops you could need. On the ground floor are scant remnants of the town's third wall. (Notice the 1353 etching showing Bern as it looked the year it entered the Swiss Federation.) The fortified wall was replaced in the 19th century by the train station. All city buses and trams come and go from here.

• *From the train station TI, cross Bahnhofplatz, walk 50 yards, and turn left (around the church) onto Spitalgasse. This marks the start of one long street (with four names)—the spine of both the peninsula and this walk—that rambles downhill through the heart of town to the bridge and bear pits.*

Notice the first of Bern's 11 historical **fountains,** the Bagpiper. These colorful 16th-century fountains are Bern's trademark. The city commissioned them for many reasons: to brighten up the cityscape of gray stone buildings, to show off the town's wealth, and to remind citizens of great local heroes and events. They also gave local artists something to work on after the Reformation deprived them of their most important patron, the Catholic Church.

• *Continue down Spitalgasse until you reach...*

**Bärenplatz:** In summer, a daily market is held on this square (busiest on Tue and Sat mornings). The street runs under the **Prison Tower** (Käfigturm)—once a part of the city wall (c. 1256). Renovated 1641–1644, the tower served as a prison until 1897 (*Käfig* means "cage"). Notice how the hand on the clock really is a hand— and how it was built in a slower-paced era, when just an hour hand told time concisely enough. The bears on the tower are from Bern's coat of arms. Live ones await you at the end of this walk.

To the left (100 yards), you'll see the **Dutch Tower.** Swiss soldiers were famous mercenaries who fought all over Europe. Returning from a battle in the Netherlands, the soldiers brought

# Welcome to Bern Walk

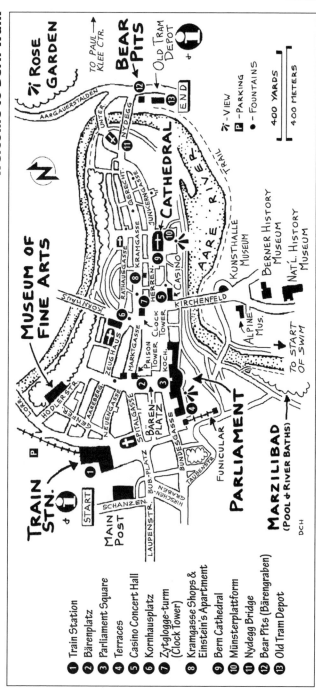

1 Train Station
2 Bärenplatz
3 Parliament Square
4 Terraces
5 Casino Concert Hall
6 Kornhausplatz
7 Zytglogge-turm (Clock Tower)
8 Kramgasse Shops & Einstein's Apartment
9 Bern Cathedral
10 Münsterplattform
11 Nydegg Bridge
12 Bear Pits (Bärengraben)
13 Old Tram Depot

back the habit of smoking. But smoking was forbidden within the city walls of Bern—so they hid in this tower to smoke secretly. (European smokers expect that, with current trends, this tower may regain its historic function within just a few years.)

Farther left is a modern and controversial **fountain** by the Swiss surrealist Meret Oppenheim. Made in 1983, it symbolizes growth and life, and is supposed to demonstrate communication between an object of art and the beholder. It worked well...too well, in fact, as most citizens immediately communicated their dislike and wanted it destroyed. But Bern's politicians proved braver than expected, and the fountain survived. Time has transformed Oppenheim's gray concrete column into a multicolored pillar decorated with moss, grass, and flowers. Locals like it only in the winter, when it's covered with ice. The grand building beyond the fountain—once the city orphanage—is the police station.

As each of the town's successive walls was torn down, they provided Bern with vast, people-friendly swaths of land which function as elongated "squares"—popular today for markets and outdoor cafés.

• *With your back to the modern fountain, stroll to the end of Bärenplatz, filled with market stalls and lined with fun places to eat (see "Eating," page 108). The big building you'll see from the square is the...*

**Parliament (Bundeshaus):** You may brush elbows with some high-powered legislators, but you wouldn't know it—everything looks very casual for a national capital. The fine granite plaza in front of the parliament (built in 2004 to replace a parking lot) is a favorite spot for demonstrations. Facing the square on the left is the Swiss National Bank—this country's Fort Knox, with piles of gold buried under the square.

Standing in front of the Parliament, check out the statuary. The woman on the top of the building represents political independence, the one on the left (under the "1291") stands for freedom, and the one on the right (1848) symbolizes peace.

Drop by the welcoming glass pavilion (left side, under the arcade) and pick up the generous literature on the Swiss government. Its bicameral system was inspired by the US Constitution, with one big difference: Executive power is shared by a committee of seven, with a rotating ceremonial president and a passion for consensus. This is a mechanism to avoid power grabs by any single individual...a safeguard that the Swiss love.

The Parliament building is currently under renovation. During this time, probably until January 2008, no guided tours are available (tel. 031-322-8522, www.parliament.ch).

• *Continuing past the Parliament info kiosk, walk around behind the Parliament to the...*

**Terraces:** From here, you have a commanding view over the Aare River and Bern's biggest swimming pool, the **Marzilibad.** On a clear day, you can see the peaks of the Eiger, Mönch, and Jungfrau (see Gimmelwald chapter)—and the far less imposing "mountain" of Bern, the **Gurten.** The Gurten is the city's favorite recreation spot, offering music festivals in summer and very modest skiing opportunities for children in winter.

Follow the tree-lined pedestrian lane left a few hundred yards to Kirchenfeld Bridge (great river views from halfway across, many museums just across). The **Casino** isn't for gamblers—it's the home of Bern's Symphony Orchestra.

• *With your back to the river, follow the tram tracks down another swath of land created by the removal of a city wall, to...*

**Kornhausplatz:** This square is ornamented by the colorful **Ogre** (*Chindlifresser,* "child-eater") fountain. Two legends try to explain this gruesome sight. It's either a folkloric representation of the Greek god Chronos, or a figure that was intended to scare children off the former city walls. The building behind on the left used to be the granary, and now houses the modern public library and the huge Kornhauskeller.

Wander down the stairs into the **Kornhauskeller.** Once the vast city wine cellar, now an Italian restaurant (see "Eating," page 108), this cellar was built in high Baroque style (1718) and renovated with paintings inspired by the Pre-Raphaelites in 1897. The 12 columns show traditional costumes of Bernese women.

• *Back on Kornhausplatz, step under the clock tower where Marktgasse becomes Kramgasse to see the fancy clock ornamenting its downhill side.*

**Zytglogge-Turm:** Bern's famous clock tower was part of the original wall marking the first gate to the city (c. 1250). The clock, which dates back to 1530, performs four minutes before each hour: The happy jester comes to life, Father Time turns his hourglass,

the rooster crows (in German, that's "kee-kee-ree-kee" rather than "cock-a-doodle-doo"), and the golden man on top hammers the bell. Apparently, this non-event was considered entertaining five centuries ago.

To pass the time waiting for the action, read the TI's leaflet explaining what's so interesting about the fancy old clock (the golden hour hand is an hour behind for half the year because of the modern innovation of daylight saving time). You can determine the zodiac, today's date, and the stage of the moon—look at the black-and-gold orb. Enthusiasts can tour the medieval mechanics—early Swiss engineering at its best—and see the billows that enable the old rooster to crow (10 SF, 50-min tour, May–Oct daily at 14:30, also at 17:30 July–Aug, buy ticket from guide).

Under the clock are the old regional measurements (Swiss foot, the bigger Bernese foot, and the *elle,* or "elbow," which was the distance from the elbow to the fingertip) and the official meter and double meter. It took a strong man like Napoleon to bring consistency to measurements in Europe, and he replaced the many goofy feet and elbows of medieval Europe with the metric system used today (c. 1800).

• *Continue your stroll down the main drag...*

**Kramgasse:** Bern has wide streets like this one, but not many squares. In the Middle Ages, craftsmen exhibited their goods on the sidewalks under simple roofs. Eventually, these were formalized, buildings expanded out, and arcades evolved.

The lanes of old Bern are lined with more than three miles of arcades, providing lots of arcaded shopping opportunities. This is my kind of shopping town: Prices are so high, there's no danger of buying (shops generally open Mon–Fri 9:00–18:30, Thu later, Sat 8:00–16:00, closed Sun).

Most shops are underneath the arcades, but don't miss the ones in the **cellars** that you can access only from the main road. The cellars, marked by old-time hatches, were originally for storing potatoes and coal, and later, wine. People said "merry Bern" was floating on wine, just as Venice was floating on water. The merry times ended in 1798, when the French invaded (and drank all the wine). The cellars were once again used for potatoes, and the city got a new nickname: "sad Bern." Napoleon's soldiers not only liberated Bern from its wine, but also from the tremendous treasury the city was known for. Napoleon used money looted from Bern to finance his Egyptian crusade.

The apartment that **Einstein** called home during several of his happiest and most productive years is 200 yards down Kramgasse from the clock tower (on the right, at Kramgasse 49). See period furniture, the original spiral staircase entrance, Einstein's Patent Office desk, photos, and manuscripts. The museum doesn't do much for me, but I guess everything's relative (6 SF, Mar–Sept daily 10:00–17:00;

Oct–Feb Tue–Fri 10:00–17:00, Sat 10:00–16:00, closed Sun–Mon; Kramgasse 49, tel. 031-312-0091, www.einstein-bern.ch).

• *Just below Einstein's apartment, at the Samson Fountain, turn right and crawl through the narrow Münstergässchen to the...*

**Bern Cathedral:** Bern's 15th-century Münster, Catholic-turned-Protestant, is capped with a 330-foot-tall tower, the highest in Switzerland (finished only in 1893). The church was dedicated to St. Vincent of Zaragoza. During the Reformation, religious icons were destroyed by Protestants (an act called "iconoclasm"—see page 211). This church's main portal, with its striking gold-leaf highlights, seems pretty un-Protestant. It probably survived because its theme, the Last Judgment, showed that no matter how rich you are or what rank you have in Church hierarchy, *anyone* can end up in hell (an idea Protestants dug). Condemned people are popping in the flames like lottery balls. Notice the humorous details in the commotion of people heading to hell (especially what the little green devil is doing to the sinful monk).

Cathedral entrance is free (April–Oct Tue–Sat 10:00–17:00, Sun 11:30–17:00, closed Mon; Nov–March Tue–Fri 11:00–13:00 & 14:00–16:00, Sat until 17:00, Sun 11:30–14:00, closed Mon; tel. 031-312-0462). Climb the spiral staircase 210 feet above the town for the view and the exercise (choose between two stairways: 312 or 354 steps). Elisabeth Bissig lives way up there, watching over the church, answering questions, and charging tourists 4 SF for the city view and a chance to peek at her bells.

Behind the cathedral is a terrace overlooking the river. Go toward the terrace, walking by free public WCs (industrial strength, pop in and push the buttons). Like the United States, Switzerland is dealing with a persistent drug abuse problem. Rather than fill its jails, it has tried a more compassionate approach (which hasn't worked well either): Public toilets like this one are lit by blue lights, so junkies shooting up in public can't locate their veins.

• *Continue on to the...*

**Münsterplattform:** This terrace was built, starting in the 14th century, from all kinds of "recycled" stones from older buildings. Archaeologists even unearthed some heads of statues that were victims of Reformation iconoclasts. Look down on the Aare (find the bear out on the breakwater). Notice the security nets below you. The platform used to be the favorite place for suicides—to the terror of the people living below. The Pavilion Café offers a scenic spot for a bite or drink on a sunny day.

With your back to the river, return to the main drag, Kramgasse. On the Fountain of Justice, a blindfolded figure of Justice triumphs over the mayor, pope, sultan, and emperor. A few steps above the fountain, a grate reveals a bit of the stream that

## Albert Einstein (1879–1955) in Bern

The man who changed how we see our universe made his greatest discoveries during the eight years he lived in Bern (1901–1909). Raised in Germany, Albert Einstein went to college in Zürich, hoping to eventually land a job teaching math and physics. But the young grad's GPA and resume were mediocre, so he took a temp job instead in Bern's Patent Office, inspecting and registering inventions.

Twenty-three-year-old Albert and his new bride Mileva (his college sweetheart) rented a second-floor apartment at Kramgasse 49 (today's Einstein House—see page 100), where Mileva soon gave birth to little Hans Albert. Einstein punched the clock at the Patent Office, and spent his spare time reading, hiking the Bern countryside, and thinking. At night, he'd join up with his mates—the self-named "Olympia Academy"—to smoke, drink beer, and talk math and philosophy. Outwardly, he led an ordinary life, but his thoughts were always on science's Big Questions. At home, in pubs, or at work he'd scribble down equations and ideas, filing them in his self-described "Department of Theoretical Physics"—a desk drawer in his office.

Then one warm spring day, as Einstein walked on the outskirts of Bern, it all started coming together. So began his "annus mirabilis"—the miracle year of 1905—in which the 26-year-old unknown amateur physicist quickly wrote five papers that would shock and perplex the world. Published in a major physics journal, they touched on a variety of subjects—such as how molecules move, and how light can appear as either a wave of energy or as a beam of tiny particles.

The most famous and unsettling paper, his theory of special relativity, described a world in motion. A man on a moving train and someone stationary see the world from different perspectives—that's the classic principle of relativity described by Galileo and Newton. But Einstein said there's an exception to the rule—light, whose speed always remains constant whether it's on a moving train or on the ground. So a man on a moving train and one at rest will never agree on what they observe...yet they're both right. The discrepancies only become obvious as

used to flow open down the middle of the peninsula, providing people with a handy disposal system.

• *From here, it's a straight stretch to the bridge at the end of the old town...*

**Nydegg Bridge:** Look downstream from the Nydegg Bridge. To your left is the site of the original town castle (now a church). The small bridge below is the oldest in Bern (once the only bridge crossing the Aare here). Above on the ridge (just behind and to the

the train travels close to the speed of light. Then, while the man on the train thinks everything is normal, the man on the ground sees the train shrink, train clocks slow down, and the man on the train stop aging!

Einstein's papers drew little initial interest and a measure of skepticism. (Einstein did get a promotion in the Patent Office—from "technical expert third class" to "technical expert second class.") But over time, other physicists grasped the significance of Einstein's work, seeing how he took earlier findings, wove them together, and did the math that explained it. Subsequent experiments proved that, in fact, even Einstein's most bizarre assertions are correct. Time on a fast-moving jet really does slow down (hence, those interminable intercontinental flights).

Einstein was invited to lecture at the local university, though he was still working nine-to-five at the Patent Office. In his spare time, he worked on his next project, general relativity. He theorized that gravity is not a force that attracts things but a curving of space—like a bowling ball on a soft mattress—that affects the motion of nearby objects. In 1909, Einstein's growing reputation won him a job offer to teach in Zürich, and he quit the Patent Office and left Bern for good.

Einstein would never again approach the creative level of his days in Bern. In 1922, he won the Nobel Prize for work done during the 1905 "annus mirabilis." Albert and Mileva split, and he remarried. When Hitler took power in Germany (1933), Einstein—a pacifist and a Jew—left Europe for America. His curly black hair had turned white, and his aging face became a pop-culture icon of genius—pipe, moustache, basset-hound eyes, and halo of frizzy white hair.

In 1939, Einstein wrote a letter to President Roosevelt theorizing that the tiniest particle of matter could be converted into an enormous amount of energy. The principle was one he'd discovered back in 1905—that energy is equivalent to mass times the speed of light squared (a very big number). And so, $E = mc^2$ became the atomic bomb, from an idea hatched in the pubs and arcaded streets of Bern.

right of the pointy spire) is the Rose Garden, a restaurant capping the ridge with fine views. And just upstream stands the site of the original Lindt chocolate factory.

• *Continue across the bridge to reach the...*

**Bear Pits (Bärengraben):** The symbol of Bern is the bear, and some lively ones frolic in these big, barren, concrete pits, to the delight of locals and tourists alike (daily 9:30–17:00 in summer, closed off-season). You may see graffiti from the B.L.M. (Bear

Liberation Movement), which, through its terrorist acts, has forced a reluctant city government to give the sad-eyed bears better living conditions.

• *Behind the pits is the...*

**Old Tram Depot:** This depot hosts a tourist center (TI, free video on the city, brewery restaurant/café with terrace). Its excellent multimedia show, complete with an animated town model and marching Napoleonic-era soldiers, illustrates the history and wonders of Bern. Worth the time, the 20-minute show is more interesting than the bears. You can enter late, as the last half is only beauty shots of the town, with no language barrier (free, uncomfortable benches, show in English once hourly—see schedule—or ask for a printed script, daily June–Sept 9:00–18:00, March–May and Oct 10:00–16:00, shorter hours in winter).

Up the pathway is the **Rose Garden** (Rosengarten), a restaurant offering basic, reasonably priced food and a great city view (for this option and more, see "Eating," page 109).

From the Old Tram Depot, it's an easy trip on tram #12 back to the station (1.90 SF). If wandering back through town, be sure to get off into the quieter side lanes, which have a fascinating and entertaining array of shops and little eateries.

## SIGHTS AND ACTIVITIES

▲▲**The Berner Swim**—For something to write home about, join the local merchants, students, and carp in a float down the Aare River. The Bernese, proud of their very clean river and their basic ruddiness, have a tradition—sort of a wet, urban *paseo*. On summer days, they hike upstream five to 30 minutes, then float back down to the excellent (and free) riverside baths and pools (Marzilibad) just below the Parliament building. While the locals make it look easy, this can be dangerous—the current is swift. If you miss the last pole, you're history (start stroking over to it well in advance).

If a float down the river is a bit much, you're welcome to enjoy just the Marzilibad, or you can try the other popular free pool, Lorrainebad (downstream, on the other side of town, where the Aare flows much slower—a good spot for beginners). If a quick taste of the river is not enough, you can raft all the way from Thun (near Interlaken) to Bern (details at TI).

▲▲**Museum of Fine Arts (Kunstmuseum)**—While it features 1,000 years of local art and some Impressionism, the museum's real hit is its fabulous collection of Paul Klee's playful paintings. If you don't know Klee, I'd love to introduce you (7 SF, covered by BernCard and Swiss Pass—see page 4, no English inside but pick up free English map/brochure, Tue 10:00–21:00, Wed–Sun 10:00–17:00, closed Mon, 4 blocks north of station, Holdergasse 12, tel. 031-328-0944).

▲**Paul Klee Center (Zentrum Paul Klee)**—This museum is dedi-

cated solely to the art of Paul Klee, with about 200 of his pieces on display (out of a collection of 4,000). It's the best place in the world to experience and learn about this modernist painter of lively, almost childlike art. In addition to the impressive collection and temporary exhibits, the museum offers a creative, educational children's museum, where young artists can draw and play, surrounded by original Klee paintings (15 SF for 1-hour workshop at 10:00, 12:00, 14:00, or 16:00).

The building, by star Italian architect Renzo Piano, is an attraction in itself. It's formed like "waves" rolling from the surrounding hills, with the waves forming pavilions. The Klee collection is on the top two floors. Downstairs you'll find cafés, an art database, a movie about building the museum, a cozy hangout, and the children's museum. Pick up a free English-language booklet when purchasing your ticket (14 SF, covered by BernCard and Swiss Pass—see page 4, 16–20 SF includes special exhibits, Tue–Sun 10:00–17:00, Thu until 21:00, closed Mon, take bus #12—operating only during museum opening hours—from train station to Zentrum Paul Klee stop, Monument im Fruchtland 3, www.paulkleezentrum.ch).

**Other Bern Museums**—Across the bridge from the Parliament building on Helvetiaplatz are several museums (Alpine, Berner History, Communication, Natural History, Rifle, and Kunsthalle contemporary art) that sound more interesting than they are (all covered by BernCard and Swiss Pass—see page 4, most open Tue–Sun 10:00–17:00, closed Mon, www.museen-bern.ch). The TI produces a pamphlet explaining all the museums.

# SLEEPING

These places are listed in geographical order from the train station. The first is a block south of it, and the rest are in the old town just past Bärenplatz, about a five-minute walk away.

**$$$ Hotel National** is well-located, with 45 fine rooms; some come with street noise, so request a quiet room (S-70–85 SF, Sb-90 SF, D-120 SF, Db-150–160 SF, smaller fifth-floor rooms—which are just fine—are about 20 SF less, apartment-205–265 SF, extra bed-40 SF, elevator, Internet access, Hirschengraben 24, tel. 031-381-1988, fax 031-381-6878, www.nationalbern.ch, info @nationalbern.ch).

**$$$ Hotel Continental** has 40 bright and comfy, Nordic-flavored rooms and a cheery breakfast room with a sun terrace (Sb-130 SF, Db-180 SF, Tb-210 SF; cheaper Fri–Sun: Sb-110 SF, Db-150 SF, Tb-180 SF elevator, Zeughausgasse 27, tel. 031-329-2121, fax 031-329-2199, new owners).

**$$$ Hotel Goldener Schlüssel** is an old, basic, crank-'em-out hotel with 29 rooms, right in the city center (S-90 SF, Sb-118 SF, D-132 SF, Db-158 SF, Tb-205 SF, extra bed-50 SF, elevator, Rathausgasse 72, tel. 031-311-0216, fax 031-311-5688, www .goldener-schluessel.ch, info@goldener-schluessel.ch).

**$ Backpackers Hotel Glocke** rents the cheapest beds in the old town (beds in 4- to 6-bed dorms-31 SF, D-78 SF, includes sheets, cheaper off-season; no breakfast, but kitchen available, non-smoking, Internet access in lobby, laundry, kitchen, reception open 8:00–11:00 & 15:00–22:00, Rathausgasse 75, tel. 031-311-3771, fax 031-311-1008, www.bernbackpackers.com, info@bernbackpackers .com).

**$ Bern Youth Hostel** is a big, institutional place below the Parliament building near the river (dorm bed-36.50 SF, D-89 SF,

---

## Sleep Code

**(1.25 SF = about $1, country code: 41)**
**S** = Single, **D** = Double/Twin, **T** = Triple, **Q** = Quad, **b** = bathroom, **s** = shower only. Unless otherwise noted, credit cards are accepted, English is spoken, and breakfast is included.

To help you sort easily through these listings, I've divided the rooms into three categories, based on the price for a standard double room with bath:

$$$ **Higher Priced**—Most rooms 150 SF or more.
$$ **Moderately Priced**—Most rooms between 90–150 SF.
$ **Lower Priced**—Most rooms 90 SF or less.

# Bern Hotels and Restaurants

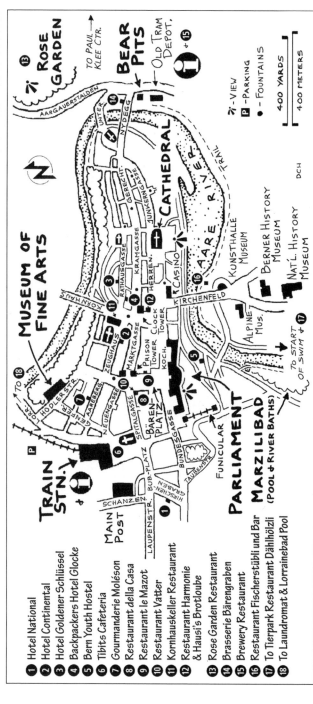

1. Hotel National
2. Hotel Continental
3. Hotel Goldener Schlüssel
4. Backpackers Hotel Glocke
5. Bern Youth Hostel
6. Tibits Cafeteria
7. Gourmanderie Moléson
8. Restaurant della Casa
9. Restaurant le Mazot
10. Restaurant Vatter
11. Kornhauskeller Restaurant
12. Restaurant Harmonie & Hausi's Brotloube
13. Rose Garden Restaurant
14. Brasserie Bärengraben
15. Brewery Restaurant
16. Restaurant Fischerstübli und Bar
17. To Tierpark Restaurant Dählhölzli
18. To Laundromat & Lorrainebad Pool

reception open 7:00–10:00 & 15:00–24:00, Weihergasse 4, tel. 031-311-6316, www.jugibern.ch, info@jugibern.ch).

# EATING

## Between the Station and Bärenplatz

**Tibits,** a self-service buffet in the train station building, offers a huge variety of vegetarian-only salads and sandwiches, plus two different hot dishes. Help yourself to a plate and pile it on. The price is by weight: An average helping will cost you about 20 SF (3.70 SF per 100 grams, 6.50 SF for soup and bread, variety of sandwiches for 7 SF, "juice of the month"-4.50–6.50 SF, Mon–Sat 6:30–23:30, Sun 8:00–23:00, Bahnhofplatz 10, tel. 031-312-9111).

**Gourmanderie Moléson** is a long, skinny, bistro-type place serving traditional Swiss dishes, *tartes flambées* (Alsatian pizzas-25 SF), vegetarian meals, and two-course lunch deals for 25 SF. The dressy and very Swiss interior can be a bit smoky, but tables tumble out into the street (Mon–Fri 11:30–14:30 & 18:00–23:30, Sat 18:00–23:30, closed Sun, Aarbergergasse 24, tel. 031-311-4463).

**Restaurant della Casa,** a traditional Swiss place with Old World ambience inside and a few tables on the sidewalk outside, has daily specials scrawled on chalkboards throughout. While not cheap, it's been a neighborhood favorite for generations (25–35-SF plates, closed Sun, between Parliament and the station at Schauplatzgasse 16, tel. 031-311-2142).

## Around Bärenplatz

**Restaurant le Mazot** is popular with locals, who come to enjoy the mountain cuisine of French Switzerland. It offers a huge selection of *Rösti* (20 SF), fondues (25 SF), raclette, and other hearty alpine dishes from a user-friendly menu. You can sit inside (woody, mountain-hut ambience, with the smell of melted cheese and tobacco) or enjoy some fine people-watching on the traffic-free square outside (daily, Bärenplatz 5, tel. 031-311-7088).

**Restaurant Vatter** is exclusively organic—serving mostly vegetarian, lots of Indian cuisine, and some meat dishes. It's a fresh, mod place with a terrace overlooking the lively Bärenplatz. The restaurant is above an organic produce store (25-SF plates, closed Sun, Bärenplatz 2, tel. 031-312-5171).

## Around Kornhausplatz

**Kornhauskeller,** decorated with colorful mural paintings (see description on page 99), is a splurge. It's in the cellar of the old granary, originally built to house the state's wine cellar. This dressy, pricey Italian place offers lunch specials and a fine antipasto bar for those on a budget. Make a meal out of the 16-SF or 24-SF plate, telling the waiter exactly what you'd like (30-SF plates, Mon–Sat 11:45–14:30 & 18:00–24:00, Sun 18:00–23:30, Kornhausplatz 18, tel. 031-327-7272).

## Near the Cathedral

**Restaurant Harmonie,** owned by the Gyger family since 1915, is one of the oldest and most traditional places in town. It offers filling Swiss cuisine and is the favorite lunch spot for Swiss politicians (daily specials, 30-SF plates, closed Sat–Sun, Hotelgasse 3, tel. 031-311-3840).

**Hausi's Brotloube** is a bakery stocked with everything you need—sandwiches, salads, fruit, drinks, and pastries—to put together a first-class picnic for the nearby Münsterplattform (Mon–Fri 6:30–18:30, Sat 6:30–13:00, closed Sun, next to Café Harmonie at Münstergasse 74).

## Near the Bear Pits

Many finish their town walk at the bear pits, and have worked up an appetite. You have three fine options here.

**Rose Garden Restaurant** is good for city views and a light meal, salad, or tea and cakes with local grannies (March–Oct daily 9:00–24:00, closed off-season, walk up Aargauerstalden tel. 031-331-3206).

**Brasserie Bärengraben,** tight and dressy, is popular with local businesspeople at lunch (18.50-SF lunch specials, immediately over the bridge opposite the bears).

**Brewery Restaurant** offers seating in their big, bright, and boisterous brewery, or on their leafy terrace overlooking the town and river. It's quick and not too expensive (fast and healthy 18-SF lunch plates, in Old Tram Depot behind the bears).

## At the Aare River

**Restaurant Fischerstübli und Bar,** specializing in fish, is the perfect place to be on a hot summer day (daily, weekends only in evening, Gerberngasse 41, tel. 031-311-5367).

**Tierpark Restaurant Dählhölzli** is probably the most popular family hangout around when it's sunny. The huge outdoor terrace is divided into a full-service restaurant (marked with tablecloths) and a cheaper self-service section. Next to it is the Dählhölzli Zoo, where children can ride ponies and pet all kinds of animals while parents rest. Before you sit down, check if the chair is dry—this is also a favorite stop for the Aare swimmers to warm up with a cup of coffee. Don't be surprised to find guests in swimsuits and waiters who gracefully accept wet bills (March–Sept 8:00–18:00, Oct–Feb 9:00–17:00, Dalmaziquai 151a, tel. 031-351-1894, www .daehlhoelzli.ch).

## TRANSPORTATION CONNECTIONS

**From Bern by Train to: Murten** (hourly, 40 min, some transfer in Kerzers), **Lausanne** (2/hr, 70 min), **Interlaken** (2/hr, 50 min), **Luzern** (hourly, 1 hr; or 2/hr with transfer in Olten, 1.5 hrs), **Zürich** (2/hr, 1–1.25 hrs), **Fribourg** in Switzerland (2/hr, 30 min), **Freiburg** in Germany (hourly, 2 hrs, some direct, some transfer in Basel), **Zermatt** (hourly, 3.25 hrs, transfer in Brig), **Montreux** (2/hr, 1.5 hrs, transfer in Lausanne**), Lugano** (hourly, 4 hrs, transfer in Luzern, Olten, or Zürich), **Appenzell** (hourly, 3.25 hrs, transfer in Gossau), **Munich** (4/day, 5.5 hrs, more with multiple transfers), **Frankfurt** (hourly, 4.5 hrs), **Salzburg** (4/day, 7.25 hrs, transfer in Zürich), **Paris** (6/day, 6 hrs). Train info: toll tel. 0900-300-3004 or www.rail.ch.

### Route Tips for Drivers

**Interlaken to Bern:** From Interlaken, catch the autobahn (direction: Spiez, Thun, then Bern). Circle Bern on the autobahn, taking the fourth Bern exit, Neufeld Bern. Signs to *Zentrum* take you to Bern Bahnhof. Turn right just before the station into the Bahnhof Parkplatz (45-min meter parking outside, all-day lot inside, 2–4 SF/hr, depending on time of entry). You're just an escalator ride away from a great TI and Switzerland's capital.

**Heading to Murten from Bern:** From the station, drive out of Bern following signs for *Lausanne*, then follow the green signs to *Neuchâtel* and *Murten*. The autobahn ends 20 miles later in Murten.

# Murten

The finest medieval ramparts in Switzerland surround the 5,000 people of Murten (or Morat, if you're speaking French). We're on the linguistic cusp of Switzerland: 25 percent of Murten speaks French; a few miles to the southwest, nearly everyone does.

Murten is a totally charming mini-Bern with lively streets, the middle one nicely arcaded with breezy outdoor cafés and elegant shops (many closed Mon). Its castle is romantically set, overlooking Lake Murten and the rolling vineyards of gentle Mount Vully in the distance. Spend a night here and have dinner with a local Vully wine, white or rosé. Murten is touristic, but seems to be enjoyed mostly by its own people.

Make time for nearby Avenches (see page 121). While quaint today, the town was once a powerful Roman capital—as its ruins attest.

## ORIENTATION

### Tourist Information

Murten's TI is just inside the city walls at the eastern end of town (opposite end from station; May–Sept Mon–Fri 9:00–12:00 & 14:00–18:00, Sat 10:00–15:00, closed Sun; July–Aug also Sun 10:00–14:00, Oct–April shorter hours and closed weekends, Französische Kirchgasse 6, tel. 026-670-5112, www.murtentourismus.ch). Get a free map and ask about sights, biking, and boat trips.

### Arrival in Murten

**By Train:** To reach the town from the station (a 5-min walk), exit to the right, take the first left, walk up Bahnhofstrasse, then turn right through the town gate. Murten is a tiny town...a delight on foot.

**By Car:** You can park overnight in the old town for free (18:00–10:00). During the day, don't park inside the gates; Murten's brown-clad parking cops are infamous. Park in the lot near the castle and Co-op supermarket (5 SF/day includes in-and-out privileges, 16 SF for your entire stay if you don't move your car, 45 SF/1 week in-and-out, take ticket and pay at hotel or police station). Get the latest advice on parking from your hotelier.

### Helpful Hints

**Internet Access:** Try **A&A Computer** (Mon and Fri 9:00–12:00 & 14:00–18:30, Sat 9:00–13:00, closed Tue–Thu and Sun, behind station, past Peugeot garage, at Engelhardstrasse 6, tel. 026-670-0520).

**Post Office:** It's across the street from the train station.

**Laundry:** None in town.

**Local Guide:** Mary Brunisholz, an American who married into this part of Switzerland, is an excellent guide with a car (150–200 SF/half-day, mobile 078-601-7040, mary.brunisholz @vtxnet.ch).

## SELF-GUIDED WALK

### Welcome to Murten

This introductory walk will give you the lay of the land, and a lesson on the historic 15th-century Battle of Murten.

• *Start your walk just below the town's main gate at the public school, where you see a statue of the feisty local leader...*

**Adrian von Bubenberg:** Burgundy was the aggressive power of the day, and this Murten native stopped the power grab of the 15th century by beating Charles the Bold. Adrian von Bubenberg stood here and looked across the lake at the distant peaks of the Jura Mountains—the historic border between the Swiss and the French. (More on the battle a little later.)

The earliest Swiss clockmakers were from those Jura Mountains. Look at the **clock tower**—where's the little hand? As part of its lease, the restaurant below takes responsibility for hand-winding the clock each day, as it has since 1712. That's the Bern gate—so called because it opens up onto the road to Bern. The tiny grated window in the mighty door is a security window.

• *Rather than enter the gate, go right instead. Head along the outside of the wall, around the first turret, and look for the cannon balls.*

These cannon balls were left in the wall to remind townsfolk of their incredible victory over the Burgundians—like an Alamo with a happy ending.

• *Belly up to the lakeview terrace*

Across the way is **Mount Vully** (mohn voo-yee)—one big vineyard, and a mecca for lovers of Swiss white wine. The lowlands to the right—a rich former lakebed—are the heart of the fertile Three Lakes Region (lakes Biel, Neuchâtel, and Murten). The lush farmland is called the "vegetable garden of Switzerland" for its soil, which yields more than 60 varieties of produce.

The ancient Celtic "Helvet" tribe recognized the fertility of this land and settled here. The Romans likewise made this land a priority in establishing their colony of Helvetia. (Today, Switzerland is officially known as Confederation Helvetica—the "CH" you see on bumper stickers.)

• *Check out the small **church**.*

Foreseeing a showdown with Burgundy, Adrian von Bubenberg had the town walls strengthened. As three-quarters of the town were German-speaking, they took a vote and decided to tear down the French church to get more stones. (This little church was rebuilt for the French-speaking community six years after its big one was demolished.) As the Calvinist Reformation swept through Catholic Switzerland in the early 16th century, churches like this were stripped of their rich paintings, sculptures, and stained glass. The altar became a Bible on a table, and pulpits became the focus. The emphasis was teaching the word of God. In this church, about the only exception to the "no distractions"

# Murten

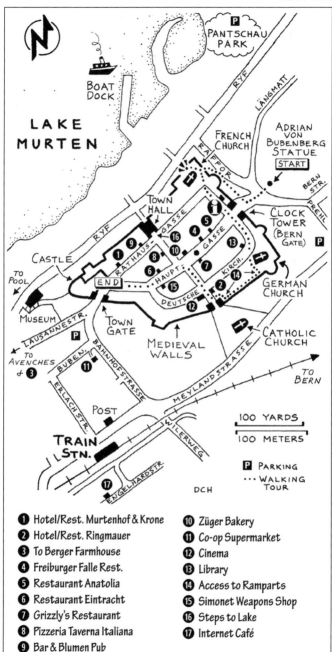

1. Hotel/Rest. Murtenhof & Krone
2. Hotel/Rest. Ringmauer
3. To Berger Farmhouse
4. Freiburger Falle Rest.
5. Restaurant Anatolia
6. Restaurant Eintracht
7. Grizzly's Restaurant
8. Pizzeria Taverna Italiana
9. Bar & Blumen Pub
10. Züger Bakery
11. Co-op Supermarket
12. Cinema
13. Library
14. Access to Ramparts
15. Simonet Weapons Shop
16. Steps to Lake
17. Internet Café

rule are tiny stained-glass coats of arms—heraldry of the wealthy families who helped fund its construction.

• *From here, you'll walk across town. Walk past the TI, the Bern Tower, and up the lane to the library (on right, #31).*

Notice that along with being a "Bibliothek," the **library** is also a "Ludothek." This means parents can check out toys and games for their children, rather than spend their hard-earned money keeping massive places like "Toys 'R' Us" in business. Across the street, the typically Bernese little **Web Husli** shows off its old-time loom. The door is perfect for short people—if you're five-feet five-inches, stand tall on the threshold. After a 14th-century fire burned down the wooden town, future building was limited to the characteristic yellow Jura stone (like the library). Around the corner (left) just past the town's morgue, is the public WC.

• *Continue straight ahead to the...*

**German Church:** Murten's German church, built in 1710, is also post–Reformation Protestant simple. As the town is on the border between two cantons (Bern and Fribourg), for 400 years its rule was shared: Every five years, it would flip between cantons. Arrangements like this didn't sit well with Napoleon, and around 1800, he made it firmly a part of nearby Fribourg.

Inside, notice the big stucco relief (center of ceiling) with two seals: the bear for Bern and the three castles for Fribourg. The Protestant passion for Bible study is also evident in this church. The pulpit was carved from a single trunk of oak in 1460. Explore the choir (circle of seats for big shots) behind the altar. Find Adrian von Bubenberg's seat. (Hint: The window above shows the war hero in red, with his victorious local yokels in their alpine red-knit hats...underdogs whupping the Burgundians.) Pull up the seat and rest on the misericord—a lazy but permissible alternative when everyone stands during a long service. Notice that the two prime seats do double duty (on the right hand of the preacher sat the leader of Bern or Fribourg—depending on who happened to be ruling that year). To computer gamers, the stained-glass depiction of the crucifixion feels proto-Tetris (c. 1926).

• *Leaving the church, hook left around the back. Finger the limestone and sandstone tombstones, quarried from Mount Vully for noble families. Then climb the creaky stairs onto the ramparts and walk about 50 yards.*

**Rampart Ramble:** Murten's only required sightseeing is to scramble the ramparts (free, open daily until 21:00). Survey the town. Note the uniformity of Murten. Paint your place the wrong color, and you may be instructed to redo it—at your own expense. Scanning the countless chimneys, think of the enforced conformity that comes with living in a small town (and find the one oddball). Telephone and electricity wires are all underground. Look back at the roof of the German church. A color-blindness test is built into its tiles. (If you can find the six-sided "star of David"—not a Jewish symbol in this case, but recalling the star that guided the wise men to Bethlehem on the first Christmas—you're okay.)

• *Continue to the tower. Climb the steps for a commanding town and lake view.*

With your back to the lake, look inland and imagine the action on June 22, 1476. Mighty Charles the Bold, with his 20,000 well-armed Burgundians, was camped on the hill (with the divided forest) for 10 days, laying siege to the town of 2,000. Runners were sent out from the town to gather help. A makeshift army of about 10,000 villagers gathered on the hills to the left. Just as George Washington attacked when the Redcoats were celebrating Christmas, the Swiss swooped in as the Burgundians were still hungover from a big Midsummer Night's Eve bash. It was pouring rain—a muddy, bloody mess. Almost all 20,000 Burgundians were slaughtered—many driven into the lake with their armor to drown (try swimming in a coat of mail). For centuries, French bones would wash ashore. Charles the (no-longer-so-) Bold barely got away on a very fast horse.

This victory demonstrated to the Swiss the advantages of *E Pluribus Unum,* and the assemblage of the many still-fiercely independent Swiss cantons into the Confederation Helvetica snowballed. In this sweet little corner, an influential battle in European history had been fought. Burgundian power ebbed, and Europe got to know a new nation...Switzerland.

• *Walk a bit farther along the wall and descend at the next tower (across from Café-Pension Ringmauer).*

The stairs lead to a fine old clock mechanism from 1816. Once powering the big clock in the City Hall tower, it spent decades in an Ikea-like to-be-assembled pile—gathering dust in an attic. An old local, recognizing a good challenge, reassembled it into perfect working order (1991). Notice how the gearbox powers three different clock faces, and how the old hand crank raises the stones that power the clock. The white face determines the clock's time—which rings on the quarter-hour.

• *Step outside the wall, where you'll see the Catholic church (1886), private gardens along the wall, and the different stages of the wall's construction.*

The first phase was built with large river stones, some arranged in a neat fishbone pattern. Later, the town ran out of money, and the next stage shows pebbles and rubble mixed with a rough concrete. And finally, when the town prospered again, they finished the wall with finely cut sandstone.

• *Walk back into town, stopping on the first corner at the fire station-turned–community–cinema.*

Local shareholders are thanked with their names on the door. Pop into the charming theater—80 plush, red seats. Notice what's playing tonight (see "Nightlife," below). At this corner, spin slowly, admiring the town's fine shutters, and think of something tour guide-ish to say about them.

• *Then, continue a block to the...*

**Main Street:** In the 19th century, Murten's townsfolk used one of three water fountains on this street. Enjoy the colorful store signs as they still hang out their shingles in the traditional fashion. Bakery and *pâtisserie* competition on this street is fierce. Drop into one for the local specialties: *Nidlechueche*, a sweet, doughy cream tart (3.20 SF per slice); and *Seelander Zwetschen*, a chocolate-covered prune truffle with liqueur.

Near the top of the main street, **Simonet Weapons** sells all the latest knives by Victorinox. There's the green stay-glow, and even a model with a memory stick for the outdoorsman with a laptop. At the top of the street (#16), Murten's oldest house has fine paintings under its eaves. There's some nice *Schmuck* (jewelry) two doors to the right.

• *Farther to the right, at the top of town, step into...*

**Murten Castle:** The town castle, which houses the police station in a former prison (closed to the public), shows off an impressive gun from 1882 and a fine lake view. The nearby museum is not worth your time or money, but steps lead from there down to the lake.

## ACTIVITIES

**Lake Activities**—To get down to Murten's lazy lakefront, find the access just past the castle, or, more centrally, at Rathausstrasse 17

(a block from Hotel Murtenhof). Just past the grassy breakwater is Pantschau, a big park. The park is flanked by cheap self-service eateries (such as La Chaloupe, with salad bar and crêpes) and the Beach House (with better lakeside seating). There's mini-golf, windsurfing gear rental and instruction, an open-air summer film fest, and a fine lakeside promenade.

**One-Hour Cruise (with Hiking Option):** Promenade Tour du Lac trips go about six times a day through the summer (13 SF without stops, 15 SF with stopover privileges, 4/day Oct–April, call to confirm off-season, tel. 032-329-8811 or 032-729-9600; TI can help).

Consider stopping in the small town of Praz on the French-speaking shore. From there, you have two good options: You could hike through vineyards up Mount Vully—where a bench and fine lake and Alp views await—and return on the lake with your same ticket. Or you can walk from Praz back to Murten, clockwise around the lake (2 hrs, 3.80 SF for boat from Murten to Praz).

**Half-Day Three Lakes Cruise:** Consider sailing on all three lakes of the region on a one-way, three-hour trip (involving one train connection). Boats leave the town of Biel (an easy train ride from Murten) daily at 9:45, cruise through Lake Biel, connect with canals to lakes Neuchâtel and Murten, and stop at several small medieval villages along the way. The boat arrives in Murten at 13:00, then turns around and heads back along the same route at 14:30, arriving in Biel at 18:20 (one-way-45 SF, round-trip-90 SF but a 52-SF "day card" covers the trip, details at TI or call BSG, tel. 032-329-8811 or 032-729-9600, www.bielersee.ch or www.navig .ch). There are two trips per day in each direction, each involving a Murten–Biel train connection (1/hr, 1-hour trip).

**Swimming Pool**—The Olympic-size public swimming pool is outside of town next to the lake, just past the castle (6 SF, daily July–Aug 9:00–21:00, early summer and fall 9:30–19:00, closed in winter and spring).

**Biking**—The Three Lakes region has 100 miles of signposted bike paths (well-described in TI's brochures). Pick up a free map or buy a top-notch one. The best easy ride circles the lake and Mount Vully (through vineyards and, if you like, to the summit for a good view). You can rent **bikes** at train-station ticket counters (23 SF/half-day, 31 SF/day, 5 SF less with Eurailpass or Swiss Pass, includes helmets, daily 6:30–23:00). Ask about being dropped off with your bike—or dropping off your bike—at another station, which opens up interesting options (7 SF extra, limited to a few stations).

# NIGHTLIFE

**Movies**—Murten's cute little community co-op theater plays movies nightly (15 SF, Schulgasse 18). Movies are shown in their original language (capital letter indicates the soundtrack language, small letters indicate subtitles—e.g., "Efd" means "English with French and *Deutsch* subtitles").

**Theater am See** hosts a lakeside summer film festival with outdoor screenings of a different movie each night (early July–early Aug, details at TI).

**Pubs**—There are plenty of inviting pubs and nightclubs in town. The **Bar and Blumen** sells flowers by day (check out the edelweiss), and  drinks with a lake view by night (next to Town Hall and Hotel Murtenhof). The main street has an Irish bar and several other nightspots. The bar just outside the Bern Tower is popular with locals.

## SLEEPING

**(1.25 SF = about $1, country code: 41)**
This adorable town is no secret. July through mid-September (especially on weekends) is peak time—make a reservation and expect maximum prices. When price ranges are given in the hotel listings, it means that prices vary depending on the season, type of room, or view. For a youth hostel, you'll have to sleep in nearby Avenches (see page 122).

**$$$ Hotel Murtenhof and Krone,** a worthwhile splurge, has 54 nicely appointed rooms—each a stylish mix of old and new. The Krone section of the hotel has smaller, less-expensive rooms, and a cozy, spacious lounge. This place is well-run by the Joachim family—Theodore, Jutta, and their son Marc (Sb-120 SF, small Db-140, big Db-230 SF, Tb-200 SF, family rooms, in mid-Sept–May ask for a 10 percent discount with this book, elevator, Internet access, next to castle at Rathausgasse 1–5, tel. 026-672-9030, fax 026-672-9039, www.murtenhof.ch, info@murtenhof.ch). They have the best lakeview restaurant in town (see below).

**$$ Hotel Ringmauer** (German for "Ramparts") is friendly and characteristic, with a fun mix of modern decor in a traditional setting. Showers and toilets are within a dash of all 14 rooms (S-60 SF, D-110 SF, Db-120 SF, T-145 SF, Q-165 SF, attached restaurant, near town wall farthest from lake, Deutsche Kirchgasse 2, tel. 026-670-1101, fax 026-672-2083).

**$ Berger Farmhouse** is the choice if "Green Acres is the place" for you. Consider a night in a barn (literally) at the big, traditional Berger-Aegerter family farm. Frau Berger, who speaks German and French, fills a big room with six single beds (and can add up to four more). There's no plumbing—you use a bathroom in the family building next door. The place is generally empty, so you're likely to have it all to yourself—surrounded by hay, old farm tools, and the noise of animals (May–Nov only because there's no heat, 30 SF per bed with breakfast, she'll cook dinner for 15 SF by request, family deals, includes sheets but no towels, a third of the way to Avenches, a mile or so south of Murten, on the main road just before Greng, look for the sign, Lindenweg 2, tel. 026-670-1407).

# EATING

Eating in Murten is a joy. I'd stroll the main drag up one side and down the other to survey the action before making a choice. For elegance and a lake view, it's the Murtenhof. There are several good options right on the lake a 10-minute walk from the town center. Budget eaters can picnic or find a salad bar. Bakeries make good sandwiches, but they close by about 18:00.

Anything called "Seelander" or mentioning "three lakes" is typical of this Three Lakes region. Traditional restaurants serve *Egli-Filets,* the very popular perch "from the lake" (these days actually caught in Bodensee—Lake Constance in English—up by the German border). As this is the "vegetable garden of Switzerland," restaurants pride themselves on offering good veggies. You'll want a glass of wonderfully smooth and refreshing white Vully (voo-yee) wine with your meal (about 4 SF per glass).

**Restaurant Murtenhof,** with a covered terrace giving diners a comfortable and classy lakeside setting regardless of the weather, serves "updated Three Lakes cuisine" and several vegetarian choices. Sipping a glass of local white wine with the right travel partner, while gazing across the lake at hillside vineyards as the sun sets, is one of Europe's fine moments. Their fresh and tasty "catch of the day" (while not *Egli*) actually *is* from the lake (19 SF). To be sure you get the limited lakeside seating, call in a reservation at 026-672-9030 (salad bar, March–Nov Tue–Sun 11:00–23:00, closed Mon and Dec–Feb). The recorded sheep baaah-ing on the soundtrack adds to the place's rustic elegance.

**Ringmauer Restaurant** is a good bet for French cuisine and decadent desserts, offering a dressy section (40-SF plates, 78-SF five-course fixed-price meal) and a cheaper zone (30-SF plates, 17.50-SF daily special). It has fine outdoor seating on a quiet, picturesque lane, but the indoor section can be smoky—a good sign, indicating it's a local favorite. They serve top-end local wine by the glass (closed Sun evenings and Mon, Deutsche Kirchgasse 2, tel. 026-670-1101).

Fun-loving **Freiburger Falle** serves all the old *Fribourgeoise* traditions, such as meat on a hot stone (36 SF), fondue, and so on—in a characteristic cellar under the main street. You'll eat under alphorn and castle-style chandeliers (it hides under the Irish pub at Hauptgasse 43, tel. 026-672-1222, Bruno Lüscher).

**Restaurant Anatolia** is a Turkish place with crayon-quality menus posted everywhere and rather high prices for ethnic food. Still, it's much loved by locals for its fresh ingredients, good cooking, and charming owner, Mehmet. Eat indoors or out, with a fine main-drag view (20–25 SF, Hauptgasse 45, tel. 026-670-2868).

**Restaurant Eintracht** serves local cuisine from a fun menu, including old-time chef specials. If there is a down-and-dirty, horse-meat-cookin' local hangout in town, this is it (15–25-SF plates, half portions available, healthy specials, vineyard ambience or streetside seating, closed Wed, closes Sun at 18:00, Hauptgasse 19, tel. 026-670-2240).

**Grizzly's Restaurant,** perfect for those in need of a quick trip back home, is a playful, enthusiastic place with an enticing menu of North American delicacies. The Yukon-chic interior comes with totem poles, buckskins, and rock and roll. The outside offers the finest seats on the main street (fresh salads, trappers' spare ribs, vegetarian options, Tue–Sat 11:00–23:30, closed Sun–Mon, reservations smart, Hauptgasse 24, tel. 026-670-0787). As the menu says, "If the meal's not ready in 10 minutes, it will be in 15. If it's not on the table in 15 minutes, have another beer."

*Pizza:* Murten has two pizzerias. The one on the main street has better views, but locals prefer **Pizzeria Taverna Italiana** as a better value (17-SF daily specials, 20-SF pizza and pasta, 15-SF pizzas to go, daily 10:00–14:00 & 17:00–23:00, near Hotel Murtenhof at Kreuzgasse 4, tel. 026-670-2122).

*Bakeries:* The main street has four bakeries, all with ample charm. **Züger** (at Hauptgasse 33) has a tea room and offers daily indoor seating and pleasant outside seats. They have delicate, local-style, open-face sandwiches and a wide variety of salads for around 14 SF (Wed–Sat and Mon 7:00–18:30, Sun 7:45–18:30, closed Tue).

*Supermarket:* The giant **Co-op** (with a cafeteria) towers between the train station and city center (Mon–Thu 8:00–19:00, Fri 8:00–20:00, Sat 7:30–16:00, closed Sun).

## TRANSPORTATION CONNECTIONS

**From Murten by Train to: Avenches** (hourly, 10 min, direction: Payern), **Bern** (hourly, 30 min, most require a transfer in Kerzers), **Fribourg** in Switzerland (hourly, 30 min), **Lausanne** (hourly, 90 min, generally transfer in Fribourg), **Zürich** (2/hr, 1.75–2.25 hrs, transfer in Bern, Fribourg, or Kerzers). Train info: toll tel. 0900-300-3004.

### Route Tips for Drivers
**Murten to Lake Geneva (50 miles):** The autobahn from Bern to Lausanne/Lake Geneva makes everything speedy (see Lake Geneva chapter). Murten and Avenches are 10 minutes off the autobahn. Broc, Bulle, and Gruyères are within sight of each other and the autobahn. It takes about an hour to drive from Murten to Montreux. The autobahn (direction: Simplon) takes you high above Montreux (pull off at great viewpoint rest stop) and Château

de Chillon. For the castle, take the first exit east of the castle (Villeneuve). Signs direct you along the lake back to the castle.

# Near Murten: Avenches

Avenches, four miles south of Murten, was once Aventicum, the Roman capital of Helvetica. Today, it's a quaint little town with an ancient theater taking a bite out of it. From the town spreads a vast field of sparse Roman ruins.

With a pleasant, small-town French ambience, Avenches (ah-vahnsh) is a quieter, less expensive place to stay than Murten. Just a few minutes away by train, it also makes an easy day trip. The **TI** (Mon–Fri 8:00–12:00 & 13:30–17:30, Sat 9:30–12:30, closed Sun, tel. 026-676-9922, www.avenches.ch) and the town are a seven-minute uphill walk from the station.

## Roman Avenches

Aventicum was a Roman capital, with a population of 20,000. The Romans appreciated its strategic crossroads location, fertile land,

and comfortable climate (several times voted "most livable place to retire"). While the population of today's Avenches could barely fill the well-worn ruins of their Roman amphitheater, Aventicum was once one of the largest cities of the Roman Empire. Everything sits on Roman ruins, which were nearly quarried to oblivion until the 19th century, when its scant remains were saved. Today, things are carefully preserved. Metal detectors must be registered here. Mothers, knowing that turning up anything ancient will bring on the archaeologists, yell at their kids, "Don't dig!" Even the benches on the main street are bits of a 2,000-year-old temple cornice.

There are five Roman sights: the amphitheater, a lone tower, a sanctuary and a theater in a field outside of town, and a museum.

The **amphitheater,** or arena, which once seated 18,000, is the largest Roman ruin in Switzerland (free, always open). While the gladiator action is no more, it's still busy with an annual opera festival and other musical events. At the top of the amphitheater (just past the museum entrance), scan the surrounding countryside. All the farmland was once a walled Roman town of about 20,000 people. The **tower** on the ridge (on left)—the only one remaining of the original 73 towers—marks where the wall once stood. In the middle, past the lone standing column of the **sanctuary,** you can see the small **theater** ruins (see below).

The **Roman museum** fills a medieval tower attached to the amphitheater in town with three fascinating floors of Roman artifacts. Good students borrow the extensive English catalog, which affords a fairly intimate look at domestic life here back then. Don't miss the glass, mosaics, and a gold bust of Marcus Aurelius (A.D. 80) found in an old Roman sewer in 1939 (4 SF, April–Sept Tue–Sun 10:00–12:00 & 13:00–17:00, closed Mon; Oct–March Tue–Sun 14:00–17:00, closed Mon).

Perhaps the best Aventicum experience is to spend some quiet time at sunset pondering the evocative **Roman theater** (Théâtre Romaine) and **sanctuary** in the fields, a half-mile walk out of town (free, always open, tiny free car park at the site). The single column marks "Du Cigognier"—nicknamed the "stork sanctuary" (c. 1700) for the stork nest it supported. As the site was a quarry until the 19th century, almost nothing remains.

## SLEEPING

**(1.25 SF = about $1, country code: 41)**
**$$$ Hotel Couronne** is an Old World, three-star place with a modern interior. It sits grandly on the main square of little Avenches, where Yves and Isabelle Faivre rent 12 charming, bright rooms (Db-160–210 SF depending on size, next to TI, tel. 026-675-5414, www.lacouronne.ch).

**$** Friendly **Elisabeth Clement-Arnold** rents a room in her house (D-50 SF first night, then 40 SF per night, cash only, bathroom is yours alone but down the hall, often nobody home until 19:00, reserve by e-mail, rue Centrale 5, tel. & fax 026-675-3031, eckadima@hotmail.com).

**$** The Avenches **IYHF hostel,** the only hostel in the area, is a beauty. It's run by the Dhyaf family, has four- to 10-bed rooms, and includes breakfast, a homey TV room, table tennis, a big backyard, and a very quiet setting near the Roman theater (32 SF for dorm bed in 4-bed room, 29 SF in 6- to 10-bed room, 36 SF per person for S or D and 34 SF per person for T when available, non-members pay 6 SF extra, office open 7:00–9:30 & 17:00–22:00, no curfew, 3 blocks from center at medieval *lavoir,* or laundry, Rue du Lavoir 5, tel. 026-675-2666, fax 026-675-2717, avenches@youthhostel.ch). If you're on a tight budget and have a car, this place is a great option.

# GIMMELWALD

## and the BERNER OBERLAND

Frolic and hike high above the stress and clouds of the real world. Take a vacation from your busy vacation. Recharge your touristic batteries high in the Alps, where distant avalanches, cowbells, the fluff of a down comforter, the whistle of marmots, and the crunchy footsteps of happy hikers are the dominant sounds. If the weather's good (and your budget's healthy), ride a gondola from the traffic-free village of Gimmelwald to a hearty breakfast at Schilthorn's 10,000-foot-elevation, revolving Piz Gloria restaurant. Linger among alpine whitecaps before riding, hiking, or parasailing down 5,000 feet to Mürren and home to Gimmelwald.

Your gateway to the rugged Berner Oberland is the grand old resort town of Interlaken. Near Interlaken is Switzerland's open-air folk museum, Ballenberg, where you can climb through traditional houses from every corner of this diverse country.

Ah, but the weather's fine and the Alps beckon. Head deep into the heart of the Alps, and ride the cable car to the stop just this side of heaven—Gimmelwald.

### Planning Your Time

Rather than tackle a checklist of famous Swiss mountains and resorts, choose one region to savor: the Berner Oberland.

Interlaken is the administrative headquarters and a fine transportation hub of this region. Use it for business—banking, post office, laundry, shopping—and as a springboard for alpine thrills. (Note that at higher altitudes, many hotels, restaurants, and shops are closed between Easter and late May.) At your hotel, pick up a free guest card for small discounts on some museums and sights (such as the Swiss Open-Air Folk Museum at Ballenberg).

# Berner Oberland

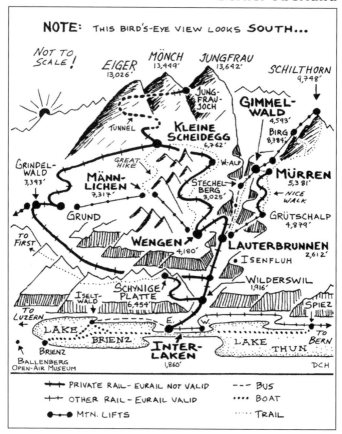

NOTE: THIS BIRD'S-EYE VIEW LOOKS SOUTH...

NOT TO SCALE!

EIGER 13,026'
MÖNCH 13,449'
JUNGFRAU 13,642'
SCHILTHORN 9,748'
JUNG-FRAU-JOCH
GIMMEL-WALD 4,593'
BIRG 8,784'
TUNNEL
KLEINE SCHEIDEGG 6,762'
W. ALP
MÜRREN 5,381'
GRINDEL-WALD 3,393'
GREAT HIKE
MÄNN-LICHEN 7,317'
STECHEL-BERG 3,025'
NICE WALK
TO FIRST
GRUND
GRÜTSCHALP 4,879'
WENGEN 4,180'
LAUTERBRUNNEN 2,612'
ISENFLUH
SCHYNIGE PLATTE 6,454'
WILDERSWIL 1,916'
ISELT-WALD
TO LUZERN
SPIEZ
TO BERN
LAKE BRIENZ
E.
W.
LAKE THUN
BRIENZ
BALLENBERG OPEN-AIR MUSEUM
INTER-LAKEN 1,860'
DCH

PRIVATE RAIL - EURAIL NOT VALID — BUS
OTHER RAIL - EURAIL VALID ···· BOAT
MTN. LIFTS ······ TRAIL

With decent weather, explore the two areas that tower above either side of the Lauterbrunnen Valley, south of Interlaken: Kleine Scheidegg/Jungfrau and Mürren/Schilthorn. To check the weather, call the Interlaken TI (tel. 033-826-5300), ask a local, or visit www.swisspanorama.com (entire area), www.jungfraubahn .ch (for icy Jungfraujoch, accessed by train), or www.schilthorn.ch (for Schilthorn peak, accessed by lift).

The best overnight options are the rustic hamlet of Gimmelwald, the resort town of Mürren, or (for accommodations without the expense and headache of mountain lifts) the village of Lauterbrunnen, on the valley floor. Ideally, spend three nights, with a day exploring each side of the valley.

## Alpine Lifts in the Berner Oberland

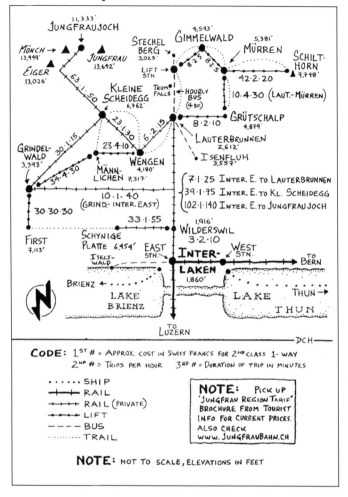

**CODE:** 1ST # = APPROX. COST IN SWISS FRANCS FOR 2ND CLASS 1-WAY
2ND # = TRIPS PER HOUR    3RD # = DURATION OF TRIP IN MINUTES

······· SHIP
┼─┼─┼ RAIL
┼┼┼┼ RAIL (PRIVATE)
•─┼─• LIFT
─ ─ ─ BUS
········ TRAIL

**NOTE:** PICK UP "JUNGFRAU REGION TARIF" BROCHURE FROM TOURIST INFO FOR CURRENT PRICES. ALSO CHECK WWW.JUNGFRAUBAHN.CH

**NOTE:** NOT TO SCALE, ELEVATIONS IN FEET

For the fastest look, consider a night in Gimmelwald, breakfast at the Schilthorn, an afternoon doing the Männlichen–Wengen hike, and an evening or night train out. What? A nature-lover not spending the night high in the Alps? Alpus interruptus.

## Getting Around the Berner Oberland

For more than 100 years, this region has been the target of nature-worshipping pilgrims. And Swiss engineers and visionaries have made the most exciting alpine perches accessible...

**By Lifts and Trains:** Part of the fun—and most of the expense—here is riding the many lifts (gondolas and cable cars).

Generally lifts are not covered by train passes, but a Eurailpass or Swiss railpass gives you a 50 percent discount on even the highest lifts (without the loss of a flexi-day of your pass). Ask about discounts for early-morning and late-afternoon trips, youths, seniors, families, groups, and those staying a while. The Junior Card for families pays for itself in the first hour of trains and lifts: Children under 16 travel free with parents (20 SF/one child, 40 SF/two or more children; available at Swiss train stations). Get a list of discounts and the free fare and time schedule at any Swiss train station. If you're staying a week, you can save money with the **Berner Oberland Pass** (220 SF, includes 3 days of unlimited travel and 4 days of half-price fares on all trains, buses, and lifts) or the **Jungfraubahnen Pass** (190 SF, or 140 SF with Swiss Pass, covers 6 days of unlimited transportation in Jungfrau region except pricey Jungfraujoch train, tel. 033-828-7233).

Study the "Alpine Lifts in the Berner Oberland" chart on page 124. Lifts generally go at least twice hourly, from about 7:00 until about 20:00 (sneak preview: www.jungfraubahn.ch). For a complete schedule of all trains, lifts, buses, and boats, pick up the regional timetable (2 SF at any station).

**By Car:** Lauterbrunnen, Stechelberg, Isenfluh, and Interlaken are all accessible by car. You can't drive to Gimmelwald, Mürren, Wengen, or Kleine Scheidegg—but don't let that stop you from staying up in the mountains; park the car and zip up on a lift. To catch the lift to Gimmelwald, Mürren, and the Schilthorn, park at the cable-car station in Stechelberg (parking: 2 SF/2 hrs, 6 SF/day, see page 137 for more information). To catch the train to Wengen or Kleine Scheidegg, park at the train station in Lauterbrunnen (parking: 2 SF/2 hrs, 9 SF/day).

# Interlaken

When the 19th-century Romantics redefined mountains as something more than cold and troublesome obstacles, Interlaken became the original alpine resort. Ever since, tourists have flocked to the Alps "because they're there." Interlaken's glory days are long gone, its elegant old hotels eclipsed by the new, more jet-setty alpine resorts. Today, its shops are filled with chocolate bars, Swiss Army knives, and sunburned backpackers.

## ORIENTATION

Efficient Interlaken (pop. 5,500) is a good administrative and shopping center. Take care of business, give the town a quick look, and view the live TV coverage of the Jungfrau and Schilthorn weather in the window of the Schilthornbahn office on the main street (at Höheweg 2). Then head for the hills. Stay in Interlaken only if you suffer from Alptitude sickness.

## Tourist Information

The TI has good information on the region, advice on alpine lift discounts, and a room-finding service (July–Sept Mon–Fri 8:00–18:30, Sat 8:00–17:00, Sun 10:00–12:00 & 17:00–19:00; Oct–June Mon–Fri 8:00–18:00, Sat 8:00–16:00, closed Sun; attached to Hotel Metropole on the main street between West and East stations, a 10-min stroll from either, Höheweg 37; tel. 033-826-5300, www.interlakentourism.ch). Good mini-versions of Interlaken/Jungfrau region maps are included in the many free transportation and hiking brochures. Pick up a Bern map if that's your next destination. The TI organizes free walks on Mondays at 17:00 in the summer (call to confirm).

## Arrival in Interlaken

Interlaken has two train stations: East (Ost) and West. All trains stop at both East and West stations. If heading for higher-altitude villages, get off at the East station. For hotels in Interlaken, get off at the West station. The West station also has a helpful and friendly train information desk (travel center for in-depth rail questions: Mon–Fri 9:00–12:00 & 13:30–18:30, Sat 9:00–12:00 & 13:30–17:00, closed Sun; ticket windows open daily 6:40–21:00; tel. 033-826-4750). Ask about discount passes, special fares, railpass discounts, and schedules for the scenic mountain trains. There's a fair exchange booth next to the ticket windows (daily 6:40–20:00).

It's a pleasant 20-minute walk between the West and East stations, or there's an easy, frequent train connection (3/hr, 2.80 SF). From the East station, private trains take you deep into the mountainous Jungfrau region (see "Transportation Connections," page 137).

## Helpful Hints

**Closed Days:** On Sundays and holidays, small-town Switzerland is quiet. Hotels are open, and lifts and trains run, but many stores are closed.

**Telephones:** Phone booths cluster outside the post office near the West station. For efficiency, buy a phone card from a newsstand or train station ticket window. (If you'll be staying in Gimmelwald, note that its sole public phone—at the gondola station—takes only cards, not coins.)

**Laundry:** Friendly Helen Schmocker's **Wäscherei** has a change machine, soap, English instructions, and a riverside location (open daily 7:00–22:00 for self-service: load-6 SF; open for full service Mon–Fri 8:00–12:00 & 13:30–18:00, Sat until 16:00, closed Sun, drop off in the morning and pick up that afternoon: load-12 SF; from the main street take Marktgasse over two bridges to Beatenbergstrasse 5, tel. 033-822-1566).

**Local Guidebook:** Don Chmura's Lauterbrunnen guidebook gives history, folk life, flora, fauna, and hiking information (sold throughout the Lauterbrunnen Valley, 8 SF).

**Bike Rental:** You can rent bikes at either train station (23 SF/half day, 31 SF/day, 5 SF less with Eurailpass or Swiss Pass, daily 8:30–12:00 & 13:00–18:30).

## SELF-GUIDED WALK

### Welcome to Interlaken

Most visitors use Interlaken as a springboard for high-altitude thrills (and rightly so). But the town itself has history and scenic charm, and is worth a short walk. This 45-minute stroll circles from the West train station down the main drag to the big meadow, past the casino, along the river to the oldest part of town (historically a neighboring town called Unterseen), and back to the station.

• *From the West train station, walk along...*

**Bahnhofstrasse:** This main drag, which turns into Höheweg as it continues east, cuts straight through the town center from the West train station to the East station. The best Swiss souvenir shopping is along this Bahnhofstrasse stretch (things get more expensive on the Höheweg stretch, near the fancy hotels). Tchibo makes the best take-out coffee in town (Starbucks-style). At the roundabout is the handy post office (with free public WCs) and Loeb, Interlaken's only department store. Just behind the post office on Marktgasse, the hardware store stocks real cowbells (both ornate and plain). At Höheweg 2, the TV in the window of the Schilthornbahn office shows the weather up top.

• *On your right is...*

**Höhematte Park:** This "high meadow," or Höhematte (but generally referred to simply as "the park"), marks the beginning of Interlaken's fancy hotel row. Hotels like the Victoria-Jungfrau hearken back to the days when Interlaken was *the* original alpine resort. The first grand hotels were built here to enjoy the views of the Jungfrau in the distance. (Today, the Jungfraus getting the most attention are next door, at Hooters.)

The park originated as farmland of the monastery that pre-dated the town (marked today by the steeples of both the Catholic and Protestant churches—neither of any sightseeing interest). The actual **monastery site** is now home to the City Hall, courthouse, and city administration building. With the Reformation in 1528, the monastery was shut down, and its land was taken by the state. Later, when the land was being eyed by developers, the town's leading hotels and business families bought it and established that it would never be used for commercial buildings (a very early example of smart town planning). There was talk of building a parking lot under it, but the water table here, between the two lakes, is too high. Today, this is a fine place to stroll, hang out on the park benches or at Restaurant Schuh, and watch the parasailors gracefully land.

From the park, turn left into the grounds of **Casino Kursaal,** where, at the top of each hour, dwarfs ring the toadstools on the flower clock. The Kursaal, originally a kind of 19th-century fat farm, is now both a casino (passport but no tie required) and a convention center that hosts musical events and nightly folklore shows through the summer (fun yodeling with lots of audience participation, details at the TI).

• *Follow the path left of the Kursaal to the river (huge public swimming pool just over the river). Walk downstream under the train track and cross the pedestrian bridge, stopping in the middle to enjoy the view.*

**Aare River:** The Aare River is Switzerland's longest. It connects Lake Brienz and Lake Thun (with an 18-foot altitude difference—this short stretch has quite a flow). Then it tumbles out of Lake Thun, heading for Bern and ultimately into the Rhine. Its level is controlled by several sluices. In the distance, a church bell tower marks a different parish and the neighborhood of Unterseen, which shares the town's name, but in German: *Unterseen* means "lower lakes." Behind the spire is the pointy summit of the Niesen (like so many Swiss peaks, capped with a restaurant and accessible by a lift). Stroll downstream along the far side of the river to the church spire. The delightful riverside walk is lined by fine residences. Notice that your Jungfrau view now includes the Jungfraujoch observation deck (the little brown bump in the ridge just left of the peak).

• *At the next bridge, turn right to the town square lined with 17th-century houses on one side and a modern strip on the other.*

**Unterseen:** This was a town when Interlaken was only a monastery. The church is not worth touring. A block away, the (generally empty) **Town History Museum/Museum of Tourism** shows off classic posters, fascinating photos of the construction of the Jungfraujoch, and exhibits on folk life, crafts, and winter sports—all well-described in English (5 SF, May–mid-Oct Tue–Sun 14:00–17:00, closed Mon and mid-Oct–April, Obergasse 26).

**Return to Station:** From Unterseen, cross the river on Spielmatte, and you're a few minutes' walk from your starting point. On the second bridge, notice the border between the two towns, or parishes, marked by their respective heraldic emblems (each with

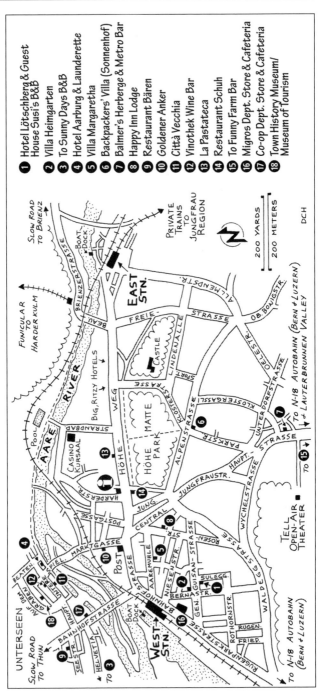

**Interlaken**

1. Hotel Lötschberg & Guest House Susi's B&B
2. Villa Heimgarten
3. To Sunny Days B&B
4. Hotel Aarburg & Launderette
5. Villa Margaretha
6. Backpackers' Villa (Sonnenhof)
7. Balmer's Herberge & Metro Bar
8. Happy Inn Lodge
9. Restaurant Bären
10. Goldener Anker
11. Citta Vecchia
12. Vinothek Wine Bar
13. La Pastateca
14. Restaurant Schuh
15. To Funny Farm Bar
16. Migros Dept. Store & Cafeteria
17. Co-op Dept. Store & Cafeteria
18. Town History Museum/ Museum of Tourism

DCH

an ibex, or wild mountain goat). A block or so later, on the left, is the Marktplatz. The river originally ran through this square. The town used to be called "Aaremühle" ("Aare mill") for the mill that was here. But in the 19th century, town fathers made a key marketing decision: Since "Aaremühle" was too difficult for English tourists to pronounce, they changed the name to "Interlaken."

# SIGHTS AND ACTIVITIES

## Near Interlaken

**Boat Trips**—"Interlaken" is literally "between the lakes" of Thun and Brienz. You can explore these lakes on a lazy boat trip (8/day mid-June–mid-Sept, fewer off-season, free with Eurailpass or Eurail Selectpass but uses a flexi-day, schedules at TI or at BLS Travel Center in West station, tel. 033-826-4760 or 033-334-5211). The boats on **Lake Thun** (10/day, 2 hours to Thun, 4 hours return, 51 SF round-trip) stop at the St. Beatus Höhlen caves (30 min away, see below) and two visit-worthy towns: Spiez (1 hour) and Thun (1.75 hours). The boats on **Lake Brienz** (3 hours, 36 SF round-trip) stop at the super-cute village of Iseltwald (45 min away) and at Brienz (1.25 hours away, near Ballenberg Open-Air Folk Museum—described below).

**St. Beatus Höhlen caves** on Lake Thun can be visited with a guided tour (17 SF, 60 min, 2/hr, April–mid-Oct daily 10:30–17:00, closed mid-Oct–March, tel. 033-841-1643, www.beatushoehlen .ch). The best excursion plan: Ride the bus from Interlaken (20-min ride, line #21, depart West station at :19 past the hour); tour the caves; take the short, steep hike down to lake; and return by boat (8.40 SF one-way, 30 min to Interlaken, see above).

**Adventure Trips**—For the adventurer with money and little concern for personal safety, several companies offer high-adrenaline trips such as rafting, canyoning (rappelling down watery gorges), bungee jumping, and paragliding. Costs range from 160 SF to 205 SF (river rafting plus bungee jump-205 SF, paragliding-160 SF, tandem hang gliding-180 SF). Interlaken companies include Alpin Raft (tel. 033-823-4100, www.alpinraft.com) and Outdoor Interlaken (tel. 033-826-7719, www.outdoor-interlaken.ch). For an overview of your options, visit www.interlakenadventure.com or study the racks of brochures at most TIs and hotels (everyone's getting a cut of this lucrative industry).

Recent fatal accidents jolted the adventure-sport business in the Berner Oberland, leading to a more professional respect for the risks involved. In May 2000, an American died bungee jumping from the Stechelberg–Mürren cable car (the operator used a 180-meter rope for a 100-meter jump). In July 1999, 21 tourists died canyoning on the Saxetenbach River, 10 miles from Interlaken;

they were battered and drowned by a flash flood filled with debris. (The monument just outside Wilderswil on the Saxeten Road is stirring.) Enjoying nature up close comes with risks. Adventure sports increase those risks dramatically. Use good judgment.

▲▲Swiss Open-Air Folk Museum at Ballenberg—Across Lake Brienz from Interlaken, the Swiss Open-Air Museum of Vernacular Architecture, Country Life, and Crafts in the Berner Oberland is a rich collection of traditional and historic farmhouses from every region of the country. Each house is carefully furnished, and many feature traditional craftspeople at work. The sprawling 50-acre park, laid out roughly as a huge Swiss map (Italian Swiss in the south, Appenzell in the east, and so on), is a natural preserve providing a wonderful setting for this culture-on-a-lazy-Susan look at Switzerland.

The Thurgau house (#621) has an interesting wattle-and-daub (half-timbered construction) display, and house #331 has a fun bread museum and farmers' shop. There's cheesemaking (near the east entry), traditional farm animals (like very furry-legged roosters, near the merry-go-round in the center), and a chocolate shop (under the restaurant on the east side).

An outdoor cafeteria with reasonable prices is inside the west entrance, and fresh bread, sausage, mountain cheese, and other goodies are on sale in several houses. Picnic tables and grills with free firewood are scattered throughout the park.

The little wooden village of Brienzwiler (near the east entrance) is a museum in itself, with a lovely pint-size church.

**Cost, Hours, Information:** 18 SF, half-price after 16:00, 16 SF with guest card, covered by Swiss Pass (see page 4). A RailAway combo-ticket, available at either Interlaken station, includes transportation to and from Ballenberg and your admission (38 SF from West station, 35.20 SF from East, add 12.60 SF to return by boat instead). The houses are open daily May–Oct 10:00–17:00, but the park stays open later. Craft demonstration schedules are listed just inside entry. Use the 2-SF map/guide. The more expensive picture book is a better souvenir than guide. Tel. 033-952-1030, www.ballenberg.ch.

**Getting There from Interlaken:** Take the train from either of Interlaken's train stations to Brienz (hourly, 30 min, 8.60 SF one-way from West station). From Brienz, catch a bus to Ballenberg (10 min, 3.20 SF one-way) or hike (45 min, slightly uphill). Consider returning by boat (Brienz boat dock next to train station, one-way to Interlaken-21 SF). Trains also run occasionally from Interlaken to Brienzwiler, a 20-min uphill walk to the museum (every 2 hours, 30 min, 9.80 SF one-way from West station).

**Castles and Forts**—A few impressively well-kept and welcoming old castles in the Interlaken area are worth considering for day trips by boat, bus, or car.

**Thun Castle** (Schloss Thun), built between 1180 and 1190 by the Dukes of Zähringer, has a five-floor historical museum offering insights into the cultural development of the region over a period of some 4,000 years. From the corner turrets of the castle, you are rewarded with a spectacular view of the city of Thun, the lake, and the Alps (7 SF, 5 SF with guest card, April–Oct daily 10:00–17:00, Feb–March daily 13:00–16:00, Nov–Jan Sun only 13:00–16:00, www.schlossthun.ch).

**Hünegg Castle** (Schloss Hünegg) in Hilterfingen (farther along Lake Thun, towards Interlaken) contains a museum exhibiting furnished rooms from the second half of the 19th century. The castle is situated in a beautiful wooded park (8 SF, 7 SF with guest card, mid-May–mid-Oct Mon–Sat 14:00–17:00, Sun 10:00–12:00 & 14:00–17:00, closed off-season, www.schlosshuenegg.ch).

**Oberhofen Castle** (Schloss Oberhofen) is for those interested in gardens. Its beautifully landscaped park with exotic trees is a delight (free, mid-March–mid-Nov daily from 9:00 until dusk, closed in winter). The museum in the castle depicts domestic life in the 16th through 19th centuries, including a Turkish smoking room and a medieval chapel (7 SF, 5 SF with guest card, mid-May–mid-Oct Mon 14:00–17:00, Tue–Sun 11:00–17:00, closed off-season, tel. 033-243-1235).

For a more modern fort, consider visiting the **WWII Swiss Infantry Bunker** in Beatenbucht. From the cable car station there, walk uphill for five minutes to the first bend, keep straight for 10 yards, and walk behind the camouflage at the first right turn.

## NIGHTLIFE

For counterculture with a reggae beat, check out **Funny Farm** (past Balmer's Herberge hostel, in Matten). The young frat-party dance scene rages at the **Metro Bar** at Balmer's (bomb-shelter disco bar, with cheap drinks and a friendly if loud atmosphere). For a stylish wine bar with local yuppies, check in at the **Vinothek,** across from Città Vecchia in Unterseen (see "Eating," below). If you can't sleep and are waiting for your prunes, try **Restaurant Schuh** on the park.

## SLEEPING

I'd head for Gimmelwald, or at least Lauterbrunnen (20 min by train or car). Interlaken is not the Alps. But if you must stay...

**$$$ Hotel Lötschberg,** with a sun terrace and 21 wonderful rooms, marked its 100th anniversary in 2006. It's run by English-speaking Susi and Fritz and is the best real hotel value in town. Happy to dispense information, these gregarious folks pride themselves on a personal touch that sets them apart from other hotels (Sb-120 SF, Db-165 SF, big Db-185 SF, extra bed-30 SF, family deals, rates about 15 percent cheaper mid-Oct–April, closed Nov–March, non-smoking, elevator, Internet access, kitchen open to guests, laundry service, bike rental; 5-min walk from West station: leaving station, turn right, after Migros at the circle go left to General-Guisanstrasse 31; tel. 033-822-2545, fax 033-822-2579, www.lotschberg.ch, hotel@lotschberg.ch). Effervescent Fritz offers cooking classes and organizes guided adventures. He does tandem hang gliding almost every day with one of his guests (guests fly with Fritz at a discount, about 20 SF cheaper than any other deal in town).

**$$ Guest House Susi's B&B** is Hotel Lötschberg's no-frills, cash-only annex, run by Fritz and Susi, offering nicely furnished, cozy rooms (Sb-105 SF, Db-135 SF; apartment with kitchenette 105 SF/2 people, 185 SF/4–5 people—minimum 3-night stay; prices about 20 percent cheaper mid-Oct–April, closed Nov–March, same contact info as Hotel Lötschberg, above).

**$$ Sunny Days B&B,** a homey, nine-room place in a residential neighborhood, is run by Dave from Britain (Sb-98–110 SF, Db-110–148 SF, prices vary with season and view, extra bed about 40 SF, Nov–late April all rooms 100–120 SF, Internet access; exit left out of West station and take first bridge to your left, after crossing the bridges turn left on Helvetiastrasse and go 3 blocks to #29; tel. 033-822-8343, www.sunnydays.ch, mail@sunnydays.ch).

**$$ Hotel Aarburg** offers 13 plain, peaceful rooms in a beautifully located but run-down old building a 10-minute walk from the West station (Sb-70 SF, Db-120 SF, 10 SF more in July–Aug, next to launderette at Beatenbergstrasse 1, tel. 033-822-2615, fax 033-822-6397, hotel-aarburg@quicknet.ch).

**$$ Villa Heimgarten** is a fine 1902 house in a quiet, handy location. While not particularly cozy, it rents seven basic rooms at a good price (Sb-50 SF, Db-90 SF, T-110 SF, Q-140 SF, 6-bed room-195 SF, the whole house can be rented for bigger groups, 5 percent off with this book in 2007, cash strongly preferred, garden, playground, 5-min walk from West station, across from Hotel Lötschberg at Bernastrasse 7, tel. 033-821-0963, fax 033-822-7479, www.villaheimgarten.ch, villaheimgarten@bluewin.ch).

**$ Villa Margaretha,** run by English-speaking Frau Kunz-Joerin, offers the best cheap beds in town. It's like grandma's big Victorian house on a residential street. Keep your room tidy, and you'll have a friend for life (D-86 SF, T-129 SF, Q-172 SF, the 3 rooms share a big bathroom, 2-night minimum, closed Oct–April,

## Sleep Code

**(1.25 SF = about $1, country code: 41)**
**S** = Single, **D** = Double/Twin, **T** = Triple, **Q** = Quad, **b** = bathroom,
**s** = shower only. Unless otherwise noted, credit cards are
accepted, English is spoken, and breakfast is included.

To help you sort easily through these listings, I've divided
the rooms into three categories, based on the price for a standard double room with bath:

$$$ **Higher Priced**—Most rooms 150 SF or more.
 $$ **Moderately Priced**—Most rooms between 90–150 SF.
  $ **Lower Priced**—Most rooms 90 SF or less.

cash only, no breakfast served but dishes and kitchenette available, lots of rules to abide by, go up small street directly in front of West station to Aarmühlestrasse 13, tel. 033-822-1813).

**$ Backpackers' Villa (Sonnenhof) Interlaken** is a creative guest house run by a Methodist church group. It's fun, youthful, and great for families, without the frat-party scene of Balmer's Herberge (listed below). Travelers of any age feel comfortable here (D-98 SF, T-135 SF, Q-156 SF, dorm beds in 5- to 7-bed rooms with lockers and sheets-35 SF per person, 5 SF more per person for rooms with toilets and Jungfrau-view balconies, includes breakfast, kitchen, garden, movies, small game room, Internet access, laundry, bike rental, free admission to public swimming pool/spa, no curfew, open all day but reception open only 7:00–11:00 & 16:00–22:00, 10-min walk from either station, across the park from TI, Alpenstrasse 16, tel. 033-826-7171, fax 033-826-7172, www.villa .ch, mail@villa.ch).

**$ Balmer's Herberge** is many people's idea of backpacker heaven. This Interlaken institution comes with movies, table tennis, a cheap launderette (4 SF/load), bar, restaurant, swapping library, Internet access, tiny grocery, bike rental, excursions, a shuttle-bus service (which meets important arriving trains), and a friendly, hardworking staff. This little Nebraska is home for those who miss their fraternity. It can be a mob scene, especially on summer weekends (dorm bed-25–29 SF, S-43 SF, D-66 SF, T-99 SF, Q-132 SF, includes sheets and breakfast, non-smoking rooms, open year-round, e-mailed reservations recommended 5 days in advance except for dorm beds, Hauptstrasse 23, in Matten, 15-min walk from either train station, tel. 033-822-1961, fax 033-823-3261, www.balmers.com, mail@balmers.ch).

**$ Happy Inn Lodge** has 15 cheap backpacker rooms above a lively, noisy restaurant a five-minute walk from the West station (dorm bed-22 SF, S-40 SF, D-80 SF, T-90–105 SF, Q-120–140 SF, breakfast-8 SF, Rosenstrasse 17, tel. 033-822-3225, fax 033-822-3268, www.happyinn.com, info@happyinn.com).

# EATING

Interlaken's two big department stores each feature reasonable self-service restaurants. **Migros** is across the street from West station (Mon–Thu 8:00–18:30, Fri 8:00–21:00, Sat 7:30–17:00, closed Sun); while the **Co-op** is across the river from the West station, on your right (Mon–Thu 8:00–18:30, Fri 8:00–21:00, Sat 7:30–17:00, closed Sun).

## In Unterseen, the Old Town Across the River

**Restaurant Bären,** in a classic low-ceilinged building with cozy indoor and fine outdoor seating, is a great value for *Rösti,* fondue, raclette, fish, traditional sausage, and salads (20-SF plates, open daily, closed Mon off-season, from West station turn left on Bahnhofstrasse and go over the river a block to Seestrasse 2, tel. 033-822-7526).

**Goldener Anker** is the local hangout—smoky, with a pool table and a few unsavory types. If you thought Interlaken was sterile, you haven't been here. Jeannette serves and René cooks, just as they have for 25 years (hearty 20-SF salads, fresh vegetables, 3 courses for 17 SF, daily from 16:00, Marktgasse 57, tel. 033-822-1672). This place sometimes hosts small concerts, and has launched some of Switzerland's top bands.

**Città Vecchia** serves the best Italian food and Italian wine in town, with seating indoors or out, on a leafy square (pizza-15 SF, pasta-20 SF, plates-30 SF, Mon and Wed–Sat 10:00–14:00 & 17:30–23:30, Sun 10:00–23:30, closed Tue, on main square in Unterseen at Untere Gasse 5, tel. 033-822-1754, Rinaldo).

## On or near the Main Drag

**La Pastateca,** at the top hotel in town (Victoria-Jungfrau), is very elegant. To sit on its terrace and watch the Jungfrau is one of the great Interlaken treats. To do it affordably, go with the super antipasto buffet (all you like from a huge spread of Italian-style treats, including lots of meat and seafood, 25 SF), or come for the "business lunch" (the buffet, plus a pasta of your choice, great bread and olive oil, bottled water, and coffee for 27 SF, available Mon–Fri 11:30–14:00). The service is formal and can be slow (daily 11:30–23:00, a block past TI, facing the park, tel. 033-828-2680).

**Restaurant Schuh,** formerly the Grand Café Schuh, retains its grand-café ambience on the best real estate in town (at the corner of the park, across from Hotel Metropole and TI). Meals are disappointing, but desserts are wonderful, and there's no better place to nurse a drink or coffee and watch the parasailors glide into the park (live schmaltzy music, newspapers, classy indoor and outdoor seating, Höheweg 56, tel. 033-822-9441).

# TRANSPORTATION CONNECTIONS

If you plan to arrive at Zürich Airport and want to head straight for Interlaken and the Alps, see the Zürich chapter (page 45). Note that Interlaken is connected to Luzern and Montreux (on Lake Geneva) via the Golden Pass scenic rail route (see Scenic Rail Journeys chapter). Train info: toll tel. 0900-300-3004 (www.rail.ch).

**From Interlaken East (Ost) by Train to: Lauterbrunnen** (hourly, 20 min, 9.40 SF each way), **Spiez** (2/hr, 20 min), **Brienz** (1–2/hr, 30–40 min), **Bern** (2/hr, 50 min), **Zürich** and **Zürich Airport** (hourly, 2–2.25 hrs, most direct but some with transfer in Bern and/or Spiez), **Luzern** (hourly, 2 hrs), **Lugano** (hourly, 5 hrs, transfer in Luzern, Zürich, or Olten), **Zermatt** (hourly, 3.5 hrs, transfer in Spiez and Brig). While there are a few long trains from Interlaken, you'll generally connect from Bern.

**From Bern by Train to: Lausanne** (2/hr, 1.25 hrs), **Murten** (hourly, 40 min, some transfer in Kerzers), **Zürich** (2/hr, 1–1.25 hrs), **Zermatt** (hourly, 3.25 hrs, transfer in Brig), **Appenzell** (hourly, 3.25 hrs, transfer in Gossau), **Munich** (hourly, 6 hrs), **Frankfurt** (hourly, 4.5 hrs), **Salzburg** (4/day, 7.25 hrs, transfer in Zürich), **Paris** (6/day, 6 hrs).

## From Interlaken to the Lauterbrunnen Valley

**By Public Transportation to Gimmelwald:** Take the train from the Interlaken East station to Lauterbrunnen (hourly, 20 min). From Lauterbrunnen, you have two options:

1. The faster, easier way—best in bad weather or at the end of a long day with lots of luggage—is to ride the postal bus from Lauterbrunnen station (3.80 SF, hourly bus departure coordinated with arrival of train, get off at Schilthornbahn stop) to Stechelberg and the base of the Schilthornbahn gondola station, where the gondola will whisk you in five thrilling minutes up to Gimmelwald (7.80 SF, departing at :10 and :40).

2. The more scenic route is to catch the cable car from Lauterbrunnen to Grütschalp, where a special scenic train *(Panorama Fahrt)* will roll you along the cliff to Mürren (total trip from Lauterbrunnen to Mürren: 30 min, 9.80 SF). From there, either walk a paved 30 minutes downhill to Gimmelwald, or walk 10 minutes across Mürren to catch the gondola down to Gimmelwald (7.80 SF).

**By Car:** You can drive to Lauterbrunnen and to Stechelberg;

## What's What in the Berner Oberland

**Allmendhubel** (AHL-mehnd-hoo-behl): Funicular from Mürren, leading to good hikes at the top (see page 151).

**Ballenberg:** Swiss Open-Air Folk Museum, on Lake Brienz (see page 132).

**Berner Oberland:** The mountainous part of the canton of Bern, sometimes referred to as "Jungfrau region." Everything else on this list is in the Berner Oberland.

**Birg** (beerg): Cable-car stop between Mürren and the Schilthorn, with a trail leading steeply down to Gimmelwald and more (see page 160).

**Brienz** (bree-ENTS): Lake on the east side of Interlaken (Brienzersee); also the name of a town on that lake.

**Eiger** (EYE-gehr): Literally "ogre," one of the three big mountains in the area (with the Mönch and Jungfrau); famous as a treacherous climbing destination.

**First:** Overlook point accessible by lift from Grindelwald; end-point of hike from Schynige Platte (see page 168).

**Gimmelwald** (GIM-mehl-vahlt): Wonderfully rustic time-warp village overlooking the Lauterbrunnen Valley; good home-base option (see page 140).

**Grindelwald** (GRIN-dehl-vahlt): Expensive resort town, not to be confused with Gimmelwald.

**Grütschalp** (GREWTSH-alp): Station at the top of the cable car from Lauterbrunnen. It's connected by train and a trail to Mürren (see page 166).

**Interlaken** (IN-tehr-lah-kehn): Big town at the "entrance" to the Berner Oberland; you'll go through here to get anywhere else in this chapter (see page 126).

**Jungfrau** (YOONG-frow): Literally "maiden," the region's highest peak (13,642 feet).

**Jungfraubahn** (YOONG-frow-bahn): Company that runs all of the trains and lifts in the area (except for the Schilthorn).

**Jungfraujoch** (YOONG-frow-yoke): High-altitude (11,300 feet) observation deck near the Jungfrau peak, accessible by train from Kleine Scheidegg.

**Kleine Scheidegg** (KLY-neh SHY-dehk): Viewpoint with breath-taking Eiger, Mönch, and Jungfrau views; has several hotels and restaurants (see page 173), plus the train station that offers pricey rides to the Jungfraujoch (page 159).

**Lauterbrunnen** (LOUT-ehr-broo-nehn): Small town in the middle of the Lauterbrunnen Valley. From here, a cable car goes up to Grütschalp—with connections to Mürren and Gimmelwald—the train runs up to Wengen and Kleine Scheidegg, and the postal bus goes to Stechelberg. For hotels and restaurants, see page 155.

**Lauterbrunnen Valley:** Valley at the heart of the Berner Oberland; most towns and activities in this chapter overlook this valley.

**Männlichen** (MAYN-likh-ehn): Overlook point with pastoral meadow and dramatic views, connected to Wengen and also to Grund (near Grindelwald) by lifts; also the starting point of an easy hike to Kleine Scheidegg with nonstop mountain views (see page 167).

**Mönch** (munkh): Literally "monk," one of the three major peaks of the region (along with Eiger and Jungfrau).

**Mürren** (MEW-rehn): Pleasant resort town near Gimmelwald, midway up the Schilthorn cable-car line; a good high-mountain home base for those who find Gimmelwald too small and rustic (see page 147).

**Schilthorn** (SHILT-horn): The 10,000-foot peak across the Lauterbrunnen Valley from the Jungfrau, reached by cable car from Stechelberg (in the valley), Mürren, and Gimmelwald; features spectacular views and the Piz Gloria revolving restaurant made famous by James Bond (see page 157).

**Schilthornbahn:** Cable-car company that operates the lift on the west side of the Lauterbrunnen Valley, connecting Stechelberg (on the valley floor) with Gimmelwald, Mürren, Birg, and the Schilthorn.

**Schynige Platte** (SHIH-nih-geh PLAH-teh): High-altitude observation point near the entrance to Lauterbrunnen Valley, reached by funicular from Wilderswil; starting point of a long but scenic hike to First (see page 168).

**Sefinen Valley** (seh-FEE-nehn): Branches off the Lauterbrunnen Valley beyond Stechelberg and Gimmelwald; good for a hike (see page 162).

**Stechelberg** (SHTEH-khehl-behrk): At the end of the Lauterbrunnen Valley, it's the starting point of the cable car leading up to Gimmelwald, Mürren, and on to the Schilthorn (for accommodations, see page 173).

**Thun** (toon): Lake to the west of Interlaken (Thunersee), and the name of a town on that lake.

**Trümmelbach** (TREW-mehl-bahkh): Striking series of waterfalls near Lauterbrunnen (see page 170).

**Wengen** (VAYNG-ehn): Resort town on Jungfrau side of Lauterbrunnen Valley; on the train line between Lauterbrunnen and Kleine Scheidegg (for hotels, see page 171).

**Wilderswil** (VIHL-dehrs-vihl): Village near entrance of the Lauterbrunnen Valley; on the train line between Interlaken and Lauterbrunnen; has funicular to Schynige Platte and trailhead to First (see page 168).

but you can't drive to Gimmelwald (park in Stechelberg and take the cable car) or to Mürren, Wengen, or Kleine Scheidegg (park in Lauterbrunnen and take the cable car to Mürren or the train to Wengen/Kleine Scheidegg). For drivers, the most direct route to Gimmelwald is via the cable car at Stechelberg. It's a 30-minute drive from Interlaken to the Stechelberg cable-car station (parking lot: 2 SF/2 hrs, 6 SF/day). Gimmelwald is the first stop above Stechelberg on the Schilthorn cable car (7.80 SF, 2/hr at :10 and :40). Note that the Schilthornbahn is closed for servicing for a week in early May and also from mid-November through early December. During this time, you'll ride the cargo cable car directly from Stechelberg to Mürren, where a small bus shuttles you down to Gimmelwald.

# Gimmelwald

Saved from developers by its "avalanche zone" classification, Gimmelwald was (before tourism) one of the poorest places in Switzerland. Its traditional economy was stuck in the hay, and its farmers—unable to make it in their disadvantaged trade—survived only by Swiss government subsidies (and working the ski lifts in the winter). For some travelers, there's little to see in the village. Others (like me) enjoy a fascinating day sitting on a bench and learning why they say, "If heaven isn't what it's cracked up to be, send me back to Gimmelwald."

Take a walk through the town. The huge, sheer cliff face that dominates your mountain views is the Schwarzmönch ("Black Monk"). The three peaks above (or behind) it are, left to right, the Eiger, Mönch, and Jungfrau. While Gimmelwald's population has dropped in the last century from 200 to about 100 residents, traditions survive. Most Gimmelwalders have one of two last names: von Allmen or Feutz. They are tough and proud. Raising hay in this rugged terrain is labor-intensive. One family harvests enough to feed only about 15 cows. But they'd have it no other way, and, unlike the absentee-landlord town of Mürren, Gimmelwald is locally owned. (When word got out that urban planners wished to develop Gimmelwald into a town of 1,000, locals pulled some strings to secure the town's bogus avalanche-zone building code.) Those same folks are happy the masses go to touristy and commercialized

## Gimmelwald

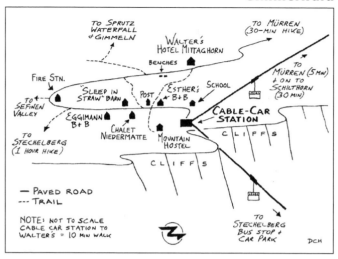

Grindelwald, just over the Kleine Scheidegg ridge. Don't confuse Gimmelwald and Grindelwald—they couldn't be more different.

## SELF-GUIDED WALK

### Welcome to Gimmelwald

Gimmelwald, though tiny, with one zigzag street, gives a fine look at a traditional Swiss mountain community.

• *Start this quick walking tour at the...*

**Cable-Car Station:** When the lift came in the 1960s, the village's back end became its front door. Gimmelwald was, and still is, a farm village. Stepping off the cable car, you see a sweet little hut. Set on stilts to keep out mice, the hut was used for storing cheese (the rocks on the rooftop keep the shingles on through wild winter winds). Behind the cheese hut stands the village schoolhouse. In Catholic Swiss towns, the biggest building is the church. In Protestant towns, it's the school. Gimmelwald's biggest building is the school (two teachers share one teaching position, 17 students, and a room that doubles as a chapel when the Protestant pastor makes his monthly visit). Don't let Gimmelwald's low-tech look fool you: In this school, each kid has his or her own Web site. In the opposite

---

## Swiss Cow Culture

Traditional Swiss cow farmers could make more money for much easier work in another profession. In a good year, farmers produce enough cheese to break even—they support their families on government subsidies. (The government supports traditional farming as much for the tourism as for the cheese.) But these farmers have made a lifestyle choice to keep tradition alive and to live high in the mountains. Rather than lose their children to the cities, Swiss farmers have the opposite problem: Kids argue over who gets to take over the family herd.

The cows' grazing ground can range in elevation by as much as 5,000 feet throughout the year. In the summer (usually mid-June), the farmer straps elaborate ceremonial bells on his cows and takes them up to a hut at high elevations. The cows hate these big bells, which can cost upwards of 2,000 SF apiece—a proud investment for a humble farmer. When the cows arrive at their summer home, the bells are hung under the eaves.

These high-elevation summer stables are called "alps." Try to find some on a Berner Oberland tourist map (e.g., Wengernalp, Grütschalp, Schiltalp). The cows stay at the alps for about 100 days. The farmers hire a team of cheesemakers to work at each alp—mostly hippies, students, and city slickers eager to spend

---

direction, just beyond the little playground, is Gimmelwald's Mountain Hostel (listed on page 146).

• *Walk up the lane 50 yards, past the shower in the phone booth, to Gimmelwald's...*

**"Times Square":** The yellow alpine "street sign" shows where you are, the altitude (4,470 feet), and how many hours *(Std.)* and minutes it takes to walk to nearby points. Most of the buildings once housed two families and are divided vertically right down the middle. The writing on the post office building is a folksy blessing: "Summer brings green, winter brings snow. The sun greets the day, the stars greet the night. This house will keep you warm. May God give us his blessings." The date indicates when it was built or rebuilt (1911). Gimmelwald has a strict building code. For instance, shutters can only be natural, green, or white. Esther's farmer shop (10 yards uphill, always open, buy things on the honor system) is worth a look.

three summer months in the mountains. Each morning, the hired hands get up at 5:00 to milk the cows, take them to pasture, and make the cheese—milking the cows again when they come home in the evening. In summer, all the milk makes alp cheese (it's too difficult to get it down to the market). In the winter, with the cows at lower altitudes, the fresh milk is sold as milk.

Every alp also has a resident herd of pigs. Cheesemaking leftovers (*Molke,* or whey) can damage the ecosystem if thrown out—but pigs love the stuff. The pigs parade up with the cows... but no one notices. Cheesemakers claim that bathing in whey improves the complexion...but maybe that's just the altitude talking.

Meanwhile, the farmers—glad to be free of their bovine responsibilities—turn their attention to making hay. The average farmer has a few huts at various altitudes, each surrounded by small hay fields. The farmer follows the seasons up into the mountains, making hay and storing it above the huts. In the fall, the cows come down from the alps and spend the winter moving from hut to hut, eating the hay the farmer spent the summer preparing for them.

Throughout the year, you'll see farmers moving their herds to various elevations. If snow is in the way, farmers sometimes use tourist gondolas to move their cows. Every two months or so, Gimmelwald farmers bring together cows that aren't doing so well and herd them into the gondola to meet the butcher in the valley below.

• *From this tiny intersection, we'll follow the town's main street (away from gondola station).*

**Main Street:** Walk up the road. Notice the announcement board: one side for tourist news, the other for local news. Cross the street and peek into the big new barn, dated 1995. This is part of the Sleep in Straw association, which rents out barn spots to travelers when the cows are in the high country. To the left of the door is a cow-scratcher. Swiss cows have legal rights (for example, in the winter, they must be taken out for exercise at least three times a week). This big barn is built in a modern style. Traditionally, barns were small (like those on the hillside high above) and closer to the hay. But with trucks and paved roads, hay can be moved more easily, and farm businesses need more cows to be viable. Still, even a well-run big farm hopes just to break even. The industry survives only with government subsidies (see "Swiss Cow Culture" sidebar, page 142).

• *Go just beyond the next barn. On your right is the...*

**Water Fountain/Trough:** This is the site of the town's historic water supply. Local kids love to bathe and wage water wars here when the cows aren't drinking from it. Now detour left down a lane about 50 yards (along a wooden fence and then past pea-patch gardens) to the next trough and the oldest building in town, Husmättli, from 1658. (The town's 17th-century buildings are mostly on the road zigzagging below town.) Study the log-cabin construction. Many are built without nails. The wood was logged up the valley and cut on the water-powered village mill (also below town). Gimmelwald heats with wood and, since the wood needs to age a couple of years to burn well, it's stacked everywhere.

• *Back on the paved road, continue uphill.*

Notice the cute cheese hut on the right (with alpine cheese for sale). It's full of strong cheese—up to three years old. On the left (at the B&B sign) is the home of Olle and Maria, the village schoolteachers. Maria runs the Lilliput shop (the "smallest shop with the greatest gifts"—handmade delights from the town and region, just ring the bell and meet Maria). Her son does a booming trade in sugar-coated almonds; her daughter competes with cookies.

• *Fifty yards farther along is the...*

**Alpenrose:** At the old schoolhouse, notice the big ceremonial cowbells hanging under the uphill eave. These swing from the necks of cows during the procession from the town to the high Alps (mid-June) and back down (about Sept 20). If the cows are gone, so are the bells—hanging from similar posts under the eaves of mountain huts in the high meadows.

• *At the end of town, notice the dramatic...*

**Sefinen Valley:** All the old homes in town are made from local wood cut from the left-hand side of this valley (shady side, slow-growing, better timber).

• *The road switches back at the...*

**Gimmelwald Fire Station:** The *Föhnwacht Reglement* sheet, posted on the fire station building, explains rules to keep the village from burning down during the fierce dry wind of the Föhn season. During this time, there's a 24-hour fire watch, and even smoking cigarettes outdoors is forbidden. Mürren was devastated by a Föhn-caused fire in the 1920s. Because villagers in Gimmelwald—mindful of the quality of their volunteer fire department—are particularly careful with fire, this is a rare village to not have had a terrible fire in its history.

Check out the other posted notices. This year's Swiss Army calendar tells reservists when and where to go. Every Swiss male does a 17-week stint in the military, then a few days a year in the reserves until about age 40. The *Schiessübungen* poster details the shooting exercises required this year. In keeping with the William Tell heritage, each Swiss man does shooting practice annually for the military (or spends three days in jail).

• *Take the...*

**High Road to Hotel Mittaghorn:** The resort town of Mürren hovers in the distance. And high on the left, notice the hay field with terraces. These are from WWII days, when Switzerland, wanting self-sufficiency, required all farmers to grow potatoes. Today, this is a festival of alpine flowers in season (best at this altitude in May and June).

• *Our walk is over. From Hotel Mittaghorn, you can return to Gimmelwald's "Times Square" via the stepped path.*

## NIGHTLIFE

Evening fun in Gimmelwald is found at the **Mountain Hostel** (offering a pool table, Internet access, lots of young Alp-aholics, and a good chance to share information on the surrounding mountains). **Walter's bar** (in Hotel Mittaghorn) is a local farmers' hangout. When they've made their hay, they come here to play. Although they look like what some people would call hicks, they speak some English and can be fun to get to know. Sit outside (benches just below the rails, 100 yards down the lane from Walter's) and watch the sun tuck the mountaintops into bed as the moon rises over the Jungfrau. If this isn't your idea of nightlife, stay in Interlaken.

## SLEEPING

**(4,593 feet, 1.25 SF = about $1, country code: 41)**

Gimmelwald is my home base in the Berner Oberland. To inhale the Alps and really hold them in, you'll sleep high in Gimmelwald, too. Poor but pleasantly stuck in the past, the village has a creaky hotel, happy hostel, a couple of B&Bs, and even a Web site (www .gimmelwald.ch). The only bad news is that the lift costs 7.80 SF each way to get here.

**$$ Maria and Olle Eggimann** rent two rooms— Gimmelwald's most comfortable—in their quirky but alpine-sleek chalet. Maria and Olle, who job-share the village's only teaching position and raise three kids of their own, offer visitors a rare and intimate peek at this community (D-120 SF, Db with kitchenette-180 SF for 2 or 3 people, optional breakfast-20 SF, cash only, guarantee your reservation in advance with a check or wire transfer equal to half the cost of your stay, last check-in 19:30, 3-night minimum; from gondola continue straight for 200 yards along the town's only road, B&B on left; tel. 033-855-3575, oeggimann @bluewin.ch).

**$$ Esther's B&B,** overlooking the main intersection of the village, is like an upscale mini-hostel, with five clean, basic, and comfortable rooms sharing two bathrooms and a great kitchen (S-45–60 SF, big D-95–105 SF, Db-90–100 SF, big T-130–180 SF, Q-170–200 SF, family room for up to 5, cash only, 2-night stays preferred, breakfast with homemade bread-15 SF, non-smoking, tel. 033-855-5488, fax 033-855-5492, www.esthersguesthouse.ch, info @esthersguesthouse.ch, some English spoken). Esther also rents two four-person **apartments** with kitchenettes in the house next door (140 SF/2 people, 190 SF/4 people; balcony suite-150 SF/2 people, 200 SF/4 people; extra bed-20 SF, check Web site for details).

**$ Hotel Mittaghorn,** the treasure of Gimmelwald, is run by Walter Mittler, a perfect Swiss gentleman. Walter's hotel is a classic, creaky, alpine-style place with memorable beds (if the bed's too lumpy or short, consider putting the mattress on the floor, or wear socks and drape the blanket over your feet), and a million-dollar view of the Jungfrau Alps. The hotel has three rooms with private showers and four rooms that share a shower (1 SF/5 min). Walter is careful not to let his place get too hectic or big, and he enjoys sensitive Back Door travelers. He runs the hotel with a little help from Rosemarie, from the village. To some, Hotel Mittaghorn is a fire waiting to happen, with a kitchen that would never pass code, bumpy beds, teeny towels, and minimal plumbing, run by an eccentric old grouch. These people enjoy Mürren, Interlaken, or Wengen, and that's where they should sleep. Be warned, you'll see more of my readers than locals here, but it's a fun crowd—an extended family (Db-80 SF, 6-SF surcharge per person for 1-night stays, cash only, open April–Oct). Reserve by telephone only, then reconfirm by phone the day before your arrival (tel. 033-855-1658, www.ricksteves.com/mittaghorn). Walter usually offers his guests a hearty 15-SF dinner at 19:30 (soup, main course, and dessert, by reservation only). Hotel Mittaghorn is at the top of Gimmelwald, a five-minute climb up the steps from the village intersection.

**$ Chalet Niedermatte** rents an apartment just 50 yards from the cable-car station (summer: Db-75 SF, Tb-100 SF, Qb-130 SF; winter: Db-130 SF, Tb-145 SF, Qb-160 SF; kitchen, laundry, reserve by e-mail and then reconfirm by e-mail 2–3 days before arrival, tel. 033-855-1662, rossbollen@hotmail.com, Liesi and Mani).

**$ Mountain Hostel** is a beehive of activity, as clean as its guests, cheap, and friendly. Phone ahead, or, to secure one of its 50 dorm beds the same day, call after 9:30 and leave your name. The hostel has low ceilings, a self-service kitchen, a mini-grocery, a free pool table, and healthy plumbing. It's mostly a college-age crowd; families and older travelers will probably feel more comfortable elsewhere. Petra Brunner has lined the porch with flowers. This relaxed hostel survives with the help of its guests. Read the signs *(Please Clean the Kitchen)*, respect Petra's rules, and leave it tidier than you found it. The place is one of those rare spots where a congenial atmosphere spontaneously combusts, and spaghetti becomes communal as it cooks (23 SF per bed in 6- to 15-bed rooms, includes sheets, showers-1 SF, no breakfast, hostel membership not required, cash only, free Internet access, laundry, 20 yards from lift station, tel. & fax 033-855-1704, www.mountainhostel.com, reserve by e-mail at mountainhostel @tcnet.ch).

**$ Schlaf im Stroh** ("Sleep in Straw") offers exactly that. After the cows head for higher ground in the summer, the friendly von Allmen family hoses out their barn and fills it with straw and budget travelers. Blankets are free, but bring your own sheet, sleep sack, or sleeping bag. No beds, no bunks, no mattresses, no kidding. Esther fluffs up your hay each night (24 SF, 18 SF for kids ages 11–15, 10 SF for kids up to age 10, cash only, includes breakfast "barn service" and a single modern bathroom and showers, open late June–mid-Oct depending on grass and snow levels, almost never full, possible manure pile outside barn door; from lift, continue straight through intersection to big modern barn marked 1995 on the right; same contact info as Esther's B&B, above).

## EATING

There are no restaurants in town, but you have a few options. The Mountain Hostel has a decent members' kitchen and makes great pizzas in the evenings (non-guests welcome). Hotel Mittaghorn serves dinner only to its guests (15 SF). Consider packing in a picnic meal from the larger towns. Mürren, a 30-minute hike away, has good restaurants and a grocery. If you need a few groceries and want to skip the hike to Mürren, you can buy the essentials—noodles, spaghetti sauce, and candy bars—at the Mountain Hostel's reception desk. Local farmers sell their produce. Esther (at the main intersection of the village) sells cheese, sausage, bread, and Gimmelwald's best yogurt—but only until the cows go up in June.

# Mürren

Mürren—pleasant as an alpine resort can be—is traffic-free and filled with bakeries, cafés, souvenirs, old-timers with walking sticks, GE employees enjoying incentive trips, and Japanese tourists making movies of each other. Its chalets are prefab-rustic. With help from a panorama, train, funicular, and cable car, hiking options are endless from Mürren. Sitting on a ledge 2,000 feet above the Lauterbrunnen Valley, surrounded by a for-tissimo chorus of mountains, the town has all the comforts of home (for a price) without the pretentiousness of more famous resorts.

Historic Mürren, which dates from 1384, has been overwhelmed by development. Still, it's a peace-ful town. There's no full-time doctor, no police officer (they call Lauterbrunnen if there's a prob-lem), and no resident priest or pas-tor. (The Protestant church—up by the TI—posts a sign showing where the region's roving pastor preaches each Sunday.) There's not even enough business to keep a bakery open full-time (Mürren's bakery is open mid-June–Sept and Dec–April)—a clear indication that this town is either lively or completely dead, depending on the season. Keep an eye open for the "Milch Express," a tiny cart that delivers fresh milk and eggs to hotels and homes throughout town.

## ORIENTATION

Mürren sits high on a ledge, overlooking the Lauterbrunnen Valley. You can walk from one end of town to the other in about 10 minutes.

There are two basic ways to get to Mürren: on the panoramic train from Grütschalp (connects via cable car to Lauterbrunnen); or on the cable car from Stechelberg (in the valley), which stops at Gimmelwald, Mürren, and continues up to the Schilthorn. The train and cable-car stations (which both have lockers) are at oppo-site ends of town.

**Tourist Information:** Mürren's TI can help you find a room and give hiking advice (July–Sept daily 8:30–19:00, Thu until 20:45, less off-season, above the village, follow signs to Sportzentrum, tel. 033-856-8686, www.wengen-muerren.ch). You can change money at the TI, or even better, use the ATM by the Co-op grocery.

### Helpful Hints

**R & R:** The slick **Sportzentrum** (sports center) that houses the TI offers a world of indoor activities (13 SF to use pool and whirl-pool; 8 SF for Gimmelwald, Lauterbrunnen, and Interlaken hotel guests; free for guests at Mürren hotels—ask your

# Mürren

1. Anfi Palace Hotel
2. Hotel Alpina & Edelweiss Cafeteria
3. Hotel/Rest. Bellevue & Launderette
4. Hotel/Rest. Jungfrau
5. Hotel/Rest. Blumental
6. Eiger Guesthouse
7. Chalet Fontana
8. Chalet Helvetia
9. Chalet Böbs
10. Stägerstübli Restaurant
11. Restaurant Hotel Eiger
12. Top Apartments (Laundry)
13. Co-op Grocery
14. Päsci's Snack Bar Bistro

— PAVED ROAD
--- TRAIL

NOT TO SCALE—
CABLE-CAR STN.
TO TRAIN STN. IS
ABOUT 10 MIN. WALK

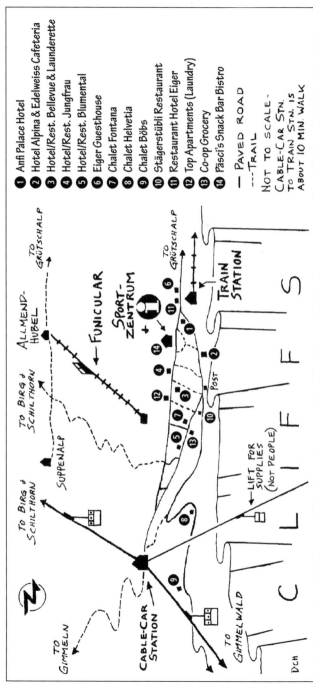

hotelier for a voucher; pool open Mon–Sat 13:00–18:45, Thu until 20:45, Sun 13:00–17:45, closed May and Nov–mid-Dec). In season, they offer squash, mini-golf, table tennis, and a fitness room.

**Internet Access:** Connect at the **TI** (see above) or **Eiger Guesthouse** (see "Sleeping," below, daily 8:00–23:00, across from train station, tel. 033-856-5460).

**Bike Rental:** Rent mountain bikes at **Stäger Sport** (bikes with helmets-25 SF/half-day, 35 SF/day, daily 9:00–17:00, closed late Oct–mid-May, in TI/Sportzentrum, tel. 033-855-2355, www.staegersport.ch). Use caution on rough stretches.

**Laundry: Hotel Bellevue** has a self-service launderette in its basement (5 SF/wash, 5 SF/dry, daily 7:00–22:00). **Top Apartments** will do your laundry by request (25 SF/load, unreliable hours: Mon–Sat 9:00–11:00 & 15:00–17:00, closed Sun, behind and across from Hotel Bellevue, look for blue triangle, call first to drop off in morning, tel. 033-855-3706).

# SELF-GUIDED WALK

## Welcome to Mürren

Mürren has long been a top ski resort, but a walk across town offers a glimpse into its past. This stroll takes you through town on the main drag, from the train station (where you'll arrive if coming from Lauterbrunnen) to the cable-car station, then back up to the Allmendhubel funicular station.

• *Start at the...*

**Train Station:** The first trains pulled into Mürren in 1891. (A circa-1911 car is permanently parked at the Grütschalp station.) A display case inside the station shows an original car from the narrow-gauge, horse-powered line that rolled fancy visitors from here into town. The current station, built in 1964, comes with impressive engineering for heavy cargo. Look out back, where a small truck can be loaded up and driven away.

• *Wander into town along the main road.*

**Stroll Under the Anfi Palace Hotel:** The towering Anfi Palace Hotel was the "Grand Palace Hotel" until it burned in 1928. Its Jugendstil Hall is the finest room in Mürren. The small wooden platform on the left—looking like a suicide springboard—is the place where snow-removal trucks dump their loads over the cliff in the winter. Look back at the meadow below the station: This is a favorite grazing spot for chamois (the animals, not the rags for washing cars). Ahead, at Edelweiss Hotel, step to the far corner of the restaurant terrace for a breathtaking view stretching from the big three (Eiger, Mönch, and Jungfrau) to the lonely cattle farm in the high alp on the right. Then look down.

Next, the Haus Montana was where Kandahar ski boots were first made in 1933 (to give the necessary support to daredevils racing from the Schilthorn to the valley floor in Mürren's infamous Inferno race). Today, the still-respected Kandahar boots are made in nearby Thun.

• *Continue toward...*

**Downtown Mürren:** You'll pass the main intersection (where the small service road leads down to Gimmelwald) and the only grocery store in town (Co-op). The tiny fire barn (Feuerwehr) has a list showing the leaders of the volunteer force and their responsibilities. The old barn behind it on the right evokes the day, not so long ago, when the town's barns housed cows. Imagine Mürren with more cows than people.

• *Reaching the far end of Mürren, you come to the...*

**Cable-Car Station:** The first cable car (goes directly to Stechelberg) is for cargo, garbage, and the (reputedly) longest bungee jumping in the world. The other takes hikers and skiers up to the Schilthorn and down to Stechelberg via Gimmelwald.

• *Hiking back along the high road, you'll enter...*

**Upper Mürren:** You'll pass Mürren's two churches, the Allmendhubel funicular station, and the Sportzentrum (with swimming pool and TI).

• *Consider riding the...*

**Mürren's Allmendhubel Funicular:** A quaint-looking but surprisingly rewarding funicular (1912, renovated in 1999) carries nature-lovers from Mürren to a perch offering a Jungfrau view that (while much lower) rivals the Schilthorn. At the station, notice the 1920s bobsled. The restaurants here (full- and self-service) have awesome views.

Allmendhubel is particularly good for families: It's cheaper than the Schilthorn. The restaurant overlooks a great playground. And the entertaining children's hike—with rough and thrilling, kid-friendly alpine rides along the way—departs from here. This is also the departure point for the North Face hike and walks to Grütschalp (see "Hikes," page 160).

## SLEEPING

**(5,381 feet, 1.25 SF = about $1, country code: 41)**

Prices for accommodations are often higher during the ski season. Many hotels and restaurants close in spring, roughly from Easter to early June, and any time between late September and mid-December.

**$$$ Hotel Alpina** is a simple, modern place with 24 comfortable rooms and a concrete feeling—a good thing, given its cliff-edge position (Sb-85 SF, Db-160 SF, Tb-200 SF, Qb-220 SF with awesome Jungfrau views and balconies, prices less off-season and without a view, outside mid-June–mid-Aug ask for a 10 percent Rick Steves discount in 2007, family rooms, homey lounge, avoid their restaurant; exit left from train station, walk 2 min downhill; tel. 033-855-1361, fax 033-855-1049, www.muerren.ch/alpina, alpina@muerren.ch, Cecilia and her son Roger).

**$$$ Hotel Bellevue** has a homey lounge, solid woodsy furniture, a great view terrace, the hunter-themed Jägerstübli restaurant, and 17 great rooms at fair rates, all with balconies and views (Sb-110 SF, Db-190 SF; special deal with this book in 2007: Db-150 SF if staying 2 nights or more except July–Aug; Internet access, tel. 033-855-1401, fax 033-855-1490, www.muerren.ch/bellevue, bellevue-crystal@bluewin.ch, Ruth and Othmar Suter).

**$$$ Hotel Jungfrau** offers 29 modern and comfortable rooms (with view: Sb-100–110 SF, Db-190–220 SF; no view: Sb-95–100 SF, Db-180–200 SF; elevator, near TI/Sportzentrum, tel. 033-856-6464, fax 033-856-6465, www.hoteljungfrau.ch, mail @hoteljungfrau.ch, Anne-Marie and Andres).

**$$$ Hotel Blumental** has 16 older but nicely furnished rooms and a fun, woodsy game/TV lounge (Sb-75–80 SF, Db-150–170 SF, 10 percent cheaper in Sept–Oct, higher prices are for July–Aug, all non-smoking rooms, attached restaurant—see listing below, tel. 033-855-1826, fax 033-855-3686, www.muerren.ch/blumental, blumental@muerren.ch, Ralph and Heidi, fourth generation in the von Allmen family).

**$$ Eiger Guesthouse** offers 14 good budget rooms. This is a friendly, creaky, easygoing home-away-from-home (S-60–65 SF, Sb-80–85 SF, D-100–110 SF, Db-130–140 SF, beds in 2- and 4-bunk rooms-40–45 SF, includes sheets and breakfast; special through 2007 with this book: D-80 SF with a 2-night minimum year-round; closed Nov and for one month after Easter, across from train station, tel. 033-856-5460, fax 033-856-5461, www .eigerguesthouse.com, info@eigerguesthouse.com, well-run by Scotsman Alan and Swiss Véronique). The restaurant serves good, reasonably priced dinners (25 SF). Its poolroom—with public Internet access—is a popular local hangout. My Switzerland Alps TV show on DVD is available in the lobby.

**$ Chalet Fontana,** run by charming Englishwoman Denise Fussell, is a rare budget option in Mürren, with simple, crispy-clean, and comfortable rooms (35–45 SF per person in small doubles or triples with breakfast and shared bathrooms, price varies with size of room, 5 SF cheaper without breakfast; one apartment with kitchen and bathroom-120 SF/2 people, 150 SF/3 people; cash only, closed Nov–April, across street from Stägerstübli restaurant in town center, tel. 033-855-4385, mobile 078-642-3485, chaletfontana@muerren.ch). If no one's home, check at the Ed

Abegglen shop next door (tel. 033-855-1245, off-season only).

**$ Chalet Helvetia,** run by Frau Hunziker, offers a homey, clean, two-bedroom apartment with bathroom, kitchen, separate entrance, and balcony from 40 SF per person (up to 4 people, no breakfast, 2-night minimum preferred, more expensive for 1-night stays, laundry service-10 SF/load; 200 yards below cable-car station on path to Gimmelwald, look for red *Zimmer* sign on right; tel. 033-855-4169, mobile 079-234-7867, chalet.helvetia@quicknet.ch).

**$ Chalet Böbs,** with terrific views, is the last house in Mürren on the road to Gimmelwald. Kitty and Albert, an alphorn player, rent three apartments: two that sleep four to five people (each with double bed, bunk bed, and twin bed) and one that sleeps two people (40 SF/person, 2-night minimum stay, kitchens, tel. 033-855-1463, mobile 078-633-6091, fax 033-855-4282, boebs@quicknet.ch).

# EATING

Many of these restaurants are in or near my recommended hotels. Outside of summer and ski season, it can be hard to find any place that's open (ask around).

**Stägerstübli** is, hands down, *the* place to eat in town. It's the only real restaurant not associated with a hotel. Located in the town center, this 1902 building was once a tearoom for rich tourists, while locals were limited to the room in the back—the nicest dining area today (15–30 SF lunches and dinners, daily 11:30–22:00, Lydia). Sitting on its terrace, you know just who's out and about in town.

**Päsci's Snack Bar Bistro** has fun, creative, and inexpensive light meals; a good selection of salads, vegetarian dishes, coffees, teas, and pastries; and impressive views (take-out available, run by a serious chef—Päsci—and Fränzi, daily 9:00–18:00, at the Sportzentrum, overlooking the ice rink).

**Hotel Blumental** specializes in typical Swiss cuisine, but also has fish, international, and vegetarian dishes. Everything is homemade and fresh (daily specials 15–24 SF, fondue-19 SF, raclette-14.50 SF, pasta-15 SF, non-smoking section, tel. 033-855-1826, see "Sleeping," above).

**Restaurant Hotel Jungfrau** is a dressy ski lodge with a modern octagonal dining room and a fine view terrace (always a 10.50-SF salad bar, 50-SF four-course meal, 23-SF cheese fondue, veggie options, nightly from 18:30, near TI/Sportzentrum, tel. 033-856-6464, see "Sleeping," above).

The **Edelweiss self-serve cafeteria** offers lunch with the most cliff-hanging dining in town—incredible views (18.50-SF hearty salads, daily 10:30–20:30, more variety—including fondue—after 18:00, next to Hotel Alpina, see "Sleeping," above).

**Restaurant Hotel Eiger** is considered one of the better places in town, with a good chef, classy indoor seating, and a terrace with a view obstructed by the station (open daily, 20-SF plates, 29-SF fixed-price meal, enticing variety of 45-SF meat fondue dinners, tel. 033-856-5454). Note that this is not the same as **Eiger Guesthouse**—which also serves good, but simpler, food (see "Sleeping," above).

**Hotel Bellevue** is atmospheric, with three dining zones: view terrace, elegant indoor, and the Jägerstübli—a cozy, well-antlered hunters' room guaranteed to disgust vegetarians. This is your best bet for game, as they buy chamois and deer direct from local hunters (lamb or game-35 SF, cheaper options as low as 13 SF, mid-June–Oct daily 11:30–14:00 & 18:00–21:00, closed off-season, tel. 033-855-1401, see "Sleeping," above).

The **Co-op** is the only grocery store in town, with good picnic fixings and sandwiches (Mon–Fri 8:00–12:00 & 13:45–18:30, Sat until 17:00, closed Sun). Given restaurant prices, this place is a godsend for those on a tight budget.

# Lauterbrunnen

Lauterbrunnen is the valley's commercial center and transportation hub. It boasts a train station (with lockers), cable car, bank, shops, and lots of hotels, and is the jumping-off point for Jungfrau and Schilthorn adventures. It's idyllic, in spite of the busy road and big buildings.

In 2006, the 114-year-old funicular between Lauterbrunnen and Grütschalp (which has a panorama train to Mürren) was closed due to shifting soil. A replacement cable car opened in January 2007.

## ORIENTATION

**Tourist Information:** Stop by the friendly TI to check the weather forecast, use the Internet, or buy any regional train or lift tickets you need (July–Aug daily 9:00–18:00; Sept–June Mon–Fri 9:00–18:00, closed Sat–Sun; 1 block up from station, tel. 033-856-8568, www.wengen-muerren.ch).

### Helpful Hints
**Medical Help:** Dr. Bruno Durrer is good and speaks English (tel. 033-856-2626).

**Internet and Laundry: Valley Hostel** on the main street

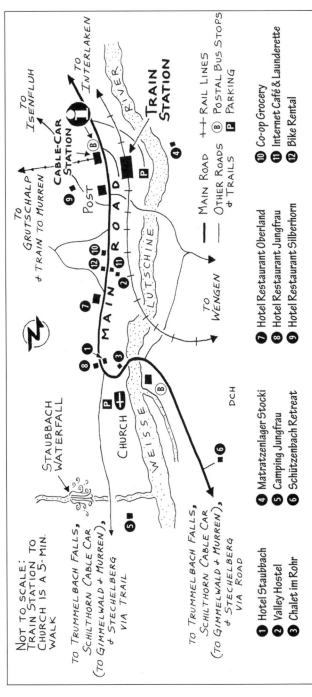

**Lauterbrunnen**

NOT TO SCALE: TRAIN STATION TO CHURCH IS A 5-MIN. WALK

STAUBBACH WATERFALL

TO TRUMMELBACH FALLS, SCHILTHORN CABLE CAR (TO GIMMELWALD + MURREN) + STECHELBERG VIA TRAIL

TO TRUMMELBACH FALLS, SCHILTHORN CABLE CAR (TO GIMMELWALD + MURREN) + STECHELBERG VIA ROAD

CHURCH

DCH

TO ISENFLUH

TO INTERLAKEN

RIVER

CABLE-CAR STATION

TRAIN STATION

Post

TO GRUTSCHALP + TRAIN TO MURREN

LUTSCHINE

TO WENGEN

WEISSE

- MAIN ROAD
-+- RAIL LINES
--- OTHER ROADS + TRAILS
Ⓑ POSTAL BUS STOPS
🄿 PARKING

❶ Hotel Staubbach
❷ Valley Hostel
❸ Chalet im Rohr
❹ Matratzenlager Stocki
❺ Camping Jungfrau
❻ Schützenbach Retreat
❼ Hotel Restaurant Oberland
❽ Hotel Restaurant Jungfrau
❾ Hotel Restaurant Silberhorn
❿ Co-op Grocery
⓫ Internet Café & Launderette
⓬ Bike Rental

runs an Internet café and a small launderette (both daily 9:00–22:00, shorter hours Nov–April; 10 SF/load includes soap, don't open dryer door until machine is finished or you'll have to pay another 5 SF to start it again; tel. 033-855-2008).

**Bike Rental:** You can rent mountain bikes at **Imboden Bike** on the main street (25-SF/4 hrs, 35-SF/day; full-suspension—reserve ahead—45-SF/half-day, 65-SF/day; daily July–Aug 9:00–18:30, Sept–June 8:30–21:00, tel. 033-855-2114).

**Grocery Store:** The **Co-op** is on the main street (Mon–Fri 8:00–12:00 & 14:00–18:30, Sat 8:00–12:00 & 13:30–17:00, closed Sun).

## SLEEPING

**(2,612 feet, 1.25 SF = about $1, country code: 41)**

**$$ Hotel Staubbach,** a big, Old World place—one of the first hotels in the valley (1890)—is being lovingly restored by hard-working American Craig and his Swiss wife, Corinne. Its 30 plain, comfortable rooms are family-friendly, there's a kids' play area, and the parking is free. Many rooms have great views (S-70 SF, Ss-80 SF, Sb-100 SF, D-90 SF, Db-120 SF, figure 50 SF/person in family rooms sleeping up to 6; 10 SF extra per room for 1-night stays, 10 SF extra for balcony rooms with valley view; elevator, 4 blocks up from station on the left, tel. 033-855-5454, fax 033-855-5484, www.staubbach.com, hotel@staubbach.com). Guests can watch a DVD of my TV show on the region in the lounge.

**$ Valley Hostel** is practical and comfortable, offering 70 inexpensive beds for quieter travelers of all ages, with a pleasant garden and the welcoming Abegglen family: Martha, Alfred, Stefan, and Fränzi (D with bunk beds-56 SF, twin D-64 SF, beds in larger family-friendly rooms-25 SF per person, breakfast-5 SF, most rooms have no sinks, non-smoking, kitchen available, cash only, 16-SF cheese fondue on request for guests 18:00–20:00, Wi-Fi, laundry, 2 blocks up from train station, tel. & fax 033-855-2008, www.valleyhostel.ch, info@valleyhostel.ch).

**$ Chalet im Rohr**—a creaky, old, woody firetrap of a place—has oodles of character (spiced with lots of Asian groups) and 50 beds in big one- to four-bed rooms that share six showers (27 SF per person, no breakfast, common kitchen, cash only, closed for 3 weeks after Easter, below church on main drag, tel. & fax 033-855-2182).

**$ Matratzenlager Stocki** is rustic and humble, with the cheapest beds in town (14 SF with sheets in easygoing little 30-bed co-ed dorm with kitchen, closed Nov–Dec, across river from station, tel. 033-855-1754, Frau Graf).

**$ *Camping:*** Two campgrounds just south of town provide 15–35-SF beds (in dorms and 2-, 4-, and 6-bed bungalows, no sheets, kitchen facilities, cash only, big English-speaking tour groups). **Mountain Holiday Park-Camping Jungfrau,** romantically situated beyond Staubbach Falls, is huge, well-organized by Hans, and also has fancy cabins (26 SF per person, tel. 033-856-2010, fax 033-856-2020, www.camping-jungfrau.ch). The park's shop, open to the public, has longer opening hours than other grocery stores in town (daily 7:30–12:00 & 16:00–20:00). **Schützenbach Retreat,** on the left just past Lauterbrunnen toward Stechelberg, is a simpler campground (tel. 033-855-1268, www .schutzenbach-retreat.ch).

## EATING

At **Hotel Restaurant Oberland,** the Nolan family takes pride in serving tasty meals from a fun menu (daily 11:30–16:00 & 17:30–21:00, tel. 033-855-1241).

**Hotel Restaurant Jungfrau,** along the main street on the right-hand side, offers a wide range of specialties served by a friendly staff (daily 12:00–14:00 & 18:00–21:00, tel. 033-855-3434, run by Brigitte Melliger).

**Hotel Restaurant Silberhorn** is the local choice for a fancy meal out (fine indoor and outdoor seating, above the cable-car station, tel. 033-856-2210).

# More in the Berner Oberland

## SIGHTS AND ACTIVITIES

### Lifts and Trains

The following lifts are both rated ▲▲▲. Doing at least one of them is an essential Berner Oberland experience.

#### The Schilthorn and a 10,000-Foot Breakfast

The Schilthornbahn carries skiers, hikers, and sightseers effortlessly to the 10,000-foot summit of the Schilthorn, where the Piz Gloria station awaits, with a solar-powered revolving restaurant, shop, and panorama terrace. Linger on top. Piz Gloria has a free "touristorama" film room with a multi-screen slide show and explosive highlights from the James Bond thriller that featured the Schilthorn (*On Her Majesty's Secret Service;* if it's not running, press the 007 button on the column in the middle of the room).

Watch paragliders set up, psych up, and take off, flying 45 minutes with the birds to distant Interlaken. (This is a tough launch point, but generally safe in the morning and late in the summer.) Walk along the ridge out back. This is a great place for a photo of you, the mountain climber.

When you ascend in the cable car, take a look at the altitude meter. (The Gimmelwald–Schilthorn hike is free, if you don't mind a 5,000-foot altitude gain.) Ask at the Schilthorn station for a cable-car souvenir decal (Schilthornbahn station in Stechelberg, tel. 033-856-2141). For another cheap thrill, ask the cable-car attendant to crank down the window (easiest on the Mürren–Birg section). Then stick your head out the window...and you're hang gliding.

You can ride up to the Schilthorn and hike down, but it's tough. For information on **hikes** from lift stations along the Schilthorn cable-car line, see "Hikes," page 160. My favorite "hike" from the Schilthorn is simply along the ridge out back, to get away from the station and be all alone on top of an Alp.

Youth hostelers—not realizing that rocks may hide just under the snow—scream down the ice fields on plastic-bag sleds from the Schilthorn mountaintop. (There's an English-speaking doctor in Lauterbrunnen.)

**Cost, Hours, Information:** The early-bird and afternoon-special cable-car tickets (61 SF round-trip before 9:00 or after 15:30) take you from Gimmelwald to the Schilthorn and back at a discount (normal rate: 81 SF, or 96 SF from the Stechelberg car park; parking-2 SF/2 hrs, 6 SF/day). These same discounted fares

are available all day long in the shoulder season (roughly May and Oct). Eurailpass and Swiss railpass holders—who get a 50 percent discount (a better deal than the early/late specials)—might as well go whenever they like, because there's no double discount. Lifts go twice hourly, and the ride (including two transfers) to the Schilthorn takes 30 minutes. For more information, including current weather conditions, see www.schilthorn .ch or call 033-826-0007.

**Breakfast at 10,000 Feet:** There's no à la carte—only a small breakfast for 15 SF (rolls and hot chocolate or coffee) or the James Bond breakfast for 22.50 SF (add egg, ham, and champagne; breakfast served 8:00–11:00). If you're going for breakfast before 9:00, consider an early-bird-plus-breakfast combo-ticket to save a few francs (round-trip from Gimmelwald:

74 SF with small breakfast/81 SF for James Bond breakfast; from Stechelberg: 85/92 SF). Ask for more hot drinks if necessary. If you're not revolving, ask them to turn on the mechanism.

## Jungfraujoch

The literal high point of any trip to the Swiss Alps is a train ride through the Eiger to the Jungfraujoch. At 11,300 feet, it's Europe's highest train station. The ride from Kleine Scheidegg takes about an hour (sit on right side for better views), including two five-minute stops at stations actually halfway up the notorious North Face of the Eiger. You have time to look out windows and marvel at how people could climb the Eiger—and how the Swiss built this

train more than a hundred years ago. The second half of the ride takes you through a tunnel inside the Eiger (some newer train cars run multilingual videos about the history of the train line).

Once you reach the top, study the Jungfraujoch chart to see your options (many of them are weather-dependent). There's a restaurant, history exhibit, ice palace (a cavern with a gallery of ice statues), and a 20-minute video that plays continuously. A tunnel leads outside, where you can ski (33 SF for gear and lift ticket), sled (free loaner discs with a 5-SF deposit), ride in a dog sled (8 SF, mornings only), or hike 45 minutes across the ice to Mönchsjochhütte (a mountain hut with a small restaurant). An elevator leads to the Sphinx observatory for the highest viewing point, from which you can see Aletsch Glacier—Europe's longest, at nearly 11 miles—stretch to the south. Remember that your body isn't used to such high altitudes. Signs posted at the top remind you to take it easy.

One of the best hikes in the region—from Männlichen to Kleine Scheidegg—could be combined with your trip up to the Jungfraujoch (see page 167).

**Cost, Hours, Information:** The first trip of the day to Jungfraujoch is discounted; ask for a Good Morning Ticket, and return from the top by noon (Nov–April you can get Good Morning rates for the first or second train and stay after noon;

train runs all year; round-trip fares to Jungfraujoch: from Kleine Scheidegg-104 SF, 80 SF for first trip of day—about 8:02; from Lauterbrunnen-154 SF, 130 SF for first trip—about 7:08; confirm times and prices, 50 percent discount for Eurailpass and Swiss railpass–holders). Pick up a leaflet on the lifts at a local TI, or call 033-828-7233 (www.jungfraubahn.ch). If it's cloudy, skip the trip; for a trilingual weather forecast from the Jungfraujoch, call 033-828-7931.

# HIKES

There are days of possible hikes from Gimmelwald and Mürren. Many are a fun combination of trails, mountain trains, and cable-car rides. I've listed them based on which side of the Lauterbrunnen Valley they're on: west (the Gimmelwald/Mürren/Schilthorn side) or east (the Jungfrau side).

## On the Gimmelwald (West) Side of the Lauterbrunnen Valley
### Hikes from the Schilthorn
While several tough trails lead down from the Schilthorn, most visitors take the cable car round-trip simply for the views (see "Lifts and Trains," above). But if you're a serious hiker, consider walking all the way down (first hike) or part of the way down (second hike) back into Gimmelwald. Don't attempt to hike down from the Schilthorn unless the trail is clear of snow. Adequate shoes and clothing (weather can change quickly) and good knees are required. (If you want to visit the Sprutz Waterfall on your way to Gimmelwald, see page 163.)

**From the Top of the Schilthorn**—To hike downhill from the Piz Gloria revolving restaurant at the peak, start at the steps to the right of the cable, which lead along a ridge between a cliff and the bowl. As you pass huge rocks and shale fields, keep an eye out for the painted rocks that mark the scant trail. Eventually, you'll hit the service road (a ski run in the winter), which is steep and not very pleasant. Passing a memorial to a woman killed by lightning in 1865, you come to the small lake called Grauseeli. Leave the gravel road and hike along the lake. From there, follow the trail (with the help of cables when necessary) to scamper along the shale in the direction of Rotstockhütte (to Gimmelwald, see next hike) or Schilttal (the valley leading directly to Mürren; follow *Mürren/Rotstockhütte* sign painted on the rock at the junction).

▲▲**Birg to Gimmelwald via Brünli**—Rather than the very long hike all the way back down into Gimmelwald, I prefer the easier (but still strenuous) hike from the intermediate cable-car station at

# Gimmelwald Area Hikes

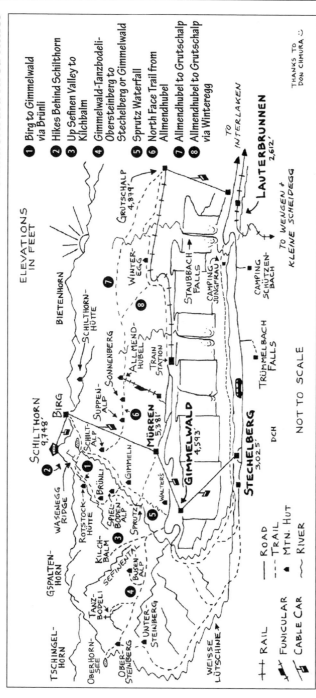

1. Birg to Gimmelwald via Brünli
2. Hikes Behind Schilthorn
3. Up Sefinen Valley to Kilchbalm
4. Gimmelwald-Tanzbodeli-Obersteinberg to Stechelberg or Gimmelwald
5. Sprutz Waterfall
6. North Face Trail from Allmendhubel
7. Allmendhubel to Grutschalp
8. Allmendhubel to Grutschalp via Winteregg

THANKS TO DON CHMURA :)

ELEVATIONS IN FEET

NOT TO SCALE

DCH

— ROAD
-- - TRAIL
▲ MTN. HUT
~ RIVER

+ RAIL
↗ FUNICULAR
⚑ CABLE CAR

Birg. This is efficiently combined with a visit to the Schilthorn (from Schilthorn summit, ride cable car halfway down, get off at Birg, and hike down from there; buy the round-trip excursion early-bird fare—which is cheaper than the Gimmelwald–Schilthorn–Birg ticket—and decide at Birg if you want to hike or ride down).

The most interesting trail from Birg to Gimmelwald is the high one via Grauseeli Lake and Wasenegg Ridge to Brünli, then down to Spielbodenalp and the Sprutz waterfall. Warning: This trail is quite steep and slippery in places, and can take four hours. Locals take their kindergartners on this hike, but it can seem dangerous to Americans unused to alpine hikes. Do not attempt this hike in snow—which you might find at this altitude, even in the peak of summer. (Get local advice.)

From the Birg lift, hike toward the Schilthorn, taking your first left down and passing along the left side of the little Grauseeli lake. From the lake, a gravelly trail leads down rough switchbacks (including a stretch where the path narrows and you can hang onto a guide cable against the cliff face) until it levels out. When you see a rock painted with arrows pointing to Mürren and Rotstockhütte, follow the path to Rotstockhütte (traditional old farm with light meals and drinks, mattress loft with cheap beds), traversing the cow-grazed mountainside.

For a thrill, follow Wasenegg Ridge. It's more scary than dangerous if you're sure-footed and can handle the 50-foot-long "tightrope" section along an extremely narrow ledge with a thousand-foot drop. This trail gets you to Brünli with the least altitude drop. (The safer, well-signposted approach to Brünli is to drop down to Rotstockhütte, then climb back up to Brünli.) The barbed-wire fence leads to the knobby little summit, where you'll enjoy an incredible 360-degree view and a chance to sign your name on the register stored in the little wooden box.

A steep trail winds directly down from Brünli toward Gimmelwald and soon hits a bigger, easy trail. The trail bends right (just before the farm/restaurant at Spielbodenalp), leading to Sprutz. Walk under the Sprutz waterfall, then follow a steep, wooded trail that deposits you in a meadow of flowers at the top side of Gimmelwald.

## Hikes from Gimmelwald
**▲Up Sefinen Valley to Kilchbalm**—An easy trail from Gimmelwald is up the Sefinen Valley (Sefinental). This is a good rainy-weather hike, as you can go as far as you like. After two hours and a gain of only 800 feet, you hit the end of the trail and Kilchbalm, a dramatic bowl of glacier fields. Note that snow can make this trail unsafe, even into the summer (ask locally for infor-

mation), and there's no food or drink along the way.

From the Gimmelwald fire station, walk about 100 yards down the paved Stechelberg road. Leave it on the dirt Sefinental road, which becomes a lane, then a trail. You'll cross a raging river and pass a firing range where locals practice their marksmanship (Fri and Sat evenings; the *danger of fire* sign refers to live bullets). Follow signs to Kilchbalm into a forest, along a river, and finally to the glacier fields.

▲**Gimmelwald–Tanzbodeli–Obersteinberg–Stechelberg/ Gimmelwald**—This eight-hour, 11-mile hike is extremely rewarding, offering perfect peace, very few people, traditional alpine culture, and spectacular views. (There's no food or drink for five hours, so pack accordingly.) As the trail can be a bit confusing, this is best done with a good map (buy locally).

About 100 yards below the Gimmelwald firehouse, take the Sefinental dirt road (described above). As the dirt road switches back after about 30 minutes, take the right turn across the river and start your ascent, following signs to Obersteinberg. After 90 minutes of hard climbing, you have the option of a side-trip to Busenalp. This is fun if the goat and cow herder is there, as you can watch the traditional cheesemaking in action. (He appreciates a bottle of wine from hikers.) Trail markers are painted onto rocks—watch carefully. After visiting Busenalp, return to the main path.

At the *Obersteinberg 50 min/Tanzbodeli 20 min* signpost, head

for Tanzbodeli ("Dancing Floor"). This is everyone's favorite alpine perch—great for a little romance, or a picnic with breathtaking views of the Obersteinberg valley. From here, you enter a natural reserve, so you're likely to see chamois and other alpine critters. From Tanzbodeli, you return to the main trail (there's no other way out) and continue to Obersteinberg. You'll eventually hit the Mountain Hotel Obersteinberg (see "Sleeping," page 173; American expat Vickie will serve you a meal or drink).

From there, the trail leads to Hotel Tschingelhorn and back to Gimmelwald (2 hours total) or Stechelberg (bottom of Schilthorn cable car, 90 min total). About an hour later, you hit a fork in the trail and choose where you'd like your hike to end.

▲**Sprutz Waterfall**—The forest above Gimmelwald hides a powerful waterfall with a trail snaking behind it, offering a fun gorge experience. While the waterfall itself is not well-signed, it's on the

# Hiking in the Berner Oberland

This region is a wonderful place to hike, and I've listed my favorite excursions. The super-scenic walk from Männlichen to Kleine Scheidegg is the best of all worlds: It's both dramatic and relatively easy. The hike from Schynige Platte to First is spectacular, but much more challenging, as is the hike from the Birg cable-car station down to Gimmelwald—don't try either of these in bad weather. In case of rain, the lower hikes (North Face Trail from Allmendhubel; the walk from Mürren or Allmendhubel to Grütschalp; the Sefinen Valley hike from Gimmelwald; and the stroll along the Lauterbrunnen Valley) are better bets.

To do any serious hiking, you should invest in a real hiking map. Hikers can get specifics at the Mürren TI or from hoteliers. For a description of six diverse hikes on the west side of Lauterbrunnen, pick up the fine and free *Mürren–Schilthorn Hikes* brochure. This 3-D overview map of the Mürren mountainside makes a useful and attractive souvenir. For the other side of the valley, get the *Wandern Jungfraubahnen* brochure, which also has a handy 3-D overview map of hiking trails (both brochures free at stations, hotels, and TIs).

Once underway, don't mind the fences (although wires can be solar-powered electric); a hiker has the right of way in Switzerland. Don't forget a water bottle and some munchies. Trails are well-marked, with yellow signs listing destinations and the estimated time it'll take you to walk there. Refer to maps (within this chapter) as you read about the hikes.

**Weather Concerns:** Locals always seem to know the weather report (as much of their income depends on it). Clouds

Gimmelwald–Spielbodenalp trail. It's steep, through a forest, and can be very slippery when wet, but the actual crossing under the waterfall is just misty.

The hike up to Sprutz from Gimmelwald isn't worth the trip in itself, but it's handy when combined with the hike down from Birg and Brünli (see above) or the North Face Trail (see below). As you descend on either of these two hikes, the trail down to Gimmelwald splits at Spielbodenalp—to the right for the forest and the waterfall; to the left for more meadows, the hamlet of Gimmeln, and more gracefully back into Gimmelwald.

can roll in anytime, but skies are usually clearest in the morning. All over the region, TV sets are tuned to the local weather station, with real-time views from all the famous peaks. The same station airs a travelogue on the region each evening at about 21:30. You can also check the weather at www.swisspanorama.com.

**Snow:** As late as July in the Berner Oberland, snow can curtail your hiking plans (the Männlichen lift doesn't even open until the first week in June). Before setting out on any hike, get advice from a knowledgeable local. Well into the spring, and sometimes also in early fall, the high trails (Männlichen to Kleine Scheidegg, Schynige Platte to First, and anything from Schilthorn or Birg) are likely to be impassable.

**Wildlife:** As hunting is not allowed in the vicinity of any lifts, animals find comfort in places you're likely to be. Keep an eye out for chamois (called *Gemse* here)—the sure-footed "goat antelope" that lives at the top of the treeline, and goes a little lower when hungry. Spotting an ibex—a wild goat with horns, scrambling along the rocky terrain—is another Berner Oberland thrill. You'll also encounter marmot, big alpine mice (like 2-pound squirrels) who get really fat each summer, planning to sleep underground for six months through the winter. These burrowing rodents are fun to watch, and if you sit still, they don't see you. You'll hear them whistle. Your best viewing place is above Allmendhubel, in the meadow above the highest hut in Blumental.

**Nordic Walking:** You may wonder about the Germans you'll see with their walking sticks *(Alpenstock)*. This is trying to be the next craze: Nordic walking. Enthusiasts claim Nordic walking is an all-body workout, activating 90 percent of your muscles and burning a third more calories than "normal" walking, while cutting way back on the strain on your back and knees when going downhill. To do it right requires proper instruction. Sticks can be rented at some outdoor shops.

## Hikes from Mürren/Allmendhubel

▲▲**North Face Trail from Allmendhubel**—For a pleasant, mainly downhill, two-hour hike (4 miles, from 6,385 feet to 5,375 feet), ride the Allmendhubel funicular up from Mürren (7.40 SF, much cheaper than Schilthorn, good restaurant at top). From there, follow the well-signed route circling around to Mürren (or cut off at Spielbodenalp, near the end, and descend into Gimmelwald via the Sprutz Waterfall). Just follow the blue signs. You'll enjoy great views, flowery meadows, mountain huts, and a dozen information boards along the way, describing the fascinating climbing history of the great peaks around you.

Along the trail, you'll pass four farms (technically "alps," as they are only open in the summer) that serve meals and drinks. Sonnenberg was allowed to break the all-wood code with concrete for protection against avalanches. Suppenalp is quainter. Lean against the house with a salad, soup, or sandwich and enjoy the view.

Notice how older huts are built into the protected side of rocks and outcroppings, in anticipation of avalanches. Above Suppenalp, Blumental ("Flower Valley") is hopping with marmots. Because hunters are not allowed near lifts, animals have learned that these are safe places to hang out—giving tourists a better chance of spotting them.

The trail leads up and over to a group of huts called Schiltalp. If the poles under the eve have bells, the cows are up. If not, the cows are still at the lower farm. Half the cows in Gimmelwald (about 100) spend their summers here. In July, August, and September, you can watch cheese being made and have a snack or drink. Thirty years

ago, each family had its own hut. Labor was cheap and available. Today, it's a communal thing, with several families sharing the expense of a single cow herder. Cow herders are master cheesemakers, and have veterinary skills, too.

From Schiltalp, the trail winds gracefully down to Spielbodenalp—a farm with lots going on (open May–mid-Oct Fri–Wed, closed Thu, good menu, 31-SF dorm beds with breakfast). From there, you can finish the North Face trail (continuing down and left through meadows and the hamlet of Gimmeln, then back to Mürren, with more historic signposts); or cut off right (descending steeply through a thick forest and under the dramatic Sprutz Waterfall into Gimmelwald—see Sprutz Waterfall, above, for details).

▲**Allmendhubel/Mürren to Grütschalp**—For a not-too-tough, two-hour walk with great Jungfrau views, ride the funicular from Mürren to Allmendhubel (6,344 feet) and walk to Grütschalp (a drop of about 1,500 feet), where you can catch the panorama train back to Mürren. An easier version is the lower Bergweg from Allmendhubel to Grütschalp via Winteregg and its cheese farm. For a super-easy family stroll with grand views, walk from Mürren just above the train tracks to either Winteregg (40 min, restaurant, playground, train station) or Grütschalp (60 min, train station), then catch the panorama train back to Mürren.

## Hikes on the Jungfrau (East) Side of the Lauterbrunnen Valley

▲▲▲**The Männlichen–Kleine Scheidegg Hike**—This is my favorite easy alpine hike (2.5 miles, 1.5 hours, 900-foot altitude drop to Kleine Scheidegg). It's entertaining all the way, with glorious Jungfrau, Eiger, and Mönch views. That's the Young Maiden being protected from the Ogre by the Monk. (These days, that could be problematic.) Trails may be snowbound into June; ask about conditions at the lift stations or local TIs. If the Männlichen lift is closed, you can take the train straight from Lauterbrunnen to Kleine Scheidegg (see Jungfraujoch under "Lifts and Trains," page 159).

If the weather's good, descend from Gimmelwald bright and early to Stechelberg. From here, get to the Lauterbrunnen train station by postal bus (3.80 SF, covered by Swiss Pass, bus is synchronized to depart with the arrival of each lift) or by car (parking at the large, multistory pay lot behind the Lauterbrunnen station- 2 SF/2 hrs, 9 SF/day). At Lauterbrunnen, buy a train ticket to Männlichen (29 SF one-way). If hiking down from Männlichen to Wengen via Kleine Scheidegg (the complete hike described in this listing), you'll buy a ticket from Lauterbrunnen to Männlichen, then from Wengen back to Lauterbrunnen, for 32 SF. Sit on the right side of the train for great waterfall views on your way up to Wengen. In Wengen, walk across town (buy a picnic, but don't waste time here if it's sunny—you can linger after your hike) and catch the Männlichen lift to the top of the ridge high above you (lift departs every 15 min, beginning the first week of June). Note that the lift can be open even if the trail is closed; confirm that the trail is open before ascending.

From the top of Wengen–Männlichen lift station, turn left and hike uphill 20 minutes to the little peak (Männlichen Gipfel, 7,500 feet) for that king- or queen-of-the-mountain feeling. Then take an easy hour's walk—facing spectacular alpine panorama  views—to Kleine Scheidegg for a picnic or restaurant lunch. To start the hike, leave the Wengen–Männlichen lift station to the right. Walk past the second Männlichen lift station (this one leads to Grindelwald, the touristy town in the valley to your left). Ahead of you in the distance, left to right, are the north faces of the Eiger, Mönch, and Jungfrau; in the foreground is the Tschuggen peak, and just behind it, the Lauberhorn. This hike takes you around the left (east) side of this ridge. Simply follow the signs for Kleine Scheidegg, and you'll be there in about an hour—a little more for gawkers, picnickers, and photographers. You might have to tip-toe through streams of melted snow—or some small snow banks, even well into the summer—but the path is well-marked, well-maintained, and mostly level all the way to Kleine Scheidegg.

About 35 minutes into the hike, you'll reach a bunch of benches and a shelter with incredible unobstructed views of all three peaks—the perfect picnic spot. Fifteen minutes later on the left, you'll see the first sign of civilization: Restaurant Grindelwaldblick, offering a handy terrace lunch stop with tasty, hearty, and reasonable food (open daily, closed Dec and May, see "Sleeping and Eating in Kleine Scheidegg," page 173). After 10 more minutes, you'll be at the Kleine Scheidegg train station, with plenty of other lunch options (including Bahnhof Buffet, see "Sleeping and Eating in Kleine Scheidegg," page 173).

From Kleine Scheidegg, you can catch the train to "the top of Europe" (see Jungfraujoch information, page 159). Or head downhill, riding the train or hiking (30 gorgeous min to Wengernalp station, a little farther to the Allmend stop; 60 more steep min from there into the town of Wengen). The alpine views might be accompanied by the valley-filling mellow sound of alphorns and distant avalanches.

If the weather turns bad or you run out of steam, catch the train at any of the stations along the way. After Wengernalp, the trail to Wengen is steep and, though not dangerous, requires a good set of knees. Wengen is a good shopping town. (For accommodations, see "Sleeping in Wengen," page 171.) The boring final descent from Wengen to Lauterbrunnen is knee-killer steep—catch the train.

▲▲**Schynige Platte to First**—The best day I've had hiking in the Berner Oberland was when I made this demanding six-hour ridge walk, with Lake Brienz on one side and all that Jungfrau beauty on the other. Start at Wilderswil train station (just above Interlaken) and catch the little train up to Schynige Platte (6,560 feet). The high point is Faulhorn (8,790 feet, with its famous mountaintop hotel). Hike to a small mini-gondola called "First" (7,110 feet), then ride down to Grindelwald and catch a train back to your starting point, Wilderswil. Or, if you have a regional train pass (or no car but endless money), take the long, scenic return trip to Gimmelwald: From Grindelwald, take the lift up to Männlichen, do the hike to Kleine Scheidegg and Wengen (see above), then head down into Lauterbrunnen and on to Gimmelwald.

For a shorter (3-hour) ridge walk, consider the well-signposted Panoramaweg, a loop from Schynige Platte to Daub Peak.

The alpine flower park (4 SF, 3 SF with guest card, at the Schynige Platte station) offers a delightful stroll through several hundred alpine flowers (best in summer) including a chance to see edelweiss growing in the wild.

Lowa, a leading local manufacturer of top-end hiking boots, has a promotional booth at the Schynige Platte station providing free loaner boots to hikers who'd like to give their boots a try. They are already broken in, but bring thick socks (or buy them there).

If hiking here, be mindful of the last lifts (which can be as early as 16:30). Climbing from First (7,113 feet) to Schynige Platte (6,454 feet) gives you a later departure down and less climbing.

## Mountain Biking

Mountain biking is popular and accepted, as long as you stay on the clearly marked mountain-bike paths.

A good but challenging ride is the round-trip Mürren Loop that runs from Mürren to Gimmelwald, down the Sefinen Valley to Stechelberg, along the dreamy bike path left of the river to Lauterbrunnen, up by cable car to Grütschalp (bike costs-7.80 SF), and back through a working cheese farm to Mürren.

You can rent bikes in Mürren (Stäger Sport, 35 SF/day includes helmet, daily 9:00–17:00, closed late Oct–mid-May, in TI/Sportzentrum, tel. 033-855-2355, www.staegersport.ch) or in

Lauterbrunnen (Imboden Bike, 25 SF/4 hrs, 35 SF/ day; call ahead to reserve a full-suspension bike: 45 SF/half-day, 65 SF/day; daily July–Aug 8:30–21:00, Sept–June 9:00–18:30, tel. 033-855-2114). The Lauterbrunnen shop is often open when the Mürren one isn't. It costs 2.50 SF per segment to take a bike onto the gondola.

You can also bike the Lauterbrunnen Valley from Lauterbrunnen to Interlaken. It's a gentle downhill ride via a peaceful bike path across the river from the road (don't bike on the road). Rent a bike at Lauterbrunnen (see above), bike to Interlaken, and return to Lauterbrunnen by train (to take bike on train, pay about 4 SF extra). Or rent a bike at either Interlaken station, take the train to Lauterbrunnen, and ride back.

## Rainy-Day Options

When it rains here, locals joke that they're washing the mountains. If clouds roll in, don't despair. They can roll out just as quickly. With good rain gear and the right choice of trail, a hike in the rain can be thoroughly enjoyable, with surprise views popping out all around you as the clouds break. And there are plenty of good bad-weather options.

▲▲**Cloudy-Day Lauterbrunnen Valley Walk**—Try the easy trails and pleasant walks along the floor of the Lauterbrunnen Valley. For a smell-the-cows-and-flowers lowland walk—ideal for a cloudy day, weary body, or tight budget—follow the riverside trail from Stechelberg's Schilthornbahn station (left of river) for three miles downhill to Lauterbrunnen's Staubbach Falls, near the town church (you can reverse the route, but it's a gradual uphill to Stechelberg). Detour to Trümmelbach Falls (described below) en route. There's a fine, paved, car-free, riverside path all the way (popular with bikers). In this "Valley of Many Waterfalls" (literally), you'll see cone-like mounds piled against the sides of the cliffs, formed by centuries of rocks hurled by tumbling rivers.

If you're staying in Gimmelwald: Take the lift down to Stechelberg (5 min), then walk to Lauterbrunnen, detouring to Trümmelbach Falls shortly after Stechelberg (15 min to falls, another 45 min to Lauterbrunnen). To return to Gimmelwald from Lauterbrunnen, take the cable car up to Grütschalp (10 min), then either walk (90 min to Gimmelwald) or take the panorama train (15 min) to Mürren. From Mürren, it's a downhill walk (30 min) to Gimmelwald. (This loop trip can be reversed.)

Note that this is an El Dorado of base-jumping (parachuting off of cliffs), and each season the bodies of thrill-seekers plummet to the valley floor. They hike to the top of a cliff, leap off—falling as long as they can (this provides the rush)—and then pull the rip-cord to release a tiny parachute, hoping it will break their fall and a gust won't dash them into the mountainside.

▲**Trümmelbach Falls**—If all the waterfalls have you intrigued, sneak a behind-the-scenes look at the valley's most powerful, Trümmelbach Falls (11 SF, daily July–Aug 8:30–18:00, April–June and Sept–Nov 9:00–17:00, closed off-season, on Lauterbrunnen-Stechelberg road, take postal bus from Lauterbrunnen TI or Stechelberg gondola station, tel. 033-855-3232, www.truemmelbach .ch). You'll ride an elevator up through the mountain and climb through several caves (wet, with lots of stairs, and—for some—claustrophobic) to see the melt from the Eiger,

Mönch, and Jungfrau grinding like God's bandsaw through the mountain at the rate of up to 5,200 gallons a second (that's 20,000 liters—nearly double the beer consumption at Oktoberfest). The upper area is the best; if your legs ache, skip the lower falls and ride down on the elevator.

**Lauterbrunnen Folk Museum (Heimatmuseum)**—This humble collection, in Lauterbrunnen, shows off the local folk culture and two centuries of mountaineering. You'll see lots of lace, exhibits on cheese and woodworking, and classic old photos (free if you're staying in the region, 3 SF otherwise, mid-June–mid-Oct Tue, Thu, and Sat–Sun 14:00–17:30, closed off-season, just over bridge and below church at the far end of town, tel. 033-855-3586 or 033-855-1388).

**Mürren Activities**—This low-key alpine resort town offers a variety of rainy-day options, from its shops to its slick Sportzentrum (sports center) with pools, steam baths, squash, and a fitness center (details on page 148). On Wednesday nights at 20:30 from June through August, Mürren's Sportzentrum hosts a lively free cultural night with alpenhorns, folk music, and local wine.

**Interlaken Activities**—For more rainy-day options, see "Sights and Activities—Near Interlaken," page 131.

## SLEEPING AND EATING

In addition to my listings in Interlaken, Gimmelwald, Mürren, and Lauterbrunnen, consider these nearby places.

### Sleeping in Wengen
**(4,180 feet, 1.25 SF = about $1, country code: 41)**
Wengen—a bigger, fancier Mürren on the other side of the valley—has plenty of grand hotels, many shops, tennis courts, minigolf, and terrific views. This traffic-free resort is an easy train ride above Lauterbrunnen and halfway up to Kleine Scheidegg and Männlichen, and offers more activities for those needing distraction from the scenery. Hiking is better from Mürren and Gimmelwald. The **TI** is one block from the station; go up to the main drag, turn left, and look ahead on the left (June–Sept and Dec–mid-April daily 9:00–18:00; mid-April–May and Oct–Nov Mon–Fri 9:00–18:00, closed Sat–Sun; Internet access in lobby; tel. 033-855-1414, www.wengen-muerren.ch).

### Sleeping Above the Train Station
**$$$ Hotel Berghaus,** in a quiet area a five-minute walk from the main street, offers 19 rooms above a fine restaurant specializing in fish (Sb-86–117 SF, Db-172–234 SF, 5 percent discount with this book and cash through 2007, elevator, Internet access; call

on phone at station hotel board for free pickup, or walk up street across from Bernerhof Hotel, bear right and then left at fork, 200 yards more past church on the left; tel. 033-855-2151, fax 033-855-3820, www.wengen.com/hotel/berghaus, berghaus@wengen.com, Fontana family).

**$$$ Hotel Schönegg,** on Wengen's main drag, is a centrally located splurge, decorated with antiques and old wood (Sb-100–110 SF, Db-200–220 SF; higher July–Aug: Sb-115–125 SF, Db-230–250 SF; non-smoking rooms, all rooms have balconies and great views, cozy family room with fireplace, Internet access in lobby, good restaurant with big terrace, look for big yellow hotel on main drag near TI, tel. 033-855-3422, fax 033-855-4233, www.hotel-schoenegg.ch, mail@hotel-schoenegg.ch, Herr und Frau Berthod).

## Sleeping Below the Train Station

The first two listings are bright, cheery, family-friendly, and five minutes below the station: Leave the station toward the Co-op store, turn right and go under the rail bridge, bear right (paved path) at the fork, and follow the road down and around.

**$$$ Bären Hotel,** run by friendly Therese and Willy Brunner, offers 14 tidy rooms with perky, bright-orange bathrooms. Their newly redone restaurant is bright and inviting, offering garden-fresh Swiss cuisine (daily specials for 15.50 SF; Sb-80 SF, Db-150 SF, Tb-210 SF, dinner-20 SF more, family rooms, Internet access, tel. 033-855-1419, fax 033-855-1525, www.baeren-wengen.ch, info@baeren-wengen.ch).

**$$ Familienhotel Edelweiss** has 25 bright rooms, lots of fun public spaces, a Christian emphasis, and a jittery Chihuahua named Speedy (Sb-70–75 SF, Db-140–150 SF, non-smoking, elevator, great family rooms, TV lounge, game room, meeting room, kids' playroom, tel. 033-855-2388, fax 033-855-4288, www.edelweisswengen.ch, edelweiss@vch.ch, Bärtschi family).

**$$ Clare and Andy's Chalet (Trogihalten)** offers three rustic, low-ceilinged rooms (1-room studio: Sb-56 SF, Db-90 SF; 2-room suite: Sb/Db-106 SF, Tb-145 SF, Qb-188 SF; 4-room flat: Tb-159 SF, Qb-192 SF, 6-bed apartment-294 SF; breakfast-15 SF, dinner by request-35 SF, 4-night minimum preferred, prices higher for shorter stays, cash only, all rooms with balconies; leave station to the left and follow paved path next to Bernerhof Hotel downhill, steep 5-min hike; tel. & fax 033-855-1712, mobile 079-423-7813, www.chaletwengen.ch, info@chaletwengen.ch, Clare is English, Andy is Swiss).

**$ Backpackers' Old Lodge** is centrally located and offers cheap beds (25 SF per bed with sheets in a 6-bed dorm; S-45 SF, D-90 SF, T-105 SF, Q-140, 10 percent off with this book in 2007, optional breakfast-7 SF, kitchens available; walk from station toward the Co-op store, before rail bridge turn left; tel. 033-855-1573, mobile 078-745-5850, www.oldlodge.ch, info@oldlodge.ch, Angela).

## Sleeping and Eating at Kleine Scheidegg
**(6,762 feet, 1.25 SF = about $1, country code: 41)**
Confirm price and availability before ascending. Both places serve meals.

**$$ Restaurant Bahnhof** invites you to sleep face-to-face with the Eiger (dorm bed-51 SF with breakfast, 69 SF includes dinner as well, D-167 SF with breakfast and dinner; in the train station building, tel. 033-828-7828, fax 033-828-7830, www.roestizza.ch, info@bahnhof-scheidegg.ch).

**$ Restaurant Grindelwaldblick,** a 10-minute hike from the train station, really gets you up into the mountains (38 SF per bed in 12-bed room, includes sheets, closed Nov and May, tel. 033-855-1374, fax 033-855-4205, www.grindelwaldblick.ch).

## Sleeping in Stechelberg
**(3,025 feet, 1.25 SF = about $1, country code: 41)**
Stechelberg is the hamlet at the end of Lauterbrunnen Valley, at the base of the lift to Gimmelwald, Mürren, and the Schilthorn.

**$$ Hotel Stechelberg,** at road's end, is surrounded by waterfalls and vertical rock, with a garden terrace and 20 quiet rooms—half in a creaky old building, half in a concrete, no-character new building (D-86–104 SF, Db-130, Db with balcony-158 SF, T-147 SF, Tb-186 SF, Q-176 SF, Qb-234 SF, postal bus stops here, tel. 033-855-2921, fax 033-855-4438, www.hotel-stechelberg .ch, hotel@stechelberg.ch).

## Sleeping in Obersteinberg
**(5,900 feet, 1.25 SF = about $1, country code: 41)**
**$$** Here's a wild idea: **Mountain Hotel Obersteinberg** is a working alpine farm with cheese, cows, a mule shuttling up food once a day, and an American (Vickie) who fell in love with a mountain man. It's a 2.5-hour hike from either Stechelberg or Gimmelwald. They rent 12 primitive rooms and a bunch of loft beds. There's no shower, no hot water, and only meager solar-panel electricity. Candles light up the night, and you can take a hot-water bottle to bed if necessary (S-83 SF, D-166 SF, includes linen, sheetless dorm beds-66 SF, these prices include breakfast and dinner, without meals S-37 SF, D-74 SF, dorm beds-20 SF, closed Oct–May, tel. 033-855-2033). The place is filled with locals and Germans on weekends, but it's all yours on weekdays. Why not hike there from Gimmelwald and leave the Alps a day later?

## Sleeping in Isenfluh
**(3,560 feet, 1.25 SF = about $1, country code: 41)**

The yellow postal bus takes you up on a spectacular road, through a long and narrow tunnel to the tiny hamlet of Isenfluh, which is even smaller than Gimmelwald and offers better views (3.80 SF one-way; from Lauterbrunnen train station: almost hourly at :50, from Interlaken: 4 buses/day; some buses require reservations—especially the first or last ride of the day, tel. 079-788-5120).

**$$ Hotel Restaurant Waldrand** has a decent restaurant (including great fresh salads) and four reasonable rooms (Db-140–160 SF, Tb-190 SF, cash only, includes breakfast, tel. 033-855-1227, fax 033-855-1392, www.hotel-waldrand.ch, info@hotel-waldrand .ch, Vreni and Urs Werthmüller).

# ZERMATT
## and the MATTERHORN

There's just something about that Matterhorn, the most recognizable mountain on the planet. Anyone who says, "You've seen one mountain, you've seen them all," hasn't laid eyes on this pointy, craggy peak. The Matterhorn seems to have a nearly mystical draw for people—it's the Stonehenge of Switzerland.

Oh, and there's a town, too. Zermatt, a little burg of 5,500 people, might well be the most touristy resort in Switzerland. While there are pockets of traditional charm, virtually everyone you meet in Zermatt earns a living one way or another from those who flock here for a peek of the peak. Aside from the stone quarries you'll pass on the way, tourism is Zermatt's only industry.

Be warned that Zermatt is a one-mountain town. If you have time for only one mountainous region on your trip, I'd suggest the more interesting Berner Oberland over Zermatt (for specifics, see sidebar on page 177). Many visitors find Zermatt touristy and overrated, especially considering its inconvenient location (at the end of a long, dead-end valley in the southwest corner of the country). And if you make the long trek and find only cloudy weather, there's little else to do...other than wish for a T-shirt that reads, "I went all the way to Zermatt and didn't even see the lousy Matterhorn."

## Planning Your Time

On a two-week trip in Switzerland, I'd suggest two nights and the better part of two days in Zermatt if the weather's good. (To check the weather, call the Zermatt TI at tel. 027-966-8100, www .zermatt.ch.) For efficient sightseeing, arrive or leave on the Glacier Express; it's an all-day, cross-country scenic train ride to Chur, which has good connections to Zürich and elsewhere in northeast Switzerland (see Scenic Rail Journeys chapter).

# ORIENTATION

Zermatt (elevation 5,265 feet) lies at the end of the Nikolaital Valley, along the Mattervispa River in the shadow of the mighty Matterhorn (14,690 feet, "Cervino" in Italian).

The train station is at the bottom of town, a few steps from the main drag, Bahnhofstrasse. As you stand in front of the station with the tracks at your back, the heart of the village is to your right. Lifts to thrilling Matterhorn viewpoints leave from near the train station: The train up to Gornergrat is across the street and to your left, the station for the underground train/gondola/cable car to Rothorn is a few blocks ahead and to the left along the river, and the gondola/cable car station up to Klein Matterhorn is through the village to your right across the river (about three-quarters of a mile away). Details on all of these are listed below.

Zermatt brags that its streets are traffic-free. Well, not quite. Electric cars (big golf carts) buzz around the streets like four-wheeled Vespas, some with surprisingly aggressive drivers. Watch your step.

Addresses are generally not used in this small town. To find your hotel, use the map in this chapter, follow the free map from the TI, look for signs, or ask a local.

## Tourist Information

Zermatt's TI is right at the train station (mid-June–Oct Mon–Sat 8:30–18:00, Sun 8:30–12:00 & 13:30–18:00; Nov–mid-June Mon–Sat 8:30–12:00 & 13:30–18:00, Sun 9:30–12:00 & 16:00–18:00; tel. 027-966-8100, www.zermatt.ch). They offer a variety of handy, free resources: an extremely detailed map that labels every building in town; a magazine with hotels and lift schedules and prices; an events brochure; and a thick, directory-type information booklet. You can also buy hiking maps here, including a basic overview map of the region (2 SF, helpful for orientation to the region even if you're not hiking), a more detailed map for serious hikers (25.90 SF), and the good *Discovering Zermatt on Foot* hiking guide (29.50 SF, comes with the same basic map the TI sells separately for 2 SF).

Once a week, there's a free one-hour village **walking tour** in English. This is a good rainy-day option; ask for the schedule at the TI.

**Internet Access:** You'll see coin-op Internet stations all over town. The going rate is 12 SF per hour.

# Zermatt vs. the Berner Oberland

I've said for years that the Berner Oberland offers far more high-mountain travel thrills than the Zermatt area (see Gimmelwald and the Berner Oberland chapter). And I still stand by that—if you're going to only one alpine hideaway in Switzerland, the Berner Oberland is tops. But if you're trying to make up your mind, here are a few comparisons:

The Berner Oberland is relatively easy to reach, thanks to its more central location in the country and its good rail connections to Bern and Luzern. Zermatt is farther off the beaten track, at the end of a dead-end valley near the Italian border—and the final approach by train (from Brig) is run by a private company, not covered by your Eurailpass (though it is covered by the Swiss Pass—see page 4).

Zermatt is essentially one town focused on a single mountain. The Berner Oberland is an entire alpine region, with many towns and villages to visit—from the bustling administrative center of Interlaken to the tiny, traditional village of Gimmelwald. In Zermatt, most accommodations options are in the town itself. But in the Berner Oberland, you have your choice of places to sleep—in a resort town or humble village; in the valley or on a ledge overlooking the mountains.

As for sightseeing, the best part of the Berner Oberland is the Lauterbrunnen Valley, with great high-altitude attractions on both sides (the Jungfraujoch on one side, the Schilthorn on the other), plus other enjoyable lifts, towns, and hikes. Zermatt doesn't have nearly the same diversity. Budget travelers appreciate the Berner Oberland's cheaper accommodations and the discount given on mountain lifts to Eurailpass holders (unlike in Zermatt).

Both areas are touristy, but there are more traditional tidbits of the authentic Swiss countryside in the Berner Oberland than in Zermatt. The Berner Oberland also offers a wider variety of activities than Zermatt. On a rainy day, you can poke around one of the traditional villages (like Gimmelwald) or the bigger town of Interlaken, or walk through the thundering Trümmelbach Falls.

You can tell where my heart lies. Still, if you've seen the Berner Oberland already, or if you want to sample two different mountain areas of Switzerland, Zermatt is worth a visit. And the Matterhorn is really something else—it's the reason this place is known around the world.

# Zermatt

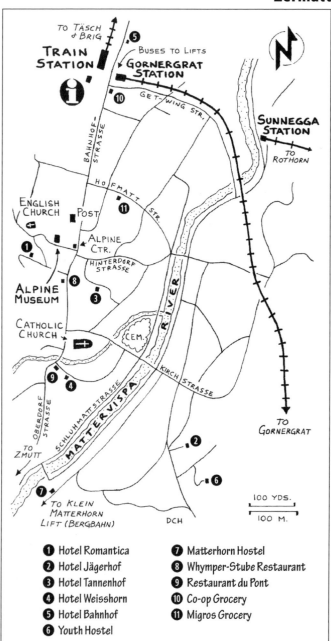

1  Hotel Romantica
2  Hotel Jägerhof
3  Hotel Tannenhof
4  Hotel Weisshorn
5  Hotel Bahnhof
6  Youth Hostel
7  Matterhorn Hostel
8  Whymper-Stube Restaurant
9  Restaurant du Pont
10  Co-op Grocery
11  Migros Grocery

## Arrival in Zermatt

Zermatt's small train station is conveniently located in the middle of town; the TI is immediately to the right as you leave the tracks, and you'll also stumble on to a stand of Elektro-taxis right out front (see below).

Cars are not allowed in Zermatt. Drivers park in the huge lot at Täsch, a few miles before Zermatt (11 SF/day), then take the shuttle train into town (7.80 SF one-way, runs every 20 min until 23:00).

## Getting Around Zermatt

Even though Zermatt is "traffic-free," there are ways to get around town faster than on foot. Two different electric **bus** lines depart across from the train station: One line goes to Bergbahn, the lift station for Klein Matterhorn (2.50 SF, or free with lift ticket, about every 10 min), and the other goes to the cliff-hanging neighborhood above that station, called Winkelmatten (3.20 SF, about every 20 min). The buses are marked with their destination and make a few stops along the way before heading back to the station (when they're marked *Bahnhof*).

You can also hire your own **Elektro-taxi** (about 10 SF for anywhere in the heart of town, extra charge for luggage and rides at night, taxi stand in front of train station), or call **Taxi Zermatt** (mobile 084-811-1212).

# SIGHTS AND ACTIVITIES

## In Zermatt

The town itself is short on attractions. On rainy days, the TI can only shrug, poignantly promote the Alpine Museum, or suggest that you go swimming in one of the big hotel pools.

**Wander the Town**—Zermatt is charming enough, despite its single-mindedness about catching the tourist dollar. The streets are lined with chalet after chalet. Just off
the main drag, you'll spot small stands of traditional shacks set on stone stilts to keep out mice (called *mazots;* look for them around Hotel Romantica, or near the river in the Hinterdorf area). You'll also spot a handful of churches, including the big landmark Catholic Church (can't miss it on Bahnhofstrasse) or the smaller English Church (built for the many British mountaineers who have flocked to this region; above and behind the Alpine Museum).

▲**Alpine Museum (Alpines Museum)**—This cute little museum, squeezed into two floors of a creaky old building, is worth a visit on a rainy day. Pick up the free English flier, and twist your way around the stuffed alpine fauna, exploring the history of Zermatt and the Matterhorn. You'll find out why Teddy Roosevelt climbed the famous peak before he was president. The reliefs of the mountain (and surrounding region) offer a helpful topographic perspective. There's a morbid room displaying artifacts found after deadly accidents, and a room dedicated to July 14, 1865—the day the Matterhorn was finally conquered by a team of seven climbers. (Tragically, four of them died on the descent.) Upstairs are a couple of reproductions of rugged mountain-hut interiors, along with exhibits on glaciology, axes, and skiing (8 SF, covered by Swiss Pass—see page 4; July–Aug daily 10:00–12:00 & 15:00–18:00; June and Sept daily 10:00–12:00 & 16:00–18:00; Oct–May Mon–Sat 16:30–18:30, closed Sun; well-signed off Bahnhofstrasse near the big Catholic Church, Tempel 6, tel. 027-967-4100). This fun but expensive museum is cramped in its current quarters; for years, they've been trying to move it to a bigger home, but so far, they lack the funding.

**Goat Parade**—A charming and unusual little event takes place each day in summer, as a small flock of local "blackneck" goats are herded through the center of town on the way to pasture (daily July–mid-Aug at around 9:00, and back home again at about 17:00). These furry goats, which are unique to the surrounding Upper Valais region, have a black head and shoulders, a white rear end, and long horns.

## High-Mountain Excursions from Zermatt

You have four options for lifts up and out of Zermatt:

    1. A cable-car ride to the highest lift station in Europe, **Klein Matterhorn** (not the "real" Matterhorn).

    2. A side spur off the Klein Matterhorn line leading to **Schwarzsee,** with some of the closest views you'll get of the Matterhorn.

    3. An underground funicular, then gondola, then cable car to **Rothorn,** with classic Matterhorn views.

    4. A train up to **Gornergrat,** for good views down on a glacier.

    The first trip leads to a snowy wonderland, year-round skiing slopes, and a cave carved into the ice. The other three will take you to pristine pastures with alpine lakes and Matterhorn vistas.

    **Pass Prices:** If the weather's clear and your pockets are deep, consider springing for a **Peak Pass,** which gives you unlimited access to all of these lifts; unfortunately, the minimum length of the pass is three days, so it's a bad value for a one- or two-day

## Zermatt Area

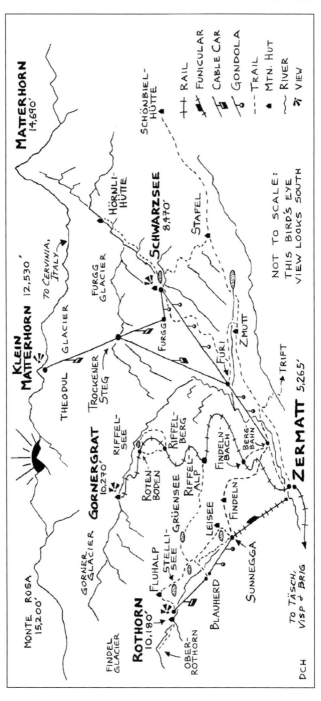

MONTE ROSA 15,200'

MATTERHORN 14,690'

KLEIN MATTERHORN 12,530'

SCHÖNBIEL-HÜTTE

HÖRNLI-HÜTTE

SCHWARZSEE 8,470'

STAFEL

FURGG GLACIER

THEODUL GLACIER

TROCKENER STEG

FURGG

FURI

ZMUTT

TRIFT

TO CERVINIA, ITALY

GORNERGRAT 10,270'

RIFFEL-SEE

RIFFEL-BERG

ROTEN-BODEN

RIFFEL-ALP

FINDELN-BACH

BERG-BAHN

ZERMATT 5,265'

GORNER GLACIER

STELLI-SEE

GRÜENSEE

LEISEE

FINDELN

SUNNEGGA

TO TÄSCH, VISP & BRIG

ROTHORN 10,180'

FLUHALP

FINDEL GLACIER

OBER-ROTHORN

BLAUHERD

NOT TO SCALE: THIS BIRD'S EYE VIEW LOOKS SOUTH

RAIL

FUNICULAR

CABLE CAR

GONDOLA

TRAIL

MTN. HUT

RIVER

VIEW

DCH

## What's What in Zermatt

**Bergbahn:** Lift station in Zermatt for Klein Matterhorn.

**Blauherd:** Upper station on the Sunnegga-to-Blauherd gondola; lower station on the Blauherd-to-Rothorn cable car, with good access to hikes, including the Marmot hike.

**Findelnbach:** Station stop on the train from Zermatt up to Gornergrat.

**Fluhalp:** Small settlement known for its good restaurant, accessible by hike from the Blauherd station.

**Furi:** Upper station on the gondola from Zermatt; lower station on a different gondola to Schwarzsee and a cable car to Trockener Steg.

**Glacier Palace:** Free sight at Klein Matterhorn, a hole dug into a glacier with ice sculptures and exhibits.

**Gorner Glacier:** Glacier that lies between Gornergrat and Klein Matterhorn.

**Gornergrat:** Viewpoint (10,270 feet) between Klein Matterhorn and Rothorn. At the upper station of a train from Zermatt, it offers views of the Gorner Glacier, Matterhorn, and Monte Rosa.

**Gourmetweg** (Gourmet hike): Hike from Sunnegga down to Zermatt via Findeln through larch forests.

**Hinterdorf:** Attractive old quarter of Zermatt by the river with old chalets and traditional *mazots* (buildings on stone stilts).

**Klein Matterhorn:** At 12,530 feet, the highest cable-car station in Europe, with great views of the Alps; always snow-covered.

**Matterhorn:** Mountain peak whose shape forms the textbook example of a "horn," which indicates that bowl-shaped valleys (cirques) were carved into the peak by several glaciers

---

visit (3 days-168 SF, 4 days-192 SF, 5 days-216 SF). The two-day **Panoramic Pass,** available only in summer, is a better deal—including Klein Matterhorn, Schwarzsee, and Rothorn (but not Gornergrat) for 130 SF. You can purchase passes at the TI or at lift stations.

**Individual Tickets:** Buy individual tickets directly at the lift stations. If you go after 14:30, you'll save about 20 percent on individual fares to Klein Matterhorn, Schwarzsee, or Rothorn—always ask (valid mid-June–late Sept). Eurailpass-holders do not get a discount on Zermatt lifts, but Swiss Pass–holders get 50 percent off. For more information, see www.matterhornparadise.ch.

**For Skiers:** Note that the descriptions and lift schedules in this section apply only to the summer season. If you're a skier, ask the Zermatt TI about specifics for your visit.

▲▲**Klein Matterhorn (12,530 feet) and Schwarzsee (8,470 feet)**—To really get your high-altitude high, zip up to the highest

on all sides.

**Monte Rosa:** Tallest peak in Switzerland (15,200 feet).

**Murmelweg** (Marmot hike): Hike from Blauherd down to Sunnegga through marmot habitat.

**Nikolaital Valley:** Deepest valley in Switzerland, with the town of Zermatt at its upper end.

**Riffelalp:** Station stop on the train from Zermatt up to Gornergrat.

**Riffelberg:** Station stop on the train from Zermatt up to Gornergrat.

**Riffelsee:** Lake below the Rotenboden station.

**Rotenboden:** Station stop on the train from Zermatt up to Gornergrat.

**Rothorn:** Upper station of the Blauherd-to-Rothorn cable car, offering the most classic views of the Matterhorn.

**Schwarzsee:** Alpine lake at an elevation of 8,470 feet and a gondola station; the closest you can easily get to the Matterhorn.

**Stafel:** Village along the hike from Schwarzsee down to Furi.

**Stellisee:** Alpine lake along a hike from Blauherd.

**Sunnegga:** Upper station on the underground funicular from Zermatt, and the lower station of the Sunnegga-to-Blauherd gondola; offers good access to hikes.

**Trockener Steg:** Upper station on the Schwarzsee-to-Trockener Steg gondola; lower station on the Trockener Steg-to-Klein Matterhorn cable car.

**Winkelmatten:** Cliff-hanging neighborhood above the Bergbahn lift station in Zermatt.

cable-car station in Europe, at Klein ("Little") Matterhorn. From way up here, the Matterhorn is just one of many cut-glass peaks; this is your best chance for a bird's-eye panorama of the Alps without hiking. But note that some visitors are disappointed by this particular view—since it's not the classic Matterhorn profile on all the postcard racks (for that, head to Rothorn—see below).

You'll reach Klein Matterhorn in three parts. First, you'll take a small, six-seat gondola on a six-minute ride over pretty glacier-carved foothills to the Furi station. (From Furi, you can take a different gondola to Schwarzsee—see below.) Then you'll take a larger cable car up to Trockener Steg. Finally, you'll board the last cable car up to Klein Matterhorn; on the left are great views down on glaciers and across to the Gornergrat train station. All the way up, you'll see plenty of ski lifts and picturesque little chalets. The area around Klein Matterhorn stays snow-covered all year long, making it a popular place for summer skiers.

Once up top, non-skiers have two sightseeing options: the observation deck and the Glacier Palace. As you leave the lift, follow the hall branching to the left, and take the elevator to the **observation deck** (12,200 feet). Exit the elevator and walk another 100 steps up to stunning panoramas. On a clear day, you can see Italy and France (including Mont Blanc, Europe's highest peak).

If you follow the hall from the lift all the way to the end, you'll reach the Panorama Bar and the exit. Go outside and walk a few steps downhill to the low-profile entrance of the **Glacier Palace,** marked *Gletschergrotte* (free, daily 9:00–15:45). This place brags that it's the "highest glacial grotto in the world"—a claim that makes  other high-altitude glacial grottos seethe with envy. The "Palace" is basically a big hole dug into the glacier, allowing you to walk deep inside. As you wander, you'll see ice sculptures (including the Matterhorn and some flowers encased in ice) and some lack-luster exhibits about glaciers, local wines, and "glacier fleas" (a.k.a. "springtails," little bugs that live up here). You can also wriggle into an actual crevasse.

Rather than going all the way to Klein Matterhorn, you could take the gondola from Furi to the alpine lake **Schwarzsee.** While a much lower elevation (8,470 feet), this area is the closest you can get to the Matterhorn (though it lacks the big-picture alpine pan-orama that the other lift excursions offer). You can also do this on your way back down from Klein Matterhorn (when you reach Furi, follow signs to *Schwarzsee* instead of *Zermatt,* 29 SF round-trip for just this segment from Furi to Schwarzsee and back to Furi, 19.50 SF one-way). Several popular hiking trails lead from here back down to the valley (see below).

**Hikes:** There are no hikes from the very top of Klein Matterhorn, since it's covered with snow year-round. The best hike on this series of lifts is at Schwarzsee. From the Schwarzsee lift station, the hike directly down to Furi is quite steep; a longer but easier and more enjoyable route is to hike down to Stafel, then on to Furi, where you can catch the gondola back to Zermatt (or con-tinue to Zermatt on foot). Plan on the better part of a day for this excursion; easier hikes are described below.

**Cost, Hours, Location:** Zermatt to Klein Matterhorn costs 84 SF round-trip (55 SF one-way); Zermatt to Schwarzsee is 43 SF round-trip (28 SF one-way). If you plan to do both, you'll save money by getting the Matterhorn Pass, which includes both Klein Matterhorn and Schwarzsee for 84 SF (which is like getting a trip to Schwarzsee for free). The Matterhorn Pass, sold at the lift station, is a good deal if this combo-trip is the only one you plan to do in the area; the Peak and Panoramic passes mentioned above cover this combo-trip and more.

The trip up to Klein Matterhorn is open daily year-round (generally Sept–June 8:30–16:05, July–Aug 7:00–16:20). The gondola from Furi to Schwarzsee doesn't run off-season (June and Sept–Oct 8:40–16:30, July–Aug 8:00–17:00, closed Nov–May). If the weather's iffy, confirm that the entire route (all the way to Klein Matterhorn) is open before you ascend—upper segments can close if it's too windy. The elevator to the Klein Matterhorn station is about three-quarters of a mile upriver from the train station (simply follow the river, or catch an electric bus marked *Klein Matterhorn* or *Schwarzsee* in front of the Gornergrat train station, across from the main train station).

▲▲**Rothorn (10,180 feet)**—While actually farther away from the famous peak than the other lifts described, Rothorn offers *the* classic Matterhorn view. When Matt Lauer wanted the best shot of the Matterhorn to broadcast on the *Today* show, he came here (and brought along some alphorn players). The passage up to Rothorn has three parts: first, an underground funicular to Sunnegga (eight cold minutes, bring a sweater), then a gondola to Blauherd, and finally, a cable car to Rothorn. All along the way are typical glacial lakes, offering a picturesque foreground for your Matterhorn photos.

**Hikes:** You have plenty of easy options for walking around the lakes up here. Get details at the TI before you ascend. Perhaps the best is the mostly level hike from the Blauherd station, around the Rothorn peak, past the Stellisee, to the restaurant at Fluhalp, then back again. If only the Sunnegga lift is open, it's still worthwhile to go for hiking and a great view of the Matterhorn (14 SF one-way). Try the 40-minute Marmot hike (Murmelweg) up to Blauherd—for a good chance of spotting these fuzzy mountain mammals—or hike from Sunnegga down to Zermatt. The Gourmetweg hike (allow 75 min) takes you through larch forests, and the path is covered with soft, fragrant pine needles.

**Cost, Hours, Location:** 59 SF round-trip, 38 SF one-way. In summer, you can get to Rothorn or Blauherd only from mid-June–mid-Sept (daily 8:00–16:40); the lower segment, to Sunnegga, is open longer (late May–early Oct). The whole shebang is open and ready for skiers in winter. The station for the underground funicular from Zermatt is across the river from the train station, just downstream from the Gornergrat train tracks.

▲▲**Gornergrat (10,270 feet)**—This viewpoint is somewhere between Klein Matterhorn and Rothorn—both geographically and in terms of your experience. A train takes you from Zermatt up to

Gornergrat in about 45 minutes, with stops at other stations along the way (Findelnbach, Riffelalp, Riffelberg, and Rotenboden). On the way up, sit on the right-hand side for good Matterhorn vistas. At Gornergrat, you'll enjoy a sweeping alpine panorama with great views of the Matterhorn (though it's not the perfect profile that you see from Rothorn). What's distinctive about Gornergrat is that it offers the best views of the Gorner Glacier that runs between it and Klein Matterhorn. It also gets you up close to the *other* big mountain in the neighborhood—actually taller than the Matterhorn—the Monte Rosa. This towering behemoth is the highest point in Switzerland (15,200 feet).

**Hikes:** The best option is to take the train from Gornergrat back to the Rotenboden station, where you can enjoy the pretty Riffelsee lake. Then walk down to the Riffelberg station and take the train back into Zermatt.

**Cost, Hours, Location:** 72 SF round-trip, 36 SF one-way. Two or three trains leave hourly mid-June–Sept, starting at about 8:00 and ending at 20:00 (fewer trains and shorter hours off-season, tel. 027-921-4712, www.gornergrat.ch). The Gornergrat train station is right across the street from Zermatt's train station.

**Other Mountain Activities**—Aside from hiking and views, adventure-seeking travelers have even more opportunities for alpine thrills near Zermatt. **Parasailing** is an expensive but unforgettable experience, best at Rothorn (about 190 SF, Air Taxi/Air Born, tel. 027-967-6744, www.paragliding-zermatt.ch). The hills above Zermatt are laced with great **mountain-bike** paths, as well (get specifics from TI).

## SLEEPING

Little Zermatt has more than a hundred hotels—and all of them are expensive. This is a resort town, plain and simple, where even the budget bunks cost big bucks. I've scrutinized the options and presented you with the best deals I could find. I've listed peak summer rates (generally highest July–Aug). You'll pay less at most places in shoulder season, like June and October, and more during ski season (Dec–mid-Jan). When there's a range, higher prices are for busy times, and lower prices are when it's slow (unless otherwise noted). Many hotels close in the shoulder season. Some begin to close as early as mid-April. They reopen beginning in early May, but some stay on vacation until late June. Of course, several hotels are open year-round.

## Sleep Code

**(1.25 SF = about $1, country code: 41)**
**S** = Single, **D** = Double/Twin, **T** = Triple, **Q** = Quad, **b** = bathroom,
**s** = shower only. Unless otherwise noted, credit cards are accepted, English is spoken, and breakfast is included.

To help you sort easily through these listings, I've divided the rooms into three categories, based on the price for a standard double room with bath:

$$$ **Higher Priced**—Most rooms 150 SF or more.
$$ **Moderately Priced**—Most rooms between 110–150 SF.
$ **Lower Priced**—Most rooms 110 SF or less.

**$$$ Hotel Romantica,** a few scenic steps up from the main street, offers 15 rooms in a flower-dappled chalet surrounded by old-fashioned huts. If you like all those huts, consider sleeping in one—this hotel has converted two of them into accommodations, which cost about the same as a standard double room. Both have tiny interiors with two stories: sitting room and modern bathroom downstairs, loft bedroom upstairs. Choose between the very low-ceilinged and rustic hut (cozy and romantic) or the hut with more modern finishes (Sb-78–85 SF, Db-150–200 SF, prices depend on demand and length of stay, tel. 027-966-2650, fax 027-966-2655, www.reconline.ch/romantica, romantica.zermatt@reconline.ch, Cremonini family).

**$$$ Hotel Jägerhof** has 48 homey rooms with new bathrooms and lots of charm. It's a little farther from the center, across the river towards the Klein Matterhorn lift station (Sb-86 SF, Db-172 SF, most doubles have balconies, elevator, Internet access, tel. 027-966-3800, fax 027-966-3808, www.hoteljaegerhofzermatt.ch, jaegerhof@zermatt.ch, Perren family).

**$$ Hotel Tannenhof** is a great value hiding a few steps off the main drag. Its 23 rooms are small, tight, and woody, without much character, but the location is good and the place is well-run (S-50 SF, Sb-80 SF, D-100 SF, Db-120–130 SF, T-120 SF, tel. 027-967-3188, fax 027-967-3173, www.tannenhof.zermatt.info, tannenhof @zermatt.info, Schaller family).

**$$ Hotel Weisshorn** offers 17 basic but comfortable rooms over a restaurant, right in the heart of town. The rooms are nothing special, but the rates are reasonable (S-61 SF, Sb-76 SF, D-106 SF, Db-134–140 SF, T-147 SF, Am Bach 6, tel. 027-967-1112, fax 027-967-3839, welcome@weisshorn-zermatt.ch).

**$ Hotel Bahnhof,** with 17 tidy rooms (and three dorm rooms) and some worn carpeting, could be Zermatt's best value. The basement features a relaxing lounge, dining room, and guests' kitchen. It's professionally run and conveniently located across the street from the train station (dorm bed-33 SF, S-65 SF, Sb-76 SF, D-90 SF, Db-104 SF, Qb-180 SF, no breakfast, laundry facilities, lockers, tel. 027-967-2406, fax 027-967-7216, www.hotelbahnhof .com, welcome@hotelbahnhof.com).

$ Zermatt's official **Youth Hostel** is sparkling new, looking over town from a perch high above the river. It's slick and super-modern, with key cards and bathrooms inside most rooms (or down the hall). The hostel is an especially good deal since the rates include breakfast and dinner—a real plus in expensive Zermatt (prices per person: in 8-bed room-47 SF, in 6-bed room with bath-room-52 SF, in 4-bed room without bathroom-57 SF, in 4-bed room with bathroom-60 SF, in twin D-60 SF, in D with one big bed-75 SF, in Db with one big bed-85 SF, all rates include sheets, Internet access in lobby, no age limit, no curfew, Staldenweg 5, tel. 027-967-2320, fax 027-967-5306, www.youthhostel.ch/zermatt, zermatt@youthhostel.ch). From the station, take the bus marked *Winkelmatten* to the Luchre stop (3.20 SF); the hostel is a steep hike up from there (follow the signs with the international hostel symbol).

$ **Matterhorn Hostel** is a more low-key, easygoing place overlooking the river. Their mission is to provide cheap beds in an expensive town, and they deliver. The floor plan is claustropho-bic, with not an inch of wasted space: 10 dorm rooms with graffiti decor are upstairs; the lounge and showers are in the basement; and a tiny Internet nook (free access) is tucked under the spiral staircase (bed in 6- to 8-bed dorm-33 SF, in 4-bed room-38 SF, in 2- or 3-bed room-43 SF, 4 SF/night discount if you stay four or more nights, breakfast-7 SF, towel rental-2 SF, closed 10:00–16:00, or 11:00–16:00 in peak season, Schluhmattstrasse 32, tel. 027-968-1919, fax 027-968-1915, www.matterhornhostel.com, info @matterhornhostel.com). It's a 10-minute walk from the train sta-tion on the way to the Klein Matterhorn lift station, right on the river. Take the bus to the Bergbahn/Klein Matterhorn lift station (2.50 SF), then take the elevator up to the cable-car station and walk one block down the hill.

# EATING

Zermatt's restaurants are as expensive as its hotels. If there's a cheap snack bar–type place here, I didn't find it (unless you count McDonald's). There are several handy bakeries and grocery stores for buying a picnic, and the streets are lined with restaurants featuring garish signs, interchangeable menus, and high prices. Simply wander down the main drag (Bahnhofstrasse) and pick the place that looks best. I ate well without breaking the bank at the two eateries listed below. They're obvious and touristy (with Japanese signs outside), but the prices and food are acceptable—and I noticed several locals mixed in with the out-of-towners.

**Whymper-Stube,** named for the first brave soul to conquer the Matterhorn, specializes in cheese dishes—that means fondue (about 25 SF per person) and raclette (8 SF per serving, two servings is enough for most). While American and Japanese tourists photograph each other eating fondue, six barstools in the corner are warmed by local regulars (kitchen open daily 12:00–14:00 & 18:00–22:00 but fondue and cold dishes are served daily 11:00–22:00, friendly staff, on Bahnhofstrasse, on the right just before the big church, tel. 027-967-2296).

**Restaurant du Pont** claims to be the oldest restaurant in town. Note that it doesn't claim to be the best. Its ambience—with low ceilings and Swiss folk sayings on the walls—beats the food (fondue for two-44 SF, *Rösti* for about 15 SF, open daily, on Bahnhofstrasse at end of square with big Catholic Church, tel. 027-967-4343).

*Grocery Stores:* **Co-op** is across from the train station (Mon–Sat 8:15–19:00, Sun 16:00–19:00). **Migros** is across from the tennis courts on Hinterdorf Strasse (Mon–Fri 8:30–12:30 & 14:00–18:30, Sat 8:30–18:30, Sun 16:00–18:30).

# TRANSPORTATION CONNECTIONS

Zermatt is at the end of the dead-end Nikolaital Valley, which you can only reach on a private rail line. This train, operated by the Matterhorn Gotthard Railway (www.mgbahn.ch), connects Zermatt to Brig hourly (80 min, second-class fares: 33 SF one-way, 66 SF round-trip, covered by Swiss Pass, Eurailpass not valid or discounted). In Brig, the Matterhorn Gotthard Railway station is just across the street from the Swiss Rail station. From here, you can easily connect to destinations all over the country. If you're coming from or going to Lausanne or Montreux, you'll save time changing trains in Visp, which lies between Zermatt and Brig (Zermatt–Lausanne via Visp: hourly, 3 hrs).

**From Brig by Train to: Bern** (at least hourly, 1.5 hrs), **Zürich** (at least hourly, 2.75 hrs, some with transfer in Bern), **Lausanne** (hourly, 1.75 hrs; faster to transfer in Visp), **Interlaken** (at least hourly, 1.75 hrs, transfer in Spiez), **Luzern** (at least hourly, 3 hrs, transfer in Bern).

**By Glacier Express to Eastern Switzerland:** In summer, four trains depart Zermatt daily and arc scenically on high-altitude tracks over the middle of Switzerland to the east. All of these Glacier Express trains go through **Chur** (6 hrs) and some continue to **Davos** or **St. Moritz** (8 hrs total to either). In winter, there's one train per day in each direction. These trains do not require a transfer in Brig. For more details, see the Scenic Rail Journeys chapter on page 253.

# APPENZELL

Welcome to cowbell country. In the moo-mel-low and storybook-friendly Appenzell region, you'll find the warm, intimate side of the land of staggering, icy Alps. Savor Appenzell's cozy, small-town atmosphere.

Appenzell is Switzerland's most traditional region...and the butt of jokes because of it. Entire villages meet in town squares like Appenzell town's Landsgemeindeplatz to vote (an event featured on most postcard racks). Until 1989, the women of Appenzell couldn't vote on local issues. But lately, the region has become more progressive. In 2000, its schools were the first to make English—rather than French—mandatory.

A gentle beauty blankets this region of green, rolling hills, watched over by the 8,200-foot peak of Mount Säntis. As you travel, you'll enjoy an ever-changing parade of finely carved chalets, traditional villages, and cows moaning, "Milk me." While farmers' bikini-clad daughters make hay, old ladies with scythes walk the steep roads, looking as if they just pushed the Grim Reaper down the hill. When locals are asked about Appenzell cheese, they clench their fists as they answer, "It's the best." (It is, without any doubt, the smelliest.)

If you're here in late August or early September, there's a good chance you'll get in on (or at least have your road blocked by) the ceremonial procession of flower-bedecked cows and whistling herders in formal, traditional costumes. The festive march

---

### Appenzell Card

If you stay for several days in the region, you'll receive a card from your hotel that covers all local train trips (on trains operated by Appenzeller Bahnen, as far as St. Gallen), free rides on three different cable cars, free admission to local museums, a free ride on the Kronberg luge, a discounted rate on the PubliCar shuttle service (3 SF), and more. The card is free of charge, but only if you're staying for a minimum period of time (possibly three nights, more likely four nights in 2007). Hotels and some smaller pensions offer the card; ask when you reserve.

---

down from the high pastures is a spontaneous move by the herding families, and when they finally do burst into town (a slow-motion Swiss Pamplona), locals young and old become children again, running joyously into the streets.

## Planning Your Time

On a two-week trip through Switzerland, save a day for the Appenzell region. This pastoral area offers a good first look at Switzerland—but would be an anticlimax after the rugged Berner Oberland or Matterhorn. If you have only a week or less in Switzerland, skip the subtle charms of Appenzell and head instead for the high mountains.

In the Appenzell region, I prefer overnighting up on Ebenalp. But the accommodations are a little rustic for some travelers, who prefer the comfort of hotels and *Zimmer* in Appenzell town.

## Getting Around Appenzell

By car, Appenzell is a breeze. Using public transportation, you can easily get to Appenzell town and Ebenalp, but connections beyond those destinations are sparse.

The center of the region is Appenzell town, connected by **train** with Wasserauen (near Ebenalp; hourly except 2/hr during rush hour, 20 min) and Herisau (same train, opposite direction, 40 min). From Herisau, bigger trains depart hourly for St. Gallen (20 min), Zürich (1.5 hrs), and Luzern (2 hrs). The Appenzell–Herisau train also stops at Urnäsch (20 min). Regional **buses** connect towns several times a day; for schedules, check with the TI or the post office.

Appenzell's shuttle service, **PubliCar**, takes passengers to locations—such as Stein—not serviced by buses (for Appenzell to Stein, figure about 8.40 SF, or 3 SF with Swiss Pass or Appenzell Card). To reserve, inquire at the TI or call 0800-553-060.

### Appenzell Region

# Appenzell Town

In this traditional town, kids play "barn" instead of "house," while Mom and Dad watch yodeling on TV. The town center is a painfully cute pedestrian zone that delights tourists born to shop.

## ORIENTATION

### Tourist Information

The TI is on the main street at Hauptgasse 4 (May–mid-Oct Mon–Fri 9:00–12:00 & 13:30–18:00, Sat–Sun 10:00–12:00 & 14:00–17:00; mid-Oct–April Mon–Fri 9:00–12:00 & 14:00–17:00, Sat–Sun 14:00–17:00; tel. 071-788-9641). For information on the greater Appenzell region, call 071-898-3300 or check out www .appenzell.ch.

## Arrival in Appenzell Town

From the train station, take Postgasse up to Postplatz, then follow Poststrasse up to Hauptgasse where you'll run directly into the TI. If arriving by car, park in the lot by the brewery. Walk across the bridge and veer right onto the main drag, Hauptgasse, which leads through town to Landsgemeindeplatz. You'll see a large church on your right with the TI and Appenzeller Folklore Museum just past it.

## Helpful Hints

**Blue Monday:** Appenzell's museums are closed, but hiking and biking are good any day the sun shines. Luges run every day—rain, snow, or shine.

**Internet Access:** Use the computers at the library on the church square (Tue–Wed 14:00–17:00, Thu 14:00–16:00, Fri 17:00–20:00, Sat 9:30–11:30, closed Sun–Mon).

**Post Office:** It's in front of the train station.

**Bike Rental:** Rent wheels at the train station (20 SF/half-day, 25 SF/day, return bike by 18:30). Most hotels rent bikes or can arrange a rental for you. For mountain bikes, go to the bike shop of **Elmar Neff** (20 SF/half-day, 30 SF/day, Mon–Fri 7:30–12:00 & 13:15–18:30, Sat 7:30–12:00 & 13:15–16:00, closed Sun, Hauptgasse 58, tel. 071-787-3477).

# SIGHTS AND ACTIVITIES

## In Appenzell Town

▲**Folk Music**—Free folk music concerts take place every Thursday (mid-June–mid-Oct) at 18:30 in City Hall, and every Wednesday at 20:00 at Hotel Hof Weissbad. You can also sometimes find live music at local restaurants—ask at the TI.

▲**Appenzeller Folklore Museum (Appenzeller Volkskunde Museum)**—The folk museum next to the TI provides an excellent look at the local cow culture. Ride the elevator to the sixth floor and work your way down through living rooms and displays of traditional costumes, art, and crafts (7 SF, covered by Swiss Pass—see page 4, ask to borrow English handbook, April–Oct daily 10:00–12:00 & 14:00–17:00; Nov–March Tue–Sun 14:00–17:00, closed Mon).

**Modern Art Museums**—Appenzell has two modern/contemporary-art exhibits in great settings. Each one costs 9 SF, but a 15-SF combo-ticket gets you into both (also covered by Swiss Pass—see page 4, Tue–Fri 10:00–12:00 & 14:00–17:00, Sat–Sun 11:00–17:00, closed Mon, www.museumliner.ch): **Museum Liner** is a silver-clad modern building right behind the train tracks (Unterrainstrasse 5, tel. 071-788-1800) and **Kunsthalle Ziegelhütte** is at Ziegeleistrasse 14 (tel. 071-788-1860).

## Appenzell Town

- ❶ Hotel Adler
- ❷ Restaurant Hotel Traube
- ❸ To Haus Lydia & Gästezimmer Koller-Rempfler
- ❹ Hotel/Rest. Appenzell
- ❺ Restaurant Marktplatz
- ❻ Gasthaus Hof
- ❼ To Gasthaus Freudenberg

## Hiking

Appenzell makes a fine home base for hiking. The TI has several flyers about easy walks in the region. I've recommended two possibilities below.

**Appenzell to Wasserauen**—This two-hour walk, which takes you to the foot of the Ebenalp cable car (see page 201), begins near the parish church in Appenzell, and leads along the creek through meadows and forests. The path is well-marked. Once you reach Wasserauen, you can take the cable car up to Ebenalp, or simply hop on the train back to Appenzell.

**Barefoot Walk (Barfussweg)**—This 90-minute path between Jakobsbad and Appenzell offers a surprising and unusual experience...yes, with your shoes off. The path leads over meadows, through creeks, and on stretches of asphalted road. Two specially designed fountains along the way will refresh your feet. The path follows the philosophy of 19th-century therapist Sebastian Kneipp, who sought to treat medical conditions with water of different temperatures and pressures. For details on the hike, ask the TI.

## Near Appenzell Town

▲**Stein**—The town of Stein has the **Appenzell Showcase Cheese Dairy** (Appenzell Schaukäserei, Mon–Fri 9:00–19:00, Sat–Sun 9:00–19:00, cheesemaking normally 9:00–14:00, tel. 071-368-5070, www.showcheese.ch). It's fast, free, smelly, and well-explained by the 15-minute English video and free English brochure with cheese recipes (ask for the brochure at the cheese counter). The lady at the cheese counter loves to cut it so you can sample it. The dairy also sells yogurt and cheap boxes of cold iced tea. The restaurant serves powerful cheese specialties.

Stein's great **folk moo-seum** (Appenzeller Volkskunde Museum) is next door. With old-fashioned cheesemaking demonstrations, peasant houses, fascinating embroidering machinery, cow art, and folk-craft demonstrations, this museum is fun, but not worth the 7 SF if you've seen the similar folk museum in Appenzell town (covered by Swiss Pass—see page 4, Mon 13:30–17:00, Tue–Sat 10:00–12:00 & 13:30–17:00, Sun 10:00–17:00, Nov–March no demos but museum open, tel. 071-368-5056, www.appenzeller-museum-stein.ch).

Without a car, the only way to get to Stein is by PubliCar (see "Getting Around Appenzell," page 192).

▲**Urnäsch**—This appealing one-street town has Europe's cutest museum. The Appenzell Museum, on the town square, brings this region's folk customs to life. Warm and homey, it's a happy little honeycomb of Appenzeller culture. A 20-minute movie in English explains four of the major regional festivals (6 SF, covered by Swiss Pass—see page 4, April–Oct daily 13:30–17:00, Nov–March open only if you call ahead, winter entry fee-20 SF for groups smaller than 4, guided tour-20 SF plus entry, good English brochure, tel. 071-364-2322).

**Kronberg Luge Ride (Bobbahn)**—Between Appenzell and Urnäsch, in the village of Jakobsbad, you can enjoy this bobsled ride roughly spring through fall. Each sled has seatbelts and can carry two people. Two handles at the side allow you to control the speed: push to accelerate, pull to brake. Respect the *Bremsen!* signs—which suggest when to brake—and don't come too close to the sled in front of you. Since they're mounted on rails, the sleds can run in rainy or snowy weather. One ride lasts about seven minutes (9 SF per sled for adults, 6 SF per sled for kids, 81 SF/10 rides, 153 SF/20 rides, 270 SF/40 rides, multiple-ride cards shareable, daily 9:00–18:00, until 17:00 in fall, closed off-season, tel. 071-794-1289, www.kronberg.ch).

## SLEEPING

Sleep in touristy Appenzell town if you want comfort—but for a rustic, high-altitude thrill, I love the low-tech, no-shower dorms at Ebenalp (see page 201). Appenzell town is small, and the hotels are central. All hotels offer the Appenzell Card (described on page 192) to guests who stay a specified number of nights. The *Zimmer* are six blocks from the town center.

**$$$ Hotel Adler,** above a delicious café/bakery with the best croissants in town (daily 7:30–19:30, closed Wed Nov–June), offers two kinds of rooms: modern or traditional Appenzeller (with lamps imitating the traditional local headwear). Helpful Franz Leu, proud to be an Appenzeller, has turned the halls and traditional rooms of his hotel into a museum of regional art and culture (Sb-80–105 SF, Db-170–190 SF, suite-240–260 SF, elevator, Herr Leu can arrange bike rentals for guests, between TI and bridge on Adlerplatz, tel. 071-787-1389, fax 071-787-1365, www.adlerhotel .ch).

**$$$ Restaurant Hotel Traube,** two blocks from the TI, is cozy, with seven tastefully decorated rooms above a fine restaurant. The friendly Hunziker family has welcomed guests here for three generations (Sb-85–110 SF, Db-150–170 SF, Marktgasse 7, tel. 071-787-1407, fax 071-787-2419, www.hotel-traube.ch, info @hotel-traube.ch). Don't confuse Hotel Traube ("grape" in German) with the similarly named Hotel Taube ("dove") nearby.

---

### Sleep Code

**(1.25 SF = about $1, country code: 41)**
**S** = Single, **D** = Double/Twin, **T** = Triple, **Q** = Quad, **b** = bathroom, **s** = shower only. Unless otherwise noted, credit cards are accepted, English is spoken, and breakfast is included.

To help you sort easily through these listings, I've divided the rooms into three categories, based on the price for a standard double room with bath:

$$$  **Higher Priced**—Most rooms 100 SF or more.
 $$  **Moderately Priced**—Most rooms between 50–100 SF.
  $  **Lower Priced**—Most rooms 50 SF or less.

---

*Zimmer*: To experience a pleasant Swiss suburban neighborhood, consider the following: **$$ Haus Lydia,** a six-room, Appenzell-style home filled with tourist information and a woodsy folk atmosphere, is on the edge of town and includes a garden and a powerful mountain view. Its crisp, renovated rooms are a fine value if you have a car or don't mind a 20-minute walk from the town center (Sb-60 SF, Db-94 SF, great breakfast; east of town over bridge, past Mercedes-Esso station, take next right and go 600 yards, Eggerstandenstrasse 53; tel. 071-787-4233, fax 071-367-2170, www.hauslydia.ch, contact@hauslydia.ch, friendly Frau Mock-Inauen). She also rents a roomy apartment by the week (Db-82–89 SF, breakfast extra). **$$ Gästezimmer Koller-Rempfler** is a family-friendly, five-room, traditional place several blocks before Haus Lydia, a little closer to the town center (Db-90–95 SF, Tb-120 SF, cash only, Eggerstandenstrasse 9, tel. 071-787-2117, niklauskoller @hotmail.com).

## EATING

The Appenzeller beer is good, famous, and about the only thing cheap in the region. Ideally, eat an early dinner up on Ebenalp at **Berggasthaus Aescher,** even if you're staying in Appenzell town (see page 192; last lift down at 19:00 July–mid Sept, 18:00 mid-May–June and mid-Sept–mid-Oct, 17:00 mid-Oct–mid-May).

In Appenzell town, many good restaurants cluster around Landsgemeindeplatz, where residents gather the last Sunday of each April to vote on local issues by show of hands. (The rest of the year, it's a parking lot.) The first four restaurants are within a block of this town square, just a few blocks up Hauptgasse from the TI (away from the bridge). All restaurants are open daily from about 8:00 to 24:00 unless otherwise noted.

**Restaurant Hotel Traube** offers pleasant dining indoors or out, with fresh ingredients and a wide selection of traditional Swiss and Appenzeller meals (20-SF plates, Tue–Sun 9:00–24:00, closed Mon, veggie options, see "Sleeping," above).

**Hotel Appenzell** serves fine salads and vegetarian dishes for about 22 SF (meat dishes also available, at corner of square closest to TI, tel. 071-788-1515).

**Restaurant Marktplatz** is filled with locals playing cards in a traditional Appenzeller atmosphere. It prides itself on being the first non-smoking restaurant in Appenzell (closed Thu, on small parking lot across from Landsgemeindeplatz fountain, walk around white building with horse head, tel. 071-787-1204).

**Gasthaus Hof** offers a huge variety of specials, including cheese dishes that give the place an unforgettable aroma (fondue-20–24 SF, healthy salad dishes, meat "vitamin corner" meals-15–33

SF, cold meals-15–22 SF, next to Hotel Appenzell, tel. 071-787-4030, www.gasthaus-hof.ch).

**Gasthaus Freudenberg** has reasonably priced meals and great views over Appenzell from outdoor tables. It's a 15-minute uphill walk from the town center (healthy *Fitnessteller*-20–35 SF, veggie dishes-12–17 SF, summer grill special-20–34 SF, closed Wed and Nov; go under train station, turn right, and follow yellow signs to Freudenberg; tel. 071-787-1240).

## TRANSPORTATION CONNECTIONS

**From Appenzell Town by Train to: Wasserauen** (near Ebenalp, described below; 1–2/hr, 20 min), **Zürich** (2/hr, 1.75 hrs with change in Gossau, 2.25 hrs with change in St. Gallen), **Chur** (hourly, 2.5 hrs, transfer in St. Gallen), **Luzern** (hourly, 2.75 hrs, change in Herisau), **Bern** (hourly, 3.25 hrs, transfer in Gossau), **Interlaken** (hourly, 4.5 hrs, 2 transfers including Gossau or St. Gallen and Zürich or Bern), **Lausanne** (2/hr, 5 hrs, transfer in Gossau or St. Gallen), **Munich** (3/day, 4.5 hrs, transfer in St. Gallen).

### Route Tips For Drivers
**Appenzell to Interlaken/Gimmelwald (120 miles):** It's a three-hour drive from Appenzell to Ballenberg (Swiss Open-Air Folk Museum), and another hour from there to the Gimmelwald lift. Head out of Appenzell town following signs to Herisau/Wattwil. A few scenic miles out of town, in Stein, *Schaukäserei* signs direct you to the Appenzell Showcase Cheese Dairy (see page 196). From there, head for Wattwil. Drive through Ricken into the town of Rapperswil. Once you're in Rapperswil, follow the green signs to Gotthard/Zürich over the long bridge, then continue south, following signs to Einsiedeln and Gotthard. You'll go through the town of Schwyz, the historic core of Switzerland that gave its name to the country.

From Brunnen, one of the busiest, most impressive, and most expensive-to-build roads in Switzerland wings you along the Urnersee. It's dangerously scenic, so stop at the parking place after the first tunnel (on right, opposite Stoos turnoff), where you can enjoy the view and a rare Turkish toilet. Follow signs to Gotthard through Flüelen, then take the autobahn to Luzern, vanishing into a long tunnel that should make you feel a little better about your 40-SF autobahn sticker. Exit at Stans-Nord (signs to Interlaken). Go south along the Alpnachersee toward Sarnen. Continue past Sarnensee to Brienzwiler before Brienz. A sign at Brienzwiler will direct you to the Freilichtmuseum Ballenberg (Swiss Open-Air Folk Museum)/Ballenberg Ost. You can park here, but I prefer the west entrance, a few minutes down the road near Brienz.

From Brienzwiler, take the autobahn to Interlaken along the south side of Lake Brienz. Cruise through the old resort town, down Interlaken's main street. From the Interlaken East train station (Ost Bahnhof), drive past the cow pasture—with a great Eiger–Jungfrau view on your left and grand old hotels, the TI, post office, and banks on your right—to the Interlaken west train station (West Bahnhof) at the opposite end of town. If stopping in Interlaken, park there. Otherwise, follow signs to Lauterbrunnen. Gimmelwald is a 30-minute drive and a five-minute cable-car ride away (see Gimmelwald chapter).

**Side-Trip Through Liechtenstein:** If you must see the tiny and touristy country of Liechtenstein, take this 30-minute detour: From Feldkirch, drive south on E77 (follow *FL* signs) and go through Schaan to Vaduz, the capital. Park near City Hall, post office, and TI. Passports can be stamped (for 2 SF) in the TI (Mon–Fri 9:00–17:00, Sat–Sun get your stamp at the info desk behind City Hall, tel. from Switzerland 00423/232-1443). Liechtenstein's banks (open until 16:30) sell Swiss francs at uniform and acceptable rates. The prince looks down on his 4-by-12-mile country from his castle, a 20-minute hike above Vaduz (castle interior closed to visitors, but offers a fine view; catch trail from Café Berg). To leave Liechtenstein, cross the Rhine at Rotenboden, immediately enter the autobahn, drive north from Sevelen to the Oberriet exit, and check another country off your list.

# Ebenalp

This cliff-hanging hut is a thin-air alternative to Appenzell town. Ride the lift from Wasserauen, five miles south of Appenzell town by road or rail line, to Ebenalp (5,380 feet). On the way up (left side), you'll get a sneak preview of Ebenalp's cave church and the cliffside boardwalk that leads to the guest house. From the top, you'll enjoy a sweeping view all the way to Lake Constance (Bodensee).

Leaving the lift, take a 12-minute hike through a prehistoric cave (slippery and dimly lit—hold the railing, and you'll soon return to daylight), past a hermit's home (a tiny museum, always open) and the 400-year-old Wildkirchli cave church (hermit monks lived there 1658–1853), to a 170-year-old guest house built precariously into the cliff. Originally a hut housing farmers, goats, and cows, it evolved into a guest house for pilgrims coming to the monks for spiritual guidance. Today, Berggasthaus Aescher welcomes tourists, offering cheap dorm beds and hot, hearty plates of *Rösti* (see "Sleeping and Eating," below).

The region is a hit with hikers who make the circuit of mountain hotels. There are 24 hotels, each a day's hike apart. All originated as alpine farms. Of these, Berggasthaus Aescher is the oldest and smallest.

From Ebenalp's sunny cliffside perch, you can almost

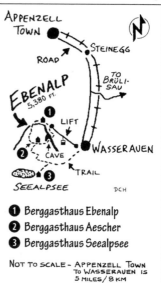

**Ebenalp**

❶ Berggasthaus Ebenalp
❷ Berggasthaus Aescher
❸ Berggasthaus Seealpsee

NOT TO SCALE – APPENZELL TOWN TO WASSERAUEN IS 5 MILES / 8 KM

hear the cows munching on the far side of the valley. Only the paragliders, like neon jellyfish, tag your world as 21st-century. In the distance, nestled below Säntis peak, is the isolated Seealpsee lake. The one-hour hike down to the lake is steep but pleasurable (take left at first fork below guest house).

**Getting There:** The Ebenalp lift runs at least twice hourly (18 SF up, 25 SF round-trip, half-price with Swiss Pass, July–mid-Sept 7:30–19:00, mid-May–June and mid-Sept–mid-Oct 7:30–18:00, mid-Oct–mid-May 9:00–17:00, closed for 2 weeks in both April and Nov for maintenance, free and reportedly safe parking at lift, free hiking brochure, tel. 071-799-1212, www.ebenalp.ch).

## SLEEPING AND EATING

There's no reason to sleep in Appenzell town. The Ebenalp lift, across from the tiny Wasserauen train station, is a few minutes' drive or a 10-minute train ride south.

**$$$ Berggasthaus Ebenalp** sits atop the mountains just above the lift. Its refurbished rooms are booked long in advance for Saturdays, but are otherwise empty (4-, 6-, or 8-bed dorms with comforters-33 SF per person; D-112 SF, coin-op shower, tel. 071-799-1194, Sutter family).

**$$$ Berggasthaus Seealpsee** is on the idyllic alpine lake

Seealpsee, a hike up a private road from the Wasserauen train station (loft dorm beds with sheets-30 SF, S-50 SF, Sb-65 SF, D-100 SF, Db-130 SF, showers-2 SF, tel. 071-799-1140, fax 071-799-1820, www.seealpsee.ch, berggasthaus@seealpsee.ch, Dörig family).

**$ Berggasthaus Aescher** (see photo on page 200) promises a memorable experience. The 170-year-old house has only rainwater and no shower. Friday and Saturday nights sometimes have great live music, but are often crowded and noisy, with up to 45 people, and parties going into the wee hours. Monday through Thursday, you'll normally get a small, woody dorm to yourself. The hut is actually built into the cliff; its back wall is the rock itself. From the toilet, you can study this alpine architecture. Sip your coffee on the deck, sheltered from drips by the gnarly overhang 100 feet above. The guest book goes back to 1940, there's a fun drawer filled with an alpine percussion section, and the piano in the comfortable dining/living room was brought in by helicopter. Claudia can show you rock-climbing charts. For a strenuous 45-minute predinner hike, copy the goats: Take the high trail toward the lake, circle clockwise up toward the peak and the lift, then hike down the way you originally came (dorm bed-35 SF, includes breakfast and comforter, no towels or showers available, dinner-14–22 SF, no credit cards but euros and traveler's checks accepted, closed Nov–April, 12 min by steep trail below top of lift, tel. 071-799-1142, www.aescher-ai.ch, reserve by phone, run by Claudia and Beny Knechtle-Wyss and their five children—Bernhardt-age 22, Reto-21, Lukas-18, Lilian-17, and Dominik-15—plus three pigs, 35 sheep, three donkeys, 20 rabbits, and two dogs).

# LAKE GENEVA
## and FRENCH SWITZERLAND

Lake Geneva, in the southwest corner of the country, is the Swiss Riviera. Separating France and Switzerland, the lake is surrounded by Alps and lined with a collage of castles, museums, spas, resort towns, and vineyards. Its crowds, therefore, are understandable. This area is so beautiful that Charlie Chaplin and Idi Amin both chose it as their second home.

French is the predominant language at Lake Geneva ("Lac Léman" in French, "Genfersee" in German). To establish a better connection with the locals, see the "French Survival Phrases" in the appendix, *s'il vous plaît*.

Skip the big, dull city of Geneva; instead, sleep in fun, breezy Lausanne. Explore the romantic Château de Chillon and stylishly syncopated Montreux. The French Swiss countryside offers up chocolates, vineyards, Gruyère cheese, and a fine folk museum.

## Planning Your Time

On a quick trip, you can get a good overview of Lake Geneva's highlights in a day or less. Lausanne makes the best home base. If

you're in a hurry, make a beeline for Château de Chillon. With more time, lazily float your way between Lausanne and Chillon on a scenic boat cruise, and get lost in Lausanne's old town and unique museums (the Olympics and Art Brut museums are best). If you have a car, explore some of the countryside options to the north (handiest if you're driving between here and Bern or Murten; see "French Swiss Countryside," page 221).

## Getting Around Lake Geneva

**Trains** easily connect towns along Lake Geneva. Take the faster Direct trains if you're going between larger cities, such as Lausanne or Montreux, or the slower Régional or REV trains if you're heading for a smaller destination, such as Château de Chillon or Villeneuve (check the TV screens in the station for *Direct*, *Régional*, or *REV* to find the right train).

**Boats** carry visitors to all sights of importance. Daily boat trips (4/day in each direction May–Sept, fewer off-season) connect Lausanne with Vevey (60 min, 16.40 SF), Montreux (80 min, 21.20 SF), and Château de Chillon (90 min, 22.60 SF). First class costs about a third more and gets you passage on the deck up top, where you should scramble for the first-come, first-served chairs. You can sail free with a Eurailpass or Swiss Pass, but it uses up a travel day of a flexipass; to avoid giving up a day, take an afternoon cruise on the same day you arrive by train in the morning. (Tel. 0848-811-848, www.cgn.ch.)

The short cruise between Montreux and Château de Chillon is fun. The pretty town of Vevey gives you the most scenic 60-minute boat ride from Lausanne and a 30-minute ride from Chillon, and makes an enjoyable destination. Evian, immediately across from Lausanne, is the French spa town famous for its mineral water. Boats go hourly (30 min, passport required) filled with people ready to enjoy its spa and tour its mineral-water facilities.

# Lausanne

Lausanne is the most interesting city on the lake, proudly dubbing itself the "Olympic Capital" (it's been home to the International Olympic Committee since 1915). Amble along the serene lakefront promenade, stroll through the three-tiered, colorful old town, explore the sculptures at Olympic Park, and visit the remarkable Collection de l'Art Brut. Take a peek at the Gothic Cathedral and climb its tower for the view.

The Romans founded Lausanne on the lakefront—but with the fall of Rome and the rise of the barbarians, the first Lausanners fled for the hills, establishing today's old town. The Roman site was abandoned (scant ruins today), but in the age of tourism, the

# Lausanne

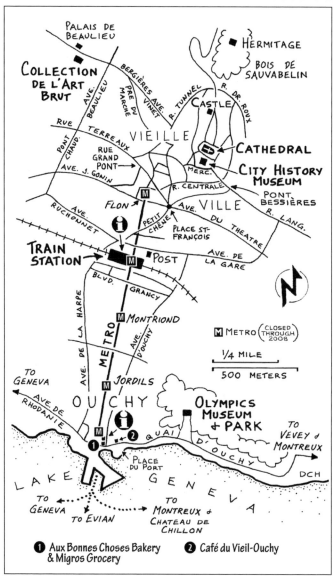

❶ Aux Bonnes Choses Bakery & Migros Grocery

❷ Café du Vieil-Ouchy

waterfront—a district called Ouchy—thrived. So the city has a design problem that goes back 1,500 years: two charming zones separated by a nondescript residential/industrial urban mess.

Thankfully, the waterfront and the old town are easily linked by a steep and handy Métro line.

Lausanne has the energy and cultural sophistication of a city larger than its 125,000 people (300,000 in greater Lausanne). A progressive city government (with a mayor from the Green Party) that subsidizes art and culture, and a university with plenty of foreign students carbonate the place with a youthful spirit. That spirit shows itself in Lausanne's notoriety as a haven for inline skating and skateboarding.

## ORIENTATION

The tourist's Lausanne has two parts: 1) The lakefront **Ouchy** (oo-shee), with good restaurants and the Olympics Museum; and 2) the **old town,** or *vieille ville* (vee-yay veel), with creaky Old World charm and other fine museums, directly uphill from the lake. The train station is located between the two neighborhoods, and everything's connected by the Métrobus (while the funicular Métro is under construction through Dec 2008).

Be careful to pronounce Lausanne correctly (loh-ZAHN), and don't confuse it with Luzern.

### Tourist Information

Lausanne has two TIs: one is in the train station (daily 9:00–19:00) and the other is at the lakefront Ouchy Métro stop, in a blue pavilion (daily April–Sept 9:00–20:00, Oct–March 9:00–18:00, tel. 021-613-7373, www.lausanne-tourisme.ch).

At either TI, ask about **walking tours** in English (10 SF, free for students and seniors, 1.5 hrs, May–Sept Mon–Sat usually at 10:00 and 15:00, in English only if there's a guide and demand, meet in front of City Hall at Place de la Palud, call 021-321-7766 to confirm time and language). Also, check if any free **concerts** are scheduled at the cathedral.

### Arrival in Lausanne

**By Train:** The train station is midway between the old town and the lakefront. This sounds inconvenient, but the Métrobus takes you either up to the old town or down to the lake in about two minutes, with departures every seven minutes. For most recommended hotels, take the Métrobus to the Montbenon stop (or, when the funicular Métro is reopened, take it to the Lausanne-Flon stop). Cross the street and walk on the pedestrian bridge until Rue du Grand-Pont. Cross again and you're in the old town. It seems confusing only until you do it. A **taxi** from the train station to your hotel runs about 15 SF.

**By Car:** Drivers headed for the old town should exit the autoroute at Lausanne Centre, following signs to *Centre* and *Riponne* (the downtown underground parking garage). If you want the lakefront, take the freeway to Ouchy (where it ends), and you'll find a big pay lot. Coming from Montreux, the smaller road (follow blue signs) leads you along the lakeshore directly into Lausanne.

## Helpful Hints

**Market Days:** On Wednesday and Saturday mornings, produce stands fill the pedestrian streets of the old town. Saturday is flea market day on Place de la Riponne.

**Internet Access:** Get online at **Quanta** (daily 9:00–24:00, across street from train station and above McDonald's at Place de la Gare 4) or **Cyberland** (daily 9:00–24:00, in old town, just over pedestrian walkway at Rue du Grand-Pont 10).

**Laundry: Quick-Wash** is well-run and handy to the train station (Mon–Fri 7:30–20:30, Sat–Sun 9:00–20:30, self-service only, change machine, good English instructions, below train station at Boulevard de Grancy 44, at corner with Passage de Montriond, tel. 079-449-3761).

**Bike Rental:** Lausanne, along with Zürich and Bern, now offers free bikes. Get a bike at **Lausanne Roule,** at Place de la Riponne (April–Oct daily 7:30–21:30; from the train station, head uphill on the main street, passing the stop for buses #5, #6, and #8; leave picture ID and 20-SF deposit, mobile 076-411-8378, www.lausanneroule.ch). Don't use a bike in town—use it to explore the lakeside, vineyards, and villages. It's a three-hour lakefront pedal to Montreux.

You can rent a bike at Lausanne's train-station baggage office (23 SF/half-day, 31 SF/day, 5 SF less with Eurailpass or Swiss Pass, daily 8:30–19:00, reserve ahead on weekends, tel. 051-224-2162, www.rentabike.ch). Ask about dropping off the bike at a different train station (7 SF extra, limited to a few stations).

In Ouchy, **Delacombaz Sport & Action** rents bikes and inline skates, but has erratic opening times (bikes cost 10 SF first hour, then 2 SF every 15 min, next to Ouchy Métro station, tel. 079-606-2761, www.delacombaz.ch).

**Late-Night Groceries:** The train station has a grocery store open long hours (daily 6:00–24:00).

## Getting Around Lausanne

Lausanne is steeper than it is big. A five-stop funicular Métro system connects the lakefront (stop called **Ouchy,** with boat landing) with the train station **(Gare-CFF)** and the upper part of Lausanne (*vieille ville* or *centre ville,* stop called **Lausanne-Flon**).

While the Métro is under construction (probably until Dec 2008), a Métrobus connects the various stops as follows: From the lakeside Ouchy stop, the Métrobus heads uphill, stopping first at the Gare-CFF stop at the train station, then continuing to Montbenon, which is right behind the Lausanne-Flon stop (runs every 7 min, 6:00–24:00).

Your ticket choices are 1.80 SF (good for three city bus stops or two Métrobus stops), 2.40 SF (good for 1 hour of buses and Métrobus), or 7 SF (24-hr pass for buses and Métrobus). Buy bus tickets from the TI, ticket windows, or ticket machines; the machines, while modern-looking, don't give change (dropping in a big coin is a costly mistake). For buses, buy tickets before boarding from the white-and-yellow machine at the bus stop. Your Eurailpass is not good on public transportation in Lausanne (except lake boats—see above).

**Taxis** are pricey—figure 15 SF for a short ride.

# SELF-GUIDED WALK

## A Stroll Through Old Lausanne

There's no way to see this town without lots of climbing. Locals are used to it (enjoy the firm legs). This self-guided stroll introduces you to Lausanne's charming old town *(vieille ville)*. It's a big counterclockwise circle, taking you from the Church of St. Francis up to the cathedral (and castle just beyond), then more or less back to the starting point. While you can begin this walk at the Church of St. Francis (skip down to the "Place St-François" section, below), most visitors will arrive at the Lausanne-Flon Métro station.

**Rue du Grand-Pont:** From the Métrobus Montbenon stop (behind the Métro funicular's Lausanne-Flon stop), walk to the high pedestrian bridge. This leads to the main thoroughfare through the city, Rue du Grand-Pont. Orient yourself from midway across the pedestrian bridge (Passerelle du Flon). Below you stretches Flon—until recently, a down-and-dirty industrial zone. Now, the old warehouses are renovated and throb at night with trendy bars, restaurants, theaters, and discos. The recommended Louis Vinothèque is immediately below (see page 218). The only reminder of the mills that once churned here is the name of the

# Old Lausanne Walk

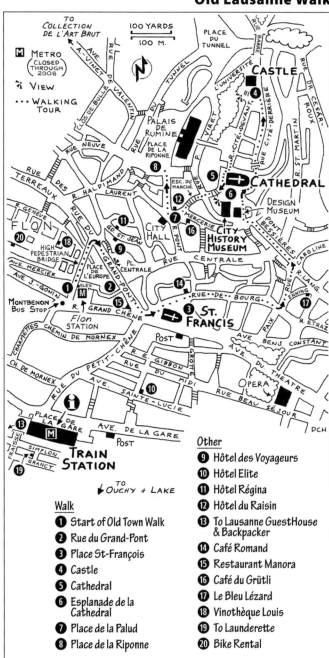

**Walk**
1. Start of Old Town Walk
2. Rue du Grand-Pont
3. Place St-François
4. Castle
5. Cathedral
6. Esplanade de la Cathedral
7. Place de la Palud
8. Place de la Riponne

**Other**
9. Hôtel des Voyageurs
10. Hôtel Elite
11. Hôtel Régina
12. Hôtel du Raisin
13. To Lausanne GuestHouse & Backpacker
14. Café Romand
15. Restaurant Manora
16. Café du Grütli
17. Le Bleu Lézard
18. Vinothèque Louis
19. To Launderette
20. Bike Rental

hottest dance club in town: MàD (stands for "Moulin à Danse," or "Dance at the Mill," Rue de Genève 23, tel. 021-340-6969). The huge construction site is a new Métro line—a super-high-tech job that will zip from Flon to the top of town (due for completion by the end of 2008).

• *Walk to where the pedestrian bridge hits the busy street. Head for the green copper spire of the Church of St. Francis (to the right). As you walk along Rue du Grand-Pont, enjoy fine views of the cathedral on your left; you'll see the Métro construction below on your right.*

**Place St-François:** The Church of St. Francis marks the town's center and transportation hub, with the grand post office and banks on the right. The church is Gothic, founded by Franciscans in the 13th century. But in 1536, it went Protestant—and was gutted of decorations. Later, a grand Baroque organ was installed. (Note that bus #2 goes from here to the Collection de l'Art Brut—see page 213.)

Head uphill (passing to the left of the church) up Lausanne's pedestrianized "Fifth Avenue," Rue de Bourg—home to the finest shops. When the street ends, turn left, continuing uphill and over the bridge toward the cathedral. The railing on the bridge is psychologically designed to discourage suicidal people from leaping. While Switzerland seems to have it all, life here can be stressful—or even depressing. In fact, between Christmas and New Year's, social workers are stationed on this bridge with soup and coffee to counsel and comfort the distraught people who congregate here, contemplating ending it all.

Walking toward the cathedral, you'll notice that Lausanne's old town—filled with administration buildings, offices, schools, and apartments—is subdued compared to most other European old towns, which are lively with lots of eateries.

• *Climb past the cathedral (we'll come back) and continue up the cobbled Rue Cité-Derrière to the summit of the old town, where you'll find the...*

**Castle:** Lausanne's castle is closed to the public, but the views are free. The statue celebrates Major Davel, a local William Tell–like hero. In 1536, the Bernese swept into this region (Canton Vaud) and took over, converting it to Protestantism and ruling it for two centuries. In 1723, Davel's heroic attempt to free his country ended in his decapitation. Only in 1798 was Napoleon able to free Vaud. In 1803, the region entered the Swiss Federation.

Walk downhill (toward the big, blocky cathedral tower). Halfway to the church on your right is the **Cantonal High School** (called "gymnasium" here). One of two great buildings from the Bernese period, this was built as a school to train a new kind of Christian leader after the Reformation. This was the first French-speaking Protestant school (c. 1590)—predating similar schools

in Geneva (which, under the leadership of John Calvin, was the center of the Swiss Reformation).

• *Continue to the...*

**Cathedral:** This is the biggest church in Switzerland, at more than 300 feet long. Go inside (free, April–Sept Mon–Fri 7:00–19:00, Sat–Sun 8:00–19:00, Oct–March daily until 17:30; tower and welcome center open April–Sept Mon–Sat 8:30–11:45 & 13:30–18:00, Sun 14:00–18:00, Oct–March daily until 17:00).

This is an **Evangelical Reform Church,** meaning that it belongs to the tradition of early Protestant reformer John Calvin—and like its founder, it remains very strict (members aren't allowed to dance, or even to have buckles on their shoes). Iconoclasm, the removal of religious symbols, suited the Calvinists well (see page 101). The once-ornate cathedral, originally dedicated to Mary, was cleared of all its statues and decorations. Its frescoes were plastered over, and its fine windows were trashed and replaced by plain ones (the colored windows were added in the 20th century).

The **pipe organ** is American-made by Fisk, a Boston company that won the commission. Locals love their organ and figure its cost (four million SF) was money well spent. There are many free concerts here, generally held on Friday evenings. Look back at its 6,700 pipes—the "stiletto in Oz" design represents the wings of angels. (The old pipes now toot in a church in Gdańsk, Poland.)

The **rose window** in the south transept has the church's only surviving 13th-century glass. The rest of the glass dates from the early 1900s. The north transept has some dreamy blue Art Nouveau scenes. Below the rose window (and just to the left) is the Mary Chapel—once the most elaborate in the church. In 1536, it was scraped clean of anything fancy or hinting of the Virgin Mary. Look at the bits of surviving original paint, and imagine the church in its colorful glory six centuries ago.

The **Painted Portal** (on the right side of the nave, the church's main entrance in the Middle Ages) is being renovated. It's remarkable for its painted Gothic statuary: Jesus overseeing the coronation of Mary. The panels below illustrate Mary's death and Assumption.

For a grand view of nearly the entire lake—and lots of Alps—climb the 225-step **tower** (2 SF, April–Sept Mon–Sat 8:30–11:30 & 13:30–17:30, Sun 14:00–17:30, Oct–March daily until 16:30).

As the city was originally built of wood, it burned down several times. Since the Middle Ages, a **watchman** has lived in the church's tower. His job: to watch for fires and to call out the hours.

The city is made of stone today—so there's little danger of fire—and people now sport watches of their own. Nevertheless, Lausanne's night watchman, the last one of his kind in Switzerland, still calls out the hours. Each night on the hour, from 22:00 to 2:00 in the morning, he steps onto his balcony and hollers. His first announcement: "I am the watchman. I am the watchman. We just had 10 o'clock. We just had 10 o'clock."

• *Back outside, belly up to the fine viewpoint immediately in front of the cathedral.*

**Esplanade de la Cathedral:** On a clear day, look behind the spire of the Church of St. Francis to see the French Alps (Chamonix and Mont Blanc, over there somewhere, are just out of sight). Evian, the famous French spa town, is immediately opposite Lausanne. On the right, the soft, rolling Jura Mountains, which mark the border of France and Switzerland, stretch all the way from Lake Geneva to Germany.

• *Notice that the City History Museum is across the square from the cathedral (see "Sights," below). Now's a good time to visit. Then go from the cathedral to...*

**Place de la Palud and Place de la Riponne:** A covered wooden staircase (Escaliers du Marché) leads down from the cathedral. You'll pass Le Barbare ("The Barbarian"), a pub famous for its fine hot chocolate, and the recommended Café du Grütli (see "Eating," page 217). Place de la Palud (pictured on page 206) is marked by its colorful Fountain of Justice (with the blindfolded figure of Justice holding her sword and scales...commanding fairness as she stands triumphantly over kings and bishops). Imagine the neighborhood moms sending kids here to fetch water in the days before plumbing. The City Hall is the other fine Bernese building in town (1685, on right). Uphill from City Hall, Rue Madeleine leads to our last stop, the vast and modern Place Riponne. The Palais du Rumine (former university), overlooking the square, now houses a collection of museums (all of which you may skip).

• *Your tour is over. Now enjoy some of Lausanne's fine museums.*

## SIGHTS AND ACTIVITIES

### In the Old Town

▲▲**City History Museum**—Facing the cathedral, this museum traces life in Lausanne from Roman times to the present with many fascinating displays. You'll see exhibits on music (from the time of Bach), the Reformation and its roots, the cathedral before Calvin, the Bernese epoch (Protestant, 1536–1798), and the beginnings of the modern era.

The highlight for many is the 1:200-scale model of Lausanne in the 17th century (based on an engraving from 1638—see copy on wall). You're viewing the town from the perspective of the lakefront district of Ouchy, with the Church of St. Francis in the foreground. You can see river valleys that have since been obliterated by the modern city. The little water mills mark the birthplace of industrial Flon. While the city's walls are long gone, its vineyards survive. (When you enter the museum, request to hear the 18-minute recorded English commentary on the model, and they'll book you a time.) Adjacent rooms show the construction of the Grand-Pont and an interesting collection of historic photos (8 SF includes helpful audioguide, covered by Swiss Pass—see page 4, Tue–Thu 11:00–18:00, Fri–Sun 11:00–17:00, closed Mon, Place de la Cathédrale 4, tel. 021-315-4101, www.lausanne.ch/mhl).

▲▲**Collection de l'Art Brut**—This well-displayed, thought-provoking collection shows art produced by untrained artists, many labeled (and even locked up) by society as "criminal" or "insane." Read thumbnail biographies of these outsiders (posted next to their works), and then enjoy their unbridled creativity.

In 1945, the artist Jean Dubuffet began collecting art he called "Brut"—untrained, ignoring rules, highly original, produced by people "free from artistic culture and free from fashion tendencies." In the 1970s, he donated his huge collection to Lausanne, which now displays 30,000 works by 500 artists—loners, mavericks, fringe people, prisoners, and mental-ward patients. Dubuffet said, "The art does not lie in beds ready-made for it. It runs away when its name is called. It wants to be incognito" (8 SF, covered by Swiss Pass—see page 4, Tue–Sun 11:00–18:00, closed Mon except July–Aug; bus #3 from station, direction: Bellevaux, stop: Beaulieu; or bus #2, direction: Desert, stop: Jomini; each bus stops within 100 yards of museum, Avenue des Bergières 11, tel. 021-315-2570, www.artbrut.ch).

## In Ouchy, Lausanne's Waterfront

The charm of Lausanne lies on its lakefront. The handy Métrobus connects Ouchy with the train station and the old town every seven minutes. Within 100 yards of the Ouchy Métro stop, you'll find everything (except shopping opportunities and a sandy beach): TI, bike rental, boat dock, the start of the lakeside promenade, and a park. The place is lively from Easter through October, and dead otherwise.

A big C-shaped **weathervane** stands on the breakwater. Identify which of the four winds is blowing by lining the "C" up with semicircle cutouts in the four granite pillars (crouch). By matching the "C" with the pillar that creates a perfect "O," you learn the prevailing wind. Nearby, notice the solar-powered **Aquarel tour boats,** which run quietly, smoothly, slowly, and green (7 SF, 30-min tours, www.lausanne.ch/aquarel). Lausanne's current mayor, from the Green Party, is making environmentalism popular. Speaking of green, this city has more green space per inhabitant (300 square feet) than nearly any city in Europe.

▲▲**Olympic Park and Museum**—This beautiful park and high-tech museum celebrate the colorful history of the Olympic Games. The expensive but excellent museum is a thrill for Olympics

buffs—and plenty of fun for those of us who just watch every two years. Given the informative English descriptions and many thrilling video clips to see, plan on spending two hours here (15 SF, family-35 SF, covered by Swiss Pass—see page 4, audio-guide-3 SF, May–Sept daily 9:00–18:00, Oct–April closed Mon; from Ouchy Métro stop, turn left and walk 5 min to Quai d'Ouchy 1, then ride the outdoor rolling staircase; tel. 021-621-6511, www.olympic.org). As you enter, note the time of the next six-minute introductory video—it's worth watching.

The museum celebrates Pierre de Coubertin, who in 1894 founded the International Olympic Committee and restarted the games after a 1,500-year lapse. The Olympic spirit is one of peace. Coubertin acknowledged that to ask nations to love each other was naive, but to ask them to respect one another is a realistic and worthy goal.

The ground floor traces the history of the Games, from ancient Greek artifacts to a century's worth of ceremonial torches. Upstairs are medals and highlights from each Olympiad, and historic, well-described equipment used for various Olympic events (find Jesse Owens' spiky jumping shoe from 1936—a design that led to the first Adidas; Carl Lewis' shoes from L.A. in 1984; the Michael Jordan–signed basketball from the 1992 Barcelona "Dream Team"; and Cathy Freeman's shoes from the 2000 Sydney games). At the top of the museum, you'll find a lakeview terrace and swanky restaurant (healthy *plat du jour* for 19 SF).

In the basement is a 3-D theater (called "Salle Nagano"; note the posted movie times as you buy your ticket, and plan accordingly) and an extensive film archive of suspenseful moments in the history of the Games (roughly 5 min each, 450 to choose from). Your ticket includes two of these mini-documentaries—if enthralled, you can buy three more for 5 SF.

Pauper athletes can enjoy much of the complex for free. Walk through the spiraling core of the complex for a sense of the action. Then enjoy the park's Olympic flame (in front of museum), athletic monuments, and lake views (take escalator to top, ask in museum for free brochure explaining sculptures, and wander back down to lake; avoid the café in the park).

## Near Lausanne: Lakeside and Vineyard Excursions on Foot or Bike

A delightful promenade stretches in both directions from the Ouchy Métro stop. The best easy **walk** is east (left as you face the lake, 75 min to Lutry). From Lutry, you can catch the train back to Lausanne (hourly, 8 min). If you hike, bring the TI's *Discover the Terraces of Lavaux* flier (describes several hikes, including this one). The trail is marked with blue plaques explaining in English the flora, fauna, and culture you're enjoying.

Picturesque **vineyards** abound along the lake near Lausanne. My favorite plan: a 5- to 10-minute train ride to Chexbres or Grandvaux, then a walk through the villages—following the yellow signs—toward Lutry for stunning views of Lake Geneva. From Lutry, hop the train back to Lausanne (hourly, 8 min).

The best **bike path** goes west (after sharing with cars for half a mile, the trail leaves the road and hugs the shoreline all the way to Morges). You'll pass Vidy (with its Roman ruins—just foundations, free), the headquarters of the International Olympic Committee (not open to the public), lots of sports facilities, and finally just peaceful lakefront parkland stretching to Morges (about 6 miles away, easy return by boat or train).

## SLEEPING

Lausanne hotels are expensive. The only cheap doubles are at the Lausanne GuestHouse. The Régina, Voyageurs, and Raisin hotels are in the old town (take the Métrobus up to the Montbenon stop, cross the street and walk on the pedestrian bridge, cross Rue du Grand-Pont, walk up Rue Pichard, and take the first right). The Elite and Lausanne GuestHouse are closer to the train station.

**$$$ Hôtel des Voyageurs,** part of the Comfort chain, has 33 predictable rooms across the street from Hôtel Régina (below). It lacks Régina's charm, but it's in an equally good location (Sb-140 SF, Db-185 SF, Tb-205 SF, about 10 percent cheaper July–Aug and on weekends, non-smoking rooms, elevator, Internet access, Rue Grand Saint-Jean 19, tel. 021-319-9111, fax 021-319-9112, www.voyageurs.ch, hotel@voyageurs.ch).

---

## Sleep Code

**(1.25 SF = about $1, country code: 41)**

**S** = Single, **D** = Double/Twin, **T** = Triple, **Q** = Quad, **b** = bathroom, **s** = shower only. Unless otherwise noted, credit cards are accepted, English is spoken, and breakfast is included.

To help you sort easily through these listings, I've divided the rooms into three categories, based on the price for a standard double room with bath:

$$$ **Higher Priced**—Most rooms 170 SF or more.
$$ **Moderately Priced**—Most rooms between 100–170 SF.
$ **Lower Priced**—Most rooms 100 SF or less.

---

**$$$ Hôtel Elite,** run by the Zufferey family, is on a quiet, leafy, residential street just above the train station. Its 33 rooms are pleasant and modern (Sb-140 SF, Db-180–250 SF depending on size and view, Tb-210–265 SF, non-smoking rooms, elevator; from station, cross the street and go uphill around McDonald's, take first right to Avenue Sainte-Luce 1; tel. 021-320-2361, fax 021-320-3963, www.elite-lausanne.ch, info@elite-lausanne.ch).

**$$ Hôtel Régina,** on a steep pedestrian street immersed in old-town charm, is a find: 36 comfy, remodeled rooms, hospitable hosts (Michel and Dora), and a great location (Sb-128 SF, Db-168 SF, Tb-208 SF, suites-165–325 SF depending on number of people, 10 percent less Fri–Sun if staying at least 2 nights, cheaper in winter, non-smoking rooms, Internet access, Rue Grand Saint-Jean 18, tel. 021-320-2441, fax 021-320-2529, www.hotel-regina.ch, info@hotel-regina.ch).

**$$ Hôtel du Raisin,** an old, old, Old World dive with no English and dingy, faded furnishings, has 12 rooms in a fine but noisy location on a lively square in the old town (S-55 SF, Ss-70 SF, D-120 SF, Ds-140 SF, attached restaurant with sidewalk café, Place de la Palud 19, tel. & fax 021-312-2756).

**$ Lausanne GuestHouse & Backpacker** has got to be one of Switzerland's best hostels. This elegant, century-old house, which offers dorm beds and private rooms, turns its back on the train tracks. All of its rooms overlook the lake on the quiet side (bunk in 4-bed dorm-35 SF, S-80 SF, Sb-90 SF, D-88 SF, Db-100 SF, no breakfast, no smoking, no curfew, reception open 7:30–12:00 & 15:00–22:00, Internet access, lockers, laundry, bike rental, kitchen, garden, parking; 5-min walk from train station: leave out the back by track 9, go down the stairs and turn right to Epinettes 4; tel. 021-601-8000, www.lausanne-guesthouse.ch, info@lausanne-guesthouse.ch).

# EATING

## In Ouchy

The lakeside Ouchy district is *the* place to relax. Immediately in front of the Métro stop is a fun zone with fountains, parks, playgrounds, promenades, and restaurants. The only good, budget eating option is a picnic with the local office gang on any of the many inviting benches or scenic lakeside perches. **Aux Bonnes Choses** is a small bakery with a heart for picnickers, offering good sandwiches, salads, pastries, and drinks to go. This is infinitely better than the lousy kiosk options in the waterfront park (daily 6:30–19:00, 5-SF salads Mon–Fri only, left as you exit Métro, Place de la Navigation 2, tel. 021-617-8857). Another good spot to shop for your picnic is the **Migros** grocery store on Avenue de Rhodanie (daily 8:00–21:45).

**Café du Vieil-Ouchy,** charming and reasonably priced, seems a bit out of place among all the fancy and expensive restaurants. It offers traditional Swiss cuisine, including cheese fondue and hash brown–like *Rösti* (16–22-SF entrées, Thu–Mon 11:30–14:30 & 17:30–22:00, closed Tue–Wed, Place du Port 3, tel. 021-616-2194).

## In the Old Town

**Café Romand** is a classic Swiss brasserie—plain, smoky, and filled with natives enjoying hearty French Swiss home cooking. Local students, pensioners, and businessmen sit under old-time photos in this characteristic yet simple eatery like they own the place (20–25-SF plates, Swiss white wines by the glass and carafe—see list of what bottles are open behind bar, daily specials, closed Sun, hiding behind the Pizza Hut at Place St-François 2, tel. 021-312-6375).

**Restaurant Manora** is part of a modern, self-service chain offering a quick and healthy series of buffet lines where you grab what looks good: hot meals, salads (4.90-SF, 7.90-SF, and 9.40-SF plates), fancy fruit juices, desserts, and so on (Mon–Sat 6:45–22:45, Sun 7:45–22:45, where Rue du Grand-Pont hits Place St-François).

**Café du Grütli** (named for the meadow where Switzerland was born) offers typical French Swiss cuisine near Place de la Palud. Choose from three tempting areas to eat: outside on a cozy cobbled lane; ground-floor, circa-1850, Parisian-bistro style; or upstairs, with antlers and the ambience of a 13th-century castle. As the owner's family is into hunting, you'll find game on the menu (20–30-SF plates, Mon–Sat 9:00–14:30 & 18:00–23:00, closed Sun, Rue de la Mercerie 4, tel. 021-312-9493).

**Le Bleu Lézard** has great French cuisine, a typical French atmosphere, and a trendy clientele that appreciates its candlelit, bohemian interior and fun outdoor porch (20-SF salads, good veggie options, daily 7:00–24:00, open later on weekends, smoky interior, jazz bar downstairs, Rue Enning 10, tel. 021-321-3830).

**Vinothèque Louis** is primarily a wine bar, where you can choose from 40 different wines available by the glass (and many more by the bottle). To order appetizers, see their short "tapas" menu. To make your wine choice easier, take advantage of their clever color code, classifying wines by their character. Browse among the many bottles (take-away prices and drink-in prices marked), and take your favorite into the bistro. The ground floor has the *vinothèque* and bistro, with tasty and beautifully presented Mediterranean dishes (25–35-SF plates, 17–22-SF daily specials, strong on vegetables). Locals sip their wine and hang out on the big modern sun terrace (daily 10:00–1:00 in the morning; below the pedestrian bridge, down the elevator, across from Flon Métro stop at Place de l'Europe 9; tel. 021-213-0300). The top floor has the expensive Restaurant Gastronomique (65–120-SF fixed-price meals).

## TRANSPORTATION CONNECTIONS

**From Lausanne by Train to: Montreux** (4/hr, 25 min), **Château de Chillon** (hourly, 35 min on REV train), **Geneva** (3/hr, 40 min), **Bern** (2/hr, 70 min), **Murten** (hourly, 90 min, change in Fribourg, Neuchâtel, or Payerne), **Basel** (hourly, 2 hrs, change in Bern or Biel), **Interlaken** (hourly, 2.25 hrs, transfer in Bern; or go via Golden Pass scenic route, with transfers in Montreux and Zweisimmen—see Scenic Rail Journeys chapter on page 253), **Luzern** (hourly, 2.5 hrs; more frequent with transfer in Olten; or go via Golden Pass route—see Scenic Rail Journeys chapter), **Zürich** (2/hr, 2.5 hrs), **Zermatt** (hourly, 3 hrs, change in Visp—not Brig, unless connecting to Glacier Express), **Lyon** (almost hourly, 2.75–3.25 hrs, transfer in Geneva), **Chamonix** (every 2 hrs, 2.5 hrs, change in Martigny and Le Châtelard-Frontière), **Paris** (6/day, 4 hrs), **Milan** (6/day, 3.25–4 hrs). Train info: toll tel. 0900-300-3004.

# Château de Chillon

This medieval castle, set wistfully at the edge of Lake Geneva, is a ▲▲▲ joy. Remarkably well-preserved, it has never been damaged or destroyed—always inhabited, always maintained. The Savoy family (their seal is the skinny red cross on the towers) enlarged it to its current state in the 13th century, when this was a prime location—at a crossroads of a major trade route from England and France to Rome.

Château de Chillon (shee-yon) was the Savoys' fortress and

residence, with four big halls (a major status symbol) and impractically large lakeview windows (because their powerful navy could defend against possible attack from the water). But when the Bernese invaded in 1536, the castle was conquered in just two days, and the new governor made Château de Chillon his residence (and a Counter-Reformation prison). With the help of Napoleon, the French-speaking people on Lake Geneva finally kicked out their German-speaking Bernese oppressors in 1798. The castle became—and remains—the property of the Canton of Vaud. It's been used as an armory, a warehouse, a prison, a hospital, and a tourist attraction. Rousseau's writings first drew attention to the castle, inspiring visits by Romantics such as Lord Byron and Victor Hugo, plus other notables, including Dickens, Goethe, and Hemingway.

Follow the free English brochure from one fascinating room to the next. Enjoy the castle's tingly views, dank prison, battle-scarred weapons, simple Swiss-style mobile furniture, and 700-year-old toilets (Rooms 15 and 22). Bonivard's Prison (Room 7) is named for a renegade Savoy who was tortured here for five years (lashed to the fifth column from the entrance). When the Romantic poet Lord Byron came to visit, Bonivard's story inspired him to write *The Prisoner of Chillon,* which vividly recounts a prisoner's dark and solitary life ("And mine has been the fate of those/To whom the goodly earth and air/Are bann'd, and barr'd—forbidden fare"; full text available in the gift shop). You can still see where Byron scratched his name in a column (third from entrance, covered by glass). The chapel (Room 18) uses projectors to simulate the original frescoes. Models in room 24 explain the construction of the castle. Remember the grand views from the lakeside windows? Notice the small slits facing the road on the landside (courtyard, Room 25), which are more practical for defense. The 130-step climb to the top of the keep (Room 32) isn't worth the time or sweat. Stroll the patrol ramparts, then curl up on a windowsill to enjoy the lake.

**Cost, Hours, Information:** 10 SF, covered by Swiss Pass (see page 4), April–Sept daily 9:00–18:00, shorter hours off-season, easy parking, tel. 021-966-8910, www.chillon.ch. Guided tours in English are usually available for individuals at 11:30 and 15:30 for an extra 6 SF (mid-June–mid-Sept).

**Getting to Château de Chillon:** The castle sits at the eastern tip of Lake Geneva, about 20 miles east of Lausanne (and about a mile east of Montreux).

From Lausanne, you can connect to the castle using a combination of various methods: train, bus, boat, and hike.

The hourly **REV train** (direction: Villeneuve, 35 min, 10.40 SF) takes you directly to the station at Veytaux-Chillon, a few minutes' walk along the lake (ideal for picnicking) from the castle.

The faster and more frequent **Direct train** whisks you to Montreux (2/hr, 20 min, 9.80 SF), where you transfer to a bus. From the Montreux station, cross Avenue des Alpes and go down the stairs. Cross the street and find the blue bus stop on your right, where you can hop **bus #1** to Château de Chillon (3 SF, direction: Villeneuve, stop: Chillon; buy tickets from machine on board, first select the fare, which is A for *Adulte*, then the destination: zone 1). You can also **hike** the one mile from Montreux to Château de Chillon.

To return to Lausanne, simply reverse the directions (catch the train from the Veytaux-Chillon station back to Lausanne—trains leave hourly at :26 past the hour—or hop the bus from Château de Chillon to Montreux, direction: Vevey, stop: Escaliers de la Gare, take handy escalator up to the station and catch the train the rest of the way to Lausanne).

A slower but more scenic route is by **boat** between Château de Chillon and Montreux or Vevey, connecting to Lausanne with trains. For a longer trip, sail one-way between Château de Chillon and Lausanne (90 min). True *See*farers would prefer a round-trip (see "Getting Around Lake Geneva," page 204).

# Montreux

This expensive resort has a famous jazz festival each July. The lakeside promenade takes you along parks, palm trees, *crêperies,* ice-cream stands, modern sculptures, and the Friday produce market. In the center, meet the statue of Freddie Mercury, who had strong bonds with Montreux. His band, Queen, bought the local Mountain Recording Studios in 1978.

The wonderful Montreux **TI** has tons of brochures and extensive information about the region, excursions, and a list of moderately priced rooms in the center (Mon–Fri 9:00–18:00, Sat–Sun 10:00–17:00, tel. 084-886-8484, www.montreux-vevey.com). In summer, you can take a 90-minute **walking tour** of the city (10 SF, April–Sept Wed–Sat at 10:00, no tours Sun–Tue or Oct–March, meet in front of TI, call TI to confirm).

For Internet access, try **Cyberworld,** located in the Hollywood cinema complex a few blocks north of the TI (3 SF/15 min, Mon–Fri 12:00–23:00, Sat 13:00–23:00, Sun 15:00–22:00, Grand-Rue 90).

For an easy way to see several sights in the French Swiss countryside, including the town of Gruyères and the chocolate factory in Broc, take a ride from Montreux on the **Chocolate Train** (described on page 222).

If you're driving from Montreux to Lausanne, consider visiting the **Corniche de Lavaux.** This rugged, sometimes frightening Swiss Wine Road swerves through picturesque towns and the stingy vineyards that produce Lake Geneva's tasty but expensive wine. From Montreux, go west along the lake through Vevey, following blue signs to *Lausanne* along the waterfront and taking the Moudon/Chexbres exit. Be sure to explore some of the smaller roads. **Hikers** can take the boat to Cully and explore on foot from there.

## SLEEPING

### In and near Montreux

**$$ Hôtel Elite** has seen better days, but its 23 rooms are clean and refurbished, with new bathrooms and double-paned windows that keep out noise. You can have your breakfast on the little terrace in back. The modest buffet reminds you that you're in the French part of Switzerland, where breakfast consists of a cup of coffee and a croissant (Sb-80–110 SF, Db-140–170 SF, elevator, 8-min walk from train station on main street, Avenue du Casino 25, tel. 021-966-0303, fax 021-966-0310, www.montreux.ch/elite, hotel .elite@vtx.ch).

**$ Montreux Youth Hostel** is on the lake, a 10-minute stroll north of Château de Chillon (dorm bed-31.50 SF, D-88 SF, non-members pay 6 SF extra, 14.50-SF meals available; check-in 17:00–22:00; Passage de l'Auberge 8, tel. 021-963-4934, fax 021-963-2729, www.youthhostel.ch/montreux, montreux@youthhostel.ch).

**$ Backpackers Riviera Lodge,** centrally located on the main square in nearby Vevey, offers cheap beds in a 19th-century townhouse on the lake. Guests receive the Riviera Card, which covers transportation and up to 50 percent off on various museums, including Château de Chillon (dorm bed-27 SF, D-88 SF, breakfast-8 SF, kitchen, Internet access, 3-min walk from station, Place du Marché 5, tel. 021-923-8040, www.rivieralodge.ch, info@rivieralodge.ch).

# French Swiss Countryside

The sublime French Swiss countryside is sprinkled with crystal-clear lakes, tasty chocolates, smelly cheese, and sleepy cows. If you're traveling between Murten, Lausanne, and Interlaken (see map on page 222), take time for a few of the countryside's sights, tastes, and smells.

## French Switzerland

## Getting Around the French Swiss Countryside

This region is ideal by car. By public transportation, it's more difficult. Cross-country **buses** use Fribourg and Bulle as hubs: Bulle–Gruyères (2/day, 15 min), Fribourg–Bulle (hourly, 30 min). The **train** is definitely the best bet between Bulle and Gruyères (hourly, 7 min), and is also handy between Bulle and Broc (hourly, 10 min).

For an easy all-day side-trip from Lake Geneva, consider hopping on the **Chocolate Train** in Montreux. The train carries either panoramic or old-time "belle époque" coaches. It leaves from Montreux at 9:35 and begins by following the same route as the Golden Pass (see Scenic Rail Journeys chapter). You'll be served coffee and a croissant while enjoying the scenic ride. At 10:45, the train stops to visit the Gruyères cheese factory (described on page 224). From there, a bus takes you up to the picturesque old town of Gruyères for a visit to the castle (included) and some time for lunch (on your own). Then the journey continues to the town of Broc, where you'll tour the Cailler Chocolate Factory (including a film and chocolate tasting; described below). The train returns to Montreux at 17:52 (85.40 SF, first class only, 25 SF reservation fee with first-class Swiss Pass, June–Oct Mon and Wed, departs from Montreux at 9:35, tel. 0900-245-245, from other countries dial 41-840-245-245, www.mob.ch).

For a **tour** of the region, consider GTK Tours, based in Bern (see page 95).

## Bulle

On your way to the Fribourger Alps, stop in the town of Bulle, which has a charming, distinctly French ambience. On Tuesdays, the weekly produce-and-craft market fills the center of town. The market gets bigger and more colorful in summer, when many vendors wear their traditional costumes and sell handmade crafts. The castle on the main square is closed to the public; it houses the police department.

The **TI** is located between the castle and the train station; follow the blue signs (Mon–Fri 9:00–12:00 & 13:30–18:30, Sat 9:00–12:00, closed Sun, tel. 084-842-4424, www.info-bulle.ch).

▲▲**Musée Gruèrien**—The museum, a two-minute walk through the castle grounds, is worth a visit. Somehow this unassuming little town built a refreshing, cheery folk museum that manages to teach you all about life in these parts and leave you feeling very good (6 SF, free English guidebook, Tue–Sat 10:00–12:00 & 14:00–17:00, Sun 14:00–17:00, closed Mon, tel. 026-912-7260, www.musee-gruerien.ch). When it's over, the guide reminds you, "The Golden Book of Visitors awaits your signature and comments. Don't you think this museum deserves another visit? Thank you!"

## Cailler Chocolate Factory

To fight their image of being a boring "old grannies" chocolate, Cailler invited famous designers to reinvent the brand. Wonderful new chocolate creations resulted. The winner of the competition was Parisian Jean Nouvel (the architect responsible for Luzern's Culture and Conference Center). Nouvel also designed imaginative displays for the factory. Visitors wander through chocolate-dark corridors while films and slide shows explain the production and shipment of chocolate. In one room, you can taste almonds or hazelnuts, crumble a cocoa bean in the palm of your hand, and touch a block of cocoa butter. In the tasting room, friendly employees are happy to answer your questions as you sample the new creations from elegant trays (4 SF, April–Oct Mon–Fri 9:30–16:00, closed Sat–Sun and Nov–March, groups of 4 or more should call a day in advance to reserve, located in sweet-smelling town of Broc, follow signs to *Nestlé* and *Broc Fabrique,* tel. 026-921-5151, www.cailler.ch).

## Gruyères

This ultratouristy town, famous
for its cheese and rated ▲, fills its
fortified hilltop like a bouquet.
Its ramparts are a park, and the
ancient buildings serve tourists.
Hotels here are expensive. The
TI is at the town entrance (daily
9:30–12:15 & 13:00–17:30).

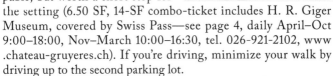

**Castle**—Gruyères' castle is skip-
pable, but worth a short stop for
the setting (6.50 SF, 14-SF combo-ticket includes H. R. Giger
Museum, covered by Swiss Pass—see page 4, daily April–Oct
9:00–18:00, Nov–March 10:00–16:30, tel. 026-921-2102, www
.chateau-gruyeres.ch). If you're driving, minimize your walk by
driving up to the second parking lot.

**H. R. Giger Museum**—This museum, a spooky, offbeat contrast
to idyllic Gruyères, is dedicated to the Swiss artist who designed
the monsters in the *Alien* movies. Not for the faint of heart, this
museum shares those movies' dark aesthetic (10 SF, 14-SF combo-
ticket includes castle, covered by Swiss Pass, daily 9:00–18:00,
www.hrgigermuseum.com).

**Gruyères Fromageries**—There are two very different cheesemaking exhibits to choose from in and near Gruyères—one is old and
up in the hills, and the other is new and handy. Both are worth
▲▲. The cute cheese shop in the modern center has lunches and
picnic goodies.

    **Ye Olde Cheesemaker:** Five miles above Gruyères, a dark
and smoky 17th-century farmhouse in Moléson gives a fun look
at the traditional, smelly way of crafting cheese in a huge caul-
dron over an open fire (3 SF, mid-May–mid-Oct daily 9:30–18:00,
closed off-season, cheese actually made at 10:00 and 14:30, tel.
026-921-1044, www.fromagerie-alpage.ch, TI tel. 026-921-8500,
www.moleson.ch).

    **New Cheese Factory:** Closer and modern, the cheese-produc-
tion center at the foot of Gruyères town (follow *Fromagerie* signs)
opens its doors to tourists. Admission includes a sample of three
varieties of Gruyère cheese and an English audioguide—punch
444 for English, then the number listed next to the displays (5 SF,
daily 9:00–19:00, tel. 026-921-8400, www.lamaisondugruyere.ch).

## Glacier des Diablerets

For a grand alpine trip to the tip of a 10,000-foot peak, take the
three-part lift from Reusch or Col du Pillon. The trip takes about
90 minutes and costs 54 SF. Stay for lunch. From the top, you can
see the Matterhorn and a bit of Mont Blanc, the Alps' highest

peak. This is a good chance to do some summer skiing (normally expensive and a major headache). A lift ticket and rental skis, poles, boots, and coat cost about 65 SF. The slopes close at 14:00 during the summer, and at 17:00 from October through April.

The base of the lift is a two-hour drive from Murten or Gimmelwald. Your best public-transportation bet is to catch an early train to Diablerets with a transfer in Aigle. Then bus to Col du Pillon (7/day) and take the cable car to the top (last departure at 16:00). For more ski information, call 024-492-0923 or check www.glacier3000.ch.

## Taveyanne

This remote hamlet—worth ▲▲—is a huddle of log cabins used by cowherds in the summer. Taveyanne is two miles off the main road between Col de la Croix and Villars (a small sign points down a tiny road to a jumble of huts and snoozing cows stranded at 5,000 feet). The hamlet's old bar is a restaurant, serving a tiny community of vacationers and hikers.

The town's inn is **$ Refuge de Taveyanne** (from 1882), where the Seibenthal family serves meals in a rustic setting with no electricity, low ceilings, and a huge, charred fireplace. Consider sleeping in their primitive five-mattress loft (14 SF, D-30 SF, cash only, access by a ladder outside, bathroom outside, closed Mon–Tue except July–Aug, closed Nov–April, tel. 024-498-1947). It's a fine opportunity to really get to know prize-winning cows.

# LUGANO

The town of Lugano, the leading city of the Italian-speaking Swiss canton of Ticino, gives you Switzerland with an Italian accent. The town (population 53,000) sprawls luxuriously along the shores of Lake Lugano. Just a short, scenic train ride over the Alps from the German and French regions of Switzerland, Lugano has a splashy, zesty, Mediterranean ambience. It attracts vacationers from the rainy north with its sunshine, lush vegetation, inviting lake, and shopping. While many travelers come here for the fancy boutiques, others make this a base for hiking, cruising the lake, and passing lazy afternoons in its many gardens. While its mountains are not mighty, its beaches are lousy, and it can feel a little geriatric, Lugano has a unique charm that merits at least a short visit.

## Planning Your Time

Lugano lies conveniently at the intersection of the William Tell Express and the Bernina Express—two of Switzerland's more scenic train rides. Blitz sightseers arrive on the William Tell one day and take off on the Bernina Express the next. If relaxing is on your itinerary, spend two nights and a full day here, arriving and departing on the scenic trains.

# ORIENTATION

The old town is on Lake Lugano, which is bordered by promenades and parks. A funicular connects the old town on the lakeside with the train station above. Nearly everything in this chapter is within a five-minute walk of the base of the funicular.

Note that most people in Lugano speak Italian; you're surrounded on three sides by Italy (see "Italian Survival Phrases" in the appendix). In this corner of Switzerland, a *Strasse* (or road) becomes a *Via,* and a *Platz* (or square) become a *Piazza.*

## Tourist Information

Lugano's TI faces the boat dock a couple of blocks below the funicular (Mon–Fri 9:00–19:00, Sat 9:00–17:00, Sun 10:00–15:00, Palazzo Civico, Riva Albertolli, tel. 091-913-3232, fax 091-922-7653, www.lugano-tourism.ch). The TI offers **walking tours** (free, Sun, Mon, and Wed at 9:30, 2.25 hours).

## Arrival in Lugano

The train station has lockers (4 SF, under the tracks, always accessible), a less convenient and pricier baggage-storage counter (7 SF, short hours), ATMs, a convenient grocery (Shop Aperto di Lugano, daily 6:00–22:00), and a room-finding service, but no real TI. The easiest way to get to the town below is by funicular (1.10 SF, free with Swiss Pass, daily 5:20–23:50, every 5 min).

## Helpful Hints

**Internet Access: Mondailpay,** at Via Canova 9, is the only real Internet café in town. At **Burger King,** any meal is a happy meal for those with e-mail concerns—it comes with 30 minutes of free Internet access (lakefront, on Piazza R. Rezzonico).

**Local Guide: Christa Branchi** teaches enthusiastically about her home town (200 SF/half-day, 300 SF/day, tel. 091-606-3302, christabranchi@hotmail.com).

# SELF-GUIDED WALK

## Welcome to Lugano

While many might think a guided walk of resorty Lugano is absurd, there's actually some interesting history hiding out. This short stroll gets you well-oriented and covers the essentials. Start on Piazza Cioccaro, at the base of the funicular (which connects the train station with the town center).

• *Walk downhill 50 yards to the right, into...*

**Via Pessina:** In this tangled and colorful little corner (under flags of all 26 Swiss cantons) are several small shops run by Signor

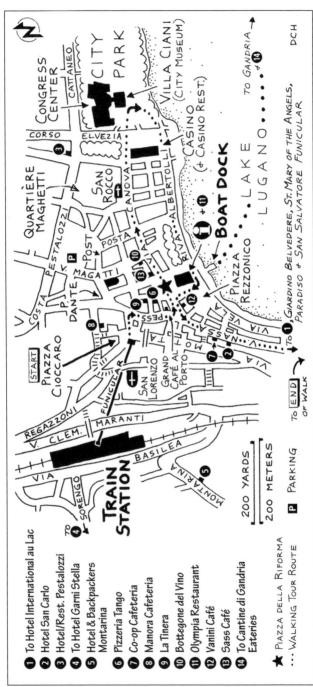

## Lugano Center

CONGRESS CENTER

CITY PARK

CATTANEO

VILLA CIANI (CITY MUSEUM)

CORSO

ELVEZIA

CASINO (+ CASINO REST.)

QUARTIÈRE MAGHETTI

SAN ROCCO

CANOVA

ALBERTOLLI

BOAT DOCK

LAKE LUGANO

COSTA

PESTALOZZI

POST

P.V. MAGATTI

POSTA

RIVA

PIAZZA REZZONICO

TO GANDRIA

TO GIARDINO BELVEDERE, ST. MARY OF THE ANGELS, PARADISO & SAN SALVATORE FUNICULAR

P. DANTE

PESS

VIA VELA

VIA NASSA

START PIAZZA CIOCCARO

FUNICULAR

SAN LORENZO

GRAND CAFÉ AL PORTO

TO END OF WALK

REGAZZONI

V. CLEM.

MARANTI

BASILEA

VIA SORENGO

TRAIN STATION

MONTARINA

TO

200 YARDS

200 METERS

P PARKING

DCH

1 To Hotel International au Lac
2 Hotel San Carlo
3 Hotel/Rest. Pestalozzi
4 To Hotel Garni Stella
5 Hotel & Backpackers Montarina
6 Pizzeria Tango
7 Co-op Cafeteria
8 Manora Cafeteria
9 La Tinera
10 Bottegone del Vino
11 Olympia Restaurant
12 Vanini Café
13 Sass Café
14 To Cantine di Gandria Eateries

★ PIAZZA DELLA RIFORMA
··· WALKING TOUR ROUTE

Gabbani. Go in the wine shop (marked *Bottega del Vino*). Its ceiling is mossy with *boccalini* (traditional quarter-liter wine carafes, typical of the rustic grottos of Ticino).

• *Farther down, at Via Pessina 3, is...*

**Grand Café al Porto:** This venerable institution is both Lugano's best spot for cakes and coffee and the most historic café in town (daily 8:00–18:30). The *1803* above the fireplace is the date it opened—and also when Ticino joined the Swiss Federation. Once a convent (notice the fine *sgraffito* facade), the café evokes the 19th-century days when Giuseppe Mazzini and fellow Italian patriots would huddle here—safely over the border—planning their next move to unify Italy. Much later, as World War II wound down, U.S. dignitary Allen Welsh Dulles met right here with Nazi and Italian representatives to organize a graceful end to the war and prevent the Germans from ruining Italy with a scorched-earth retreat. And in more carefree times, this is where Clark Gable and Sofia Loren dipped cookies in their coffee.

• *Just past Grand Café al Porto, take a left into...*

**Piazza della Riforma:** This square is Lugano's living room. The city is proudly liberal, even today, as the name of its main square implies. Its progressive spirit from the days of the Risorgimento (Italian unification) survives today as Lugano remains one of the most liberal-voting cities in Switzerland. This square—with geraniums cascading on all sides—hosts an open-air cinema, markets (Tue and Fri), and local festivals.

• *Facing City Hall, go left (past the* farmacia*) down...*

**Via Canova:** This road leads directly to the city park. Along the way, you pass the creamy, elegant little Church of San Rocco. Its rich frescoes celebrate the saint responsible for protecting the city against the plague. Behind that is the Quartière Maghetti, an entire city block turned into a popular mall—lots of shops and fun eateries by day and a lively, youthful bar scene after hours.

• *Via Canova dead-ends at a pink palace in the...*

**City Park (Parco Civico Villa Ciani):** The park's centerpiece, the Villa Ciani, houses the city museum. Sprawling from here along the lake is a lush park filled with modern art and exotic trees from around the world. Its water gate evokes the 19th century, when this was the private domain of aristocrats. The flower beds are organized to show off maximum color all year long. It's lit at night and particularly good for a late, romantic stroll (open daily 6:30–23:30).

• *From the City Park, walk back to the town center along the...*

**Waterfront:** The casino restaurant overlooks the lake. Ride its glass *elevatore* up and down for a fun and free view. Then continue strolling through the arcade or under the mulberry trees (a favorite of silk worms, dating from the time when silk was a local industry)

## The Story of Lugano

Lugano's history is tied to its strategic position: where the Italian world is pressed up against the Alps, and just below the most convenient alpine passes. The Celts crossed the Alps here and left their mark. The ancient Romans were here, too—the oldest sacred building in Switzerland is an early Christian baptistery on this lake.

In 1220, when the first road over the Gotthard Pass was built, the Swiss took an interest in acquiring the Italian-speaking region of Ticino, leading to a battle for control. The nearby town of Bellinzona is named not for the Italian *bella* ("beautiful"), but for the Latin *bellum* ("war")—and this truly was a medieval war zone. Several castles in Bellinzona recall a pivotal Swiss victory in 1513. With this success, the Swiss gained a toehold in Ticino.

But the feisty region maintained its independence. In 1798, Ticino even stood up to Napoleon by creating an independent Republic of Ticino. But the people of Ticino were unable to rule themselves peacefully, and five years later (in 1803), they decided to join the Swiss Federation. With that event, the present-day borders of Switzerland were finally established.

In the 19th century, Lugano—Italian-speaking, just a short trip from Milan, yet safely over the border in Switzerland—provided a refuge and staging ground for intellectual Italian revolutionaries. They'd meet here to plan the Risorgimento, the struggle for Italian unification (c. 1840–1869). Later in the 19th century, tourism arrived and the grand lakefront hotels were built.

Today, Lugano is second among Swiss cities only to Zürich in the number of banks. It's easy for Italians and others with suitcases of hard cash—black money—to swing by and take advantage of the secret bank accounts. (Locals claim George H. W. Bush stops by about annually.) But the mentality here remains Italian. Rather than the Zürich model ("live to work"), the people of Lugano brag that they work to live.

until you reach the boat dock opposite the TI.

• *A block inland from the TI is Piazza della Riforma again. The first left is...*

**Via Nassa:** This is one of Lugano's main shopping streets. Stow your guidebook and just enjoy the wandering, window-shopping, and people-watching for several blocks. It's fun to assume that half the briefcases you pass are filled with cash. Along this gauntlet of boutiques and jewelry shops under typical Lombardi arcades, notice all the clocks. If you're trying to get away from time...this is

## Lugano

a nightmare. At #22, the Co-op department store (closed Sun) has good selection of Swiss chocolates (just inside the door on the left) and a handy top-floor cafeteria (lunch only, great views).

• *Follow Via Nassa until it dead-ends at a small but historic church.*

**Church of St. Mary of the Angels (Chiesa Santa Maria degli Angioli):** This unpretentious little lakefront church, which dates from 1499, was part of a monastery (next door, described below). Inside the church, you'll find the city's best frescoes. Bernardino Luini (from Milan) painted *The Passion and Crucifixion of Christ* and *The Last Supper* in 1529. After enjoying the gentle expressions and calm beauty of his art, you'll understand why Luini is nicknamed the "Raphael of the North."

*The Passion and Crucifixion of Christ,* the artistic highlight of all Ticino and the finest Renaissance fresco in Switzerland, is on the wall that separates the nave from the altar area. Follow the action as the scenes from Christ's passion are played out, from Jesus being crowned with thorns (left) to the doubting apostle Thomas touching Jesus' wound after his resurrection. The central and dominating theme is the crucifixion. The work is riddled with symbolism. For instance, at the base of the cross, notice the skull and femur of Adam, as well as his rib (from which Eve was created). Worshippers saw this and remembered that without Adam and Eve's first sin, none of the terrible action in the rest of the fresco would have been necessary. Luini spent a decade working on this. Take an extremely close-up look at the fresco technique.

The altar is rich and unusual with its wooden inlay work. *The Last Supper* (back left wall) was sliced off a wall of the monks' dining hall and put on canvas to be hung here.

• *On the lakefront across from the church begins the...*

**Giardino Belvedere:** This delightful little garden park is an open-air modern-art museum. The building facing it was once a monastery, then the Grand Hotel Palace. This first grand hotel on the lake was radical in that it actually faced the lake. From here, survey the scene. Paradiso, the big hotel zone with its 80-foot-high fountain, is a 15-minute walk along the lakeside. From there, the San Salvatore lift zips sightseers to the summit (described below). The ridge across the lake marks the border of Italy.

## ACTIVITIES

### San Salvatore: Lugano's Best 360-Degree Mountaintop View

Lugano is a base from which several relatively small peaks can be conquered sweat-free by lifts. At about 3,000 feet, Lake Lugano's

mountains are unimpressive compared to the mightier Alps farther north. Still, if you want the complete Lugano experience, you need to enjoy the commanding mountaintop views over the lake.

San Salvatore is the easiest and most rewarding peak. You'll begin at Paradiso (a 15-min walk from Lugano, or take bus #1 from the Lugano TI). From there, a funicular slides you from up and up (20 SF round-trip, 12-min ride, departs on the half-hour, daily June–Aug 8:30–23:00, April–May and Sept 8:30–18:30, late March and Oct–mid-Nov 8:30–17:00, closed mid-Nov–mid-March, www.montesansalvatore.ch). At the top, you'll find a self-serve cafeteria (closes at 18:00), a fancy restaurant (way overpriced, and after dark you have no views), a playground, and excellent viewpoints. From the lift, be sure to climb five more minutes to the actual summit, where you'll find a small church. Then climb to the rooftop of the church for an incredible 360-degree view.

## Cruising Lake Lugano with a Stop in Gandria

Lake Lugano is made to order for a boat trip. Along with pedal boats and simple cruises from village to village, there are fancier excursions (a lunch trip, a grand tour, a shopping excursion into Italy, and an evening dinner cruise). For details, ask at the TI.

**One-Hour Loop Trip:** The best basic trip is the one-hour circle from Lugano. This cruise stops at several desolate restaurants and hamlets along the far side of the lake, visits Gandria (a peaceful and picturesque little fishing town with several romantic view restaurants), then returns to Lugano (20 SF round-trip including stopovers, or 12 SF for one segment). You can get off and hike. The far side of the lake has a trail lacing together several little grottos and hamlets (each with a boat stop) with hiking times and directions clearly marked. For information on the hike, ask the TI, your hotel, or even the guys on the boat. Carefully note when the next boat comes by and exactly where it stops (as this can be confusing).

**Cantine di Gandria** has two characteristic *trattorias* and wine grottos—great for a rustic meal or just a snack and a drink (note they close on different days, so at least one is sure to be open on any given day). A five-minute walk from Cantine di Gandria takes you to the **Customs Museum** (Museo Doganale) with underwhelming exhibits on customs and smuggling (free, no English but worth a 10-min visit, April–Oct daily 13:30–17:30, closed Nov–March). Boats stop alternately at Cantine di Gandria and Museo Doganale.

**Gandria** is the most intriguing stop. This dense cluster of fishing houses hangs over the lake with a few lazy and romantic hotels

and several inviting restaurants. **Restaurant Miralago Gandria** is immediately above the ferry dock (mediocre food, fair prices, extremely romantic setting, closed Wed, tel. 091-971-4361). You can lob bits of bread to the hungry birds, rewarding the ones who fly high circles by your lakeside table. **Locanda Gandriesi** has better cooking but is farther from the boat dock and birds. If stopping here, you can walk back to Lugano (great 45-min lakeside path before hitting the Castagnola suburb of Lugano and a boring 30-min walk along streets into town). To enjoy just the more interesting part of the walk, catch bus #1 from the Castagnola post office.

**Half-Day Plan:** Here's a pleasant way to spend a late afternoon and evening (confirm boat times before departing): 16:00-Walk from Lugano to Paradiso, 16:15-Catch the boat from Paradiso to

---

## Sleep Code

**(1.25 SF = about $1, country code: 41)**
**S** = Single, **D** = Double/Twin, **T** = Triple, **Q** = Quad, **b** = bathroom,
**s** = shower only. Unless otherwise noted, credit cards are accepted, English is spoken, and breakfast is included.

To help you sort easily through these listings, I've divided the rooms into three categories, based on the price for a standard double room with bath:

$$$ **Higher Priced**—Most rooms 200 SF or more.
$$ **Moderately Priced**—Most rooms between 120–200 SF.
$ **Lower Priced**—Most rooms 120 SF or less.

---

Cantine di Gandria to visit the Customs Museum and enjoy a glass of wine at the nearby Grotto di Theresa, 18:00-Take the boat from the Museo Doganale stop to Gandria and have an early dinner in Gandria (at Miralago Gandria—early diners always get lakeside tables), 19:15-Catch the boat to Paradiso (next one not until 22:15). Once at Paradiso, walk to the San Salvatore lift, ride the lift to the summit of the mountain (best at twilight but disappointing after dark), ride back down, and walk along the lake from Paradiso back to Lugano.

## SLEEPING

### In Lugano's Old Town

$$$ **Hotel International au Lac** is a classic, pricey old hotel with 80 rooms and some Lake Lugano views. It's conveniently and scenically located where pedestrian-only Via Nassa hits the lake. Four generations of Schmids have maintained the early-20th-century ambience since 1906, with old photos, inviting lounges, antique furniture, and—it seems—many of their original guests (Sb-120–185 SF, Db-200–298 SF depending on size and view, Tb-270 SF, family-friendly, Internet access, terrace restaurant, fun view seats on balcony of bar, swimming pool, parking-20 SF/day, Via Nassa 68, tel. 091-922-7541, fax 091-922-7544, www.hotel-international.ch, info@hotel-international.ch).

$$ **Hotel San Carlo,** also on the pedestrian-only shopping street, but closer to the center, rents 22 small but cheerful rooms. This welcoming place is run by Anna Martina and Beppe. The flamboyant Italian-mod design within its old walls is fun and refreshing (Ss-95 SF, Sb-120 SF, Ds-140 SF, Db-160 SF, cheaper off-season, non-smoking rooms, elevator, Via Nassa 28, tel. 091-922-7107, fax 091-922-8022, sancarlo@ticino.com).

**$$ Hotel Pestalozzi,** near the city park, is plain and vaguely institutional. It offers fresh, modern rooms with a woody Nordic touch and some lake views (S-64 SF, Sb-98 SF, D-108 SF, Db-168 SF, lakeview Db-178 SF, elevator; good restaurant—see "Eating," below; Piazza Indipendenza 9, tel. 091-921-4646, fax 091-922-2045, www.attuale.com/pestalozzi.html, pestalo@bluewin.ch). Though a bit of a walk from the train station funicular, this hotel is a particularly good value.

## Near the Train Station
**$$ Hotel Garni Stella,** a wonderful little oasis, offers 14 rooms between slick office buildings just behind the train station. Owner Antoinette Burkhard's love of modern art is evident, with statues on the patio and fun paintings throughout (Sb-110 SF, Db-160 SF, 5 percent discount with this book in 2007, some rooms have terraces, Internet access, swimming pool; exit the station at rear, follow tracks right for 50 yards, take the first left uphill, then turn left to Via F. Borromini 5; tel. 091-966-3370, fax 091-966-6755, www.hotel-stella.ch, info@hotel-stella.ch).

**$ Hotel & Backpackers Montarina,** a creaky old mansion in a palm garden overlooking the lake, rents 24 huge antique double rooms and 140 dorm beds (dorm bed in 6- to 16-bed room with sheets-30 SF, S-70 SF, Sb-80 SF, D-100 SF, Db-120 SF, breakfast buffet-12 SF, Internet access, reception open 7:30–23:00, lockers, small kitchen, swimming pool, free parking, Via Montarina 1, tel. 091-966-7272, fax 091-966-0017, www.montarina.com, info@montarina.com). As you exit the train station at the rear, walk left along the tracks, and you'll see the pink buildings and the big sign.

# EATING

My recommended restaurants are all in the old town. Lugano is not the best place for lakeside dining. For better value, cross the lake to the remote little grotto restaurants, or visit the town of Gandria (both options described on page 233). If enjoying the wine, realize that you'll pay the same per liter for the little one-deciliter (about 3.5 oz) glasses as you do for the big half-liter (about 17 oz) carafes—so go with the small glasses and try several different wines. Experiment. The Ticino merlot is great.

**Pizzeria Tango** serves Italian cuisine with Ticino influence and a helpful waitstaff. While a few of its tables face the busy main square, its interior and the tables facing a quiet little square on the back may be more inviting (25-SF daily plates, 15–20-SF pizzas, open daily until very late, Piazza della Riforma, tel. 091-922-2701).

**Co-op Cafeteria,** midway along the Via Nassa pedestrian mall, has an elegant-as-cafeterias-go dining area on its top floor with a pretty rooftop terrace (Mon–Sat 11:30–14:30, closed Sun, Via Nassa 22).

**Manora** is an easy self-service restaurant offering healthful food and indoor and outdoor seating. It's in the Manor supermarket on Piazza Dante Alighieri (100 yards from bottom of train station funicular; daily 7:30–22:00).

**La Tinera,** beloved by locals, serves affordable, traditional Ticinese cuisine. It's tucked away in an old wine cellar, with heavy wooden furniture and a display of wine bottles and antique copper cookware (meat dishes-20–30 SF, smaller dishes-13 SF, Mon–Sat 8:30–15:00 & 17:30–23:00, closed Sun, Via dei Gorini, behind Piazza della Riforma, tel. 091-923-5219).

**Restaurante Pestalozzi,** close to the city park, is a stylish belle époque restaurant serving reasonably priced meals in a smoke-free and alcohol-free setting (15-SF daily specials, open daily 18:30–21:30, Piazza Indipendenza 9, tel. 091-921-4646).

**Bottegone del Vino** is an expensive little eatery appreciated for its fine wine. The menu is small and rustic, the wine is excellent, and the ambience is of a quality wine bar. Sitting here you feel "in the know"—but order carefully, as prices really add up (Mon–Sat until 24:00, closed Sun, a block off Piazza della Riforma at Via Magatti 3, tel. 091-922-7689).

*Around Piazza della Riforma:* In addition to Pizzeria Tango (described above), several other restaurants offer decent food and great people-watching from outdoor tables on the square. Consider **Sass Café** (classy wine bar with 18-SF daily specials and 30-SF à la carte items), **Olympia** (19-SF pastas, 30-SF main dishes, below City Hall, the mayor's fave), and **Vanini Cafe** (tops for coffee and desserts; try the *marron glace*—candied chestnuts).

## TRANSPORTATION CONNECTIONS

Lugano is a long detour from virtually anywhere else in Switzerland. It's best connected to other Swiss destinations by scenic trains: the **William Tell Express** (train-and-boat combination to Luzern) or the **Bernina Express** (bus-and-train combination to eastern Switzerland). The Bernina Express bus leaves for Tirano near Lugano's train station (200 yards to the left as you leave the station, see chart at station). More details about these trips are in the Scenic Rail Journeys chapter on page 253.

**From Lugano by Train to: Luzern** (hourly, 3 hrs), **Zürich** (hourly, 3 hrs, some with easy change in Arth-Goldau), (hourly, 5 hrs, transfer in Luzern, Zürich, or Olten), **Bern** (hourly, 4 hrs, transfer in Luzern, Zürich, or Olten), **Milan** (hourly, 1.5 hrs).

**From Lugano to Milan's Airports:** The closest major airports to Lugano are actually in Italy, near the city of Milan: Malpensa Airport and Linate Airport (www.sea-aeroportimilano.it). To reach either, first take the 1.5-hour train to Milan's Central Station. From that station, cheap and easy shuttle buses leave about every 15 minutes for both Malpensa and Linate.

# PONTRESINA, SAMEDAN, AND ST. MORITZ

High in the mountains of the canton called Graubünden, in the southeast corner of Switzerland, two valleys meet, carving out a picturesque region called the Upper Engadine ("Oberengadin" in German). This area is rich with rugged mountain scenery and colorful folk traditions, and is a handy stopover for tourists taking the scenic Bernina Express.

While there may not seem to be a lot of history here, the trained eye sees it everywhere. Celtic people inhabited this region centuries before Christ. The hillsides are still terraced, recalling the hard work that came with farming up here in ancient times. History is in the region's unique language, too: Romansh is a vulgar form of Latin that arrived here with the Etruscans, who were chased here as Rome expanded. Town names date back to various invaders. For instance, "Pontresina" comes from "Bridge of the Saracens."

The most famous town here is the glitzy ski resort of St. Moritz, but for a more authentic Back Door experience, head for Pontresina or Samedan—where workaday Swiss people go to find some high-altitude fun. In these towns, you don't find English newspapers—an indication that while there are many visitors, most are from nearby.

## Planning Your Time

The three towns in this chapter—Pontresina, Samedan, and St. Moritz—form a convenient little triangle, each about 10 minutes apart by train. With a full day here and some good planning, you can sample all three, and throw in a hike to boot. This area isn't worth a long detour, but it happens to link two scenic rail trips: the

## Pontresina, Samedan, and St. Moritz Area

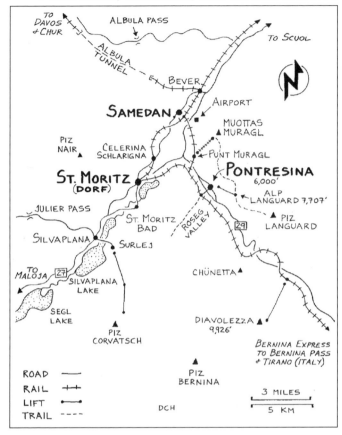

Bernina Express and the Glacier Express (see Scenic Rail Journeys chapter). Hop off the train, set up a home base, explore—then continue on your way.

This remote region has two distinct tourist seasons: summer (June–Oct) and winter (Dec–March). Outside of these seasons, many places are closed and the area can feel dead.

# Pontresina

Pontresina—a popular winter and summer mountain resort with about 2,000 residents—makes a good Graubünden home base. At 6,000 feet above sea level on a wind-protected terrace overlooking the Bernina Valley, Pontresina faces southwest and enjoys plenty of sunshine. Popular trails through its larch forests offer spectacular views of the 13,000-foot Piz Bernina peak and the immense Morteratsch glacier.

Pontresina's first tourists, mostly German and British, arrived in the 1850s. For a while, it was a summer-only destination. But by the early 1900s, the Muottas Muragl railway was inaugurated, the first grand hotels were built, and tourists began showing up in winter, too.

## ORIENTATION

Pontresina sits above a river overlooking its valley. Virtually everything of interest (except the train station) is along Via Maistra (may-strah), which means "Main Street" in Romansh.

**Tourist Information:** The TI is in the heart of town in the slick new Rondo Culture and Congress Center (July–Aug Mon–Fri 8:30–18:00, Sat 8:30–12:00 & 15:00–18:00, Sun 16:00–18:00, shorter hours off-season, tel. 081-838-8300, fax 081-838-8310, www.pontresina.com).

### Arrival in Pontresina

The train station lies at the foot of the town. You can take a 10-minute uphill walk to the city center, following the white signs to Pontresina. Or, easier, take bus #1 or #2 to Pontresina Post (2/hr, 2.80 SF, free with Swiss Pass, buy ticket at counter inside train station). Walking the 10 minutes from Pontresina back down to the train station on Via da Mulin offers spectacular gorge views along the way.

### Helpful Hints

**Internet Access:** You'll find public Internet terminals at **Hotel Post** (8 SF/30 min, daily 8:00–21:00, closed in May, Via Maistra) and **Hotel Saratz** (5 SF/30 min, June–Sept open 24/7, closed Oct–May, opposite TI on Via Maistra). Most hotels offer Internet access (generally for a fee) to their guests.

**Local Guide: Ulla Währer** is a charming and knowledgeable local guide (100 SF/1 hour, 150 SF/2 hours, 180 SF/4 hours, 300 SF/day, tel. 081-832-1381, ulla.waehrer@freesurf.ch).

## SIGHTS AND ACTIVITIES

**Church of St. Mary**—Above town, next to the five-sided, 13th-century Spaniola Tower, stands this remarkable little church (limited hours, generally July–Oct Mon–Fri 15:30–17:30, closed Sat–Sun). Faded 13th-century, Byzantine-inspired frescoes survive on the west wall. The other walls and ceiling were richly decorated by an Italian workshop (1497). The bright colors are original;

# Graubünden

Switzerland's biggest canton, isolated by high mountain ranges, is also one of its most conservative. The name Graubünden goes back to 1395, when a group of farmers wearing gray clothes organized themselves in the "Gray League" to fight for their autonomy. This fiercely independent region didn't join the Swiss Confederation until 1803.

People in Graubünden believe the best way to control nature is to obey it. Passionate about their environment, they purify all dirty water before returning it to the rivers. Locals are currently going through the expensive process of removing canals (built to direct streams and rivers) and allowing the water to choose its own course once again. The natives love their beautiful countryside and cherish their customs—predictably voting against EU membership and other issues that might compromise Swiss neutrality and self-determination.

Graubünden has three official languages: German, Italian, and Romansh (an ancient dialect that comes directly from Latin). You'll overhear conversations where one person speaks Italian, the other replies in German, a third butts in with Romansh...and everybody understands each other. On the trains, the announcements are in German and Romansh.

Graubünden cuisine is hearty. Try *Pizokel*, a *Spätzle*-like creation of cheesy flour dumplings. In fall, you might find *Pizokel* made from chestnut flour and served with wild mushroom stew. The Graubünden's air-dried beef, *Bündnerfleisch*—very expensive and sliced paper-thin—is popular throughout Switzerland. *Capuns* are cabbage leaves stuffed with a mix of dough, leeks, bacon, onion, and air-dried beef. *Bündner Gerstensuppe* is a creamy barley and vegetable soup. For a Graubünden dessert, it's got to be *Nusstorte*, a rich walnut cake.

it's never been repainted. The frescoes depict the legend of Mary Magdalene and (above) the story of Lazarus' resurrection. Imagine this church packed with illiterate villagers five centuries ago.

**Alpine Museum**—This little museum is worth a quick visit. Situated in an old Engadine town house, it offers exhibits on the development of alpine mountain climbing, the regional mining industry, hunting, and local animals. About 130 of the 250 different bird species found in the Upper Engadine are shown here. Listen to the recorded songs of 60 different birds on their primitive aviary jukebox. The 20-minute slideshow is in German and makes you feel like a wimp. Still, it's interesting for its images of "the mountain experience" (5 SF, June–Oct Mon–Sat 16:00–18:00, closed Sun, Via Maistra).

## Pontresina

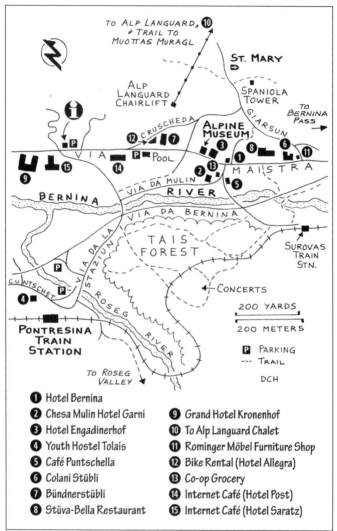

1. Hotel Bernina
2. Chesa Mulin Hotel Garni
3. Hotel Engadinerhof
4. Youth Hostel Tolais
5. Café Puntschella
6. Colani Stübli
7. Bündnerstübli
8. Stüva-Bella Restaurant
9. Grand Hotel Kronenhof
10. To Alp Languard Chalet
11. Rominger Möbel Furniture Shop
12. Bike Rental (Hotel Allegra)
13. Co-op Grocery
14. Internet Café (Hotel Post)
15. Internet Café (Hotel Saratz)

**Biking**—Several sports stores rent bicycles, inline skates, tennis rackets, and other gear. **Fähndrich Sport** rents good mountain bikes with various suspensions (20–25 SF/half-day, 30–40 SF/day, helmets-7 SF/half-day, 10 SF/day, Mon–Sat 8:00–12:00 & 14:00–18:30, closed Sun except July–Aug, at Hotel Allegra on Via Maistra, tel. 081-842-7155, www.faehndrich-sport.ch). **Flying Cycles,** at the Pontresina train station, rents a huge selection of mountain bikes and fun, easy-to-learn electric-powered bikes (23

SF/half-day, 35 SF/day, helmets-8 SF, daily 8:30–18:30, tel. 081-834-5750). Riding the train to the Bernina Pass and biking nine miles back into town is just one of many fun biking options.

**Bus #2 Joyride**—Bus #2 runs scenically back and forth through the valley's towns and villages (2/hr, 2.80 SF). Consider it for a cheap survey of the neighborhood while connecting the three main towns. Just hop on and pay the driver or flash your Swiss Pass.

**Music**—Free summer classical music concerts are offered in the Tais Forest across the river, and (on rainy days) in the Grand Hotel Kronenhof (daily at 11:00, mid-June–mid-Sept, confirm and get details at TI).

**Swimming**—The covered public pool on Via Maistra (7 SF, Mon–Fri 10:00–21:00, Sat–Sun 10:00–19:00) also has a sauna (mixed daily except Thu, when it's women-only; 14 SF, includes pool entrance).

## Hiking

Pontresina is a hiker's paradise. The town boasts Switzerland's largest mountaineering school and has a good reputation for adventure sports. Shops lining Via Maistra rent all kinds of sports gear.

Upper Engadine trails come with high altitudes. Hikers should bring the appropriate gear (solid shoes, sun protection, windbreaker, hat, and water). Even in summer, with cold winds blowing down from the snow-capped mountains, it can get cold—especially on chairlifts. The sun is strong and the air is thin, so use sunscreen. Hiking trails are marked according to their difficulty. Yellow signs indicate easy hikes and walks. White-and-red signs indicate more demanding hikes, where real hiking boots are in order. Blue signs indicate alpine routes that require serious gear (these dangerous trails include rock climbing and glacier crossings).

The flowers in the Alps are protected; pick one, and you may be fined. Some meadows are also protected for haymaking. Signs ask you to stick to the trails, as trampled grass is hard to cut.

The TI has a great free brochure with a panoramic map listing the region's many hikes. Of the 80 hikes it lists and describes, consider this one first...

**Pontresina to Muottas Muragl to Alp Languard**—For maximum alpine thrills per calorie burned, consider this three-hour hike. It comes with grand views and takes you gradually down 1,000 feet in altitude. From Pontresina (6,000 feet), catch bus #1 or #2 (2/hr,

2.80 SF) to the Muottas Muragl funicular (19 SF one-way, 29-SF combo-ticket also covers your trip back down to Pontresina on the Alp Languard lift, see below for details).

The funicular lifts you to a lofty restaurant (8,105 feet), from where you hike over to Alp Languard (7,710 feet). Midway, there's a great soup or coffee-and-cakes stop (ask for the WC key for a fun alpine memory). Each year, a different appreciation-of-nature theme is displayed along this trail. Keep your eyes open for ibex, bighorn stags, and marmots.

At Alp Languard, a chalet serves reasonably priced traditional meals (see page 247). From Alp Languard, hike or ride the lift down to Pontresina (lift covered by 29-SF Muottas Muragl combo-ticket described above, runs daily 8:30–17:30).

**Other Hikes**—A fun way to explore the nearby Roseg Valley and marvel at its glacier (from a distance) is to hike two hours up the valley and take the horse-drawn "omnibus" back to Pontresina (reservations required, June–Oct departures at fixed hours, 22 SF one-way, 32 SF round-trip, Luigi Costa, tel. 081-842-6057). You can also rent a private carriage (100 SF one-way, 150 SF round-trip).

Consider taking the train up to the Bernina Pass (7,000 feet), hike around for a couple of hours, then take the train back—or, to get even higher, ride the cable car from the Bernina Pass up to Diavolezza (9,930 feet, 21 SF one-way, 30 SF round-trip, 2/hr, daily 8:30–17:00).

The TI offers various guided hikes with themes, such as "Experiencing Wilderness with Marmots and Ibex," which are free for tourists overnighting in Pontresina—ask for a guest card from your hotel—though you'll need to pay for the cable-car ride (13 SF one-way, 20 SF return, 3–4 hikes per week, reservations required). While the hikes are guided in German, some mountaineers speak English and can be hired privately through the TI.

## Near Pontresina: Muottas Muragl

This impressive alpine perch (8,105 feet) overlooking Samedan is accessible by foot (from Pontresina) or by funicular. To reach the funicular, you can either take bus #1 or #2 from Pontresina, or you can catch the train between Pontresina and Samedan and get off at Punt Muragl (it's a request-only stop, press the green button, or it won't stop). The funicular dates from 1907 (19 SF one-way, 27 SF round-trip, 29-SF combo-ticket lets you go up this funicular and down the Alp Languard lift, 2/hr, daily 8:00–23:00, cheaper after 18:00).

Once up top on Muottas Muragl, you can hike, lounge around on deck chairs (10-SF rental), have a meal (self-service or pricey but good restaurant), or even spend the night. Keep an eye out for alpine animals.

*Sleeping at Muottas Muragl:* **$$ Alpine Hotel Muottas Muragl** offers a secluded overnight high in the Alps. When the lift takes the last tourist down, things become as peaceful as the Alps can be. Rooms are clean and simple (open June–Oct only, S-78 SF, S with view-88 SF, D-136 SF, D with view-156 SF, Q-232 SF, tel. 081-842-8232, fax 081-842-8290, www.muottasmuragl.ch, info@muottasmuragl.ch).

## SHOPPING

Many sports and souvenir shops line Via Maistra. A typical product from the Upper Engadine is furniture carved from Arven pine (a.k.a. Scotch pine). The pine, special to this region, starts out light, darkens with time, and has spots where the branches used to be. Look for the tree's characteristic five-needle clusters when hiking.

**Rominger Möbel,** a local furniture store, makes the Arven pine furniture it sells. Its upstairs showroom is like a modern Engadine home show—walking among hand-carved beds, tables, and dressers gives you a sense of good living high in this remote corner of Switzerland (closed Sun, 5-min walk from town center on Via Maistra in the direction of Bernina Pass, tel. 081-842-6263, www.rominger.ch).

## SLEEPING

**$$$ Hotel Bernina,** a well-run and woody three-star place, feels like high quality, from the friendly pick-up at the station to the traditionally clad waitresses who serve your breakfast coffee. Its rooms are a fine value for this area (Sb-95–135 SF, Db-180–260 SF depending on room and season, tel. 081-838-8686, fax 081-838-8687, www.hotelbernina.ch, info@hotelbernina.ch).

**$$$ Chesa Mulin Hotel Garni,** below the main street, offers modern, bright, and comfortable rooms, each with a painting depicting a local legend. An inviting sitting area with open fireplace and library makes bad weather tolerable. The friendly Isepponi-Schmid family takes good care of their guests (Sb-114 SF, Db-198 SF, sauna, sundeck, Via da Mulin 107, tel. 081-838-8200, fax 081-838-8230, www.chesa-mulin.ch, info@chesa-mulin.ch).

**$$ Hotel Engadinerhof,** while less cozy, can be a good value. Its 75 rooms gather around a sprawling and classic Old World lounge. The cheaper sink-only rooms ("Category A") are clean and have well-preserved furniture from the 1930s (S-60 SF, D-110 SF). "Category B" offers the same old-fashioned rooms, plus antique bathrooms (Sb-80 SF, Db-150 SF). "Category C" gets you modern rooms (Sb-90 SF, Db-170 SF; Internet access, Via Maistra, tel.

## Sleep Code

**(1.25 SF = about $1, country code: 41)**
**S** = Single, **D** = Double/Twin, **T** = Triple, **Q** = Quad, **b** = bathroom,
**s** = shower only. Unless otherwise noted, credit cards are
accepted, English is spoken, and breakfast is included.

To help you sort easily through these listings, I've divided
the rooms into three categories, based on the price for a standard double room with bath:

$$$ **Higher Priced**—Most rooms 180 SF or more.
$$ **Moderately Priced**—Most rooms between 130–180 SF.
$ **Lower Priced**—Most rooms 130 SF or less.

Most hotels in this region have a severe cancellation policy (30
days in advance with no penalty, but thereafter, you'll generally have to pay for the entire period you reserved).

081-839-3100, fax 081-839-3200, www.engadinerhof.com, info
@engadinerhof.com).

**$ Youth Hostel Tolais** rents 120 beds across the street from
the train station. There's no curfew, and guests have 24-hour access
(though check-in is limited to 16:00–18:30 & 19:30–22:00, check-
out is 7:30–10:00; dorm bed-47–57 SF, D-138 SF; price includes
sheets, breakfast, and dinner; 7 SF less for breakfast only, members
pay 6 SF less per day, self-serve restaurant, game and TV room, tel.
081-842-7223, fax 081-842-7031, www.youthhostel.ch/pontresina,
pontresina@youthhostel.ch).

## EATING

Virtually all restaurants in Pontresina are part of a hotel, apart
from a few bakeries that serve reasonably priced meals. Picnickers
will seek out the **Co-op** grocery, between the train station and the
town center on Via da Mulin (Mon–Fri 8:00–12:15 & 14:00–18:30,
Sat 8:00–17:00, closed Sun).

**Café Puntschella** is the local favorite for good, healthy, reasonably priced, local-style dishes, a 12-SF salad bar, and great desserts. With a no-frills diner ambience, it offers indoor and outdoor
seating and an entertaining menu (Engadine specialties-15 SF,
pastas-14 SF, salads-11–15 SF, daily 7:30–21:30, shorter hours off-
season, Via da Mulin, tel. 081-838-8030, www.puntschella.ch).

**Colani Stübli,** a cozy eatery, serves regional and seasonal
specialties (17 SF for local dishes such as *Krautpizokel* and *Capuns,*

daily lunch special-20 SF, entrées-30–40 SF, daily 11:30–14:00 & 18:00–21:00, smaller dishes after 21:00, at Hotel Steinbock on Via Maistra, tel. 081-839-3626).

**Bündnerstübli** dishes up hearty, traditional meals with fish and game in a woody, Old World setting. Half portions are no problem. Consider being adventurous with the traditional appetizers, which work as main plates (fish and game-35 SF, vegetarian dishes-16–20 SF, *Fitnessteller*-28 SF, daily 18:00–21:30, at Hotel Rosatsch, Via Maistra 71, tel. 081-838-9800).

*Elegant Five-Star Hotel Dining Rooms:* Pontresina's two top hotels each have wonderful restaurants in sumptuous dining rooms. **Stüva-Bella Restaurant** is expensive and exclusive, with a flair for serving inventive and light regional and international cuisine. Their 85-SF five-course fixed-price meal is a good splurge, but you'll be amazed at how well you can eat with only their 9-SF salad bar and a cheese plate (soups-12 SF, entrées-40–50 SF, June–Sept and Jan–March daily 19:00–22:30, closed April–May and Oct–Dec, in Hotel Walther on Via Maistra, tel. 081-839-3636). **Grand Hotel Kronenhof** dominates the town and has public rooms fit for a Vienna palace. It's less accommodating to anyone concerned about price, but its dining room is so elegant that even a budget traveler could consider its 85-SF five-course fixed-price meal a reasonable splurge (Via Maistra, tel. 081-830-3030, www.kronenhof.com).

*Eating Above Pontresina:* **Alp Languard Chalet,** at the top of the lift (7,710 feet up—see "Hiking," page 243), serves affordable meals with unbeatable views (raclette-15 SF, daily special-18 SF, June–Oct daily 8:30–16:00, tel. 079-682-1511).

# Samedan

Little Samedan (sah-MAY-dehn) offers the best possible peek at Upper Engadine culture and architecture. This village, which has the most traditional Engadine architecture of the three towns, is the historic capital of the valley. Romansh remains its first language.

**Tourist Information:** Samedan's TI is on Via Plazzet (Mon–Fri 8:00–12:00 & 13:30–18:00, Sat until 17:00, closed Sun, also closed Sat off-season, tel. 081-851-0060, www.samedan.ch).

## SELF-GUIDED WALK

### Samedan Town Stroll

There's little to do in Samedan other than relax and enjoy a stroll. For a short hike from the town center, walk uphill on Surtuor, following the white sign for *Kath. Kirch*.

The 13th-century, castle-like **stone tower** was the private tower of a noble family. From its wooden balcony, they'd oversee festivities in their little domain.

The next house up, at **#12,** dates from 1656. This X-shaped house is in the form of a St. Andrew's cross, made of extended roof beams. This was a popular way to bless homes here. Notice the sturdy beam ends—roofs were built to support heavy stones and snow. Houses come with Romansh names. You'll see *Chesa Juzi* (Juzi's House) and *Chesa dals 3 Frers* (House of the Three Brothers).

The **Catholic Church** (neo-Romanesque from 1910, with a bell dating back to 1505) stands at the top of the town. From here, survey the surrounding slopes. Notice the ancient terracing from Celtic peoples. Continue uphill, passing the ski lift, and pause at the yellow benches for the gorgeous view. Samedan lies at the point where the two valleys of the Inn and Flaz Rivers merge. From here, the Inn River continues through Innsbruck before joining the Danube.

Huff and puff the thin air (you're at 6,000 feet) to the dramatically situated Protestant **Church of St. Peter.** The Romanesque bell tower (c. 1100) predates today's late Gothic church (c. 1480; now a burial church, generally closed to tourists).

Benches line the cemetery walls and offer sunny, wind-protected picnic spots. Beneath you stretches the highest-altitude airport in Europe, a favorite among gliders (launched by a yellow truck with a huge winch, rather than an airplane).

## SLEEPING AND EATING

While Pontresina has more eating and sleeping options (see page 237), Samedan hoards the lion's share of this valley's Graubünden quaintness.

**$$ Hotel Post** dates back to the days when people stopped here to warm up and change horses rather than to play golf and ski. Renting nine comfy, woody rooms, it's one of the few places with rustic character left in town (open June–Sept; Sb-75 SF, Db-150 SF, good restaurant, near train station, tel. 081-852-5354, fax 081-852-4692, www.poestli-samedan.ch, hotelpostsamedan@bluewin.ch).

**$$$ Hotel Bernina,** a grand hotel next to Hotel Post, will be closed much of 2007 for renovation (Db-200–250 SF, call first

## Traditional Engadine Architecture

Samedan and Pontresina both have fine old traditional houses. A short stroll in either town shows plenty of tradi- tional elements and medieval ingenuity to stay warm in the harsh mountain weather. Walls are thick—typically two feet—for insulation. Notice how windows are like the narrow end of a funnel—originally covered with animal skin rather than glass. Bay windows gathered maximum precious light and came with built-in seats where women would sit to do handwork.

The structural essence of these grand farmhouses—even though thoroughly modernized—survives. You can still see the big lower door for animals, and the big upper door for hay and the carriage—with a smaller door built into it for people to get in and out while minimizing heat loss. People had the animals sleep below in the hope their rising body heat would warm the living space above. Proud noble family coats of arms still decorate buildings, as many local families can trace their heritage to the Middle Ages.

Look for the traditional Engadine *sgraffito* ornamentation on exterior walls. To make *sgraffito*, facades are covered with a layer of dark plaster, which is then covered with white or colored plaster. Decorations—which are much more durable than painted facades—are scratched within three hours through the wet white layer, so that the dark background appears. These rustic and crude decorations look modern, but have a long history.

to see if they're open, tel. 081-852-1212, fax 081-852-3606, www .hotel-bernina.ch, hotel-bernina@bluewin.ch).

*Eating:* **Hotel Post Restaurant** is a characteristic old eatery run with a passion for the local culture (Noldi's Specialties-22 SF, a fun tasting fixed-price meal for 30 SF, closed Sun). The **Bernina Pizzeria** next door is also a good value.

# St. Moritz

The oldest—and perhaps best-known—winter resort in the world, St. Moritz has long been the winter haunt of Europe's rich and famous. Its sister city says it all: Vail.

It's said that in 1864, St. Moritz hotel pioneer Johannes Badrutt invented winter tourism in the Alps. To allay his British guests' skepticism, he offered them free accommodations if the winter weather was bad. They came and enjoyed fine weather. He liquored them up, they had fun…and they brought their friends along the next year. St. Moritz hosted the Winter Olympics in 1928 and 1948.

St. Moritz itself is little more than luxury hotels and designer boutiques, though it offers livelier nightlife than surrounding towns. For the jet set, winter is prime time in St. Moritz. Summer is quieter and popular with sporty types and nature lovers. While celebrity-spotting drops way, way off in the summer, prices are more reasonable. It's also a great time for hiking and adventure sports. Visitors enjoy inline skating, polo, golf, paragliding, horseback riding, and evening concerts. Cable cars zip you to some great mountaintops.

## ORIENTATION

St. Moritz has two centers: the town (Dorf) and the spa (Bad). The Dorf is on a steep slope. The train station, at the foot of St. Moritz Dorf, is a downhill hike from the town center. St. Moritz Bad sprawls on a level plain along the lake. Along with the spa, you'll find all the sport facilities at St. Moritz Bad (covered pool, tennis courts, ice-skating hall, horseback riding facilities, and so on). Bus #3 connects Dorf, Bad, and the train station (4/hr, 2.60 SF).

### Tourist Information
The TI is in the center of St. Moritz Dorf (July–Aug Mon–Fri 9:00–18:30, Sat–Sun 9:00–12:00 & 16:00–18:00; off-season Mon–Fri 9:00–12:00 & 14:00–18:00, Sat–Sun 9:00–12:00; Plaza Mauritius, tel. 081-837-3333, fax 081-837-3366, www.stmoritz.ch).

### Arrival in St. Moritz
St. Moritz's train station is near the lake, just below the Dorf. Pick up a free map at the train information counter (lockers but no TI or bike rental at station). The train station café is a good budget eatery (9–17 SF, daily 7:00–21:00). To avoid the steep uphill hike from the train station to Dorf, hop on bus #3 (4/hr, 2.60 SF).

## Helpful Hints

**Altitude Alert:** Don't forget that St. Moritz is at a high elevation (6,090 feet); you might feel dizzy and tired, and your body needs to adapt. Top athletes from all over the world come here for altitude training before the Olympics.

**Shopping:** The **Co-op** department store and grocery are on Plaza da Scoula and Via dal Bagn (Mon–Thu 8:00–18:30, Fri 8:00–22:00, Sat 8:00–17:00, closed Sun).

# SIGHTS

**Segantini Museum**—This museum is dedicated to the ultimate painter of alpine life. Giovanni Segantini came here to get away from the misty air of Milan. The crisp alpine atmosphere was great for capturing the bright, sharp, crystal-clear mountain light. Painting in the open air with brushstrokes that invigorated his fascinating scenes, Segantini created works reminiscent of the French Impressionists. The tiny museum, which looks like a neo-Byzantine church, is actually based on Segantini's design of the Swiss Pavilion for the 1900 World's Fair in Paris—but made of local stone, rather than the originally intended steel. Segantini died young (at age 41, in 1899), and money ran out before this grandiose pavilion could be built. Segantini's masterpiece, the *Alpine Triptych*, was painted for the World's Fair, but also never completed. Segantini's ill-fated vision—both his pavilion and his life's major work—is now here, near where he settled in his thirties. His paintings are bursting with symbolism—life, nature, death. He lovingly carved the frames ornamented with the five-needled Arven pine (10 SF, June–Oct and Dec–April Tue–Sun 10:00–12:00 & 14:00–18:00, closed Mon, March–May, and Nov, take bus #2 to Via Somplaz 30, tel. 081-833-4454, www.segantini-museum.ch).

**Engadiner Museum**—The historic, domestic, and social cultures of the Engadine region are displayed in this museum. The building (from 1905) houses interiors from throughout the Engadine (such as a patrician living room, a smoky farm kitchen, and a four-poster bed), as well as an exhibit on the discovery of the spa water that put St. Moritz on the vacation map (5 SF, Mon–Fri 9:30–12:00 & 14:00–17:00, Sun 10:00–12:00, closed Sat and May, Via dal Bagn 39, take bus #3 to Via Aruons, tel. 081-833-4333).

# SLEEPING

**$ Youth Hostel Stille,** at the boring, residential eastern end of St. Moritz Bad, offers 190 beds and all the services, activities, games, and lavish extras a top-end hostel can have (dorm bed-46.50 SF, D-141 SF, Db-152 SF, price includes breakfast and three-course dinner, prices about 10 SF higher in winter, members pay 6 SF less, reception open 7:00–10:00 & 16:00–22:00, 10-min walk from bus stop on Via Sela, Via Surpunt 60, tel. 081-833-3969, fax 081-833-8046, www.youthhostel.ch/st.moritz, st.moritz@youthhostel.ch).

## EATING

As in Pontresina, most of St. Moritz's restaurants are in hotels. An exception is **Restaurant Engiadino,** famous for its raclette and fondues (35 SF, lunch specials around 19 SF, Mon–Sat 11:30–14:00 & 18:15–21:30, closed Sun, in center of St. Moritz Dorf at Plaza da Scuola).

**Veltlinerkeller,** decorated with a huge stuffed moose head, serves a variety of grilled meats and Italian specialties (lunch special-18 SF, entrées-26–30 SF, daily 9:00–14:00 & 17:00–23:00, in St. Moritz Bad at Via dal Bagn 11, tel. 081-833-4009).

**Restaurant Hauser** is the standard stop for local workers who know where to find the best-value meal in town (long hours daily, below Hotel Hauser at Via Traunter Plazzas 71, tel. 081-837-5050).

## TRANSPORTATION CONNECTIONS

**By Train: St. Moritz, Pontresina,** and **Samedan** are all connected to each other by train (hourly, 10 min, 4.60 SF). From these towns, trains go to **Chur** (hourly, 2 hrs), **Tirano** (hourly, 2.5 hrs), and **Zürich** (hourly, 3.75 hrs, transfer in Chur). From Pontresina, you may have to change in Samedan. For details on the Bernina Express and Glacier Express, see the Scenic Rail Journeys chapter.

**By Bus:** Bus #2 connects Pontresina, Punt Muragl, Samedan, and St. Moritz (2/hr, 2.80 SF).

# SCENIC RAIL JOURNEYS

*• Golden Pass • William Tell Express • Bernina Express*
*• Glacier Express*

Switzerland has one of the world's best rail networks—and many of its tracks run through some of the world's best scenery. While just about any train ride in Switzerland is photogenic, four are aggressively marketed as the most spectacular: the Golden Pass, William Tell Express, Bernina Express, and Glacier Express. If you're looking for a scenic day enjoying the Alps from the window of your train, and would like to do it in one of Switzerland's unique "panorama cars" (offering huge windows that sweep halfway across the ceiling), these journeys can be great experiences. While they aren't quite as "fantastic with countless highlights" as they're advertised to be (the high lifts in ski areas like the Berner Oberland are much higher and more breathtaking), the trains are a fun way to do some sightseeing while getting from point A to point B.

This chapter provides you with all the logistical, nuts-and-bolts information you'll need to splice each of these journeys into your itinerary. I've also included commentary on each route, describing the highlights in the direction that most travelers are likely to go. If you travel in the opposite direction, the same information still applies—just hold the book upside down.

I've also included some information about Chur, a town that's not really worth a visit, except that it lies at the intersection of the Bernina Express and Glacier Express routes. Chur makes for a handy pit stop or overnight if connecting these trips.

## Tickets

**Schedules:** In this chapter, I've tried to list the specific departure and arrival times for 2007. But these schedules are always subject to change—it's essential to confirm the times before you travel. Timetables for most of these trains appear on the Swiss Rail Web site: www.sbb.ch/en. (Also try Germany's all-Europe rail site, http://bahn.hafas.de/bin/query.exe/en.) Any train station in Switzerland can provide you with free schedules. Each scenic rail line also operates its own Web site, with even more details (listed in each section, below).

**Buying Tickets:** Tickets and reservations for all of these scenic rail lines—including those run by private rail companies—can be purchased at any train station in Switzerland. In the US, you'll pay more (about $20 per order) to get tickets and reservations through your travel agent or at www.raileurope.com. Getting your reservations before you go also limits your flexibility, as reservations made through US agents are non-changeable and nonrefundable—unlike reservations made at train stations in Europe.

**Reservations:** You can book these journeys as early as two months ahead, or as late as the day before (at any Swiss train station or on the various Web sites). The Glacier Express requires reservations. If you want to take the official tourist package for the William Tell Express or Bernina Express, reservations are also required. Reserve the Golden Pass only if you want a front-row VIP seat. To save money and maximize your flexibility, you can take standard (non-panoramic) trains on the Golden Pass, William Tell Express, and Bernina Express routes without a reservation (though the bus segment of the Bernina Express requires a reservation, it's easy to purchase from the driver on the bus). These alternatives are explained in each section below.

**Eurailpass and Swiss Pass:** Two major types of railpasses can be useful in Switzerland: A Eurailpass (or Eurail Selectpass) and a Swiss Pass. (For details on all of the options, see page 19 in the Introduction.) These railpasses cover most of your travel on the scenic rail journeys. But seat reservations always cost extra, and some trips aren't fully covered by a railpass: Even if you have a Eurailpass or Swiss Pass, you'll pay 38 SF extra for the William Tell Express package trip. However, traveling the same route on standard trains, rather than on the designated tourist trains, is fully covered by a railpass. And on the Glacier Express, two different segments of the trip are free with a Swiss Pass, but not covered by a Eurailpass (with a Eurailpass, Disentis to Brig costs 45 SF second-class; Brig to Zermatt costs 33 SF).

When booking your ticket or buying reservations, make sure the ticket agent understands what type of pass you have (if any) and exactly what trip you're taking. Confirm that you've gotten all the reservations and other tickets you need to complete your trip. While rail agents generally know what railpasses cover, sometimes they don't—leading to frustrating run-ins with conductors who

## Scenic Swiss Rail Journeys

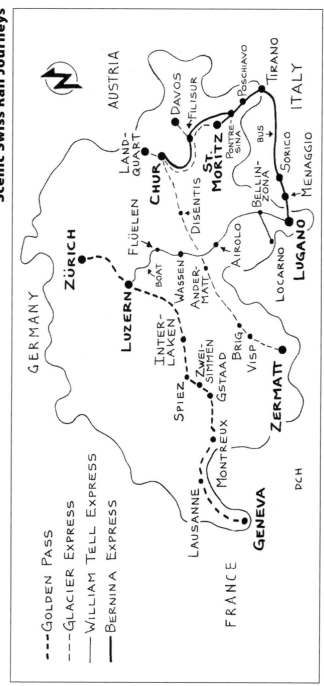

- - - Golden Pass
- - - Glacier Express
——— William Tell Express
━━━ Bernina Express

insist that you've only paid for part of your trip.

## Train Types

Various types of trains, with various types of cars, run these routes. Here are some key distinctions to look for:

**Classes:** Most trains have first- and second-class cars. In bigger train stations, a digital panel on the tracks indicates departure time, destination, and the composition of the train (that is, at which part of the platform you'll find the first- or second-class cars).

**Panoramic vs. Standard Cars:** All of the routes in this chapter offer special panoramic cars. On some trains—such as Golden Pass and Bernina Express—all of the cars are panoramic, so there's no need to splurge for first class. On other trains, such as Glacier Express and William Tell Express, you can choose between more expensive panoramic (first-class) and cheaper standard (second-class) cars.

**Panoramic cars** have huge, wrap-around windows, allowing you to see through part of the ceiling. The Golden Pass goes one better: The driver sits in a little bubble upstairs, leaving the very front of the train open for VIP seating with completely unobstructed views of what's coming up. The windows in the panoramic cars generally can't open, meaning that photographs often come with a glare, and the interior (even with air-conditioning) can heat up in sunshine.

**Standard cars** are typical train cars, featuring regular windows. With a smaller field of vision than the panoramic cars, these require a little more bobbing and weaving to enjoy the views. Aside from being cheaper, the chief advantage of the standard cars is that the windows generally can be opened, for cool air and photos without reflections. Passengers in panoramic cars are free to walk to the standard cars to open a window and snap a photo.

**Standard vs. Tourist Trains:** In many cases, standard trains operated by Swiss Rail run these same routes—more frequently, and usually less expensively (though you'll sacrifice things like fancy dining cars and souvenir keychains). Because standard trains are used by local commuters, they may stop at more stations along the route than the designed-for-tourists panoramic trains. Many travelers enjoy the flexibility of following the scenic route on standard trains, enabling them to hop off and explore a village, then hop on the next standard train that comes through—without the headache of reservations (which are almost never necessary on standard trains).

# Golden Pass

The exceptionally picturesque Golden Pass train route cuts a swath diagonally across the pristine center of Switzerland, connecting Zürich with Lake Geneva. Of all the rail journeys in this chapter, its central location—lacing together many of Switzerland's top sights—makes the Golden Pass the one you're most likely to take.

## ORIENTATION

### The Route

The Golden Pass officially runs between the cities of Zürich and Geneva, but most travelers focus on the segment between Luzern and Lake Geneva's Montreux. Better yet, hone in even more tightly—on the very best stretch, from Interlaken to Montreux.

Special panoramic cars are used between Luzern and Montreux. Because the tracks change from narrow to standard gauge to narrow again, two train changes are required (at Interlaken Ost and Zweisimmen).

**Route Breakdown:** The entire Golden Pass route (almost 8 hrs) is run by various companies and involves several train changes. Here's the breakdown.

**Zürich to Luzern:** Standard trains run by Swiss Rail (2/hr, 1 hr).

**Luzern to Interlaken Ost:** Narrow-gauge panoramic trains run by Brünig Railway (5/day, 2 hrs); also standard trains by Swiss Rail (hourly, 2 hrs).

**Interlaken Ost to Zweisimmen:** Direct panoramic trains run by Golden Pass (2/day, 1 hr); also standard trains run by Swiss Rail (at least hourly, 1.25 hrs, requires change in Spiez).

**Zweisimmen to Montreux:** Direct, narrow-gauge panoramic trains run by Golden Pass (5/day, 2 hrs); also standard trains run by Swiss Rail (9/day, 2 hrs).

**Montreux to Geneva:** Standard trains run by Swiss Rail (hourly, 1 hr).

**Planning Your Time:** Because it connects so many knock-out Swiss destinations (Zürich, Luzern, Interlaken, and Lake

Geneva)—and because it goes in both directions—the Golden Pass can be spliced into your itinerary in many different ways. I'd focus on the best stretch, using it to connect Interlaken and Lake Geneva (3 hrs total, including the lovely 2-hr segment from Zweisimmen to Montreux).

However you use it, check schedules along the way and plan your layovers strategically to maximize time on the panoramic cars. For example, if traveling from Luzern to Lake Geneva, consider taking the 8:55 panoramic train from Luzern to Interlaken Ost (arriving 10:45), then wander Interlaken and have lunch before catching the 13:25 panoramic train to Montreux (change trains in Zweisimmen at 14:23, arrive Montreux at 16:13).

## Cost and Schedule

The Golden Pass trip from Luzern to Montreux costs 67 SF second class; just the "best of" segment from Interlaken to Montreux is 47 SF. The entire ride is covered by a Eurailpass or Swiss Pass. Reservations, while not required, are recommended for summer midmorning departures and the super-scenic front seats (15 SF for front-row VIP seats, 7 SF for other seats in panoramic cars; more details under "Seating," below).

Special panoramic cars—some with front-row VIP seating—depart several times each day. Standard trains run from Spiez to Montreux every hour (2-hr trip, change trains in Zweisimmen). These regular regional trains show you the same scenery without the big windows.

**Information:** Most of the route is part of the Swiss Rail network. Special panoramic trains on the Luzern–Interlaken route are run by Brünig Railway (www.bruenig.ch). Panoramic trains on the section between Zweisimmen and Montreux are operated by MOB (Montreux–Oberland Bernois; tel. 090-024-5245, www .mob.ch). For more on the full route, see www.goldenpass.ch. An English-language guidebook describing the route is sold on the train (12 SF).

**Seating:** There are both standard and panoramic trains on the entire Luzern–Montreux route.

The lovely stretch from Zweisimmen to Montreux is covered by standard trains (9/day); trains with panoramic cars (2/day); and some special "Grande Vue" trains with both typical panoramic cars and special VIP seats (3/day May–Nov, 1/day Dec–April). On these "Grande Vue" cars, the conductor drives the train from a little domed area upstairs—leaving both the front and back of the train open for passengers. The first two rows, offering VIP seats with an unobstructed view of the pristine alpine scenery coming right at you, require a supplement of 15 SF (reserve in advance, or just grab one if available and pay the conductor on the spot). The non-supplement seats just behind the supplement seats give you a bit of the grand front view (and cheapskates have been known to grab a few free minutes up front). The panoramic cars have first- and second-class seating (with panoramic ceilings in both—no need to spring for first class, unless you want VIP seats). Cars have standard seating mixed with lounge areas with sofas, tables, and a bar.

Note that on the Luzern–Interlaken section, you'll need to choose between panoramic (first class) and non-panoramic (second class) cars.

## SELF-GUIDED TOUR

I've described only the best and most visually exciting portion of the Golden Pass journey, the three-hour stretch from Interlaken to Lake Geneva, focusing on the *crème de la crème*—the two hours between Zweisimmen and Montreux (described from north to south).

As you pull out of Interlaken, the train cruises along the south bank of **Lake Thun** (Thunersee). "Interlaken" means "between the lakes"—it's situated between the big lakes of Thun and Brienz. Before long, at the town of Spiez, you'll split off and head southwest to Zweisimmen.

Leaving Zweisimmen, you'll roll through **Simmental** valley, famous among American farmers for its top-end cows. Big farmhouses lie scattered in the lush meadows—an indication that the farmland is good here. The large wooden buildings are typical of Bernese farm architecture: housing the barn, sheltering the crops, and storing agricultural machines, all under one huge roof. Farming is heavily subsidized in Switzerland, and farmers form the strongest economical lobby. Trying to increase their modest income, many farmers have switched to exotic crops (like melons) or animals. These days, ostriches, yaks, bison, and highland cattle have become a common sight in the Swiss Alps.

Between Saanenmoser and Schonried, the train reaches its highest point (about 4,000 feet) and stops at the famous resort town of **Gstaad.** Although known as a favorite hangout for famous "backpackers," such as Monaco's Princess Caroline, Liz Taylor, Roger Moore, and Michael Jackson, the town does not offer many exciting sights. In winter, the modest ski slopes are not as crowded as the flashy nightspots, as most of the skiers are more into *après-*ski activities. Sipping their cocktails, they eye each other and discuss the latest trends in ski gear fashion. In summer, Gstaad hosts the Swiss Open tennis, polo, and golf tournaments, as well as music festivals. Violin virtuoso Yehudi Menuhin founded the Menuhin Festival here. While it started as an opportunity for young classical musicians to show their talent, today it's known for high-quality classical concerts.

Just south of Gstaad, you say *Auf Wiedersehen* to the German-speaking part of Switzerland and *Bonjour* to **French Switzerland.** The mountains are jagged. In fact, many are called *dents,* the French word for "teeth." With the change in language, you'll also see a change in culture and architecture. French-style gray stone houses are replacing half-timbered, woody, German-style chalets. The mountain airstrips—generally made for the Swiss Air Force during World War II—are used today for sightseeing flights around the Alps. The cute village of Rougemont, with its traditional chalets, is famous among the Swiss as the place where the wealthy send their girls to boarding school.

Happy **cows** spend their summers on the Alps, wandering freely and munching the fragrant herbs of these lush alpine meadows. The resulting milk is the secret ingredient for tasty Gruyère cheese. On steep hillsides here, the grass is still cut by hand. It dries in the summer sun, then is collected and stored in the barns to serve as cow salads through the winter (see "Swiss Cow Culture" sidebar in Gimmelwald chapter, page 142).

You might consider interrupting your journey in **Château d'Oex,** known for its Hot-Air Ballooning Week (last week of January). Bertrand Piccard and Brian Jones took off from here on March 1, 1999, and sailed their balloon all the way around the world. Below the train station, Le Chalet restaurant gives insight on Gruyère cheese production.

South of Château d'Oex, the valley narrows to a deep gorge. Up on the hillsides, the damage of the devastating 1999 winter storm "**Lothar**" can still be seen. Entire forests were leveled, aggravating the already precarious avalanche situation. The trees on the steep slopes stop the snow from sliding down and burying the villages. Once the trees are gone, they don't grow back. Artificial avalanche barriers need to be erected. Landslides and floods have been relatively common in recent years—an unfortunate consequence of uncontrolled deforestation and construction of vacation homes in areas that traditionally served as pastures and forestlands.

The small **lake** is dammed and used for hydroelectric power. Switzerland makes good use of its Alps for production of electricity. Although it has some nuclear power plants, 60 percent of Switzerland's energy is hydroelectric. The country exports its electricity to France and Italy.

**Montbovon** is the place to change trains if you're going to Bulle or Gruyères (see "French Swiss Countryside," page 221). After the first tunnel, an inscription on the barn to the right welcomes the traveler in the Gruyère region: *La Gruyère vous salue.*

The train winds its way uphill with more curves and tunnels than before. Passing through the **Jaman Tunnel,** you're engulfed in nearly two miles of darkness, then you emerge in another world—leaving the feudal Middle Ages and entering the 19th-century belle époque. At the village of Les Avants, one of Switzerland's oldest winter resorts, you catch the first glimpses of Lake Geneva sprawling deep underneath you and begin a steep descent. A series of sharp bends in tunnels takes you out of the mountains and down to lake level.

The architecture has even more of a French flair now that you've entered the **"Swiss Riviera."** Palm trees, vines, and many sanatoriums indicate this is a warmer climate. You're surrounded by the vineyards of the Lavaux region, famous for its white wine. The view broadens to include the French Alps of Savoy across the lake, the lakeshore of the Swiss Riviera to the west, and the broad Rhône Valley to the east. As you approach Montreux—with its grand hotels—the train meanders its way intimately through private gardens.

**Montreux** has the only train station in Europe with three different rail gauges: regular, narrow (which you're on), and very skinny (for the Rochers de Naye train, taking sightseers to a nearby peak with views less exciting than those you've just enjoyed).

From here, it's an easy train trip to Lausanne, or a quick bus ride or about a one-mile lakefront hike to Château de Chillon (see Lake Geneva chapter).

## TRANSPORTATION CONNECTIONS

**From Luzern by Train to: Zürich** (3/hr, 1 hr), **Zürich Airport** (2/hr, 1.25 hrs), **Bern** (hourly, 1 hr; or 2/hr with transfer in Olten, 1.5 hrs), **Lugano** (hourly, 3 hrs), **Chur** (hourly, 2.25 hrs, change in Thalwil).

**From Interlaken by Train to: Lauterbrunnen** (hourly, 20 min, 9.40 SF each way) **Spiez** (2/hr, 20 min), **Brienz** (1–2/hr, 30–40 min), **Bern** (2/hr, 50 min), **Zürich** and **Zürich Airport** (hourly, 2 hrs, most direct, but some with transfer in Bern and/or Spiez).

**From Montreux by Train to: Lausanne** (4/hr, 25 min), **Bern** (2/hr, 1.5 hrs, transfer in Lausanne), **Geneva** (2/hr, 1 hr).

# William Tell Express

The William Tell Express figures it deserves the most famous name in Switzerland. Tell exists only in legend, but his story—being forced to shoot an apple off his son's head because he refused to bow to the Hapsburg hat—helped inspire the Swiss to rebel against their Hapsburg rulers. The train route crosses the place where the first Swiss cantons pledged "all for one and one for all," the birthplace of the Confederation Helvetica in 1291. The trip is half by boat and half by train from Luzern to the Italian-speaking region of Ticino (the towns of Lugano and Locarno).

Don't go out of your way to do this trip. The boat ride is low-altitude and more pastoral than thrilling, and the train ride is more interesting as a lesson in Swiss engineering than impressive for its views. (Because the train cuts through the highest mountains inside the Gotthard tunnel, it only reaches 3,600 feet above sea level.)

But if you're connecting Luzern and Italian Switzerland anyway, this route is undeniably scenic. You can book the official "William Tell Express" trip, or simply buy regular tickets with none of the hoopla. I'd save money and gain flexibility by just riding the boat and train on regular departures and skip the much-promoted tourist package. Even if you don't buy the package, you can still ride the fancy panorama train (without a seat reservation) at no extra charge.

## ORIENTATION

### The Route
The William Tell Express begins with a slow boat trip on Lake Luzern from the city of Luzern to Flüelen (3.5 hrs). Then a train cuts down into the Italian-speaking canton of Ticino (2 hrs). In the town of Bellinzona, you'll choose between two end points: Lugano or Locarno (I prefer Lugano).

The 3.5-hour boat trip from Luzern to Flüelen is lazy and very pretty. As the traditional steamer blows its old-time horn, you glide by idyllic lakeside resort towns and under mighty peaks. If you're in a hurry, you can get a flavor for the lake by doing a shorter round-trip cruise during your time in Luzern. Then take the train to Flüelen (1 hr from Luzern, as opposed to 3.5 hrs by boat); you'll see essentially the same scenery as the William Tell "Express" boat, but three times faster.

Whether you ride the boat or train from Luzern, in Flüelen you can join the William Tell Express panoramic train (departs

Flüelen at 12:16 and 15:16). In Bellinzona, you can either transfer to a non-panoramic train to Lugano, or stay on the same train to Locarno.

Another option is to skip Flüelen entirely. Standard (non-panoramic) trains make the Luzern–Lugano trip along the same route hourly in each direction (3 hrs total).

## Cost and Schedule

The value of buying the official William Tell Express tourist trip (154 SF first class, 126 SF second class) is dubious. The only things that come "extra" with this pricey package are a mediocre lunch on the boat, a reserved seat on the panoramic train, a brochure about the route, and a souvenir Swiss Army–knife keychain. Travelers using a Eurailpass or Swiss Pass pay a 38-SF reservation fee to buy this official trip—but you're better off skipping the package altogether. Your railpass already covers the entire route, including the boat (but not the lunch or the seat reservation—neither of which is necessary anyway).

There are two official William Tell Express departures daily in each direction (running May–Oct only). Going north to south: The boat leaves Luzern at 9:20 and 11:25, docks in Flüelen where the panoramic train departs at 12:16 and 15:16, and arrives in Lugano at 14:46 and 17:46. Going south to north: The train departs Lugano at 10:12 and 12:12, meets the boat in Flüelen at 13:00 and 15:03, and arrives in Luzern at 16:20 and 18:25. As always, remember to confirm all times.

**Information:** The official William Tell Express departures are operated by the Lake Luzern Navigation Company (tel. 041-367-6767, www.lakelucerne.ch). For more information, see www .wilhelmtellexpress.ch.

## Helpful Hints

**Boat Ride:** If you're doing the full William Tell Express route, board the boat at pier 1 across from the Luzern train station. Present your ticket and pick up your package deal, including a lunch voucher and information flyers. There's no real baggage check on the boat; travelers just stack their backpacks and suitcases in a corner.

**Lunch:** The official William Tell Express boat trip comes with a forgettable lunch.

**Train Trip:** On the official William Tell Express train from Flüelen, you'll find first class and the panoramic car way out on the platform in sector C. Yellow slips mark which seats are reserved. If you have no reservation, take any seat without a yellow marker.

# SELF-GUIDED TOUR

Here's what you'll see if you're doing the entire William Tell Express route. If you're taking only the train, skip down to that section.

## William Tell Boat Trip

The boat trip crisscrosses **Vierwaldstättersee** (the "Lake of Four Forest Cantons"—or simply "Lake Luzern"). The trip is popular with the older generation of locals, who eat and drink their way through the lazy route. On a sunny day, you can sit on the deck enjoying the mountain views. Survey the boat before you settle on a seat—considering sun, shade, and wind.

After two hours, you sail into the **Canton of Uri** and the landscape gets rougher, the slopes steeper, and the villages fewer and more rustic. This is William Tell country. The legendary Swiss national hero represents the essence of the country's spirit, still felt today: the desire for independence from foreign rule. William Tell has been a popular muse: Schiller wrote a play about him based on ancient Swiss chronicles, and Rossini set the legend to music in an 1829 opera.

Swiss patriots get excited as the boat approaches **Rütli.** The meadow above is the birthplace of the Swiss Confederation. In 1291, three representatives of the founding cantons met here and swore allegiance to each other, against their oppressive Hapsburg neighbors. More than 700 years later, Switzerland is still a confederation—but now it's up to 26 cantons.

Some hikers choose to disembark at Rütli and head for the mystical meadow marked by a big Swiss flag. Then they follow the **Weg der Schweiz** ("Path of Switzerland"), a trail leading around the lake. Along the way, they contemplate stone signs representing each of the 26 cantons in the order they joined the union. The canton markers are spaced according to each canton's population (the 20-mile-long trail is designed to have exactly 5 millimeters for each Swiss citizen).

Later, the boat stops at **Tellskapelle.** This 16th-century frescoed chapel marks another legendary spot—where William Tell jumped ship on the way to prison and swam to freedom.

The last stop is **Flüelen,** where the panoramic train awaits.

## William Tell Train Trip

From Flüelen, the train climbs from 1,540 feet up to 3,600 feet, at the Gotthard tunnel—the primary north–south transportation route through the Alps. You enter a classic alpine world of snowcapped mountains towering above wild valleys, with narrow gorges carved by eons of angry white water. Wooden chalets, pine forests, and lush meadows dotted with munching cows complete this image of picture-perfect Central Switzerland.

The train tracks are protected from avalanches, landslides, and waterfalls by concrete galleries. Gazing out the window, you'll see some of the greatest accomplishments of Swiss road and railroad engineering. **Wassen,** marked by its striking chapel, is the climax for trainspotters—with more trains passing per minute than just about anywhere else. First, the chapel is on your right. Then the train loops around the tiny town, and the chapel is on your left. Your train disappears into a tunnel, and when you emerge, the same chapel is still there. The train actually spirals up the slopes. (The William Tell Express package comes with a schematic map that illustrates this.)

Göschenen (where you can transfer to Andermatt, and on to the Glacier Express—see page 274) is the last stop before the 9.5-mile-long **Gotthard tunnel.** After 10 minutes of rocketing through darkness, you emerge in a whole different world—a different canton (Ticino, rather than Uri) and language (Italian, rather than German). Since the 13th century—long before this tunnel was built—the Gotthard Pass has been *the* major trade route over this part of the Alps, connecting northern and southern Europe. The trade continues to rumble under rather than over the pass. These days, heavy truck traffic brings pollution and traffic jams—but little money—to Switzerland. But an ambitious new high-speed train tunnel, currently under construction, will allow shippers to transport merchandise by train and get trucks off the roads.

Welcome to **Ticino,** Switzerland's botanical garden. While the weather around Lake Luzern is often iffy, Ticino feels Mediterranean—warm and southern—making it a favorite weekend destination for the Swiss. Rather than cuckoo-clock-like chalets, the houses are now plain, square, and made of stone. Instead of conifers, the forests are full of chestnut trees. You'll see vineyards, oleander, and even palm trees. And the upcoming train stops are announced in Italian now: *"Prossima fermata...."*

While life seemed almost too good in the pristine and touristic Lake Lucerne region, here in the valley of **Leventina,** the economy is tougher. Unemployment rates are high, young folks have to commute into the cities farther south for a job, houses and roads aren't as well maintained, and window boxes no longer come with so many flowers.

As you approach **Biasca,** notice a modern square building with pebble walls on your left-hand side. This is the information center for the new 30-mile-long Gotthard Base Tunnel, which will be the longest train tunnel in the world (Tue–Sun 9:00–18:00, closed Mon, tel. 091-873-0550, www.infocentro.ch). You'll see industrial buildings and factories around Biasca.

If heading to Lugano, you may need to change trains in **Bellinzona.** (The official William Tell train continues to Locarno.) The train to Lugano passes the northern tip of Lake Maggiore and goes through a quiet, lush valley lined with picturesque villages and chestnut trees. Enjoy your time in Italian Switzerland!

## TRANSPORTATION CONNECTIONS

**From Luzern by Train to: Zürich** (3/hr, 1 hr), **Zürich Airport** (2/hr, 1.25 hrs), **Bern** (hourly, 1 hr; or 2/hr with transfer in Olten, 1.5 hrs), **Interlaken** (hourly, 2 hrs direct to Ost station), **Lausanne** (hourly, 2.5 hrs; more with transfer in Olten), **Chur** (hourly, 2.25 hrs, change in Thalwil).

**From Lugano by Train to: Zürich** (hourly, 3 hrs, some with easy change in Arth-Goldau), **Interlaken** (hourly, 5 hrs, transfer in Luzern, Zürich, or Olten), **Bern** (hourly, 4 hrs, transfer in Luzern, Zürich, or Olten). From Lugano, you can continue on to the **Bernina Express** (below).

# Bernina Express

The Bernina Express is one of the most exciting train rides through the Swiss Alps thanks to its diversity: starting with the sunny palm-tree ambience of Lugano, getting a taste of Italy along beautiful Lake Como, climbing up and over the twisting Bernina Pass, and seeing mountain towns like Pontresina before finishing up in eastern Switzerland. The little red train with panoramic cars spirals up to 7,380 feet, passing steep mountains and cliffs, glaciers, waterfalls, and a wild, rugged landscape.

## ORIENTATION

### The Route
The Bernina Express combines a bus trip through Italy with a train ride up and into the mountains. The bus begins in Lugano and runs along the west side of Italy's Lake Como, eventually arriving at Tirano, where the route continues by train. From Tirano, the train crosses back into Switzerland and twists up the steep

mountainside north, mastering a very steep grade on regular tracks (no cogwheels) en route to the most spectacular stretch: over the Bernina Pass. Then the train winds back down the other side, stops in mountain towns (such as Pontresina), and finally deposits you in your choice of towns: Chur, St. Moritz, or Davos.

The route can be reversed (Chur/St. Moritz/Davos to Tirano by train, then bus to Lugano). In fact, this way arguably provides an even better experience: Approaching Pontresina from the north is breathtaking, and it gets even better when the train gets to the Bernina Pass.

**Planning Your Time:** The trip is spectacular but long. It helps to break up the journey with an overnight or two in the Pontresina area (see Pontresina, Samedan, and St. Moritz chapter). The Bernina Express is especially enjoyable in July and August, when you can take one of the open-top yellow train cars between Tirano and St. Moritz.

If you have more time, consider taking a standard regional train along this route (rather than the official panoramic Bernina Express train). That way, you can get off as you like for hiking and exploring (see "Local Train Alternative," below).

## Cost and Schedule

A one-way trip on the Bernina Express from Lugano to Chur costs 74 SF second class, 110 SF first class. If you're only going as far as Pontresina, it's cheaper (45 SF second class, 61 SF first class). The entire trip (including the bus) is covered by a Eurailpass or a Swiss Pass, though reservations cost extra.

If you do the official Bernina Express trip, **seat reservations** are required for both the bus and the panoramic train (9 SF for train, 12 SF for bus, buy easy-to-get bus reservation from driver as you board). Remember, you can do the same stretch on a regular train without reservations (optional seat reservation-5 SF; no such option for bus).

The bus leaves daily in summer (mid-May–mid-Oct) from outside Lugano's train station at 10:15 and heads for Tirano (facing the lake with the station at your back, walk about 100 yards to the left; bus stop has yellow sign for St. Moritz and Tirano).

At 13:00, you'll arrive in Tirano. From here, trains continue north over the mountains. All trains follow the same tracks as far as Pontresina, where they fan out to three different end points: to Chur (departs Tirano 14:15, arrives Chur 18:29), to St. Moritz (departs Tirano 14:49, arrives St. Moritz 17:11), or to Davos (departs Tirano 14:34, arrives Samedan 16:44, arrives Davos 18:19). The Davos-bound train, which runs in summer only, is the only direct panoramic train from Tirano to Samedan.

If you're doing it the other way around, here are some options: From Chur, the train leaves at 8:28 and arrives in Tirano at 12:36. From St. Moritz, the train departs at 9:41, arriving in Tirano at 11:57. From Davos, the train leaves at 8:40 and reaches Tirano at 12:20. The bus from Tirano leaves at 14:25 and arrives in Lugano at 17:30. Remember to confirm all times.

In winter (mid-Oct–mid-May), the bus service stops, but the train still runs between Tirano and Chur, and Tirano and St. Moritz, but not Tirano and Davos.

**Information:** The Bernina Express is operated by Rhaetian Railway (tel. 081-288-6104, www.rhb.ch). You can buy an English guidebook about the Bernina Express on the train or at gift shops along the way (12 SF). A recorded English commentary plays on the train's loudspeaker. Lugano bus info: tel. 081-288-5454.

## Helpful Hints

**Bus Trip:** The Lugano–Tirano leg of the Bernina trip (through Italy) is on a bus. Make yourself comfortable—the seats recline, and the footrests, armrests, and individual fans give you more comfort than on a standard postal bus. There are no WCs or food on the bus, so buy your snacks and drinks before boarding (a convenient spot is the Apero shop at Lugano's train station, daily 6:00–22:00). The bus stops for a WC and snack break in Italy (accepts Swiss francs). Bags can be put under the bus. The bus trip is almost entirely through Italy.

**Train Trip:** Once you reach Tirano, you'll switch to a panoramic train. The train has five cars: one is first class only, with panoramic windows that don't open. The other four are regular cars (with non-panoramic windows that open); two have first- and second-class seating, two are second class only.

**Topless Trains:** If traveling in July or August, ask about sitting in the yellow "convertible" train cars with flip seats and no roof (they can go on the Tirano–St. Moritz tracks because there are no long tunnels). Both first- and second-class cars are panoramic, and equally good.

**Local Train Alternative:** The train segment of the Bernina Express can be done on a standard (non-panoramic) local train. These trains stop at all stations, allowing you to hop off and walk around in the beautiful scenery. You can get off at Poschiavo for a quick visit, or at the Bernina Pass for hiking, or at Diavolezza to do a cable-car trip. Alp Grüm and Ospizio Bernina are starting points for several great hikes. Train connections are easy and quick if you're just passing through.

# SELF-GUIDED TOUR

## Bernina Express Bus Trip

The bus trip is more scenic than relaxing. Lakes Lugano and Como are almost fjord-like, lined with little Italian getaways. For the best views, sit on the right-hand side (seat numbers don't seem to matter).

At first, the road takes you around Lake Lugano on narrow, windy roads, frequently honking its horn to warn oncoming traffic at tight passages. Leaving Lugano, you'll pass the town of Gandria (fun to visit from Lugano by boat—see page 233 of Lugano chapter). Shortly after Gandria, you cross the border into **Italy** (it's a nonevent—bus doesn't stop, no need to show passports). You may notice a change in architecture: While the Swiss love meticulously manicured gardens and painstakingly renovated houses, the Italians take things a bit easier.

Once the bus leaves Lake Lugano, the road broadens and takes you through modern Italian villages before hitting picturesque **Lake Como** (Lago di Como). Above the town of Menaggio are your first views of the lake. The village across the lake on the right (by the funny hump of land) is the *real* Bellagio (not the Las Vegas casino). At the nearby village of Dongo, the Italian fascist dictator Mussolini was captured at the end of World War II. Tunnels occasionally disrupt your views, but you can catch glimpses of the lush lakefront. In Gravedona, the street gets narrow enough to make getting the bus through a tight squeeze. Posh private villas and gardens line the street; look for the 12th-century Romanesque Church of Santa Maria del Tiglio. From here, the trip takes you to the tiny harbor town of Domaso. This area is touristy, with plenty of campgrounds, hotels, and swimming pools.

Shortly before noon, the bus stops for 15 minutes in **Sorico,** at the northern tip of Lake Como. You'll have a chance to use the WC and buy a snack or drink at Bar Pace (Swiss francs accepted). Check out the big photograph behind the bar—George Clooney posing with the bar's proud owner on a 2002 visit. Clooney owns a grandiose villa on Lake Como.

The bus then crosses the **"Pian di Spagna"**—famous for a tense standoff between Spanish and Swiss troops during the religious wars of the Counter-Reformation. The trip continues up the fertile **Valtellina Valley,** where some of northern Italy's white wine is produced. The sunny slopes on the left side are reserved for vineyards, the right lower slopes are for woodland, and the bottom of the valley is occupied by apple plantations. This region belonged for centuries (from 1512 until Napoleon in 1797) to Switzerland's largest canton, Graubünden. While this region is Italian today, many Swiss still think of the local Veltlin wine as their own.

**Tirano** is our next stop. In the old town, the bus passes an impressive Renaissance church (Madonna di Tirano, on the left) before arriving at the train station at 13:00. You have time for lunch and some sightseeing before hopping on the Bernina Express train (departs at 14:15 to Chur, at 14:49 to St. Moritz, at 14:34 to Davos). Or, to cram in more sightseeing, take an earlier departure on a regional train to gain time for a stop-over in the fine town of Poschiavo (described below), and catch your Bernina Express train from there later (confirm times at the Tirano station information window).

If you're interested in the Poschiavo side-trip, see below. Otherwise, skip down to the next section ("Bernina Express Train Trip, Part One").

## Poschiavo

From the Poschiavo train station, walk to the main street and turn left, following the signs to *Centro* and the TI. Cross the river over the pedestrian bridge and  continue left, then right, then left, following the *Information* signs. The main square, **Piazza Comunale,** is lined with neoclassical and neo-Gothic buildings, including an impressive Catholic church (Chiesa di San Vittore Mauro). A church stood here as early as 703, but the building has been rebuilt and renovated several times: The bell tower dates from 1202, and the Baroque front door was carved in the 1700s. Don't miss the little yellow building just before the church, with the intricate wrought-iron grills. Have a peek inside, and don't be startled by the skulls lining the walls—you're standing in front of the local ossuary.

The **TI** is located in the old Town Hall, below the 12th-century church tower. Pick up a map and the English translation for a short orientation walk: Go from the main square a block north and find the **Church of St. Ignazio.** It's ironic that this Protestant church's namesake, St. Ignatius of Loyola, was the founder of the militant Jesuit order—whose main purpose was to fight "heretic" Protestants. Notice the inscription above the central pulpit, which is fervently Protestant: *Chiesa cristiana vangelica riformata da gli errori e superstizioni umane* ("Christian evangelical church, reformed from human errors and superstitions").

But...you've got a train to catch!

## Bernina Express Train Trip, Part One: From Tirano to Pontresina

From Tirano, the train crosses the center of town before climbing up to **Brusio.** Here the train takes the famous circular viaduct, the only one in the world—an ingenious construction allowing the train to reach higher altitudes without the help of a cogwheel mechanism. As the train twists up, you can see the front and back cars curving in front of and behind you, riding over the viaduct.

Lay back and enjoy the most scenic part of the trip. You pass dark old pine forests with needle-and-moss-covered boulders. Chestnut forests, tobacco plantations, and vineyards contribute to the lush tableau. Wildflowers along the track include bright-orange lilies and mountain azaleas. The train slaloms up the steep mountain and offers more and more views of waterfalls, steep cliffs, and the Poschiavo valley and lake far below you.

Thirty minutes after leaving Poschiavo, and before you reach the Bernina Pass, you'll spot the first glacier, **Palü Gletscher** (behind the little lake of Palüsee on the left). It lies nestled between the peak Piz Varuna (11,330 feet) on the left and the eastern summit of Piz Palü on the right (12,790 feet).

The groaning of the train is a reminder that this is the only train crossing over the Alps without a tunnel. It goes right over the summit. Ospizio Bernina—at the **Bernina Pass**—marks the highest point of this trip (7,380 feet). You'll see the White Lake (Lago Bianco), whose color comes from the snowmelt, also called "glacier milk." A watershed sign (yellow, reading *Wasserscheide*) explains that this is a European continental divide: From here, rivers flow either north (towards the Inn, Danube, and finally to the Black Sea) or south (to the Adriatic Sea via the Adda and Po Rivers).

Behind the White Lake, you can see the glaciers of **Sassal Masone** and **Piz Cambrena.** This mountain pass not only separates European drainage basins, but also cultures. In winter, when the train line was more susceptible to bad-weather closures, the remote Italian-speaking valley of Poschiavo was often cut off from Switzerland, and turned itself towards its southern neighbor, the valley of Veltlin (where you were just riding the bus).

The train crosses the barren landscape and descends into the **Engadine** valley. This part of Switzerland was discovered by tourists and convalescents at the end of the 19th century. Imagine the gorgeous skiing here in the winter, which still attracts the rich and famous. After the railroad opened this secluded valley to the world, the first hotels and sanatoriums were built (the air and sunshine supposedly helped fight various diseases). Poets found their muse in the wild, romantic landscape, while painters flocked in, attracted by the quality of the light. Keep an eye out for typical Engadine architecture—small windows set in thick walls, etched *sgraffito* decorations, and carved wooden doors.

The **Montebello curve** offers you the best views over the Morteratsch glacier on the left, with the impressive peaks in the background; from left to right: the Bellavista Range (12,770 feet), Crest Agüzza (12,690 feet), and the highest peak in the canton, Mount Bernina (13,280 feet). Mount Bernina was first climbed in 1850 by a team led by rangers from the village of Schanf. Their gear consisted only of thick woolen pants, a shirt and jacket, hobnailed shoes, and a hat with a black veil to shade them from the strong sunshine.

As you continue, the tracks are lined by more and more larch trees. The milky-white waters from Lago Bianco and the Morteratsch glacier run wild in a broad riverbed alongside the tracks, as satisfied cows chew away on the meadows and waterfalls tumble down the cliffs. From the Morteratsch station, there's a fine one-hour hike to the edge of the glacier, past posts tracking the glacier's recent retreat.

Next stop: **Pontresina.** This town is a good place to break the journey (see Pontresina, Samedan, and St. Moritz chapter). Consider spending a night or two in Pontresina, exploring the quaint village of Samedan, visiting the glitzy resort of St. Moritz, and maybe doing some hiking before continuing on your way.

If you're going to **St. Moritz,** your train trip is nearly over (about 10 min after Pontresina). But on the way to **Chur** or **Davos,** there's more to see...

## Bernina Express Train Trip, Part Two: From Pontresina to Chur

Although you're leaving the glaciers behind, your trip will still lead you through magnificent mountain scenery, with steep cliffs and deep gorges.

First, you'll slide through the broad and mellow valley around Samedan, following the shortest river in Switzerland, Flazbach. On the right, look for the funicular heading up to **Muottas Muragl,** a viewpoint overlooking the valleys that come together in Samedan (for details, see page 244). This is also home to Europe's highest airport. It serves glider enthusiasts and the rich and famous who come to vacation in St. Moritz.

After Samedan, in **Bever,** the train leaves the valley and climbs to another highly spectacular leg of its journey. The section between Bever and Bergün boasts amazing engineering work. Technicians from all over the world come here to admire the diversity of spiral tunnels, looping viaducts, galleries, and bridges that span the Albula Gorge.

The train works its way up along a cheerfully splashing mountain creek, between the Arven pine and larch trees and some isolated farmhouses. The **Albula tunnel,** the highest subterranean alpine crossing in Europe, takes you up to 5,970 feet. This pass serves as another barrier between cultures and climate—the weather is often different on either side of the tunnel. Hikers can follow the tracks and read the information panels about the construction of the train line. The street along the tracks is closed in winter and considered a paradise for sledders. Every winter, 100,000 sled enthusiasts are attracted by this closed, windy road, giving them the ride of their lives on a three-mile, downhill, car-free stretch.

From **Preda,** the train loops down through five spiral tunnels and two straight tunnels, crossing nine viaducts and going under two galleries—considered the most ingenious railway line ever built. It covers almost eight miles and descends more than 1,365 feet in altitude. The village of **Bergün** will be visible three separate times as you loop around the valley. Bergün greets you with a modern public open-air swimming pool and an onion-shaped, 17th-century "Roman tower." As the train continues winding down the pretty valley, you'll often be able to see other parts of the track below or next to you. Any track you see is one you've either already been on—or will be soon...

At **Filisur,** the Bernina Express route splits again. Some trains head directly to Davos (no stops en route), while others continue to Chur. I'll continue to narrate the Chur route.

After Filisur, the Chur-bound train enters a tunnel, and an announcement reminds you to ready your camera and position yourself on the left side. Just after the tunnel, you'll cross the famous **Landwasser viaduct.** A masterpiece of engineering, its pillars were built without scaffolding. Iron towers, which formed the center of each pillar, were built first. With the help of cranes set up atop each pillar, materials were hoisted up and the brick was laid. The 425-foot-long viaduct curves elegantly in a radius of 330 feet. Below, the wild Albula River carves the dramatic gorge; above, your train's panoramic windows allow you to see the steep and rugged cliffs looming over the tracks (a particularly beautiful stretch is right after Solis). Notice how nicely the dark limestone masonry matches the surrounding landscape (it was quarried right here).

**Thusis** is the commercial hub of the broad and lush Domleschg valley. The trip takes you down along the Lower Rhine River.

Notice the many fortresses, castles, towers, and ruins along the river, a reminder that taxes were levied on the traders traveling this major route between northern and southern Europe. One of Switzerland's most popular mineral waters originates in Rhäzüns. The 13th-century castle above the town now belongs to a local chemical company.

**Reichenau** marks the confluence of the Upper and Lower Rhine. This town became wealthy from the taxes it got from the passing merchants. The 17th-century Reichenau Castle on the Lower Rhine was once used as a school, but is now privately owned.

The train follows the Rhine at the foot of Calanda Mountain to our final stop, **Chur.** You can catch the Glacier Express (explained below) from Chur or from St. Moritz (see page 252).

## TRANSPORTATION CONNECTIONS

**From Lugano by Train to: Luzern** (hourly, 3 hrs), **Zürich** (hourly, 3 hrs, some with easy change in Arth-Goldau), **Interlaken** (hourly, 5 hrs, transfer in Luzern, Zürich, or Olten), **Bern** (hourly, 4 hrs, transfer in Luzern, Zürich, or Olten).

**From Pontresina to: St. Moritz** (2 trains/hr, 15 min), **Samedan** (hourly trains, 7 min; 2 buses/hr, 20 min), **Zürich** (hourly trains, 3.5 hrs, transfer in Samedan and Chur), **Tirano** (hourly trains, 2.5 hrs; 3 panoramic trains per day in summer).

**From Chur by Train to: Zürich** (2/hr, 1.5 hrs), **Luzern** (hourly, 2.25 hrs, transfer in Thalwil).

# Glacier Express

This most promoted of the Swiss scenic rail routes travels between Zermatt in the southwest of Switzerland and various resort towns in eastern Switzerland (St. Moritz, Chur, and Davos). If you stay on for the whole ride, you'll spend almost eight hours crossing 291 bridges, going through 91 tunnels, and reaching an altitude of 6,670 feet.

While it's an impressive and famous journey, the Glacier Express is not necessarily the be-all and end-all of Swiss rail trips. Much of the journey is down in valleys (as opposed to along the sides of cliffs), meaning that high-altitude views are a little lacking. But the stark landscape, carved by the glaciers that gave the train its name, is striking. The trip offers a dramatic way to connect eastern Switzerland with tucked-away-in-the-mountains Zermatt (see Zermatt and the Matterhorn chapter).

# ORIENTATION

## The Route

The Glacier Express is a misnomer—it's hardly an express. Not only does it take its time (traveling at about 20 mph to make the full trip in almost 8 hrs), but it also makes several stops along the way. The route cuts along the southern part of Switzerland, between St. Moritz/Chur/Davos (in the east) and Zermatt (in the west). You can ride in either direction.

**Planning Your Time:** The most distinctive stretch of the trip is the high-mountain pass between Disentis and Brig. If you don't want to commit to the whole eight hours, you can try to connect a trip with this segment only (about 3 hrs). Remember that you can join or leave the trip whenever you like (for example, Chur in the east and Brig in the west link conveniently into Swiss rail lines to other major destinations).

## Cost and Schedule

You'll pay 129 SF for second class, or 215 SF for first class, between St. Moritz and Zermatt. The entire trip is covered by the Swiss Pass (except the reservation fee, described below). But a Eurailpass covers only part of the journey; two segments are privately run and not covered by Eurail (Disentis–Brig-45 SF second class; Brig–Zermatt-33 SF; plus a 5-SF fee if you buy it on the train).

If you're riding the full length of the Glacier Express sans railpass, the cost is high enough to warrant a look at the Half-Fare Travel Card, which can quickly pay for itself (99 SF for 1 month, see page 19).

Last year, the Glacier Express added spiffed-up panoramic first- and second-class cars, with air-conditioning and headsets for commentary. On these new "premium" trains, the second-class panoramic seating gets extremely crowded in summer—consider splurging on first class.

In addition to your train ticket or pass, you'll have to buy a **reservation.** The panoramic trains require a reservation fee of 30 SF (same price for first or second class). If you're not starting or ending in St. Moritz, or if you're getting off along the way, you can choose a cheaper, non-panoramic train (reservation-15 SF, 9 SF off-season). But if you want to take a direct, nonstop train between St. Moritz and Zermatt, the pricier panoramic train is your only option.

From mid-May through mid-October, four trains run daily in each direction. Going from east to west, the train begins in either St. Moritz (departs at 9:02 and 10:02) or Davos (departs at 10:10); all trains stop in Chur along the way (at 11:15, 12:15, and 12:15). A fourth train originates in Chur, departing at 11:15. Going from

# Glacier Express

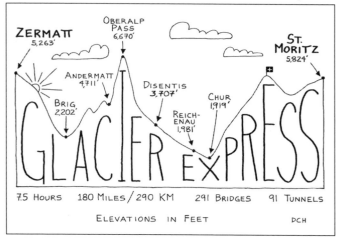

ZERMATT 5,263'
OBERALP PASS 6,670'
ST. MORITZ 5,824'
ANDERMATT 4,711'
BRIG 2,202'
DISENTIS 3,707'
CHUR 1,919'
REICH-ENAU 1,981'

GLACIER EXPRESS

7.5 HOURS    180 MILES / 290 KM    291 BRIDGES    91 TUNNELS

ELEVATIONS IN FEET                    DCH

west to east, the trains depart Zermatt at 8:48, 9:08, 9:48, and 10:08. All trains have panoramic cars. Off-season, frequency drops to one per day in each direction (east to west: departs St. Moritz at 9:02, stops in Chur at 11:15; west to east: departs Zermatt at 10:30). The train takes six hours to connect Zermatt and Chur, or eight hours for Zermatt to St. Moritz or Davos. Confirm all times before your trip.

**Information:** The Glacier Express is operated by Matterhorn Gotthard Bahn, based in Brig (Nordstrasse 20, tel. 027-927-7777, www.glacierexpress.ch or www.mgbahn.ch). There's a little recorded commentary about what you're seeing on the regular train; the headsets in the panorama cars offer more narration. For more insight, pick up a guidebook before you board, or buy the 15-SF official guide by Merian on the train.

## Helpful Hints

**Picking the Best Seat:** It's obviously more enjoyable to sit facing front. For most of the trip—including the most dramatic stretch, between Disentis and Brig—it's also slightly preferable, if you're coming from the east, to sit on the left-hand side of the train (generally seat numbers ending in 1, 2, 3, and 8), which is the right-hand side if you're coming from the west (same seat numbers). Note that if you start in Zermatt with any of the seat numbers I've mentioned, you might begin your trip facing backwards; the car will soon change direction in Brig.

**Luggage:** You'll keep your luggage with you (they don't check it through). In second class, there are luggage racks above your seat. In panoramic class, slip it between the backs of the seats.

**No-Show Bridges:** Most promotional materials show the Glacier Express train venturing across ancient aqueducts and old stone bridges. It makes for picturesque publicity. But realize that you don't see these bridges from the train itself...because you're on them.

**Eating on the Glacier Express:** The train has a fancy restaurant car that offers lunch—handy if you're in for the full eight hours. For 38 SF, you get a salad (summer) or soup (winter), a main dish, and a dessert; 26 SF buys you just the main dish (drinks cost extra). Their trademark gizmo: a tilted wine glass. Since lunch is generally served when the train is going up a steep incline (11:00–13:30), these gimmicky glasses always get a laugh. Reservations are required for lunch (request when booking your ticket).

To save a few francs, it's fine to bring your own **picnic.** Seats in panoramic cars even come with handy tables—perfect for a grocery-store feast.

## SELF-GUIDED TOUR

All Glacier Express trains—whether they begin in St. Moritz or Davos—go through Chur. I'll describe the route starting at Chur and heading toward Zermatt. (For details on most of the trip from St. Moritz to Chur, see "Bernina Express Train Trip, Part Two: From Pontresina to Chur.")

Just outside of Chur (near where the St. Moritz train line hits the Chur line), you'll be following the **Vorderrhein Gorge,** nicknamed the "Swiss Grand Canyon." It was carved by the Rhine River (though way down here in Switzerland, it's a little tyke, and not navigable). After about nine miles, the train diverges from the Rhine and enters a pastoral region called Surselva, centered on the town Ilanz. This is Romansh country, where the fourth official language of Switzerland is kept alive—barely—in communities like this one. Romansh, like French and Italian, is a Romance language—but it's more directly descended from Latin than most. From this valley (Reichenau, at roughly 2,000 feet above sea level, is the lowest altitude of the route), the big climb begins.

As you approach **Disentis,** the tracks begin to twist along the edge of a canyon—making the scenery more dramatic (a taste of what's to come). You'll pull into Disentis, with its big 17th-century Benedictine Monastery looming in your window. Your car will jiggle as the cogwheel engine is attached. This new engine has gears that can lower to latch onto the cogs of an extra rail that has grippable teeth. At 10 percent incline (that's 100 meters of gain per kilometer, or about 500 feet per mile), conventional train wheels start to slip. The solution: a cogwheel (a.k.a. rack-and-pinion drive).

You'll work your way up the mountain alongside the baby Rhine River. Just west of Sedrun is the staging ground for the excavation of the Gotthard Base Tunnel (which will run 30 miles under the mountain from Erstfeld to Bodio when it opens—God willing—in 2015). Just past Rueras, the track steepens and the train slows to allow its gears to latch into the cog rail. After Tschamut, the last inhabited place before Oberalp Pass, you enter a long series of snow sheds—designed to protect the tracks (and trains) in case an avalanche strikes. You'll emerge from the sheds at **Oberalp Pass,** the literal high point of this journey (6,670 feet), and glide along the Oberalp Lake. High above you, notice the extensive network of avalanche fences—a reminder of the many generations of Swiss farmers who have learned to live on the land. The reddish streaks you might see on the snow? Believe it or not, that's sand from the Sahara Desert—caught up in high-altitude winds and carried all the way to the Swiss Alps.

As you descend from the pass, you'll travel over, then through, the modern town of **Andermatt,** home to a Swiss Army base. Deep below you is the 9.5-mile-long Gotthard Tunnel, which takes trains unscenically from Goschenen to Airolo. In this desolate terrain, notice the huge boulders embedded in the ground, deposited there by glaciers.

Soon after, you'll go through the 9.5-mile-long Furka Basis Tunnel. While it might seem like a view-killer, realize that this tunnel—finished in 1982—made it possible for the Glacier Express to continue running through the winter. Cars are allowed onto the train to ride smoothly and safely between Realp and Oberwald. This is especially handy in the winter, when the road is closed.

You'll emerge into the region of **Goms,** with more pretty villages. The village of Fiesch/Kühboden has a cable car up to Eggishorn, boasting views of all the Alps All-Stars: the Matterhorn, Mont Blanc, Eiger, Mönch, and Jungfrau.

Soon after, the train meets up with another one of Europe's great rivers, the **Rhône.** The baby Rhône, just a bubbly little mountain stream here (originating from the once-mighty Rhône glacier nearby), flows all the way to Marseille, France, and into the Mediterranean.

Finally, you'll arrive at **Brig,** an ugly industrial town with good connections to other train lines (transfer here if you're not continuing on to Zermatt). From Brig, it's 20 miles on to Zermatt and the Matterhorn, following the craggy Nikolaital Valley. Keep an eye out for vineyards—the highest in Europe. We're out of milk country, and into wine country. At Stalden, a road leads up another valley to the resort of Saas-Fee. Shortly before the village of Randa, you pass a cone of rubble left by a huge avalanche that wiped out two miles of road and track here in 1991.

At **Täsch,** vast parking lots mark the end of the road for drivers. From here it's train only into the traffic-free terminus of this line, Zermatt. Think about how much the terrain has changed since you started the trip: from fertile farmlands, to tundra above the tree line, to this rough and rocky terrain.

As you continue along the valley, lined with quarries, you'll begin to get your first glimpses of the unmistakable shape of the **Matterhorn**—a fitting exclamation point marking the end of this long journey. **Zermatt**—with its bunker-like, avalanche-proof train station—lies just around the bend.

## TRANSPORTATION CONNECTIONS

**From Chur by Train to: Zürich** (2/hr, 1.5 hrs), **Luzern** (hourly, 2.25 hrs, transfer in Thalwil).

**From Zermatt:** Zermatt is connected to the outside world via the 80-minute train ride to Brig. Brig is also a handy place to bail out of the Glacier Express route, if you're coming from the east and not going all the way to Zermatt. If you're coming from or going to Lausanne or Montreux, you'll save time changing trains in Visp, a town between Zermatt and Brig (Zermatt-Lausanne via Visp: hourly, 3 hrs).

**From Brig by Train to: Bern** (at least hourly, 1.5 hrs), **Lausanne** (hourly, 1.75 hrs, more with change in Sion), **Interlaken** (at least hourly, 1.75 hrs, transfer in Spiez), **Luzern** (at least hourly, 3 hrs, transfer in Bern), **Zürich** (at least hourly, 2.75 hrs, some with transfer in Bern).

# Chur

The routes of the Glacier Express and the Bernina Express intersect in Chur—supposedly Switzerland's oldest and warmest town. It's a handy transportation hub for these two scenic train lines, and has a charming enough old town. Overall, Chur (pronounced "koor") is just a typical Swiss burg—fine for passing through, but not worth a detour. If you've got time to kill, you can wander up through the old town to two big churches (the Romanesque Cathedral and the Gothic Church of St. Martin), some remains of the medieval city wall, and the town museum (Rätisches Museum, 6 SF, no English descriptions). Follow the handy red signs pointing you to the attractions. Public WCs are next to the cathedral.

## ORIENTATION

Chur fans out over the foothills from the Rhine River. The newly renovated train station is at the bottom (north end) of the town center.

**Tourist Information:** The TI, in the train station, offers a free town map marked with sights, hotels, restaurants, and a convenient walking-tour route, plus a free brochure with hotel listings (Mon 13:30–18:00, Tue–Fri 8:30–18:00, Sat 9:00–12:00, closed Sun, tel. 081-252-1818, www .churtourismus.ch).

**Arrival in Chur:** To get to the old town, leave the train station and walk up Bahnhofstrasse. In two blocks, you'll reach the big roundabout at Postplatz. The old town is straight ahead.

**Internet Access:** The **library** (Kantonsbibliothek Graubünden) offers 15 minutes online for free (thereafter 2 SF/15 min, Tue and Thu 9:00–17:45, Wed and Fri 9:00–18:45, Sat 9:00–15:45, closed Sun–Mon, Karlihofplatz, tel. 081-257-2828).

## SLEEPING

Sleep here only if you must, in order to connect to one of the scenic rail lines. These moderately priced places are in the old town, an easy 10- to 15-min walk from the train station.

**Hotel Freieck** has 37 clean, tasteful rooms with wood floors and fun, old-fashioned furniture, over a low-key café (Sb-90–110 SF, Db-150–180 SF, Tb-180–230 SF, prices depend on season—highest May–mid-Oct, Reichsgasse 44–50, tel. 081-255-1515, fax 081-255-1516, www.freieck.ch, hotel@freieck.ch, Stockmann family).

**Hotel Restaurant Rebleuten,** in a 500-year-old building, overlooks a quiet little square a block off Kornplatz. The eight small, rustic rooms have worn carpets but are plenty comfortable. The hotel is warmly run by the Stöhr family (Ss-65 SF, Sb-80 SF, Db-150 SF, Pfisterplatz 1, tel. 081-257-1357, fax 081-257-1358, www.rebleuten.ch, info@rebleuten.ch).

**Hotel Franziskaner** is charming, well-located, and features newly renovated and reasonably priced rooms (S-50 SF, Ss-75–85

SF, Db-110–160 SF, Untere Gasse 29, tel. 081-252-1261, fax 081-252-1279, www.franziskaner.biz, info@franziskaner.biz).

## TRANSPORTATION CONNECTIONS

Chur is a convenient spot to catch either the Glacier Express or the Bernina Express. It also offers speedy, frequent connections to Zürich, making it an ideal junction for spicing up your trip with a scenic train.

**From Chur by Train to: Zürich** (2/hr, 1.5 hrs), **Luzern** (hourly, 2.25 hrs, transfer in Thalwil). To reach destinations in northern or western Switzerland—such as Bern, Interlaken, or Lake Geneva—you'll transfer in Zürich (see Zürich's "Transportation Connections," page 62).

# APPENDIX

## Winter Sports in Switzerland

I admit it: This is a summertime book. I've included plenty of tips on hiking, while ignoring the winter-sports scene entirely. But winter activities are an important part of the Swiss culture (and tourist industry). Here are the basics.

Skiing had its roots in Scandinavia 4,000 years ago as a method of wintertime transportation. Just a century ago, clever entrepreneurs in the Swiss Alps realized that the sport could be a profitable extension of their resorts' spring and summer seasons. Telemark (cross-country skiing) came first, then alpine (downhill) skiing, and today snowboarding rules. Generations of Swiss skiers have honed their skills on these slopes. Today's biggest names include Erica Hess, Vreni Schneider, and Maria Walliser.

You don't have to be a skier or snowboarder to enjoy Switzerland in the winter. Ski resorts offer plenty of other activities, including snowshoeing, sledding, ice skating...and shopping. Or just ride up a lift, rent a chair in the sun, and warm up with a glass of *Pflümli* (plum liqueur).

The winter-sports season begins in December and runs through Easter. During this period, hotel prices in resort towns surpass summer highs. For those who can afford them, the best winter activities are in the Berner Oberland (Mürren, Wengen, Grindelwald, and Gstaad); the southern canton of Valais (Zermatt, Saas-Fee, Crans-Montana, and Verbier); and the eastern canton of Graubünden (St. Moritz, Davos, Klosters, and Arosa).

The **Berner Oberland** offers the ultimate variety in terrain and character (see Gimmelwald and the Berner Oberland chapter). Three resort areas cluster around the Lauterbrunnen Valley. The cliff-hanging town of Mürren is a good home base, with the 10,000-foot Schilthorn peak as the backbone of its ski area (great steep sections up top, especially the Kanoneruhr; lower down, it caters to all levels, but can suffer from icy conditions or lack of snow). Across the valley, Wengen offers challenging skiing, fine accommodations, and shopping, with a complex lift system connecting it to Kleine Scheidegg, Männlichen, and Grindelwald. Each January, the World Cup ski races take place on Wengen's tough Lauberhorn run. Grindelwald, a little closer to Interlaken, is another fine base—with multiple funicular railways, cable cars, lifts, and more than 100 miles of downhill runs (www.grindelwald .com).

Farther to the west, Gstaad has more of a French accent. With a perfect location at the intersection of several valleys, it enjoys great sun exposure and a decent elevation (www.gstaad.ch). This famous, glamorous resort—mingling German coziness and French modernism—is *the* place to see and be seen. Skiing is secondary (see "Golden Pass," page 257 of Scenic Rail Journeys chapter).

The canton of **Valais** ("Valley") is known for its excellent winemaking along the banks of the Rhône, but it's also a popular skiing destination. Connected to Italy by several high-mountain passes, Valais is home to Switzerland's best-known sight: the Matterhorn. The area around the Matterhorn, including the villages of Zermatt and Saas-Fee, enjoy a high elevation and good skiing. Whereas Zermatt sits surrounded by groves of fir trees, with tacky tourist souvenir shops lining its main street (see Zermatt chapter), Saas-Fee lies in a deep valley that seems to pour out from the huge Fee ("Fairy") glacier (www.saas-fee.ch). Its town center—also very touristy—is circled by mountains, among them Switzerland's highest peak, the Dom (14,908 feet).

The resorts of Crans-Montana lack the village charm of other Swiss resorts, but offer great skiing with expansive views over the Rhône valley and the Valais Alps (www.crans-montana.ch). The resort town of Verbier is very modern (www.verbier.ch). It features a high-tech, state-of-the-art sports complex that links four valleys with Switzerland's most famous transit network, Téléverbier: 12 gondolas, five cable cars, 32 chairlifts, and 46 ski lifts, providing access to more than 250 miles of runs (www.televerbier.ch). Other activities here include rock and ice climbing, snowshoeing, and cross-country ski excursions.

The **Graubündener Alps** contain 14 different passes. St. Moritz, situated in the Upper Engadine valley, is so well-known that it's a registered trademark (see Pontresina, Samedan, and St. Moritz chapter). This resort town offers designer boutiques, luxury accommodations, a natural mineral spring spa...oh, and ski slopes, too. In addition to skiing, winter visitors to St. Moritz play polo and cricket on snow, go bobsledding on natural ice, or try *Skikjöring*—skiing pulled by riderless horses.

St. Moritz is also home to the famed Cresta Run, a difficult toboggan run that was started by a group of eccentric 19th-century invalids who were sent to Swiss hospitals to recuperate. Instead, they fled their beds, invented the toboggan, and created a treacherous route down the mountain. Screaming perilously down the slopes, members of this exclusive club were known as the fastest men on earth. The tradition continues today (www.cresta-run .com).

Other Graubünden resorts include Davos (more urban, good for hockey and Nordic skiing, www.davos.ch) and Klosters (a favorite of the British royal family, www.klosters.ch). A less-discovered, Back Door–style option is Arosa, a village whose natural beauty, isolated location, and quiet atmosphere set it apart (www .arosa.ch). Visitors to Arosa can take the train one hour from Chur or drive along a 19-mile road so twisty that it's said there's a curve for every day of the year. In this village, horse-drawn sleighs outnumber cars. The ski slopes are just five minutes from the town center, and there's also an ice arena, curling center, and racetrack, where a hot-air balloon lifts off regularly in winter.

One of my favorite Swiss memories happened one winter night on the snowy slopes of the Berner Oberland. My friend Walter (who runs Hotel Mittaghorn, see page 146) and I, warmed by hot chocolate laced with schnapps, decided to go sledding between mountain-high villages. We strapped flashlights to our heads, miner-style, and zoomed through the crisp, moonlit night.

## Let's Talk Telephones

Here's a primer on making phone calls. For information specific to Switzerland, see "Telephones" in the Introduction.

**Making Calls Within a European Country:** About half of all European countries use area codes (like we do in most of the US); the other half uses a direct-dial system without area codes.

To make calls within a country that uses a direct-dial system (Switzerland, Belgium, the Czech Republic, Denmark, France, Italy, Poland, Portugal, Norway, and Spain), dial the same number whether you're calling across the country or across the street.

In countries that use area codes (such as Austria, Britain, Finland, Germany, Ireland, the Netherlands, Sweden, Croatia, Hungary, Slovenia, and Slovakia), dial the local number when calling within a city, and add the area code if calling long-distance within the country.

**Making International Calls:** Always start with the international access code (011 if you're calling from the US or Canada, 00 from Europe), then dial the country code of the country you're calling (see chart below).

What you dial next depends on the phone system of the

# European Calling Chart

Just smile and dial, using this key:
AC = Area Code, LN = Local Number.

| European Country | Calling long distance within ... | Calling from the US or Canada to ... | Calling from a European country to ... |
|---|---|---|---|
| Austria | AC + LN | 011 + 43 + AC (without the initial zero) + LN | 00 + 43 + AC (without the initial zero) + LN |
| Belgium | LN | 011 + 32 + LN (without initial zero) | 00 + 32 + LN (without initial zero) |
| Britain | AC + LN | 011 + 44 + AC (without initial zero) + LN | 00 + 44 + AC (without initial zero) + LN |
| Croatia | AC + LN | 011 + 385 + AC (without initial zero) + LN | 00 + 385 + AC (without initial zero) + LN |
| Czech Republic | LN | 011 + 420 + LN | 00 + 420 + LN |
| Denmark | LN | 011 + 45 + LN | 00 + 45 + LN |
| Finland | AC + LN | 011 + 358 + AC (without initial zero) + LN | 999 + 358 + AC (without initial zero) + LN |
| France | LN | 011 + 33 + LN (without initial zero) | 00 + 33 + LN (without initial zero) |
| Germany | AC + LN | 011 + 49 + AC (without initial zero) + LN | 00 + 49 + AC (without initial zero) + LN |
| Greece | LN | 011 + 30 + LN | 00 + 30 + LN |
| Hungary | 06 + AC + LN | 011 + 36 + AC + LN | 00 + 36 + AC + LN |
| Ireland | AC + LN | 011 + 353 + AC (without initial zero) + LN | 00 + 353 + AC (without initial zero) + LN |
| Italy | LN | 011 + 39 + LN | 00 + 39 + LN |

| European Country | Calling long distance within ... | Calling from the US or Canada to ... | Calling from a European country to ... |
|---|---|---|---|
| Netherlands | AC + LN | 011 + 31 + AC (without initial zero) + LN | 00 + 31 + AC (without initial zero) + LN |
| Norway | LN | 011 + 47 + LN | 00 + 47 + LN |
| Poland | AC + LN | 011 + 48 + LN (without initial zero) | 00 + 48 + LN (without initial zero) |
| Portugal | LN | 011 + 351 + LN | 00 + 351 + LN |
| Slovakia | AC + LN | 011 + 421 + AC (without initial zero) + LN | 00 + 421 + AC (without initial zero) + LN |
| Slovenia | AC + LN | 011 + 386 + AC (without initial zero) + LN | 00 + 386 + AC (without initial zero) + LN |
| Spain | LN | 011 + 34 + LN | 00 + 34 + LN |
| Sweden | AC + LN | 011 + 46 + AC (without initial zero) + LN | 00 + 46 + AC (without initial zero) + LN |
| Switzerland | LN | 011 + 41 + LN (without initial zero) | 00 + 41 + LN (without initial zero) |
| Turkey | AC (if no initial zero is included, add one) + LN | 011 + 90 + AC (without initial zero) + LN | 00 + 90 + AC (without initial zero) + LN |

- The instructions above apply whether you're calling a land line or mobile phone.
- The international access codes (the first numbers you dial when making an international call) are 011 if you're calling from the US or Canada, or 00 if you're calling from anywhere in Europe.
- To call the US or Canada from Europe, dial 00, then 1 (the country code for the US and Canada), then the area code and number. In short, 00 + 1 + AC + LN = Hi, Mom!

country you're calling. If the country uses area codes, drop the initial 0 of the area code, then dial the rest of the number.

Countries that use direct-dial systems (no area codes) vary in how they're accessed internationally by phone. For instance, if you're making an international call to the Czech Republic, Denmark, Italy, Norway, Portugal, or Spain, simply dial the international access code, country code, and phone number. But if you're calling Switzerland, Belgium, or France, drop the initial zero of the phone number. Example: To call a Paris hotel (tel. 01 47 05 49 15) from Luzern, dial 00, 33 (France's country code), then 1 47 05 49 15 (phone number without the initial 0).

## Country Codes

After you've dialed the international access code (00 if you're calling from Europe, 011 from the US or Canada), dial the code of the country you're calling.

| | |
|---|---|
| Austria—43 | Italy—39 |
| Belgium—32 | Morocco—212 |
| Britain—44 | Netherlands—31 |
| Canada—1 | Norway—47 |
| Croatia—385 | Poland—48 |
| Czech Rep.—420 | Portugal—351 |
| Denmark—45 | Slovakia—421 |
| Estonia—372 | Slovenia—386 |
| Finland—358 | Spain—34 |
| France—33 | Sweden—46 |
| Germany—49 | Switzerland—41 |
| Gibraltar—350 | Turkey—90 |
| Greece—30 | US—1 |
| Ireland—353 | |

## Directory Assistance

National—111
International—191
Train info—0900-300-300

## US Embassy

**In Bern:** Jubilaeumsstrasse 93, Mon–Fri 9:00–11:30, closed Sat–Sun, tel. 031-357-7234, http://bern.usembassy.gov.

## Public Holidays and Festivals in 2007

This is a partial list of events. For more, contact the Swiss national tourist office (US tel. 877-794-8037, www.myswitzerland.com, info.usa@myswitzerland.com) and check www.whatsonwhen.com.

# 2007

### JANUARY
| S | M | T | W | T | F | S |
|---|---|---|---|---|---|---|
|   | 1 | 2 | 3 | 4 | 5 | 6 |
| 7 | 8 | 9 | 10 | 11 | 12 | 13 |
| 14 | 15 | 16 | 17 | 18 | 19 | 20 |
| 21 | 22 | 23 | 24 | 25 | 26 | 27 |
| 28 | 29 | 30 | 31 |   |   |   |

### FEBRUARY
| S | M | T | W | T | F | S |
|---|---|---|---|---|---|---|
|   |   |   |   | 1 | 2 | 3 |
| 4 | 5 | 6 | 7 | 8 | 9 | 10 |
| 11 | 12 | 13 | 14 | 15 | 16 | 17 |
| 18 | 19 | 20 | 21 | 22 | 23 | 24 |
| 25 | 26 | 27 | 28 |   |   |   |

### MARCH
| S | M | T | W | T | F | S |
|---|---|---|---|---|---|---|
|   |   |   |   | 1 | 2 | 3 |
| 4 | 5 | 6 | 7 | 8 | 9 | 10 |
| 11 | 12 | 13 | 14 | 15 | 16 | 17 |
| 18 | 19 | 20 | 21 | 22 | 23 | 24 |
| 25 | 26 | 27 | 28 | 29 | 30 | 31 |

### APRIL
| S | M | T | W | T | F | S |
|---|---|---|---|---|---|---|
| 1 | 2 | 3 | 4 | 5 | 6 | 7 |
| 8 | 9 | 10 | 11 | 12 | 13 | 14 |
| 15 | 16 | 17 | 18 | 19 | 20 | 21 |
| 22 | 23 | 24 | 25 | 26 | 27 | 28 |
| 29 | 30 |   |   |   |   |   |

### MAY
| S | M | T | W | T | F | S |
|---|---|---|---|---|---|---|
|   |   | 1 | 2 | 3 | 4 | 5 |
| 6 | 7 | 8 | 9 | 10 | 11 | 12 |
| 13 | 14 | 15 | 16 | 17 | 18 | 19 |
| 20 | 21 | 22 | 23 | 24 | 25 | 26 |
| 27 | 28 | 29 | 30 | 31 |   |   |

### JUNE
| S | M | T | W | T | F | S |
|---|---|---|---|---|---|---|
|   |   |   |   |   | 1 | 2 |
| 3 | 4 | 5 | 6 | 7 | 8 | 9 |
| 10 | 11 | 12 | 13 | 14 | 15 | 16 |
| 17 | 18 | 19 | 20 | 21 | 22 | 23 |
| 24 | 25 | 26 | 27 | 28 | 29 | 30 |

### JULY
| S | M | T | W | T | F | S |
|---|---|---|---|---|---|---|
| 1 | 2 | 3 | 4 | 5 | 6 | 7 |
| 8 | 9 | 10 | 11 | 12 | 13 | 14 |
| 15 | 16 | 17 | 18 | 19 | 20 | 21 |
| 22 | 23 | 24 | 25 | 26 | 27 | 28 |
| 29 | 30 | 31 |   |   |   |   |

### AUGUST
| S | M | T | W | T | F | S |
|---|---|---|---|---|---|---|
|   |   |   | 1 | 2 | 3 | 4 |
| 5 | 6 | 7 | 8 | 9 | 10 | 11 |
| 12 | 13 | 14 | 15 | 16 | 17 | 18 |
| 19 | 20 | 21 | 22 | 23 | 24 | 25 |
| 26 | 27 | 28 | 29 | 30 | 31 |   |

### SEPTEMBER
| S | M | T | W | T | F | S |
|---|---|---|---|---|---|---|
|   |   |   |   |   |   | 1 |
| 2 | 3 | 4 | 5 | 6 | 7 | 8 |
| 9 | 10 | 11 | 12 | 13 | 14 | 15 |
| 16 | 17 | 18 | 19 | 20 | 21 | 22 |
| 23/30 | 24 | 25 | 26 | 27 | 28 | 29 |

### OCTOBER
| S | M | T | W | T | F | S |
|---|---|---|---|---|---|---|
|   | 1 | 2 | 3 | 4 | 5 | 6 |
| 7 | 8 | 9 | 10 | 11 | 12 | 13 |
| 14 | 15 | 16 | 17 | 18 | 19 | 20 |
| 21 | 22 | 23 | 24 | 25 | 26 | 27 |
| 28 | 29 | 30 | 31 |   |   |   |

### NOVEMBER
| S | M | T | W | T | F | S |
|---|---|---|---|---|---|---|
|   |   |   |   | 1 | 2 | 3 |
| 4 | 5 | 6 | 7 | 8 | 9 | 10 |
| 11 | 12 | 13 | 14 | 15 | 16 | 17 |
| 18 | 19 | 20 | 21 | 22 | 23 | 24 |
| 25 | 26 | 27 | 28 | 29 | 30 |   |

### DECEMBER
| S | M | T | W | T | F | S |
|---|---|---|---|---|---|---|
|   |   |   |   |   |   | 1 |
| 2 | 3 | 4 | 5 | 6 | 7 | 8 |
| 9 | 10 | 11 | 12 | 13 | 14 | 15 |
| 16 | 17 | 18 | 19 | 20 | 21 | 22 |
| 23/30 | 24/31 | 25 | 26 | 27 | 28 | 29 |

| | |
|---|---|
| **Jan 1** | New Year's Day |
| **Jan 2** | Harder Potschete (parade), Interlaken |
| **Jan 6** | Epiphany (closings) |
| **Feb** | Karneval, especially celebrated in Luzern, Zürich, and Bern |
| **March 11–May 27** | International Jazz Festival (www.jazzfestivalbern.ch), Bern |
| **March 24–April 1** | International Easter Music Festival (www.lucernefestival.ch), Luzern |
| **April 6–9** | Easter Weekend |
| **April 15–16** | Sechseläuten (Spring Festival, www.sechselaeuten.ch), Zürich |
| **April 24** | Open-Air Parliament (public selection of delegates), Appenzell |
| **May 17** | Ascension Day (religious festival, closures) |

| | |
|---|---|
| **May 28** | Whit Monday (religious festival, closures) |
| **June 7–17** | Berner Tanztage (dance festival, www.tanztage.ch), Bern |
| **June 15–July 8** | Zürich Festival (www.zuercher-festspiele.ch) |
| **Late June–early Sept** | William Tell Performance (open-air theater, www.tellspiele.ch), Interlaken |
| **July 5–7** | Estival Jazz (free open-air festival, www.estivaljazz.ch), Lugano |
| **July 6–21** | Montreux International Jazz Festival (www.montreuxjazz.com) |
| **July 6–14** | City Festival (www.festivalcite.ch), Lausanne |
| **July 19–22** | Gurten Open-Air Rock Festival (www.gurtenfestival.ch) |
| **Aug 1** | Swiss National Day (parades and fireworks) |
| **Aug 10–Sept 16** | Luzern Festival (classical, www.lucernefestival.ch), Luzern |
| **Oct 5-7** | Festa d'Autunno (food and wine festival), Lugano |
| **Nov 1** | All Saints' Day |
| **Nov 19-25** | Luzern Music Festival (piano, www.lucernefestival.ch) |
| **Nov 28** | Traditional Onion Market Fair, Bern |
| **Dec** | Christmas fairs |
| **Dec 6** | St. Nicholas Day |
| **Dec 25** | Christmas (closures) |
| **Dec 26** | Boxing Day |

## Numbers and Stumblers

- Europeans write a few of their numbers differently than we do. 1 = $1$, 4 = $4$, 7 = $7$. Learn the difference or miss your train.
- In Europe, dates appear as day/month/year, so Christmas is 25/12/07.
- Commas are decimal points and decimals, commas. A dollar and a half is $1,50, and there are 5.280 feet in a mile.
- When counting with your fingers, start with your thumb. If you hold up your first finger to request one item, you'll probably get two.
- What Americans call the second floor of a building is the first floor in Europe.
- Europeans keep the left "lane" open for passing on escalators and moving sidewalks. Keep to the right.

## Metric Conversion (approximate)

| | |
|---|---|
| 1 inch = 25 millimeters | 32°F = 0°C |
| 1 foot = 0.3 meter | 82°F = about 28°C |
| 1 yard = 0.9 meter | 1 ounce = 28 grams |
| 1 mile = 1.6 kilometers | 1 kilogram = 2.2 pounds |
| 1 centimeter = 0.4 inch | 1 quart = 0.95 liter |
| 1 meter = 39.4 inches | 1 square yard = 0.8 square meter |
| 1 kilometer = 0.62 mile | 1 acre = 0.4 hectare |

## Climate

First line, average daily low; second line, average daily high; third line, days of no rain.

| | J | F | M | A | M | J | J | A | S | O | N | D |
|---|---|---|---|---|---|---|---|---|---|---|---|---|
| **Bern** | | | | | | | | | | | | |
| | 29° | 30° | 36° | 42° | 49° | 55° | 58° | 58° | 53° | 44° | 37° | 31° |
| | 38° | 42° | 51° | 59° | 66° | 73° | 77° | 76° | 69° | 58° | 47° | 40° |
| | 20 | 19 | 22 | 21 | 20 | 19 | 22 | 20 | 20 | 21 | 19 | 21 |

## Converting Temperatures: Fahrenheit and Celsius

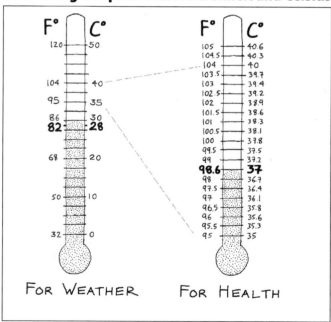

*Europe takes its temperature using the Celsius scale, while we opt for Fahrenheit. For weather, remember that 28°C is 82°F—perfect. For health, 37°C is just right.*

## Making Your Hotel Reservation

Most hotel managers know basic "hotel English." Faxing or e-mailing are the preferred methods for reserving a room. They're more accurate than telephoning and much faster than writing a letter. Use this handy form for your fax or find it online at www.ricksteves.com/reservation. Photocopy and fax away.

## One-Page Fax

To: _____ @ _____
　　　　　　*hotel*　　　　　　　　　　　　　*fax*

From: _____@ _____
　　　　　　　*name*　　　　　　　　　　　　*fax*

Today's date: _____ / _____ / _____
　　　　　　　　　*day*　　*month*　　*year*

Dear Hotel _____ ,
Please make this reservation for me:

Name: _____

Total # of people:_____ # of rooms: _____ # of nights: _____

Arriving: _____ / ____ / ____　　My time of arrival (24-hr clock): _____
　　　　　*day*　*month*　*year*　　　　(I will telephone if I will be late)

Departing: ____ / ____ / ____
　　　　　　*day*　*month*　*year*

Room(s): Single _____Double ____Twin _____Triple ____ Quad_____

With: Toilet _____ Shower_____Bath _____ Sink only _____

Special needs: View____ Quiet ____ Cheapest ____ Ground Floor ____

Please fax, mail, or e-mail confirmation of my reservation, along with the type of room reserved and the price. Please also inform me of your cancellation policy. After I hear from you, I will quickly send my credit-card information as a deposit to hold the room. Thank you.

_____
*Signature*

_____
*Name*

_____
*Address*

_____
*City*　　　　　　　　　　　*State*　　　　*Zip Code*　　*Country*

_____
*E-mail Address*

## Swiss-German Survival Phrases

When using the phonetics, pronounce ī as the long I sound in "light."

| | | |
|---|---|---|
| Hello. | **Gruetzi.** | **groyt**-see |
| Do you speak English? | **Sprechen Sie Englisch?** | **shprehkh**-ehn zee **ehng**-lish |
| Yes. / No. | **Ja. / Nein.** | yah / nīn |
| I (don't) understand. | **Ich verstehe (nicht).** | ikh fehr-**shtay**-heh (nikht) |
| Please. | **Bitte.** | **bit**-teh |
| Thank you. | **Merci.** | **mehr**-see |
| I'm sorry. | **Es tut mir leid.** | ehs toot meer līt |
| Excuse me. | **Entschuldigung.** | ehnt-**shool**-dig-oong |
| (No) problem. | **(Kein) Problem.** | (kīn) proh-**blaym** |
| (Very) good. | **(Sehr) gut.** | (zehr) goot |
| Goodbye. | **Ciao.** | chow |
| one / two | **eins / zwei** | īns / tsvī |
| three / four | **drei / vier** | drī / feer |
| five / six | **fünf / sechs** | fewnf / zehkhs |
| seven / eight | **sieben / acht** | **zee**-behn / ahkht |
| nine / ten | **neun / zehn** | noyn / tsayn |
| How much is it? | **Wieviel kostet das?** | **vee**-feel **kohs**-teht dahs |
| Write it? | **Schreiben?** | **shrī**-behn |
| Is it free? | **Ist es umsonst?** | ist ehs oom-**zohnst** |
| Included? | **Inklusive?** | in-kloo-**zee**-veh |
| Where can I buy / find...? | **Wo kann ich kaufen / finden...?** | voh kahn ikh **kow**-fehn / **fin**-dehn |
| I'd like / | **Ich hätte gern /** | ikh **heh**-teh gehrn / |
| We'd like... | **Wir hätten gern...** | veer **heh**-tehn gehrn |
| ...a room. | **...ein Zimmer.** | īn **tsim**-mer |
| ...a ticket to ___. | **...eine Fahrkarte nach ___.** | ī-neh **far**-kar-teh nahkh |
| Is it possible? | **Ist es möglich?** | ist ehs **mur**-glikh |
| Where is...? | **Wo ist...?** | voh ist |
| ...the train station | **...der Bahnhof** | dehr **bahn**-hohf |
| ...the bus station | **...der Busbahnhof** | dehr **boos**-bahn-hohf |
| ...tourist information office | **...das Touristen-informationsbüro** | dahs too-**ris**-tehn-in-for-maht-see-**ohns-bew**-roh |
| ...toilet | **...die Toilette** | dee toh-**leh**-teh |
| men | **Herren** | **hehr**-rehn |
| women | **Damen** | **dah**-mehn |
| left / right | **links / rechts** | links / rehkhts |
| straight | **geradeaus** | geh-**rah**-deh-**ows** |
| When is this open / closed? | **Um wieviel Uhr ist hier geöffnet / geschlossen?** | oom **vee**-feel oor ist heer geh-**urf**-neht / geh-**shloh**-sehn |
| At what time? | **Um wieviel Uhr?** | oom **vee**-feel oor |
| Just a moment. | **Moment.** | moh-**mehnt** |
| now / soon / later | **jetzt / bald / später** | yehtst / bahld / **shpay**-ter |
| today / tomorrow | **heute / morgen** | **hoy**-teh / **mor**-gehn |

## In the Restaurant

| | | |
|---|---|---|
| I'd like / We'd like... | Ich hätte gern / Wir hätten gern... | ikh **heh**-teh gehrn / veer **heh**-tehn gehrn |
| ...a reservation for... | ...eine Reservierung für... | **ī**-neh reh-zer-**feer**-oong fewr |
| ...a table for one / two. | ...einen Tisch für ein / zwei. | **ī**-nehn tish fewr īn / tsvī |
| Non-smoking. | Nichtraucher. | **nikht**-rowkh-er |
| Is this seat free? | Ist hier frei? | ist heer frī |
| Menu (in English), please. | Speisekarte (in Englisch), bitte. | **shpī**-zeh-kar-teh (in **ehng**-lish) **bit**-teh |
| service (not) included | Trinkgeld (nicht) inklusive | **trink**-gehlt (nikht) in-kloo-**zee**-veh |
| cover charge | Eintritt | **īn**-trit |
| to go | zum Mitnehmen | tsoom **mit**-nay-mehn |
| with / without | mit / ohne | mit / **oh**-neh |
| and / or | und / oder | oont / **oh**-der |
| menu (of the day) | (Tages-) Karte | (**tah**-gehs-) **kar**-teh |
| set meal for tourists | Touristenmenü | too-**ris**-tehn-meh-**new** |
| specialty of the house | Spezialität des Hauses | shpayt-see-ah-lee-**tayt** dehs **how**-zehs |
| appetizers | Vorspeise | **for**-shpī-zeh |
| bread | Brot | broht |
| cheese | Käse | **kay**-zeh |
| sandwich | Sandwich | **zahnd**-vich |
| soup | Suppe | **zup**-peh |
| salad | Salat | zah-**laht** |
| meat | Fleisch | flīsh |
| poultry | Geflügel | geh-**flew**-gehl |
| fish | Fisch | fish |
| seafood | Meeresfrüchte | **meh**-rehs-**frewkh**-teh |
| fruit | Obst | ohpst |
| vegetables | Gemüse | geh-**mew**-zeh |
| dessert | Nachspeise | **nahkh**-shpī-zeh |
| mineral water | Mineralwasser | min-eh-**rahl**-vah-ser |
| tap water | Leitungswasser | **lī**-toongs-vah-ser |
| milk | Milch | milkh |
| (orange) juice | (Orangen-) Saft | (oh-**rahn**-zhehn-) zahft |
| coffee | Kaffee | kah-**fay** |
| tea | Tee | tay |
| wine | Wein | vīn |
| red / white | rot / weiß | roht / vīs |
| glass / bottle | Glas / Flasche | glahs / **flah**-sheh |
| beer | Bier | beer |
| Cheers! | Prost! | prohst |
| More. / Another. | Mehr. / Noch ein. | mehr / nohkh īn |
| The same. | Das gleiche. | dahs **glīkh**-eh |
| Bill, please. | Rechnung, bitte. | **rehkh**-noong **bit**-teh |
| tip | Trinkgeld | **trink**-gehlt |
| Delicious! | Lecker! | **lehk**-er |

For more user-friendly German phrases, check out *Rick Steves' German Phrase Book and Dictionary* or *Rick Steves' French, Italian & German Phrase Book.*

## French Survival Phrases

When using the phonetics, try to nasalize the <u>n</u> sound.

| | | |
|---|---|---|
| Good day. | **Bonjour.** | bohn-zhoor |
| Mrs. / Mr. | **Madame / Monsieur** | mah-dahm / muhs-yur |
| Do you speak English? | **Parlez-vous anglais?** | par-lay-voo ah<u>n</u>-glay |
| Yes. / No. | **Oui. / Non.** | wee / noh<u>n</u> |
| I understand. | **Je comprends.** | zhuh koh<u>n</u>-prah<u>n</u> |
| I don't understand. | **Je ne comprends pas.** | zhuh nuh koh<u>n</u>-prah<u>n</u> pah |
| Please. | **S'il vous plaît.** | see voo play |
| Thank you. | **Merci.** | mehr-see |
| I'm sorry. | **Désolé.** | day-zoh-lay |
| Excuse me. | **Pardon.** | par-doh<u>n</u> |
| (No) problem. | **(Pas de) problème.** | (pah duh) proh-blehm |
| It's good. | **C'est bon.** | say boh<u>n</u> |
| Goodbye. | **Au revoir.** | oh vwahr |
| one / two | **un / deux** | uh<u>n</u> / duh |
| three / four | **trois / quatre** | twah / kah-truh |
| five / six | **cinq / six** | sa<u>n</u>k / sees |
| seven / eight | **sept / huit** | seht / weet |
| nine / ten | **neuf / dix** | nuhf / dees |
| How much is it? | **Combien?** | koh<u>n</u>-bee-a<u>n</u> |
| Write it? | **Ecrivez?** | ay-kree-vay |
| Is it free? | **C'est gratuit?** | say grah-twee |
| Included? | **Inclus?** | a<u>n</u>-klew |
| Where can I buy / find...? | **Où puis-je acheter / trouver...?** | oo pwee-zhuh ah-shuh-tay / troo-vay |
| I'd like / We'd like... | **Je voudrais / Nous voudrions...** | zhuh voo-dray / noo voo-dree-oh<u>n</u> |
| ...a room. | **...une chambre.** | ewn shah<u>n</u>-bruh |
| ...a ticket to ___. | **...un billet pour ___.** | uh<u>n</u> bee-yay poor |
| Is it possible? | **C'est possible?** | say poh-see-bluh |
| Where is...? | **Où est...?** | oo ay |
| ...the train station | **...la gare** | lah gar |
| ...the bus station | **...la gare routière** | lah gar root-yehr |
| ...tourist information | **...l'office du tourisme** | loh-fees dew too-reez-muh |
| Where are the toilets? | **Où sont les toilettes?** | oo soh<u>n</u> lay twah-leht |
| men | **hommes** | ohm |
| women | **dames** | dahm |
| left / right | **à gauche / à droite** | ah gohsh / ah dwaht |
| straight | **tout droit** | too dwah |
| When does this open / close? | **Ça ouvre / ferme à quelle heure?** | sah oo-vruh / fehrm ah kehl ur |
| At what time? | **À quelle heure?** | ah kehl ur |
| Just a moment. | **Un moment.** | uh<u>n</u> moh-mah<u>n</u> |
| now / soon / later | **maintenant / bientôt / plus tard** | ma<u>n</u>-tuh-nah<u>n</u> / bee-a<u>n</u>-toh / plew tar |
| today / tomorrow | **aujourd'hui / demain** | oh-zhoor-dwee / duh-ma<u>n</u> |

## In the Restaurant

| | | |
|---|---|---|
| I'd like / We'd like... | **Je voudrais / Nous voudrions...** | zhuh voo-dray / noo voo-dree-oh<u>n</u> |
| ...to reserve... | **...réserver...** | ray-zehr-vay |
| ...a table for one / two. | **...une table pour un / deux.** | ewn tah-bluh poor uh<u>n</u> / duh |
| Non-smoking. | **Non fumeur.** | noh<u>n</u> few-mur |
| Is this seat free? | **C'est libre?** | say lee-bruh |
| The menu (in English), please. | **La carte (en anglais),** | lah kart (ah<u>n</u> ah<u>n</u>-glay) |
| | **s'il vous plaît.** | see voo play |
| service (not) included | **service (non) compris** | sehr-vees (noh<u>n</u>) koh<u>n</u>-pree |
| to go | **à emporter** | ah ah<u>n</u>-por-tay |
| with / without | **avec / sans** | ah-vehk / sah<u>n</u> |
| and / or | **et / ou** | ay / oo |
| special of the day | **plat du jour** | plah dew zhoor |
| specialty of the house | **spécialité de la maison** | spay-see-ah-lee-tay duh lah may-zoh<u>n</u> |
| appetizers | **hors-d'oeuvre** | or-duh-vruh |
| first course (soup, salad) | **entrée** | ah<u>n</u>-tray |
| main course (meat, fish) | **plat principal** | plah pra<u>n</u>-see-pahl |
| bread | **pain** | pa<u>n</u> |
| cheese | **fromage** | froh-mahzh |
| sandwich | **sandwich** | sah<u>n</u>d-weech |
| soup | **soupe** | soop |
| salad | **salade** | sah-lahd |
| meat | **viande** | vee-ah<u>n</u>d |
| chicken | **poulet** | poo-lay |
| fish | **poisson** | pwah-soh<u>n</u> |
| seafood | **fruits de mer** | frwee duh mehr |
| fruit | **fruit** | frwee |
| vegetables | **légumes** | lay-gewm |
| dessert | **dessert** | duh-sehr |
| mineral water | **eau minérale** | oh mee-nay-rahl |
| tap water | **l'eau du robinet** | loh dew roh-bee-nay |
| milk | **lait** | lay |
| (orange) juice | **jus (d'orange)** | zhew (doh-rah<u>n</u>zh) |
| coffee | **café** | kah-fay |
| tea | **thé** | tay |
| wine | **vin** | va<u>n</u> |
| red / white | **rouge / blanc** | roozh / blah<u>n</u> |
| glass / bottle | **verre / bouteille** | vehr / boo-teh-ee |
| beer | **bière** | bee-ehr |
| Cheers! | **Santé!** | sah<u>n</u>-tay |
| More. / Another. | **Plus. / Un autre.** | plew / uh<u>n</u> oh-truh |
| The same. | **La même chose.** | lah mehm shohz |
| The bill, please. | **L'addition, s'il vous plaît.** | lah-dee-see-oh<u>n</u> see voo play |
| tip | **pourboire** | poor-bwar |
| Delicious! | **Délicieux!** | day-lee-see-uh |

For more user-friendly French phrases, check out *Rick Steves' French Phrase and Dictionary* or *Rick Steves' French, Italian & German Phrase Book.*

## Italian Survival Phrases

| | | |
|---|---|---|
| Good day. | **Buon giorno.** | bwohn JOR-noh |
| Do you speak English? | **Parla inglese?** | PAR-lah een-GLAY-zay |
| Yes. / No. | **Si. / No.** | see / noh |
| I (don't) understand. | **(Non) capisco.** | (nohn) kah-PEES-koh |
| Please. | **Per favore.** | pehr fah-VOH-ray |
| Thank you. | **Grazie.** | GRAHT-seeay |
| I'm sorry. | **Mi dispiace.** | mee dee-speeAH-chay |
| Excuse me. | **Mi scusi.** | mee SKOO-zee |
| (No) problem. | **(Non) c'è un problema.** | (nohn) cheh oon proh-BLAY-mah |
| Good. | **Va bene.** | vah BEHN-ay |
| Goodbye. | **Arrivederci.** | ah-ree-vay-DEHR-chee |
| one / two | **uno / due** | OO-noh / DOO-ay |
| three / four | **tre / quattro** | tray / KWAH-troh |
| five / six | **cinque / sei** | CHEENG-kway / SEHee |
| seven / eight | **sette / otto** | SEHT-tay / OT-toh |
| nine / ten | **nove / dieci** | NOV-ay / deeAY-chee |
| How much is it? | **Quanto costa?** | KWAHN-toh KOS-tah |
| Write it? | **Me lo scrive?** | may loh SKREE-vay |
| Is it free? | **È gratis?** | eh GRAH-tees |
| Is it included? | **È incluso?** | eh een-KLOO-zoh |
| Where can I buy / find...? | **Dove posso comprare / trovare...?** | DOH-vay POS-soh kohm-PRAH-ray / troh-VAH-ray |
| I'd like / We'd like... | **Vorrei / Vorremmo...** | vor-REHee / vor-RAY-moh |
| ...a room. | **...una camera.** | OO-nah KAH-meh-rah |
| ...a ticket to ___. | **...un biglietto per ___.** | oon beel-YEHT-toh pehr |
| Is it possible? | **È possibile?** | eh poh-SEE-bee-lay |
| Where is...? | **Dov'è...?** | DOH-veh |
| ...the train station | **...la stazione** | lah staht-seeOH-nay |
| ...the bus station | **...la stazione degli autobus** | lah staht-seeOH-nay DAYL-yee OW-toh-boos |
| ...tourist information | **...informazioni per turisti** | een-for-maht-seeOH-nee pehr too-REE-stee |
| ...the toilet | **...la toilette** | lah twah-LEHT-tay |
| men | **uomini, signori** | WOH-mee-nee, seen-YOH-ree |
| women | **donne, signore** | DON-nay, seen-YOH-ray |
| left / right | **sinistra / destra** | see-NEE-strah / DEHS-trah |
| straight | **sempre diritto** | SEHM-pray dee-REE-toh |
| When do you open / close? | **A che ora aprite / chiudete?** | ah kay OH-rah ah-PREE-tay / keeoo-DAY-tay |
| At what time? | **A che ora?** | ah kay OH-rah |
| Just a moment. | **Un momento.** | oon moh-MAYN-toh |
| now / soon / later | **adesso / presto / tardi** | ah-DEHS-soh / PREHS-toh / TAR-dee |
| today / tomorrow | **oggi / domani** | OH-jee / doh-MAH-nee |

## In the Restaurant

| | | |
|---|---|---|
| I'd like... | **Vorrei...** | vor-REHee |
| We'd like... | **Vorremmo...** | vor-RAY-moh |
| ...to reserve... | **...prenotare...** | pray-noh-TAH-ray |
| ...a table for one / two. | **...un tavolo per uno / due.** | oon TAH-voh-loh pehr OO-noh / DOO-ay |
| Non-smoking. | **Non fumare.** | nohn foo-MAH-ray |
| Is this seat free? | **È libero questo posto?** | eh LEE-bay-roh KWEHS-toh POH-stoh |
| The menu (in English), please. | **Il menù (in inglese), per favore.** | eel may-NOO (een een-GLAY-zay) pehr fah-VOH-ray |
| service (not) included | **servizio (non) incluso** | sehr-VEET-seeoh (nohn) een-KLOO-zoh |
| cover charge | **pane e coperto** | PAH-nay ay koh-PEHR-toh |
| to go | **da portar via** | dah POR-tar VEE-ah |
| with / without | **con / senza** | kohn / SEHN-sah |
| and / or | **e / o** | ay / oh |
| menu (of the day) | **menù (del giorno)** | may-NOO (dayl JOR noh) |
| specialty of the house | **specialità della casa** | spay-chah-lee-TAH DEHL-lah KAH-zah |
| first course (pasta, soup) | **primo piatto** | PREE-moh peeAH-toh |
| main course (meat, fish) | **secondo piatto** | say-KOHN-doh peeAH-toh |
| side dishes | **contorni** | kohn-TOR-nee |
| bread | **pane** | PAH-nay |
| cheese | **formaggio** | for-MAH-joh |
| sandwich | **panino** | pah-NEE-noh |
| soup | **minestra, zuppa** | mee-NEHS-trah, TSOO-pah |
| salad | **insalata** | een-sah-LAH-tah |
| meat | **carne** | KAR-nay |
| chicken | **pollo** | POH-loh |
| fish | **pesce** | PEH-shay |
| seafood | **frutti di mare** | FROO-tee dee MAH-ray |
| fruit / vegetables | **frutta / legumi** | FROO-tah / lay-GOO-mee |
| dessert | **dolci** | DOHL-chee |
| tap water | **acqua del rubinetto** | AH-kwah dayl roo-bee-NAY-toh |
| mineral water | **acqua minerale** | AH-kwah mee-nay-RAH-lay |
| milk | **latte** | LAH-tay |
| (orange) juice | **succo (d'arancia)** | SOO-koh (dah-RAHN-chah) |
| coffee / tea | **caffè / tè** | kah-FEH / teh |
| wine | **vino** | VEE-noh |
| red / white | **rosso / bianco** | ROH-soh / beeAHN-koh |
| glass / bottle | **bicchiere / bottiglia** | bee-keeAY-ray / boh-TEEL-yah |
| beer | **birra** | BEE-rah |
| Cheers! | **Cin cin!** | cheen cheen |
| More. / Another. | **Ancora un po.' / Un altro.** | ahn-KOH-rah oon poh / oon AHL-troh |
| The same. | **Lo stesso.** | loh STEHS-soh |
| The bill, please. | **Il conto, per favore.** | eel KOHN-toh pehr fah-VOH-ray |
| tip | **mancia** | MAHN-chah |
| Delicious! | **Delizioso!** | day-leet-seeOH-zoh |

For more user-friendly Italian phrases, check out *Rick Steves' Italian Phrase Book & Dictionary* or *Rick Steves' French, Italian, and German Phrase Book.*

# INDEX

# Travel smart…carry on!

**T**he latest generation of Rick Steves' carry-on travel bags is easily the best—benefiting from two decades of on-the-road attention to what really matters: maximum quality and strength; practical, flexible features; and no unnecessary frills. You won't find a better value anywhere!

### Rick Steves' Convertible Carry-On

This is the classic "back door bag" that Rick Steves lives out of for three months every summer. It's made of rugged, water-resistant 1000-denier nylon. Best of all, it converts easily from a smart-looking suitcase to a handy backpack with comfortably-curved shoulder straps and a padded waistbelt.

This roomy, versatile 9" x 21" x 14" bag has a large 2500 cubic-inch main compartment, plus three outside pockets (small, medium and huge) that are perfect for often-used items. And the cinch-tight compression straps will keep your load compact and close to your back—not sagging like a sack of potatoes.

Wishing you had even more room to bring home souvenirs? Pull open the full-perimeter expando-zipper and its capacity jumps from 2500 to 3000 cubic inches. When you want to use it as a suitcase or check it as luggage (required when "expanded"), the straps and belt hide away in a zippered compartment in the back. Choose from five great traveling colors: black, navy, blue spruce, evergreen or merlot.

### Rick Steves' 21" Roll-Aboard

At 9" x 21" x 14" our sturdy 21" Roll-Aboard is rucksack-soft in front, but the rest is lined with a hard ABS-lexan shell to give maximum protection to your belongings. We've spared no expense on moving parts, splurging on an extra-long button-release handle and big, tough inline skate wheels for easy rolling on rough surfaces.

Wishing you had even more room to bring home souvenirs? Pull open the full-perimeter expando-zipper and its capacity jumps from 2500 to 3000 cubic inches.

Rick Steves' 21" Roll-Aboard features exactly the same three-outside-pocket configuration and rugged 1000-denier nylon fabric as our Convertible Carry-On, plus a full lining and a handy "add-a-bag" strap.

Choose from five great traveling colors: black, navy, blue spruce, evergreen or merlot.

**For great deals on a wide selection of travel goodies, begin your next trip at the Rick Steves Travel Store!**

Visit the Rick Steves Travel Store at
**www.ricksteves.com**

## FREE-SPIRITED TOURS FROM
# Rick Steves

## Small Groups
## Great Guides
## No Grumps

Best of Europe ■ Family Europe
Italy ■ Village Italy ■ South Italy
France ■ Eastern Europe ■ Prague
Scotland ■ Britain ■ Ireland
Scandinavia ■ Spain-Portugal
Germany-Austria-Switzerland ■ Turkey ■ Greece ■ London-Paris
Paris ■ Venice-Florence-Rome...and much more!

Looking for a one, two, or three-week tour that's run in the Rick Steves style? Check out Rick Steves' educational, experiential tours of Europe.

Rick's tours are an excellent value compared to "mainstream" tours. Here's a taste of what you'll get...

■ **Small groups:** With just 24-28 travelers, you'll go where typical groups of 40-50 can only dream.

■ **Big buses:** You'll travel in a full-size 40-50 seat bus, with plenty of empty seats for you to spread out and be comfortable.

■ **Great guides:** Our guides are hand-picked by Rick Steves for their wealth of knowledge and giddy enthusiasm for Europe.

■ **No tips or kickbacks:** To keep your guide and driver 100% focused on giving you the best travel experience, we pay them well—and prohibit them from accepting tips and merchant kickbacks.

■ **All sightseeing:** Your tour price includes all group sightseeing, with no hidden extra charges.

■ **Central hotels:** You'll stay in Rick's favorite small, characteristic, locally-run hotels in the center of each city, within walking distance of the sights you came to see.

■ **Visit www.ricksteves.com:** You'll find all our latest itineraries, dates and prices, be able to reserve online, and request a free copy of our "Rick Steves Tour Experience" DVD!

---

# Start your trip at
# www.ricksteves.com

Rick Steves' Web site is packed with over 3,000 pages of timely travel information. It's also your gateway to getting FREE monthly travel news from Rick— and more!

## Free Monthly European Travel News

Fresh articles on Europe's most interesting destinations and happenings. Rick will even send you an e-mail every month (often direct from Europe) with his latest discoveries!

## Timely Travel Tips

Rick Steves' best money-and-stress-saving tips on trip planning, packing, transportation, hotels, health, safety, finances, hurdling the language barrier...and more.

## Travelers' Graffiti Wall

Candid advice and opinions from thousands of travelers on everything listed above, plus whatever topics are hot at the moment (discount flights, packing tips, scams...you name it).

## Rick's Annual Guide to European Railpasses

The clearest, most comprehensive guide to the confusing array of rail-pass options out there, and how to choo-choose the railpass that best fits your itinerary and budget. Then you can order your railpass (and get a bunch of great freebies) online from us!

## Great Gear at the Rick Steves Travel Store

Enjoy bargains on Rick's guidebooks, planning maps and TV series DVDs, and on his custom-designed carry-on bags, roll-aboard bags, day packs and light-packing accessories.

## Rick Steves Tours

This year more than 10,000 lucky travelers will explore Europe on a Rick Steves tour. Learn more about our 25 different one-to-three-week itineraries, read uncensored feedback from our tour alums, and sign up for your dream trip online!

## Rick on Radio and TV

Download free podcasts of our weekly *Travel with Rick Steves* public radio show; read the scripts and see video clips from public television's *Rick Steves' Europe*.

## Respect for Your Privacy

Ordering online from us is secure. When you buy something from us, join a tour, or subscribe to Rick's free monthly travel news e-mails, we promise to never share your name, information, or e-mail address with anyone else. You won't be spammed!

Have fun raising your Travel I.Q. at
**www.ricksteves.com**

# Rick Steves

## More *Savvy.* More *Surprising.* More *Fun.*

### COUNTRY GUIDES 2007

Croatia & Slovenia
England
France
Germany & Austria
Great Britain
Ireland
Italy
Portugal
Scandinavia
Spain
Switzerland

### CITY GUIDES 2007

Amsterdam, Bruges & Brussels
Florence & Tuscany
Istanbul
London
Paris
Prague & The Czech Republic
Provence & The French Riviera
Rome
Venice

### BEST OF GUIDES

Best of Eastern Europe
Best of Europe

As the #1 authority on European travel, Rick gives you inside information on what to visit, where to stay, and how to get there—economically and hassle-free.

www.ricksteves.com

## PHRASE BOOKS & DICTIONARIES

French
French, Italian & German
German
Italian
Portuguese
Spanish

## MORE EUROPE FROM RICK STEVES

Easy Access Europe
Europe 101
Europe Through the Back Door
Postcards from Europe

## RICK STEVES' EUROPE DVDs

All 43 Shows 2000-2005
Britain
Eastern Europe
France & Benelux
Germany, The Swiss Alps & Travel Skills
Ireland
Italy
Spain & Portugal

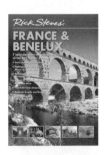

## PLANNING MAPS

Britain & Ireland
Europe
France
Germany, Austria & Switzerland
Italy
Spain & Portugal

# CREDITS

## Researcher

To help update this book, Rick relied on the help of…

### Susana Minich

Susana was born in Czechoslovakia, grew up in Switzerland, and now divides her time between Spain and Seattle. She has been guiding tours for Rick Steves since 1999. She's multilingual and has a degree in Art History with two minors: Architecture and Chocolate.

## Contributor

### Gene Openshaw

Gene is the co-author of eight Rick Steves books. For this book, he wrote material on art, history, and contemporary culture. When he's not traveling, Gene enjoys composing music, recovering from his 1973 trip to Europe with Rick, and living everyday life with his wife and daughter.

# IMAGES

| Location | Photographer |
| --- | --- |
| **Front color matter:** Gimmelwald | Dominic Bonucelli |
| **Front color matter:** Lauterbrunnen Valley | David C. Hoerlein |
| **Zürich:** View of Zürich from Limmat River | Cameron Hewitt |
| **Luzern and Central Switzerland:** Chapel Bridge | Cameron Hewitt |
| **Bern and Murten:** Bern Overview | Rick Steves |
| **Gimmelwald and the Berner Oberland:** Gimmelwald | Dominic Bonucelli |
| **Zermatt and the Matterhorn:** The Matterhorn | Susana Minich |
| **Appenzell:** Traditional Appenzell Gables | David C. Hoerlein |
| **Lake Geneva and French Switzerland:** Château Chillon | Cameron Hewitt |
| **Lugano:** Lake Lugano | Rick Steves |
| **Pontresina, Samedan, and St. Moritz:** Pontresina | Susana Minich |
| **Scenic Rail Journeys:** Bernina Express | Rick Steves |

# Rick Steves' Guidebook Series

## Country Guides

Rick Steves' Best of Europe
Rick Steves' Best of Eastern Europe
Rick Steves' Croatia & Slovenia (new in 2007)
Rick Steves' England
Rick Steves' France
Rick Steves' Germany & Austria
Rick Steves' Great Britain
Rick Steves' Ireland
Rick Steves' Italy
Rick Steves' Portugal
Rick Steves' Scandinavia
Rick Steves' Spain
Rick Steves' Switzerland

## City and Regional Guides

Rick Steves' Amsterdam, Bruges & Brussels
Rick Steves' Florence & Tuscany
Rick Steves' Istanbul (new in 2007)
Rick Steves' London
Rick Steves' Paris
Rick Steves' Prague & the Czech Republic
Rick Steves' Provence & the French Riviera
Rick Steves' Rome
Rick Steves' Venice

## Rick Steves' Phrase Books

French
German
Italian
Spanish
Portuguese
French/Italian/German

## Other Books

Rick Steves' Europe Through the Back Door
Rick Steves' Europe 101: History and Art for the Traveler
Rick Steves' Easy Access Europe
Rick Steves' Postcards from Europe
Rick Steves' European Christmas

(Avalon Travel Publishing)

Avalon Travel Publishing
1400 65th Street, Suite 250
Emeryville, CA 94608

AVALON
publishing group incorporated

Avalon Travel Publishing is an Imprint of Avalon Publishing Group, Inc.
Text © 2007, 2006, 2005, 2004, 2003, 2002 by Rick Steves. All rights reserved.
Maps © 2007 by Europe Through the Back Door. All rights reserved.
Photos are used by permission and are the property of the original copyright owners.

Printed in the United States of America by Worzalla
Second printing March 2007
Distributed by Publishers Group West
ISBN (10) 1-56691-968-1 / ISBN (13) 978-1-56691-968-5
ISSN 1552-1818

Thanks to Cameron Hewitt for writing the original information on Luzern, Zermatt, and
the Glacier Express. And thank you to my wife, Anne, for her support.

For the latest on Rick's lectures, guidebooks, tours, public radio show, and public television
series, contact Europe Through the Back Door, Box 2009, Edmonds, WA 98020, tel.
425/771-8303, fax 425/771-0833, www.ricksteves.com, rick@ricksteves.com.

**Europe Through the Back Door Managing Editor:** Risa Laib
**ETBD Editors:** Cathy McDonald, Jennifer Madison Davis, Gretchen Strauch, Jennifer
Hauseman (Senior Editor)
**Avalon Travel Publishing Series Manager and Editor:** Madhu Prasher
**Avalon Travel Publishing Editor:** Patrick Collins
**Copy Editor:** Ellie Behrstock
**Proofreader:** Kay Elliott
**Indexer:** Claire Splan
**Research Assistance:** Susana Minich
**Production & Typesetting:** Holly McGuire, Patrick David Barber
**Cover Design:** Kari Gim, Laura Mazer
**Interior Design:** Jane Musser, Amber Pirker, Laura Mazer
**Maps & Graphics:** David C. Hoerlein, Lauren Mills, Laura VanDeventer, Barb Geisler,
Mike Morgenfeld
**Photography:** Cameron Hewitt, David C. Hoerlein, Rick Steves, Susana Minich, Dominic
Bonucelli
**Front cover photos:** front image, Berner Oberland © Cameron Hewitt; back image: Basel
© Cameron Hewitt
**Front matter color photos:** p. i, Gimmelwald © Dominic Bonucelli; p. iv, Lauterbrunnen
Valley © David C. Hoerlein